MOUNTAINEERING
THE FREEDOM *of the* HILLS

THIRD EDITION

I. Ingalls Peak with dusting of new snow; Cascade Range. (Bob Gunning)

MOUNTAINEERING
THE FREEDOM *of the* HILLS

 THIRD EDITION

The Climbing Committee of The Mountaineers

Editor: PEGGY FERBER

Textbook Revision Committee:
SAM FRY, Chairman
FRED HART
SEAN RICE
JIM SANFORD
HOWARD STANSBURY

Illustrations:
ROBERT CRAM
and
RAMONA HAMMERLY

THE MOUNTAINEERS
Seattle, Washington

THE MOUNTAINEERS
Organized 1906

To explore and study the mountains, forests, and watercourses of the Northwest;

To gather into permanent form the history and traditions of this region;

To preserve by the encouragement of protective legislation or otherwise the natural beauty of Northwest America;

To make expeditions into these regions in fulfillment of the above purposes;

To encourage a spirit of good fellowship among all lovers of outdoor life.

First Edition, April 1960
Second Edition, December 1967
Third Edition, January 1974
Third Edition, Second Printing, July 1975
Third Edition, Third Printing, September 1977

COPYRIGHT © 1960, 1967, 1974
THE MOUNTAINEERS, 719 PIKE STREET,
SEATTLE, WASHINGTON 98101

MANUFACTURED IN THE UNITED STATES OF AMERICA BY
CRAFTSMAN PRESS, INC., SEATTLE, WASHINGTON

LIBRARY OF CONGRESS CATALOG CARD NO. 73-92374

ISBN 0-916890-01-5

Published simultaneously in Canada
by Mountain Craft, Box 5232
Vancouver, B.C. V6B 4B3

*

PREFACE

THE ORIGINS of *Mountaineering: The Freedom of the Hills* may be said to be lost in antiquity, or at least in early decades of the 20th century, when Puget Sounders began regularly venturing into the wilderness that surrounded their young cities and towns.

The first definable step toward the book occurred in 1934 with organization of the Climbing Course, a school since presented annually by The Mountaineers. Though European works, particularly Young's classic *Mountaincraft*, were required reading, they did not cover various subjects unique and important to American and Pacific Northwest mountaineering. To fill the gaps, outlines prepared by Course lecturers were distributed to students; eventually these were fleshed out and gathered together as the *Climber's Notebook,* subsequently published, in 1948, as the *Mountaineers Handbook.*

By 1955 tools and techniques had changed so drastically, and the Course had so grown in size and complexity, the need was felt for a new and more comprehensive textbook. Thus was undertaken the lengthy effort that culminated in 1960 with publication of the first edition of *Freedom.*

Members of the First Edition Editorial Committee were: Harvey Manning, chairman; John R. Hazle, Carl Henrikson, Nancy Bickford Miller, Thomas Miller, Franz Mohling, Rowland Tabor, and Lesley Stark Tabor. A substantial portion of the then relatively small Puget Sound climbing community participated, some 75 as writers of preliminary, revised, advanced, semifinal, and final chapter drafts, and another hundred or two as reviewers, planners, illustrators, typists, proofreaders, financiers, promoters, retailers, warehousemen, and shipping clerks. Rare was the Mountaineer climber of the period who did not have a hand in making or selling the book.

The first-edition team retired from the scene confident it had written for the ages, the sport and Course seeming to have gone about as far as they could go. However, the final wisdom of the 1950s became the archaic nonsense of the 1960s. Army and navy surplus gear from World War II wore out, replaced by sophisticated new parkas, packs, tents, boots, crampons, ropes, pitons, and whatnot. Old techniques thought to be the embodiment of perfection were refined out of all recognition; new ones were invented. Consequently, in 1964 there began another extended, strenuous effort leading in 1967 to publication of the second edition of *Freedom.*

Members of the Second Edition Editorial Committee were: John M. Davis, chairman; Tom Hallstaff, Max Hollenbeck, Jim Mitchell, Roger Neubauer, and Howard Stansbury. Though much of the first edition was retained intact, again the task force was of impressive proportions, numbering several dozen writers, uncounted reviewers and helpers. Rickety survivors of the previous committee, notably John R. Hazle, Tom Miller, and Harvey Manning unretired briefly to provide continuity. As he had with the first edition, Harvey Manning once more edited the entire text and supervised production.

Before the second edition was off the press portions already were obsolescent. There seemed no end of ingenious manufacturers offering gear that would have amazed climbers of the 1940s as much as the suggestion they would live to see man on the Moon. There also seemed no end of young athletes able to climb rings around their elders, extending capabilities of the human body almost to those of monkeys and spiders. Especially there seemed no end of people crowding the back country and the peaks, and by their crushing mass demanding a thorough re-thinking of old philosophy, a reinforced commitment to preserving the wilderness environment, a whole new ethic and style of hiking and climbing.

This third edition of *Freedom* is therefore radically different in many respects from its predecessors. Though the previous format has been followed with little change, the chapters have been rearranged to better fit contemporary Climbing Course needs and to provide a logical progression from beginning alpine travel through basic to intermediate climbing. The text has been virtually completely rewritten to correct errors and to set forth the latest concepts in equipment, technique, and ethics; few of the old chapters survive in recognizable form or content. Illustrations, as well, have been almost completely redone.

The necessity for a continuous updating of *Freedom,* urged by previous editorial committees, was again stressed in late 1970 by Max Hollenbeck, then president of The Mountaineers. Responding to the reminder, in January 1971 Climbing Committee Chairman Herman Gross appointed Sam Fry, the immediate past climbing chairman, to head the revision. A planning committee was assembled to analyze the existing book and set guidelines for the successor; Chairman Sam Fry was joined in this phase by current Climbing Chairman Sean Rice and former Climbing Chairmen Herman Gross, Chuck Heurtley, Howard Stansbury, Cal Magnusson, and Jim Sanford.

With goals defined, the Third Edition Editorial Committee took shape, centered around a Steering Committee, each member of which was assigned responsibility for a section of the book, assisted by writers and consultants as follows:

Part One, "Approaching the Peaks": chairman, Jim Sanford. "Preparation" was written by Jim Sanford, assisted by Joan Firey. "Clothing and Equipment" was thoroughly revised by Cal Magnusson, assisted by Joan Firey and Max Hollenbeck. "Camping and Sleeping" and "Alpine Cuisine" were revised by Joan Firey. "Navigation" was written by Glen Maulden, helped by Bob Bassett and Sam Fry. "Wilderness Travel" was revised by Bob Bassett, helped by Joan Firey and Max Hollenbeck.

Part Two, "Climbing Fundamentals": chairman Fred Hart wrote "Routefinding" and was assisted by Sean Rice, Mike Waddell, Bob Langenbach, Bruce Albert and Mark Wiegelt in the preparation of "Ropes and Knots," "Belaying," and "Rappelling."

Part Three, "Rock Climbing": chairman Sean Rice, with Bob Langenbach, Mike Waddell, Bruce Albert, and Mark Wiegelt, wrote the whole section. Bill Sumner reviewed several chapters. Larry Penberthy consulted on hard hats.

Part Four, "Snow and Ice Climbing": chairman Howard Stansbury was joined in revision and review by Alex Bertulis, Jim Wickwire, Ed Vervoort, Chuck Heurtley, and Sean Rice.

Part Five, "Safe Climbing": chairman, Sam Fry. "Alpine Rescue" was rewritten by Herman Gross, "Leadership and the Climbing Party" by John M. Davis and Sean Rice, and "First Aid" by Dick Mitchell, Russell Post, and Les Harms.

Part Six, "The Climbing Environment": chairman, Sam Fry. Rowland Tabor's old chapter on "Mountain Geology" was condensed by Bob Bassett, with helpful comments from Mike Heath. Ed LaChapelle updated his chapter "The Cycle of Snow." Fred Hart wrote "Mountain Weather," aided by Conway Leovy, Delmar Fadden, Stan Durst, Neal Barr, and Roger Wilcox.

The appendices were revised in only minor ways from the second edition.

Over and above the responsibilities described, all members of the Steering Committee, as well as many of the consultants, made detailed critiques of the total manuscript, notably Mike Waddell, Sean Rice, and Paul Robisch. No full listing would be possible of every person who helped with a pointed comment here, a bit of information there. As twice before, it was a true community effort.

Hundreds upon hundreds of hours were spent assembling, checking, and discussing data, writing and reviewing, revising and editing, until contents of each chapter were judged technically adequate. More hours went into collation of assembled chapters and sections to assure coherence, compatibility, and completeness. The disparity in style resulting from so massive a committee project surely requires no apology.

At the end of the line was Peggy Ferber, veteran of the *Freedom* team since first-edition days and this time around the literary editor and copy editor all in one, doomed to edit and re-edit the text over and over again. She was counseled in this herculean endeavor by Harvey Manning, who by choice took no other part in the third edition, feeling he was too far over the hill as a climber to cope with the brave new world.

The design of prior editions has been followed with little change, the layout performed by Ramona Hammerly and Peggy Ferber.

As in both previous editions, the cartoons were done by Bob Cram. Ramona Hammerly did the line drawings except for those few by Donna Cook carried over from the second edition. Sharon Gross made the sketches for "First Aid," and the illustrations for "Mountain Geology," also carried over from the second edition, were done by Ed Hanson. The index was prepared by Mary Dean Scott.

For readers unfamiliar with its past, two characteristics of *Freedom* should be noted. First, the primary purpose of the book always has been, and continues to be, to serve as textbook for the Climbing Course of The Mountaineers and the many similar schools now thriving.

Because of this, *Freedom* is not encyclopedic. No single book meets every need or desire. This one starts on a rather basic level, though not so basic as to entirely eliminate the often traumatic transition from city streets to wildland trails. It proceeds to a quite advanced level, but not to siege and solo climbing and expeditioning. A wilderness climber may very well require other books to ease his way into the sport or to progress to its more intricate aspects, and for that reason supplementary reading is suggested for many chapters. At a certain point, however, a climber should not, in any event, be learning his craft from books but from personal experience, supplemented by consultation with the masters and close study of alpine journals and periodicals.

The second noteworthy characteristic of *Freedom* is that it describes not simple climbing but *wilderness mountaineering*. Throughout these pages methods are detailed of reducing individual impact on fragile ecosystems. But wildlands must be protected not only from reckless boots, sleeping bags, and piton hammers. A single rioting bulldozer does more damage in a day than a thousand of the slobbiest walkers in a decade.

Any person who becomes a wilderness mountaineer has a deep and abiding responsibility to help preserve the wildlands. Walking softly is a fair start, but to maximize his leverage in a democracy ruled by pressure groups, a citizen must join his strength to that of others who share his ideals. Glad to say, hardly any population center lacks one or a dozen activist organizations vigorously combatting depredations of plunder-mad exploiters; new recruits are always welcome.

This book is about wild mountains. But there won't *be* any a generation or two from now unless all who value the way of life here portrayed get up on their hind legs and start yelling — in chorus.

January 1974   HARVEY MANNING

Other Books from The Mountaineers

The Alpine Lakes

Superb, full-color presentation on the wilderness heart of Washington's Cascade Mountains. Ed Cooper and Bob Gunning, in 95 outstanding color photos, portray the area's mountains, forest trails, tarns, snowfields, granite cliffs. Text describes personal experiences in exploring the Alpine Lakes. 128 pages, 10" x 13½", hardbound.

Cascade Alpine Guide

Climbing and High Routes: Columbia River to Stevens Pass. First completely detailed climbing guide to the south Cascades; prepared by Fred Beckey. Includes extensive route coverage, plus approach-route material, data on Cascade geology, weather, natural history. Over 100 pages of maps, sketches; photos with routes overprinted in red. 354 pages, 7" x 8½", flexible binding.

Climber's Guide to the Olympic Mountains

Covers every climbing and approach route on the Olympic peaks; also high alpine traverses, ski and snowshoe tours. Prepared by Olympic Mountain Rescue. 240 pages, 9 maps, 17 peak sketches with routes; flexible binding.

Routes and Rocks

Hiker's Guide to the North Cascades from Glacier Peak to Lake Chelan. Detailed descriptions of trails, off-trail high routes; with point-to-point mileages, elevations, campsites, notes on geology. By D. F. Crowder and R. W. Tabor, U. S. G. S. Plus four modified U. S. G. S. quad maps with overprint for routes, 240 pages, hardbound.

The Challenge of Rainier

Dee Molenaar's complete documentation of the climbing history of Mount Rainier, from the discovery years and the pioneering efforts to today's climbing parties. Personal anecdotes and word-portraits of guides through the various eras. Sketches, more than 100 photos, 7" x 10", hardbound.

Challenge of the North Cascades

Famed climber Fred Beckey, one of the first and most persistent explorers of the North Cascades, chronicles 30 years of adventures and climbs in a personal, highly readable style. 280 pages, 46 photos, 12 maps; hardbound.

Wildflowers of Mount Rainier and the Cascades

More than 100 full-color photos by Bob and Ira Spring of wildflowers, common and rare; authoritative text by Mary Fries. 220 pages, 7" x 8½", paperbound or hardbound.

Medicine for Mountaineering

Handbook for treating accidents, illnesses in remote areas. Compiled by climber-physicians, includes treatment of traumatic, environmental injuries; emphasizes high-altitude illnesses. 350 pages, 100 drawings, hardbound.

Mountaineering First Aid

A guide to accident response and first aid care; helpful for dealing with remote-area accidents, and preventing them. Excellent added text for outdoor safety, first aid classes. 96 pages, paperbound.

In the hikes series:

All detailed guides to trail or road-and-trail hikes, with complete descriptions, sketch maps, and scenic photos for each. Volumes are 7" x 8½", paperbound, approximately 200 pages each.

101 Hikes in the North Cascades
102 Hikes in the Alpine Lakes, South Cascades and Olympics
50 Hikes in Mount Rainier National Park
Trips and Trails, 1: Camps, Short Hikes and Viewpoints in the North Cascades and Olympics
Trips and Trails, 2: Family Camps, Short Hikes and View Roads in the South Cascades and Mt. Rainier
Footloose Around Puget Sound: 100 Walks on Beaches, Lowlands and Foothills
55 Ways to the Wilderness in Southcentral Alaska
103 Hikes in Southwestern British Columbia
Snowshoe Hikes in the Cascades and Olympics
Bicycling the Backroads Around Puget Sound

*

CONTENTS

*

PLATES

 PART ONE

Approaching the Peaks

II. Glacier Peak from Meadow Mountain trail. (Lee Mann)

1 *

PREPARATION

A MOUNTAINEER is, simply, one who seeks the freedom of the hills, full wilderness citizenship with all its privileges and rewards, but one who also accepts all its responsibilities and demands. For though mountaineering at best is exhilarating, at worst it is frustrating and discouraging and punishing, or even catastrophic to those who ignore nature's stern and impersonal rules.

Freedom of the hills lies largely in the ability of a party, whatever the size, to handle every problem of travel and living, and every emergency, with nothing more than the members can carry conveniently on their backs, plus their physical resources and the knowledge and judgment they have gained through experience.

This book is intended as an introduction to the infinite moods of the mountain world, a passport for those who wish to safely and confidently enjoy the freedom of the hills.

The Mountaineering Attitude

Though distant views of mountains may speak of adventure, they seldom more than hint at the multitudinous joys and hardships awaiting in the high places. Early on, of course, the aspiring mountaineer will assess his fondness for the totality of nature — mosquitoes as well as birds, wicked brush as well as pretty flowers, cold rain and cruel wind as well as sunshine and soft breezes. He will weigh his expected thrill of sitting on a summit against the lengthy training and strenuous effort required to get there. He will decide whether the pleasures are worth the pains, whether he wouldn't really be happier in some less exalting but less exacting recreation.

There are as many varieties of the mountaineering experience as there are mountains and mountaineers, too many to summarize except in a thick volume of philosophy and poetry, and no attempt will be made here to explore the spiritual profundities of the sport, or craft, or religion, or whatever it is. Either a person has the mountaineering "attitude" or he doesn't. If he must ask, "Why do men climb mountains?" he wouldn't understand the answer anyway.

Physical Preparation

As the novice quickly learns, ability to cope with physical and mental stress depends largely on the efficiency of organs and muscles: the better the physical condition, the better the body can supply necessary fuel and the better the chance of avoiding hazardous exhaustion. An individualized conditioning program — jogging, bicycling, swimming, or a combination — eliminates some agonies of initial mountaineering ventures.

Responsibility to the Environment

Throughout man's history mountains have epitomized remoteness, wildness, and pristinity. Tarns and meadows have symbolized delicate beauty, rugged spires, durability and timelessness. Yet today tarns are being polluted with human waste, meadows trampled by boots and crushed by sleeping bags. Even the rocks are being defaced, routes destroyed, by overzealous use of pitons and bolts.

If fragile ecosystems and structures are to be preserved — for meanings and values far beyond those of "sport," and for generations yet to be born, the mountaineer must study and understand the character of the land he travels, comprehend the vulnerability of its plants and soils and creatures, and must utilize new techniques of camping and of climbing.

The true mountaineer — climber, hillwalker, or river-watcher — walks softly through the wilderness, striving to leave not the slightest trace of his passage. He accepts the fact that privilege entails responsibility, without which freedom is only license.

Knowledge to Cope with a New World

For hiker as well as climber, mountains are a foreign environment, not necessarily hostile but certainly indifferent, and calling for knowledge rarely needed by a lowlander.

The informed mountaineer thinks of his body as a machine that burns stored fuel through the reaction of oxygen and a form of sugar, the process requiring the help of a self-manufactured enzyme principally replenished during sleep. In brief, he recognizes the importance of food, water, and rest to maintain physical and psychological strength, and in extreme cases, life itself.

He further realizes the machine functions within a strictly limited temperature range and that *hypothermia* – the lowering of the body's inner-core temperature – is an ever-present danger whenever cold, wetness, wind, and fatigue combine, and that excessive heat loss can result first in uncontrollable shivering and then increasing clumsiness, clouded judgment, and a fairly rapid descent into unconsciousness and death.

He, of course, plans his trip to accommodate the unexpected, including conditions that can lead to hypothermia. He knows wet clothing transmits heat from the body much faster than dry clothing, and that when everything is sodden, wool insulates far better than other materials; that wind alone can kill and windproof shell clothing can be a lifesaver; that an uncovered head dissipates a great deal of heat; that down clothing and sleeping bag are nearly worthless when compressed under the body and that other insulating material must be placed between him and the ground or snow on which he lies.

He carries navigation aids and has mastered their use. He observes his route constantly, not only the intricacies of the path to be negotiated on the return but the opportunities for emergency campsites. He keeps an eye out for the weather.

The wise mountaineer never stops learning more about himself and his new, foreign environment, steadily and assiduously enlarges his knowledge as if happiness and health depended on it – as frequently they do.

Judgment and Experience

Perhaps the most a mountaineering textbook can do, beyond outlining the basics of equipment and technique, is to suggest how to learn from experience; judgment, certainly, comes only with time. The more one travels in the mountains the broader his knowledge, yet repeatedly new situations arise lacking any trustworthy precedent from past hikes and climbs, times when no confident response can be automatically made, when judgment must be exercised. In this uncertainty lies much of the charm of mountaineering – the infinite variety, the elusive perfection perpetually sought but never quite attained. But in this uncertainty also lies the cause of many tragedies.

With the best of intentions it often is difficult to apply proper judgment in unanticipated circumstances. For this reason there has been developed, over many years, a standard of judgment – a mountaineers' Climbing Code – based on careful observation of the habits of skilled climbers and thoughtful analysis of accidents. With only slight adaptation the Code serves not merely climbers but all wilderness travelers.

A Standard of Judgment: A Climbing Code

A climbing party of three is the minimum, unless adequate prearranged support is available. On crevassed glaciers, two rope teams are recommended.

Carry at all times the clothing, food, and equipment necessary.

Rope up on all exposed places and for all glacier travel.

Keep the party together, and obey the leader or majority rule.

Never climb beyond your ability and knowledge.

Never let judgment be swayed by desire when choosing the route or turning back.

Leave the trip schedule with a responsible person.

Follow the precepts of sound mountaineering as set forth in textbooks of recognized merit.

Behave at all times in a manner that will not reflect unfavorably upon . . . mountaineering.

The Code rests on the principle that sensible mountaineers want strong chances of safety and success even in risky or doubtful situations; they want safeguards in case they have misjudged those chances; and they want the ability to control and minimize their exposure to grave danger. By no means a step-by-step formula for conquering summits, the Code is rather the key to safe and sane mountaineering, an expression of the boundaries the veteran mountaineer knows he must not exceed and which the newer climber must accept as his guide lest he overstep the reasoned margin of safety into the unknown. Knots he can learn in one lesson, but judgment he cannot develop except through time and trial. Therefore he *must* adhere rigidly to the Code, particularly in his first seasons, and follow it blindly if necessary even though he may not understand why; with the growth of experience he will make it his own and never stray from it as long as he climbs.

2 *

CLOTHING AND EQUIPMENT

A COMPREHENSIVE SURVEY of the garb and gear in current favor among mountaineers would require as many pages as a fair-sized encyclopedia and would try the patience of the most painstaking scholar. Witness mountain shop catalogs, invaluable guides to the newest advances in design (and prices), yet giving such a variety of choices that reading a single catalog may lead to confusion, two to bewildered irresolution, three to catatonia.

This chapter and the one following do not pretend to be definitive, but rather offer a brief summary of opinion on what is most desirable in the basic outfit of a climber, the gear he must have for even the most elementary trip. Other basic tools – and more specialized equipment – will be discussed later in the context of use.

Equipment must be kept to the safe minimum and must be just as light as is consistent with durability and versatility. Modern materials and methods of manufacture have made possible great saving in weight with no sacrifice of utility, most notably in sleeping bags and shelter; unfortunately, very often the lower the weight the higher the price.

Given unlimited funds a person can visit a mountain shop and walk out an hour later fully and superbly outfitted for the high country. The novice of ordinary means must proceed more cautiously to avoid financial disaster. However, if he has a background of hiking and camping, many of the major expenditures lie behind him, and even the lifelong urbanite finds much in his closet, basement, and kitchen that can be converted to mountain use, though perhaps only as a stopgap.

The beginner need not bog down in either confusion or bankruptcy if he takes one trip at a time, one purchase at a time, remembering there is no economy in buying cheap. Boots come first, necessary for even the simplest alpine excursion, plus warm clothing, a clutter of small and inexpensive essentials, and a rucksack to carry them. For an overnight trip, shelter and kitchenware can be improvised at small cost, but the required frame pack is a substantial investment and the indispensable sleeping bag a painful purchase. Before a person can venture onto steep snow he must have an ice ax. The climbing rope comes fairly late in the timetable since the novice will be — or should be — making his first roped climbs with an experienced companion who owns one.

The governing rule is, then, never to buy anything until the next climb demands it. By improvising, modifying, borrowing, and renting, the basic outfit can be budgeted over the entire first climbing season. In succeeding years stopgaps can be gradually replaced, all the more wisely for the delay, and specialized tools accumulated.

FOOTGEAR

Boots: Foundation of the Climber

One day of climbing may involve travel through and over streams, mud, logs, brush, meadow, and scree, stepkicking in snow, and delicate footwork on steep rock. A single pair of boots usually must suffice for all these conditions; a good climbing boot, therefore, represents a happy compromise among a number of conflicting requirements. It should be tough to withstand the scraping of rocks, stiff and solid for kicking steps in hard snow, yet comfortable enough for the approach hike. The upper must be high enough to protect the ankles in rough walking, yet allow them to flex to the extreme angles required by cramponing and slabclimbing. The sole should grip on both slippery heather and smooth rock. There must be room to wiggle the toes, but the fit must not be so loose that the foot can slip around inside, causing blisters while hiking and loss of control on small holds. It is important to remember when trying on boots for size that they should be fit with the number of socks to be worn, keeping in mind the fact that socks which seem to fill the boot to overflowing at first will pack into place around the foot in a very few minutes.

The compromise currently found best by most climbers is a 6- to 8-inch-high boot with a lug sole of fairly hard rubber. (Softer grades of rubber provide superior friction but wear rapidly.) The lug sole grips well on snow and provides excellent insulation from the cold. On all types of rock it is so satisfactory that special rock shoes are rarely needed. On the trail, jolts from stones are well-cushioned.

Fig. 1. Typical boots. *Left* to *right,* high topped boot, low boot with scree cuff, and heavy climbing boot with gusseted tongue and stiff sole.

Dozens of boot styles are available which fall within the limits of the recommended compromise. Whichever is chosen must meet still further tests of acceptability. The welt should be narrow, lest it bend on small holds and cause a slip. The upper lacing should be through hooks rather than eyelets. The top should open wide so that even when the boot is wet or frozen it can be put on with minimum struggle. Reducing the number of seams decreases the points of entry for water and lengthens boot life, since seams are susceptible to abrasion and are frequently the first part to give. Minimizing seams adds to the expense of construction but increases durability, as do double and triple layering in areas exposed to roughest wear. Especially desirable is a hard toe to prevent rock bruises and uncomfortable compression by crampon straps, and to ease the task of stepkicking.

Price is usually a fair measure of the leather quality: very inexpensive boots sometimes fall apart in a season or two; a good pair of boots will, with proper care, last several years. To prevent mildew and rot, boots should be washed off after each use, stuffed with a boot tree or paper, then thoroughly dried in a ventilated, moderately warm storage place. High temperatures are almost as damaging to leather as to human skin, and the former lacks nerve endings to warn of harm being done; the boots seen roasting by the campfire are the very ones that mysteriously disintegrate on some future climb.

Water can enter the boot not only over the top but through the leather or seams. Boots of good-quality leather, well-waterproofed, particularly at the seams, and having a tongue gussetted to the top can exclude water for a long while even when slopping around in wet snow (assuming none enters over the top). Waterproofing is best applied a day or more before the next climb to allow the preservative to soak in. The type of preservative used depends on how the leather was tanned (be sure to find out when buying): for chrome-tanned leather use silicone-base wax; for vegetable-tanned leather, wax or grease. Epoxy coating will protect the toe and seams.

Besides the "compromise" boot described, other options are available for special purposes. A boot with a soft-leather upper and flexible sole is most comfortable for trail walking and easy alpine terrain. A stiffer, double upper, heavier sole, and a hard toe are more desirable for scree and snow and moderate climbing. A very stiff upper with a reinforced sole is preferred for high-angle rock and ice; with these rigid prisons one does not so much break in the boot to fit the foot as force the suffering foot to accept the cruelties of the boot. Double- and triple-insulated boots are for cold weather and expeditionary climbing.

Socks

Wool socks are the only kind worth wearing. A light, smoothly-woven pair is usually worn next to the skin and a heavy, roughly-woven pair outside these. Some people with tender feet prefer a light cotton or nylon sock next to the skin, this in addition to the wool socks. The toes must always be free to wiggle; three tightly-packed pairs of socks give less protection from the cold than two looser ones, since compression of fibers reduces the dead-air space which is the chief source of insulation. Constriction of toes means reduced circulation and cold feet.

Insoles can be added to provide extra insulation and cushioning and to gain a snugger fit. The most common materials are felt, leather, and lambskin — all of which absorb moisture and must be taken out when drying the boot. Insoles of woven synthetic fiber are nonabsorbent, do not become matted or damp, and have a loose structure that helps ventilate the foot. Insoles *must* be in place when fitting boots for size, or can be substituted for the layer of socks they replace.

Other Footgear

Many mountaineers carry camp footgear for comfort and to give boots a chance to air or dry. Tennis shoes, rubber thong sandals, and moccasins are popular in summer, down booties for cold weather bivouacs and winter tenting. A pair of lightweight, waterproof, mukluk-style "booties" pulled on over socks or down footgear are convenient for snow camping; one pair per tent is adequate for outdoor chores and avoids the inconvenience of donning boots that have been carefully brushed of snow and stowed inside.

CLOTHING

Clothing best serves its most essential purpose of preserving body heat when worn in multiple layers: sweat-absorbent material next to the skin, insulating layers that trap stagnant air, and outer shells protecting against wind and rain. Because of the rapid changes in temperature, wind, and exertion usually experienced, garments must be quick and easy to put on or shed even under difficult conditions. Ventilation is always necessary when the body is working, since enclosing the system within an airtight layer results in condensation of perspiration and thus wet clothing.

Thickness is warmth. Table 1 is a rough guide to the total thickness of insulation, of whatever kind, required for various temperatures and activities. However, the kind of insulation used determines the actual heat-preservation value in real-life situations.

Table 1. Insulation Required for Various Situations.

Temperature	Total Thickness of Insulation (in inches)		
	Sleeping	Light Work	Heavy Work
40°F	1.5	.8	.2
0°F	2.5	1.3	.35
−40°F	3.5	1.9	.5

Cotton readily absorbs water and has virtually no insulating value when wet. *Wool*, also quite absorbent, retains its dead-air structure when wet; the weight and bulk of woolen clothing, though, make it impractical as the sole source of insulation at very low temperatures. *Down*, excellent insulation when dry, is valueless when wet. Noncellular synthetic filaments such as *polyesters* (Dacron, Fortrel) and *acrylics* (Orlon) absorb very little water and dry quickly. Spun synthetic filament (Dacron Fiberfill II) is lighter for equivalent dead-air thickness than wool, unlike down does not collapse when wet, and thus is an excellent compromise insulation for such wet regions as the Pacific Northwest.

Windproof garments are essential to minimize heat loss, and a waterproof shell is necessary to keep insulating layers dry (though it is difficult to keep moisture out and still maintain adequate ventilation).

Garments should be of loose fit for minimum constriction of movement and should lap at all points of juncture (waist, wrist, ankle, and neck) to reduce heat loss. The types of clothing chosen will vary somewhat depending on severity of weather anticipated, always allowing for the unexpected.

Table 2. Wind Chill Chart.

Wind Speed MPH	Temperature (°F)										
	50	40	30	20	10	0	−10	−20	−30	−40	−50
	Equivalent Chill Temperature										
Calm	50	40	30	20	10	0	−10	−20	−30	−40	−50
5	48	37	27	16	6	−5	−15	−26	−36	−47	−57
10	40	28	16	4	−9	−21	−33	−46	−58	−70	−83
15	36	22	9	−5	−18	−36	−45	−58	−72	−85	−99
20	32	18	4	−10	−25	−39	−53	−67	−82	−96	−110
25	30	16	0	−15	−29	−44	−59	−74	−88	−104	−118
30	28	13	−2	−18	−33	−48	−63	−79	−94	−109	−125
35	27	11	−4	−20	−35	−49	−67	−83	−98	−113	−129
40	26	10	−6	−21	−37	−53	−69	−85	−100	−116	−132
above 40	little additional effect										

Little Danger	Great	Extreme
	Danger of Freezing Exposed Flesh if Dry and Properly Clothed	

To use this table, which illustrates the intensely chilling effect of wind, find wind speed (in miles per hour) in left-hand column and temperature (in degrees F) in top row; the intersection of these is the equivalent temperature. For example, at a temperature of 0°F a breeze of 15 mph has the cooling effect of a temperature of −36°F on a calm day and pre-cautions should be taken to protect exposed flesh from frostbite. The zones shown on the table indicate the danger of frostbite to any exposed flesh of an average person in good condition whose body is properly clothed for the conditions. When the effective temperature is −25°F or less, care should be taken to minimize exposure of bare skin to wind.

Some climbers, deluded by a long spell of blind luck, claim the extra weight of raingear and spare wool clothing is an unnecessary burden; they arrogantly declare that any aggressive alpinist can generate more than enough heat, even in foul weather, only in blue jeans and thin shirt. And so the "jeans mystique" continues, and so, too, does the epidemic of hypothermia, which every year takes a victim here, a victim there, each one as surprised in his final hour as if he had been stricken by a rare and mysterious tropical disease. Many a happy-go-lucky hero of the crags, wearing only skimpy cotton and a bandolier of hardware, sooner or later comes face-to-face with the naked hatred of a sudden mountain storm and becomes another unfortunate statistic.

Below the Waist

Climbing trousers should be loose-fitting and of a closely woven, hard-finish fabric for abrasion resistance and windproofness. Wool is much preferred in a cool, wet climate. The life expectancy of pants can be extended by reinforcing the seat and perhaps the knees with patches of nylon or cotton canvas or leather, all of which are slow to dry if untreated (leather patches may be waterproofed with a good wax polish). A seat patch of coated nylon packcloth, coated side in, provides a moisture-resistant barrier during a sitting belay and for the thrill-seeker, an ever-ready go-fast for sitting glissades. Another school patches only — and with cloth — when the original trouser surface is completely breached and demands of comfort and modesty are urgent. Large pockets sewn onto trouser thighs are useful for carrying small items in frequent demand, such as mittens and snacks.

Among other alternatives are *knickers* worn with long knicker socks, a combination offering more freedom of knee flexion. Excellent climbing trousers and knickers are available commercially, but at a price; the penurious mountaineer may use old wool slacks too shoddy for city wear or Army surplus or thrift-shop wool trousers. Many climbers wear ski pants for winter climbing.

For the hardy, *shorts* travel well in the rain, keeping the long pants dry for camp, or they can be worn under *wind pants* for protection from rain, wind, brush, and excessive sun. Made of light, tough, very closely woven nylon, wind pants are cut large enough to be put on without removing boots; with side-zippers they can be easily donned even while wearing crampons. Though weighing only a few ounces and stuffing easily into a pocket, wind pants over regular trousers reduce heat loss considerably in a hard blow and shed snow easily in winter conditions. As a fringe benefit, they keep trousers dry during sitting glissades and provide a fast running surface, though the material in the seat wears rapidly. Uncoated fabrics eliminate the problem of condensation.

Waterproof *rain chaps* are pant-legs that protect the legs below the parka, poncho, or cagoule — sans seat to provide some ventilation.

"Long John" *underwear* of wool or wool-and-cotton layers is desirable for winter travel (and sleeping) and cold alpine conditions, and often is carried as emergency gear for bivouacs. Down underwear is sometimes used for the same purpose.

The boundary between trousers and boots is a critical area. *Gaiters* made of tough nylon or cotton with elastic top and bottom fit snugly over pants and boot tops to keep snow and trash out of the boot. Short gaiters, 5 or 6 inches high, are sufficient for most summer climbing and help keep gravel out of boots when short pants are worn. When deep snow is anticipated, long gaiters — to above the calf — are better. Waterproof nylon is preferred by some but is hot and causes sweating underneath, especially in the longer styles. A strap under the instep holds the gaiters down; a full-length zipper or lacing allows them to be donned without removing boots. (On winter and high-altitude climbs wet zippers may freeze overnight and be very difficult to work.)

Fig. 2. Gaiters, full length and short.

Above the Waist

A warm torso helps warm toes and fingers. The *layer system* is superbly adapted to the quick fluctuations of cold and heat typical of alpine regions: layers are added or removed one by one to keep pace with changing conditions.

An *undershirt* of open-weave material helps perspiration evaporate and when closed in by other clothing traps an additional insulating layer of air. Cotton fishnet vests are popular, but like all cotton clothing are cold when wet. Wool or part-wool undergarments are preferable though more expensive.

Shirts and sweaters provide insulation mainly by trapping air within and between themselves. Several light, loose-fitting layers are therefore more effective than one heavy garment, such as a logger's mackinaw. Shirts and sweaters should be entirely wool, slow to get wet and even then retaining much of their insulating value. At least one of the shirts should have a long tail so it will remain inside the pants and protect the midriff. Cotton sweatshirts absorb water like sponges and rapidly become worthless as insulation.

Though two layers above underwear — wool shirt and sweater — are sufficient in most climbing, Table 1 shows it is impractical to depend solely on these traditional wool garments at very low temperatures — the bulk and weight become too great. *Down clothing* has two properties — lightness and compressibility — which make it indispensable in severe cold. A down garment can be squeezed into an incredibly small volume and yet quickly regain full loft. Of course down must never be allowed to become wet since it then loses practically all its insulating value and is virtually impossible to dry while in the mountains. (As mentioned above, Dacron Fiberfill II is an alternative to down, as is Polarguard.)

During the summer, down clothing is seldom worn while in motion but many climbers carry a *down parka, sweater, vest,* or *underwear* for emergencies, bivouacs, and/or added comfort during cold hours in camp. A vest or sweater is often adequate even in winter in mild coastal climates. For cold-weather expeditionary trips where rain is rare, down parkas weighing 2 to 3 pounds are frequently used. A parka and a half-bag (elephant's foot) can in some circumstances serve in lieu of a regular sleeping bag.

Insulation is the role of shirts, sweaters, or down (or synthetic-fill) clothing. Over these in foul weather comes the *parka,* whose function is to break the wind and shed water. A completely waterproof parka is undesirable, except for light work in heavy rain, since perspiration cannot evaporate through it. The ideal parka fabric remains to be developed.

Parkas of cotton or cotton reinforced with nylon are tough, wind-resistant, and repel water reasonably well when properly treated with waterproofing substances. However, they are relatively bulky and heavy, weighing about 1½ pounds. Unlined nylon wind shirts with attached hoods are tough, wind-resistant, light, and compact enough to stuff into a pocket, but have very little resistance to rain. They are excellent for high altitudes, where rain is not a problem. However, many recent imports are loosely woven and more appropriate when worn for style around a ski lodge than for warmth on a windy ridge. Quality can be determined by trying to blow through the material and observing resistance. Additional raingear is a desirable supplement to either a cotton or a nylon parka.

A double parka consisting of two layers of cotton or one of nylon and one of cotton is a heavier combination which acts on the principle of the outer layer shedding water though saturated itself and the inner water-repellent layer becoming wet only on the surface, remaining dry on the inside even in a heavy rain, for a while at least.

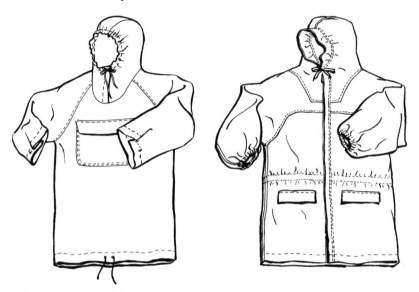

Fig. 3. Parkas. *Left,* for average conditions. *Right,* with face tunnel for more extreme conditions.

Essential to any parka is a hood that protects the head, neck, and face. The hood should be roomy enough for additional hat(s) inside and come well up over the chin. A drawstring can close a face tunnel so that only eyes and nose are uncovered. The skirt should extend nearly to the knees and there should be a drawstring at the waist and full sleeves with snaps, elastic, velcro tape or drawstrings for wrist closure. Large slash pockets on the chest, with buttons or zippers, are useful for warming hands and storing mittens, goggles, and candy bars. Some climbers prefer the pullover design, for though a front zipper allows easy control of body temperature, a zipper can jam and a parka which cannot be closed will not give full protection when really needed. Large-toothed nylon zippers are superior to small-toothed or metal zippers; though they occasionally catch material they rarely tear it and show very little tendency to freeze in cold conditions.

Raingear

When hiking or climbing in rain the choice lies between getting wet quickly with cold water from the sky or more slowly with warm water from the body. A variety of light, compact, and fairly durable raingear is available; each presents the same problem in some degree.

Full-length *ponchos* shed the rain and allow more air circulation than parkas; their major fault lies in being so cumbersome as to be restricted to camps and open trails. A coated-nylon poncho which can double as a tarp weighs about ¾ pound.

A *rain parka* and *chaps*, or a *cagoule* (a roomy, knee-length pullover parka), can be used for protection while moving in a hard rain. Coated-nylon fabrics are lightweight though delicate, and lose their waterproofness with heavy use; plastic is cheap but tears too easily to be reliable; rubberized fabric is durable and waterproof but too heavy.

Headgear

An unprotected head can account for from one-third to one-half of the body's heat loss. The head, therefore, is the first part one should cool when over-heating, and equally important, the most vital part to insulate when getting chilled (when your feet are cold — put on your hat).

Several types of headgear are often carried to serve different purposes: a *rain hat* with brim can double as sun protection, while a battered *wool felt* is hot as a sunshade but serves well in cold and rain. *Brimmed hats* keep rain from trickling down the neck but should have a tie so they will not sail away in a gust of wind.

Whatever the choice, a warm, *insulating cap* of wool or orlon to fit under the parka hood or hat is necessary for cold weather, emergencies, bivouacs, and sleeping. A *balaclava helmet* or *toque* covers the entire head and neck. Some carry a *wool scarf* for the neck area in combination with a *stocking cap*.

In the sun many use only a *sweat band* or a *handkerchief* knotted at the corners and dampened periodically with water. Others need the more complete protection of a brimmed hat with a handkerchief "tent" hanging down to protect neck and face; many "sheiks" appear in the intense sun of glacier travel. Mosquito hats are often used by the most ultra-sensitive to reduce ultraviolet exposure.

Mittens and Gloves

Mittens are better than gloves for warmth, allowing the fingers to snuggle together. A pair of heavy wool mittens, worn inside wind- and water-repellent overmitts when the situation demands, suffices for most climbing. Ideally either the inner mitt or overmitt covers the wrist and laps under or over the parka sleeve. An extra pair of wool mittens is desirable when one pair becomes soaked in rain or snow (some ski mitts have foam insulation which is effective even when wet). Leather gloves are advisable for belaying and useful in thorny brush but are difficult to waterproof and next to impossible to dry. At very low temperatures (about 0°F), exposed fingers freeze to metal — in these circumstances light silk or nylon gloves are worn under mitts and allow most tasks to be performed without exposing the skin. Fingerless wool gloves may be useful in cold-weather rock climbing; attacking army surplus wool gloves with scissors is an economical approach.

PACKS

The climber usually owns two packs: a rucksack or summit pack large enough to hold the necessities for a 1-day climb and a frame pack with a bag sufficient to carry camping gear and supplies for a week or more.

Rucksacks

Many styles of rucksacks are available, from small contoured packs just large enough to hold lunch, essentials, and extra clothing, to huge sacks that will hold hardware rack, rope, sleeping gear, and food for several days of technical climbing. In choosing a rucksack one must be sure it fits well and the capacity is suited to individual needs. Most important, the pack should be designed to carry the load high and close to the back; a slight forward lean brings the load directly over the feet so that balance is not disturbed.

Fig. 4. Carry weight high, close to the shoulders. *Left,* pack on hips, forcing a crouch. *Right,* pack high, allowing comfortable upright stance.

A waistband is helpful to prevent unpredictable lurching. Some rucksacks include a light, flexible frame for comfort and coolness but this is a matter of preference. A double bottom of nylon or leather, haul strap, and ice ax carrier are desirable for rugged climbing. Other accessories on the outside such as side pockets, flap pocket, straps for attaching rope, crampons, and skis are matters of preference and anticipated use.

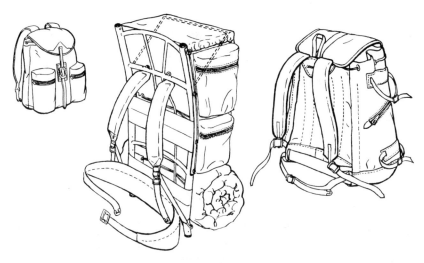

Fig. 5. Packs. *Left,* small cloth rucksack (day pack). *Center,* pack with contoured metal frame and hip band. *Right,* rucksack with interior frame (note: no exterior pockets to snag when hauling up rock faces).

Frame Packs

For loads of 30 pounds or more a frame pack is desirable. Consisting of a long, rigid frame held away from the back by taut nylon or mesh backbands or a network of strings or webbing, it allows the load to be carried high and shared among shoulders, back, and hips on well-padded shoulder straps and a wide, easily-adjustable waistband. The waistband performs a vital function in controlling the distribution of load: a snug belt places most of the weight on the hips; a loose one loads the shoulders more heavily. The frame should be fitted or adjusted so the waistband comes to the top of the hip bones when snugged up, for if the frame is too long the waistband will be too low, restricting leg movement when going uphill and not putting the proper load on the hips. A superior contrivance is a hip belt that completely encircles the pelvic girdle at a constant height with an adjustable attachment to the frame to transfer the load onto the belt.

Optimum distance between shoulder straps at the top of the frame, and the correct length of the straps, both depending on the skeletal structure of the packer, are other important features in fitting a pack correctly. With proper adjustments to torso length and size most frame sizes can be carried by anyone.

Either cotton or nylon bags are satisfactory; nylon, being somewhat lighter though inevitably more costly, dominates the market. New pack styles are coming on the market constantly, offering an infinite variety in combinations of pockets, compartments, and closure arrangements; choice is governed by individual desires. A full-length sack is preferred by some in order to have a single unit and further protect the sleeping bag from rain and brush. Packs that utilize zippers for load-carrying structure or crucial closures should be approached with caution since failure of a zipper could disable the pack.

Anything that needs to be carried can be lashed to a frame. When a rucksack is necessary for climbing it can be lashed directly to the frame in lieu of the pack sack in order to save weight.

MISCELLANEOUS EQUIPMENT

A catalog of sometimes-useful miscellany could easily run to many volumes. The checklist at the end of this chapter suggests many items that need no elaboration; others are discussed in later chapters. Some few things, however, not covered elsewhere must be carried by every climber on every trip, having been proven essential not only by demands of convenience but by the recorded history of unnecessary tragedy.

Flashlights and Headlamps

Climbs frequently begin before dawn and often end after dark. Every climber must therefore carry a reliable flashlight or headlamp on every climb.

A hand-held flashlight is relatively light and fully satisfactory if the hands are free at all times. The headlamp has important advantages on climbs where rope and ice ax place priority demands on the hands; in emergencies where the party must move over difficult terrain in the dark it can be a lifesaver.

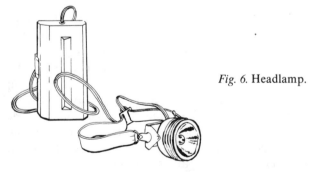

Fig. 6. Headlamp.

The choice of size and type of batteries and bulbs depends upon usage. Alkaline batteries are 50 per cent heavier than standard carbon-zinc and cost about three times as much but have a useful life two to four times longer in continuous use. However, for intermittent use the standard battery has almost the same life. At low temperatures the diffusion rate of all batteries is considerably reduced, but rewarming of batteries that have run down at low temperature gives additional life, possibly even exceeding that of new cells. Since degradation of cells occurs during the storage period — which is usually considerably longer in duration than discharge time — lower temperatures are better for storage, slowing the self-discharge reaction.

Larger batteries have greater capacity — that is, they last longer. A D-size has more capacity per unit weight, and thus greater efficiency, than a C-size battery. High-amperage bulbs draw more current, so smaller bulbs giving dimmer light last longer. A suggested safe minimum for most trips is a flashlight using two C-size carbon-zinc cells and a .27 amp bulb plus a spare set of batteries and bulb, a combination giving up to 6 hours of light in continuous usage. (A wise precaution is to reverse the batteries until the light is needed to prevent accidental discharge in the pack.) A PR4 bulb is rated at .40 candlepower and draws .27 amperes from fresh cells. A PR2 bulb produces .80 candlepower and draws .50 amperes. Bulbs with a lower amperage are available at special outlets. With a voltage of 1.8 the light is bright enough to illuminate a cross-country route; with 1.0 volt the light is adequate for following a trail.

Table 3 compares various combinations of batteries and bulbs, as tested by Recreational Equipment Inc.

Table 3. Comparative Performance of Flashlight Batteries.

| Batteries | Bulb | Continuous Burning Time Hours | | | | | | Cost Per Hour 70°F Cents | | Weight Per Hour 70°F Ounces | |
| | | 70°F | | 0°F | | *70°F | | | | | |
		1.8V	1.0V	1.8V	1.0V	1.8V	1.0V	1.8V	1.0V	1.8V	1.0V
AA Carbon Zinc	PR4	0.43	0.83	0.025	0.075	0.33	0.83	93	48	2.55	1.33
AA Alkaline	PR4	2.88	4.37	0.33	0.73	3.17	4.75	38	25	.59	.39
C Carbon Zinc	PR4	0.92	2.32	0.07	0.20	0.50	2.38	52	21	3.04	1.21
C Heavy Duty Carbon Zinc	PR4	2.75	4.12	0.83	2.13	1.92	4.77	20	13	1.02	.68
C Alkaline	PR4	9.67	15.00	0.25	2.43	8.25	9.02	13	8	.48	.31
D Carbon Zinc	PR2	1.48	3.73	0.20	1.77	1.22	4.50	32	14	4.05	1.61
D Carbon Zinc	PR4	3.33	18.25	0.58	2.07	1.67	16.25	15	3	1.80	.33
D Heavy Duty Carbon Zinc	PR2	2.50	4.50	0.18	2.27	1.58	3.85	22	12	2.40	1.33
D Heavy Duty Carbon Zinc	PR4	6.20	11.42	2.20	4.25	4.08	8.23	9	5	.96	.53
D Alkaline	PR2	11.80	19.47	0.75	4.77	8.00	13.40	13	8	.75	.45
D Alkaline	PR4	30.33	35.92	3.75	11.23	16.00	20.00	5	4.5	.29	.24

*After batteries had run down to 1.0V per pair at 0°F and then were rewarmed to room temperature.

Firestarters

An emergency supply of matches, waterproofed or stowed in a watertight container, must always be carried. Since "waterproof" matches are frequently fireproof as well, an alternative is wooden matches stored with a strip of sandpaper in an absolutely waterproof container. A stub of plumber's candle or a bit of solid chemical fuel ("heat tabs," "canned heat," "fuel rations") is indispensable to ignite wet wood, start a fire quickly in an emergency, or on a glacier when other fuel is lacking, to warm a cup of lifesaving water or juice.

Knife

In food preparation, in firebuilding, in first aid, in high-angle rock climbing — everywhere in alpine life — a knife is so essential that every climber must carry one. The traditional Boy Scout knife with two folding blades, can opener, combination screwdriver and bottle opener, and sometimes an awl, is handiest and least expensive. The similar Swiss Army knife is superior in every respect but costs more. For special purposes a hunting knife is handy, as are double-bitted axes and chainsaws, but the modest mountaineer contents himself with a modest blade.

Canteen

High peaks are usually bone-dry or solidly frozen, so each climber must carry a canteen. A 1-pint capacity generally suffices in coastal mountains; a quart is not enough in more sun-blasted ranges. Wide-mouthed poly bottles are most popular among mountaineers because they can be refilled with snow or from trickles more easily than small-mouthed bottles. With a poly bottle a climber can enjoy fruit juices untainted by the toxic metal salts generated in containers of steel or aluminum. Metal canteens do offer one major advantage over poly bottles, however: when their contents are frozen they can be thawed by holding them directly over a flame.

Sunburn Preventives

Sunlight at high altitudes has a burning capacity many times greater than at sea level — so much greater, especially on snow, that it is a threat not only to comfort but to health. Despite commercially encouraged superstition, there is no way to get a suntan without getting a sunburn, the two being inseparable parts of the same process. One can develop a tan painlessly only by controlling the length and intensity of exposure, and since the climber cannot avoid long exposure he must reduce the intensity of sunlight reaching his skin by the use of clothing wherever possible and sunburn preventives on exposed skin. Individuals vary widely in natural pigmentation and thus in toleration to exposure and in degree of protection needed. There is only one rule: the penalty for underestimation is so severe that no amount of protection can be called excessive. Tanned skin, whatever its cosmetic value, offers minor protection against the intense burning of high altitudes. More than one novice climber has gone along for weeks patiently building a tan, and on his first trip relying for protection on natural pigment found himself burned and blistered and peeled right back down to a winter white.

By far the best sun protection is clothing, and even on a hot day the discomfort of covering up is well justified. For areas that cannot be protected with clothing, actors' grease paint (clown white) or zinc-oxide pastes give virtually complete protection, and a grease base ensures against their being washed off by perspiration. One application is good for the entire climb, except where fingers and equipment rub the skin bare. The major disadvantage is that grease is somewhat difficult to remove. Alcohol base "suntan" lotions offer little protection even at moderate altitudes. There are commercial products available which, if not sweated off, effectively block ultraviolet rays.

Some people who are particularly susceptible to fever blisters around the mouth as a result of exposure to sun coat their lips completely with a total-sun-blocking cream or zinc oxide, knowing that enduring the rude remarks of their companions is preferable to spending the next weeks healing painful sores.

Glasses — Sun and Prescription

Eyes are particularly vulnerable to the brilliance of mountain skies and if unprotected can quickly be painfully burned or even permanently damaged. It is essential for the climber to have sunglasses which greatly reduce the amount of both visible light and invisible ultraviolet and infrared rays striking the eyes: passage should be no more than 10 or 15 per cent. The lenses should be very dark, but careful shopping is necessary, since many inexpensive sunglasses offered for sale on the American market are more for style than for eye protection. The design must be such as to keep light from entering at the sides and bottom, yet give adequate ventilation to prevent fogging. Extra pairs of goggles are worth carrying by any party venturing onto the blinding wastes of snowfield or glacier. In emergency a piece of cardboard with small slits can save the eye from damage, though providing minimal vision.

Climbers who need prescription glasses to obtain any clear view of their surroundings encounter special problems. Any climber so nearsighted as to have difficulty traveling treacherous terrain must always carry an extra pair in his rucksack. A good combination in bright conditions is a pair of large, well-ventilated ski goggles worn loosely over prescription lenses;

less cumbersome but again more expensive are prescription goggles.

Many climbers carry two degrees of eye protection for differing conditions: an average pair for trail and meadow travel and rock climbing, and a pair of "dark-dark" goggles for the intense glare of snow and high-altitude glacier travel.

Insect Repellents

The habits and avoidance of insects are described in Chapter 3. When they must be lived with, as is all too frequently the case, various defenses besides the swift swat may be employed. Complete coverage by clothing, including even gloves and head nets in extreme conditions, keeps out mosquitoes and flies but not no-see-ums or ticks, and in warm weather is so uncomfortable the climber may choose to take the insects on bare-knuckle style. Insect repellents may therefore be necessary.

For general-purpose use the chemical N, N-diethyl-metatoluamide (diethyl toluamide) has been judged most effective. Acting on the principle that the "touch" repulses the insect — it will land but not bite — one application to the skin of one of the stronger concentrations is effective for several hours. Protection is good against mosquitoes, flies, no-seem-ums, chiggers, and ticks. Diethyl toluamide in alcohol solution is marketed under several brand names with differing potencies (75% active ingredients being the most potent) and in differing forms such as cream, stick, aerosol spray, and foam.

Repair and Improvisation

All climbers through experience accumulate emergency kits composed of odd bits and pieces wonderfully versatile in times of trouble: an assortment of wires, tape, safety pins (of obvious value in patching broken equipment), needles (from blister-puncturing size up to sailors' awls for piercing leather), thread, razor blades, yarn, squares of patching fabric, coils of nylon string, small pliers — the list could be extended indefinitely. Generally a climber carries those items he wishes he had carried on some past climb, and though this may seem like locking the barn door after the horse is stolen, misfortunes do indeed tend to repeat themselves.

Ice Ax

The numerous uses of the ice ax and its specifications are discussed in later chapters. It is mentioned here because of its indispensability on snowfields and glaciers and snowcovered alpine trails in spring and early summer and its great value in traveling steep heather, scree, and brush and in crossing stream by footlog or ford. An ax is nearly useless and can be dangerous if carried by a person who has not practiced self-arrests on steep snow, a skill that cannot be obtained from this or any other book, but only by practice, practice, and more practice.

EQUIPMENT CHECKLIST

It is difficult on journey's eve to remember everything that may be needed. The more quickly one packs, the more easily an item may be forgotten. The seasoned climber has learned, often as not through sad experience, that a systematic run through his checklist is the only sure way, no matter how many times he has packed his sack for past trips. The following example is representative, though by no means either universal or complete; each person should make his own list. For more technical climbing he will choose specialized equipment which best satisfies his requirements and fancy. Items that may be shared in small groups are indicated by an asterisk (*); those in parentheses are optional, depending on personal preference and the nature of the trip.

Any Trip

In Pack

Ten Essentials:
map of area (in a case)
compass
flashlight with extra
    batteries and bulb
extra food
extra clothing (socks,
    mitts, sweaters, long
    underwear, scarf)
sunglasses
pocket knife
matches in waterproof
    container
candle or firestarter
first aid kit

Other:
lunch
sunburn preventive
    (lip protection)
(insect repellent)
handkerchief
toilet paper
canteen
(small insulation pad
    — to sit upon)
whistle
(altimeter)
(camera and film)
emergency shelter

Clothing

boots
socks
(gaiters)
underwear
pants
warm sweater and shirt
parka

hat(s), wool (rain, sun)
mittens, gloves
(wind pants)
(rain gear)
(shorts)
(hot weather shirt)

Overnight and Longer Trips

frame pack (rucksack)
sleeping bag
foam pad or mattress
*shelter — tent and
    accessories, tarp,
    groundsheet
*food
eating utensils (cup,
    plate, spoon)
*stove, accessories and
    fuel
*pots, accessories,
    scouring pad

*(water container)
(personal hygiene —
    toothbrush, towel)
*repair kit — pliers, wire,
    cord, razor, needle,
    thread, buttons, rivets,
    pins, etc.
(change(s) of clothing)
(down garment)
(spare underwear)
(camp footgear)

Glacier or Winter Climbs

ice ax
crampons
carabiners
slings (chest, swami,
    prusik)
(hard hat)
(avalanche cord)
*climbing rope
*(rescue pulley)
*(flukes, pickets, ice
    screws)
*(wands)
*(snow shovel)
*(igloo saw)
(snowshoes; skis, poles)
(brake bar)

additional warm clothing
    mitten shells
    extra mittens, socks
    balaclava helmet or toque
    long underwear
    (down clothing)
extra goggles
(extra candles)

additional leader gear
    (alarm timepiece)
    (group first aid)
    (headlamp and batteries)

Basic Rock Climbs

hard hat   (knee pads)
carabiners   *climbing rope
belaying gloves   *(chocks and runners,
sling rope   pitons, hammer)
(swami belt, rappel sling)   *(descending rings)
(brake bar)

Supplementary Reading:

Manning, Harvey. *Backpacking: One Step at a Time.* Seattle: Recreational
　Equipment Inc., 1972.

Current catalogs of outdoor equipment retailers. Generally available on
　request.

3 *

CAMPING AND SLEEPING

A CLIMBING CAMP is not always a comfortable, snug alpine haven, but if proximity to the summit is the determining factor a bivouac on a ledge of the mountain itself may be dictated, since the way to gain an extra hour for the climb is to camp an hour higher on the mountain. Forests ordinarily provide easy and excellent camps but often are too far below the peaks for reasonable summit attempts. Meadows above timberline offer the best sites in terms of esthetics, but because of their brief growing season are the most fragile of the mountain ecosystems.

Whatever the goal, concern for the environment should have equal weight with concern for comfort. Heathers must bloom, seed, and add their fraction of an inch of growth within a brief 2-month period, and at their exceedingly slow growth rate damage done to plants by an overnight stay can require many years of recovery. Grasses are more resilient, yet a tarp or tent left on meadow turf for a week may wipe out an entire growing season for the covered patch; moving a permanent camp every few days reduces the harm done any one spot. A rock slab is least vulnerable, and thus from this point of view, best; a sandy or gravelly flat, and open, plant-sparse areas in deep forest, in that order, are slightly less ideal.

A large proportion of long-established campsites in American mountains are on the banks of lakes and streams. However waterside plant communities are so especially delicate, and water pollution such a growing problem with the back-country population explosion of recent years, that most of these camps will have to be abandoned. Indeed, in some areas camping already is officially banned within 100 or 200 feet of highland lakes and creeks.

Timberline trees grow very slowly — some less than 10 feet tall have been found to be hundreds of years old; stoves therefore should always be carried for alpine camping.

Charms of the view and the immediate locality often influence choice of site, but microclimatology also must be given consideration: wind is the most active cooling agent and its capricious alpine behavior can be quite exasperating. Patterns of flow are often highly localized, with a full gale blasting one patch of meadow, while a few yards away the flowers droop in still and sultry air. Also to be considered is the relationship of wind to tent: pitched with the wind blowing in the open end, the tent distends, interior pressure equalizing exterior and minimizing "flap." But alpine winds are instantaneously reversible without warning — a tarp strung as a windbreak in afternoon may become a balloon after sunset. One consolation of foul weather is that storm winds are fairly consistent.

Frequently an up-slope afternoon breeze reverses at night to an icy down-slope draft from snowfields. Cold air is heavier than warm air and in settled weather flows downward like water, following valleys and collecting in depressions. Thus there is often a chill breeze down a creek or dry wash and a pool of cold air in a basin. Night air is often degrees cooler beside a river or lake than on benches or knolls above.

During a heavy, wet snowfall the snow must not be allowed to pile up on tent and fly — forces on the rigging may become excessive and bring the whole structure down on the occupants. Continual shaking of tent walls and even shoveling out under the eaves are often required.

Polyethylene ground sheets are necessary under a tarp (and under or over tent floors of non-waterproof material); normally water stays below the sheet. Sudden rains sometimes cause floods not foreseen when camp was made. Ditching, that is digging of drainage channels around tents or tarps, is not an acceptable practice; meadow turf is usually a tangle of struggling roots, severance of which can damage plants several feet away. If ground water is a problem, moving camp, though a nuisance, is the best solution.

SHELTER

In most mountains the weather is untrustworthy and huts scarce, and therefore many alpine travelers carry portable shelter. Tents and tarps both have virtues and vices, and each for some conditions is unquestionably superior. Since a party can carry one or the other but usually not both, the question of which is best for all-around use is much argued. Certainly a tent is the only shelter worthy of the name above timberline, for glacier camps, winter camping, in strong winds, and in mosquito country. Of prime importance, it can be erected almost anywhere, being a self-contained unit. The main criticism of tents is that they are either heavy or expensive and no serious mountaineer can afford the burden of a cheap, heavy tent.

Absurdly enough, shelter is often more necessary on a clear night than on a cloudy one: whenever two opposing surfaces differ in temperature, the warmer radiates heat to the colder. Since the human body is usually warmer than the night sky, exposed portions of the body or sleeping bag radiate heat and grow cold. Any shelter at all serves as a baffle: a climber sacked out under a tree may sleep cozy and warm while his companion a few feet away shivers under the stars. Clouds often reflect heat back to earth and thus have the effect of a huge tarp between sleeper and sky; the clear nights are the cold ones.

Tarps

A tarp is both light in weight and low in cost, and offers adequate shelter from all but extreme weather in lowland forests and among subalpine trees. It gives less protection than a tent from heat loss and wind but allows more convenient study of natural science and scenic splendor. On the debit side, setting up a tarp demands human ingenuity and some co-operation from the landscape.

Tarps of polyethylene are inexpensive and though not as durable as nylon, the cost is so small that frequent replacement is economically feasible. Coated-nylon tarps come with reinforced grommets sewn into sides and corners for easy rigging. Tarps lacking grommets can be rigged by tying off each corner around a small cone or pebble or with a Visklamp — a small rubber ball and a dumbbell-shaped metal gadget. Another method is permanently attached loops of nylon tape.

The most versatile size is about 9 by 12 feet, providing luxurious living room for two people and their gear and adequate for three, or even four if they are small people or very good friends. An 11- by 14-foot size will house four more comfortably. In smaller sizes the usable space approaches the vanishing point, since the outer margins of tarp-covered ground are usually only half-protected, if that.

Rigging a tarpaulin shelter is an art using only a few basic designs but unlimited variations; the architect needs imagination and experience to become a master.

The weary climber who wraps himself in the tarp as if it were a large blanket is protected from wind but generally finds himself damp from his own perspiration by morning.

The *A-tent* design resembles a true tent, the tarp being draped over a line stretched between two supports, its edges fastened down on either side. Trees, large boulders, or telescoping tent poles can be employed as end supports, but if these are lacking, either one or two bipods can be improvised, as shown in the illustration. Maximum protection in wind-driven rain is gained by rigging the tarp as close to the ground as needs for head room will allow, edges flush to the ground, anchored with a large log, rocks, or ridge of snow. The windward foot or two will be wet so ample overhang should be allowed. In calm weather the edges may be raised some distance in the air for spacious and gracious living.

The *shed roof,* with the four corners tied to anything handy, covers more floor area than the A-tent; though of no value in high wind it is ideal in mild weather or gently falling rain.

Whatever the design, a tarp must be rigged with tight lines to reduce flapping in the wind and to provide proper roof drainage. Tarp campers

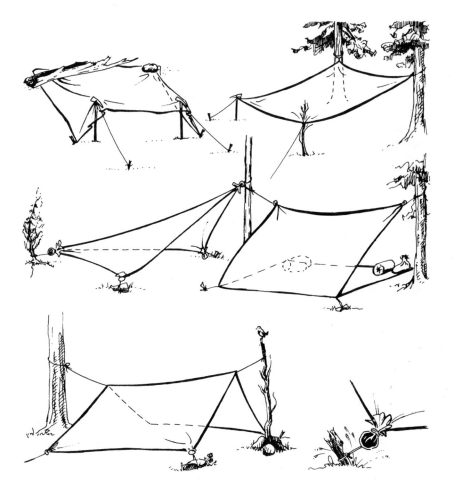

Fig. 7. Shelters improvised from tarps. Tarps without grommets can be secured by wrapping tarp edge around a small object and tying as shown in lower right.

customarily carry a considerable quantity of strong, light nylon cord to enable them to use any conceivable kind of anchor points.

When terrain allows two tarps to be pitched together the waste area is much decreased, whether the two be overlapped at or along the ridge in a giant A-tent or side by side in a shed. With such "circus tents" vast regions may be covered so that even a prolonged rain or drizzle can be outwaited in comparative freedom and comfort.

Equipment as well as climbers needs shelter. Whenever space is cramped within tent or tarp it is well to carry a number of large plastic sacks and sheets of plastic for dry storage outside. In wet mountains the few extra ounces are worth the weight.

Tents

Tents offer the greatest protection and comfort, though at considerable cost. Lightweight materials can provide housing for 2 to 4 pounds per person, including poles and hardware. The profusion of designs, sizes, weights, and materials makes choice difficult and requires many hours of poring over mountain shop catalogs. Better still is observation of tents in use; owners are generally willing to discuss the advantages and defects of their models.

The choice between a two-man or four-man version depends on the use intended. The four-man with high (6- to 7-foot) center pole affords luxurious living with the opportunity to stand, sit, and cook in comfort, profoundly helpful to morale during a long stormy spell. The size, however, gives less flexibility in choice of alpine campsites and weight is excessive when used for only two people.

A completely enclosed unit must be well ventilated and preferably should "breathe". If the tent is made of completely waterproof material, even with good ventilation, the moisture exhaled by occupants and especially from cooking condenses on the cold walls and runs down to collect in puddles on the floor. In a single windless night two persons can expel enough water vapor from lungs to drench their sleeping bags.

No one has yet built a single-wall tent that can both breathe and keep out driving rain. Old-style single-layer cotton tents, generally somewhat heavier than nylon, are satisfactory for drier areas. They breathe adequately and the closely woven fibers swell when wet so that rain runs down the outside; however touching the walls causes water to "wick" through to the inside of the tent, and wind gusts can shower occupants with each flap. Mountaineers who frequent wet wildernesses therefore prefer a double-wall design consisting of a very lightweight tent of breathable nylon and a waterproof rain fly. Most such tents have a waterproof floor and some have waterproof sidewalls to exclude rain that blows under eaves of the fly.

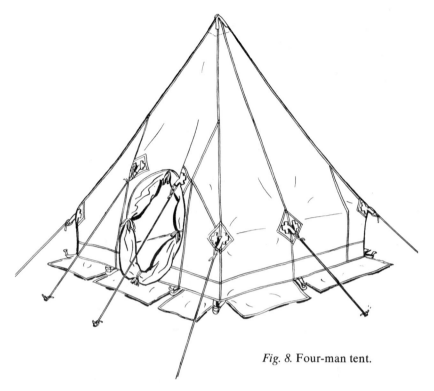

Fig. 8. Four-man tent.

One less well-known but proven design has a non-waterproof floor made of the same fabric as the walls. Lined with replaceable lightweight polyethylene sheets, it provides a convenient drainage system for water from rain, condensation, spilled soup, and wet or snowy boots and gear, all of which puddle on a waterproof floor. (It is worth noting that the coating on waterproof fabric is not permanent anyway and becomes non-waterproof with the normal wear on floors.)

The pole arrangement is a major decision: interior poles intrude into living space but are usually simpler and lighter; exterior poles provide taut sidewalls with less flap but are more complex to rig and require more hardware.

Various entrance designs offer zip doors, tunnels, and cooking alcoves. Cooking inside, protected from the wind, considerably reduces fuel consumption and may be necessary in storms. Two-man tents often have an alcove for this purpose, the living space being too small unlike four-man tents. Many options are offered in the arrangement and types of ventilation holes, windows, mosquito netting, and other features. In general the more zippers and openings the greater the weight and cost.

Fig. 9. Mountain tents. *Upper,* two-man tent with rain fly at left. *Lower,* tent with hoop-like supports.

The psychological and esthetic value of tent color is a consideration. Brighter hues are more pleasing to the tent-bound and the high reflectance and contrast have practical value to the climber seeking camp in fog or dark.

Guylines, preferably the minimum necessary to rig a tent for a hard blow, should originate from the high point of interior poles for better rigidity. In soft snow stakes may sometimes be replaced by "deadmen," bags filled with snow or rocks. Stakes themselves can be used as deadmen by burying them in a trench in a horizontal position and perpendicular to the guyline; more serviceable deadmen can be prepared in advance by drilling holes in a stake and attaching a bridle.

A fly should be designed not to touch the walls when properly rigged; where it touches, the condensation effect is the same as in a waterproof tent. The fly should come fairly close to the ground to adequately cover the tent and entrance and minimize exposure to wind-driven rain.

Snow Camps

A snow camp can be warm and comfortable, but in no other camp is insulation so important or shelter so essential. Every person who goes into the mountains must be able to provide himself with the minimum conditions for a comfortable night on snow — or at the very least for survival.

The most convenient shelter is a *tent* installed on a stamped-out platform slightly larger than the floor. In forests a natural shelter can often be found in a *tree cave*; some snow engineering, a tarp, and lots of ingenuity make a snug hideaway in the worst blow or heaviest rainstorm. In the absence of trees a similar shelter can be improvised by digging a *trench* in the snow some 4 to 6 feet deep and large enough to accommodate the party, then stretching a tarp over the top, perhaps gaining a slight pitch by anchoring one side to a ridge of snow. Though excellent in windy or rainy weather, a heavy snowfall can easily and disastrously collapse a roof so nearly flat.

A *snow cave* requires more time but provides more protection during a storm. There is absolutely no comparison between the comfort of a calm, quiet cave and a flapping, gale-swept tent. In emergencies, snow caves have so often meant survival that mountaineers consider knowledge of the construction technique mandatory.

Fig. 10. Snow cave.

Although a snow cave can be dug by hand, the job is made much easier by a lightweight shovel, with which a cave for four can be dug in an hour or so, depending on snow conditions. All that is necessary in fairly firm snow is a minimum depth of about 6 feet; a steep slope such as along a riverbank or snowdrift is desirable. The first step is to dig an entry-way into the slope deep enough to start a tunnel. Continue to dig inward about 3 feet to form the entrance, then upward to make the living area large enough for the party. The floor of the sleeping area should be above the top of the entry tunnel to trap warm air inside. The upper surfaces should be smooth and concave so that any melting snow will run down the walls rather than drip on occupants. To avoid asphyxiation, a ventilation hole is made to the outside and enlarged as necessary if the interior becomes too warm. A ground sheet on the sleeping area is necessary to keep things dry and prevent loss of equipment in the snow.

Under some conditions unsuitable for snow caves *snow-block* shelters can be constructed in A-frame designs or the traditional igloo. Proper snow consistency and a certain amount of expertise are prerequisites for this enterprise, especially the igloo.

The environmental impact of snow camping is often not immediately recognized: tin cans, leftover food and human wastes are obliterated by falling snow, only to reappear, unsightly, with the spring thaw. Pick up immediately any litter that drops in the snow and stow it away to be packed out.

BUGS

Wilderness is the occasional home of man and the permanent habitat of insects. The more lush the flowered alpine meadow, the greater the profusion of insects. Bugs are a nuisance at any hour but never more intolerable than when engaged in destroying sleep; thus they are discussed in the present context rather than any of a dozen others relevant.

There is no record of malaria or yellow fever contracted from alpine *mosquitoes* and, except in sub-Arctic ranges, little danger of being bitten to death. The bite is painless and the itching an irritation at worst, so that the hazard is chiefly mental — as is that of the Chinese water torture. The larvae hatch in water but even mud or moist humus will suffice, so that mosquitoes inhabit all but the most scorched mountains. Stimulated by warmth, they arrive with the spring snow melt, following the thaw up the mountainside and thriving until fall frosts. Fortunately most summer nights in alpine meadows are cold enough to send them to bed.

Exactly what attracts mosquitoes is not fully known. They can be observed patiently probing tree bark and stones in exploration that seems purely random. However, experiments have shown their interest and appetite are excited by carbon dioxide, by warm, moist surfaces, especially those dark in color, and by motion. When awake a traveler can minimize his personal escort of mosquitoes by fast walking and steady slapping, but when asleep his best defense is a tent guarded by netting at every orifice. Lacking a tent, complex baffles of tarps and sweaters can be arranged about the sleeping bag opening, though if the night is warm enough for mosquitoes such baffles are stifling. The ideal remedy for mosquitoes and every other flying bug is a steady breeze. Given a choice between hungry insects and a cold wind the latter is infinitely preferable.

Smallest of the fly family is the *no-see-um*, usually found in the North-west no higher than 2500 feet and almost exclusively in dank river bot-toms. Though invisible except in the dusk with the light behind it, this tiny insect gets off a most amazingly painful chew, the more unpleasant because one cannot see the creature to punish him. Wherever there is one no-see-um there are billions, every one of which can find its way into the most tightly sealed tent.

The *deer fly*, or *black fly*, resembling an ordinary house fly, and the large obscene *horse fly* or *elk fly*, both famous for their painful bites, mainly infest the upper forest zone and lush meadows, though in sultry weather they can be found deep in the forests and high on the rocks. Needing warmth for propagation, they arrive with summer and vanish with fall. They diminish in numbers, or even disappear temporarily, in the chill of a rainstorm, a good wind, or breezy shadows by a waterfall, and go quickly to sleep in all but the warmest dusk.

On approach marches in western ranges *ticks* are a nuisance if not a serious health menace. They are most abundant in the springtime of dry lands — local inquiry is advisable. The hallowed superstition that ticks drop from tree branches is false: ticks do not fly or climb or parachute. They creep along the ground, venturing sometimes 18 inches upward in search of a meal, rarely any higher except when they have found a host worth exploration. The majority can be thwarted merely by fastening the pants tightly around the boots and then watching for hitchhikers on pants legs. Formerly there was no alternative to a morning, noon, and night strip-to-the-skin-and-inspect routine, but diethyl toluamide, discussed in Chapter 2, is the first feasible repellant found that discourages ticks. Probably a thorough application to trouser legs would eliminate the need for frequent inspection.

A tick discovered during his preliminary prospecting will leave the area at a touch, being a nervous little beast. Even after an hour or so of serious drilling a gentle straightforward pull may still bring it entirely out into the open. Ticks do not "screw in" and there is no merit whatsoever to the old wives' method of "unscrewing" ticks, clockwise or counterclockwise, even though it continues to be recommended by people who should know better. Another traditional method, making a tick pull out by himself by touching his tail with gas, kerosene or a flame, is sometimes effective, as is an application of sunburn cream, insect repellent, or cooking oil.

Once deeply imbedded only surgery by razor blade or physician will do the trick. It may be less painful to take antibiotics and leave the head in the flesh like a thorn to fester and come out days or even weeks later. All remedial procedures connected with ticks are so loathsome that after camping in infested areas preventive measures should include inspection not only of bodies but of clothing, sleeping bags, tents, packs, and other equipment. Ticks can meander about a long while seeking a host and may be encountered hours or days distant from their proper home.

SLEEPING BAGS

Warmest and lightest of all conventional designs is the mummy bag: tapering toward the feet, hooded to fit over the head, and with a small face opening that can be closed with drawstrings to shut out wind. The unfortunate few suffering from claustrophobia use a rectangular bag, despite its extra weight and broad, breezy opening.

Zippers are the almost universal means of closure even though they sometimes snag the fabric or go off the trolley. Heat loss through the zipper is reduced by backing up the zipper with a tube of insulating material. Bags without zippers thus reduce weight and eliminate closure problems but complicate access.

The warmth, weight, and cost of a sleeping bag are chiefly functions of the kind and quantity of insulation — kapok, wool, Dacron, or down. Wool and kapok bags are inexpensive, but so heavy and bulky relative to warmth that neither merits consideration for backpacking. Dacron is inexpensive and for equivalent weights about halfway between wool and down in warmth; its great flaw is incompressibility, making for a very bulky roll. The best insulation, and for serious mountaineering long considered to be the only one worth consideration, is down, the soft small underfeathers of aquatic fowl. With care a good down bag lasts for years and repays its initial expense many times over in warmer nights and lighter loads. Bags using the new Dacron Fiberfill II, or similar polyesters, have just reached the market. Claims are made that weight for weight their insulation value is within 10 per cent of down and that when wet they retain 80 per cent of warmth versus 0 per cent for down. Insufficient time has elapsed for these claims to be proved, and for various design problems to be solved, but the cost is half that of a down bag of equivalent weight.

Bags are made containing anywhere from less than 1 to more than 3 pounds of down. Those with minimal insulation are mainly intended to keep a person from freezing to death on a bivouac, although hardy types aiming for lighter packs and versatility may use them in combination with a down parka; the heaviest and most expensive bags provide insulation unnecessary except in arctic conditions. At alpine camps in western American mountains 2½ pounds of down is about the average needed, though a person who sleeps cold may do well to buy a bag with more, or perhaps sleep in a suit of down or Dacron underwear.

The warmth of a sleeping bag depends on the entrapment of dead air. The loft, or inches of thickness, determines the degree of insulation. Air adjacent to the body in the cavity of the bag is heated to body temperature, the gradient decreasing towards outside-air temperature at the surface of

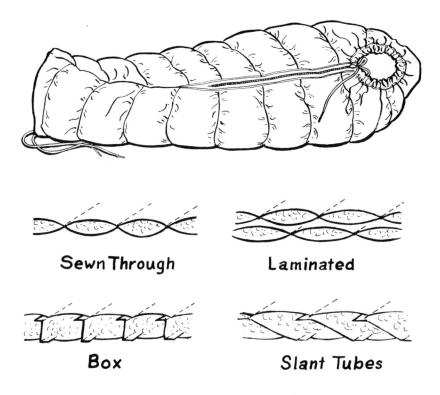

Sewn Through

Laminated

Box

Slant Tubes

Fig. 11. Sleeping bag and cross sections of construction methods.

the bag. The compressibility of down and feathers allows the bag to be rolled into a compact bundle, and so to restore loft the bag should be briskly shaken before use and occasionally aired in the sun to restore pristine fluffiness. Since down is useless underneath the body, compressing flat and losing all insulating value, the bag should be held upside down when being fluffed so the filling comes to rest on top of the sleeper.

Four methods of construction are used to keep the down uniformly distributed: sewn-through, box, slant tube, and overlapping tube. Sewn-through construction is just that — the inner cover is stitched directly to the outer, a simple and inexpensive method, but one with substantial heat loss at the seams. Box construction is more expensive but the increase in warmth is equivalent to that gained by adding a pound of down to a sewn-through bag. The most efficient and expensive designs have slant- or overlapping tube construction, offsetting the inner and outer seams to reduce the possibility of cold spots.

The ability of down or feathers to entrap dead air, and thus to insulate, depends on the integrity of the minute structure of its filaments. Two things affect these filaments and decrease their efficiency: fiber compaction from body oils and dirt, and eventual breakage of their structure from the compression of use. A removable washable liner, which adds a few ounces, or spot-cleaning of soiled areas, especially around the head of the bag, prolongs the time between cleanings. A durable outer cover adds weight but also some insulation and protection from moisture and abrasion.

Although bags may be safely dry cleaned by professionals who know how to handle bags and who use proper solvents, traces of toxic fluids may remain in the bag and if it is not thoroughly aired, can lead to sickness or even death. Dry cleaning also removes water repellant compounds from the nylon fabric; thus a bag that has been dry-cleaned more readily absorbs moisture. Bags may be hand-washed with mild soap in warm water, rinsed thoroughly to remove all traces of soap, which otherwise can compact the down, and the excess water squeezed gently out by hand or the bag spun gently in the washer. (A wet sleeping bag must be handled carefully to prevent damage to the inner structure.) It should be dried by alternately tumbling in a dryer 15 or 20 minutes at the lowest heat setting and air-drying in a shady place, with frequent shaking and turning to break up the lumps of wet down. Several days must be allowed for this process. Warning: more bags are ruined by careless washing than by any other cause.

The difficulty of drying a wet bag in the mountains dictates that every effort must be made to keep it dry. Failing that, a day in the sunshine is most effective; a campfire will not do the job except with many long patient hours and risk of damage by sparks. Moisture condensed on the bag surface in cold weather should be dried by turning the damp side up and leaving the bag spread out under the tarp or in the tent.

Wearing wet clothing to bed can result in some drying, but at the expense of a cold sleep and wet bag, and is therefore not advisable. (In good weather clothing will dry more effectively next day over a bush in camp or hung from the pack while traveling, and in bad weather it will in any event get wet again very quickly.) In cold conditions *small* clothing items, such as mittens and socks, can be taken into the bag to dry.

Closing the bag around the face allows more immediate warming of the interior, a process also speeded by undressing inside the bag. A wool hat provides additional insulation for the head, and dry socks help warm cold feet. Heat loss from exhalation can be reduced by breathing through a sweater; pulling the head inside the bag warms both quickly but adds considerably to interior moisture.

GROUND INSULATION

Since down compresses under body weight to almost nothing, additional insulation is desirable for a warm bed. On wet ground or snow, conduction of heat from the sleeper's underside is very rapid and a ground pad is essential. Extra clothing, pack frame, rope, and boots can be improvised for padding but a foam or air mattress provides more comfort.

Fig. 12. Sleeping on pack and gear.

An *air mattress* provides the softest bed for its weight and bulk; however, on snow or cold ground convection currents within the air chambers carry heat away from the body. A thin foam pad on top of the mattress increases warmth.

A relatively thin (⅜-inch) pad of *closed-cell foam*, such as *ensolite*, provides good insulation under the bag but does not readily compress. A 1½-inch-thick pad of *open-cell foam* is often used; less Spartan than ⅜-inch sheets on hard ground, it becomes quite thinly compressed under body pressure and also makes a bulky roll. Some foam products are not adaptable to temperatures below 0°F.

A 4-foot-long pad or mattress is adequate, since items of equipment can be used to support and insulate feet and legs. In very cold weather the boots should be integrated somehow into the bed to assure their not becoming frozen.

The destruction of alpine plants and the strewing of resultant dead foliage are so repugnant that bough beds are not to be considered an alternative except in the direst of emergencies. Retaining their insulation and comfort so briefly, they rarely justify the time, effort, and vandalism necessary for their construction. Modern materials are so light, versatile, comfortable, and inexpensive as to render bough beds obsolete.

BIVOUACS

In American terminology a bivouac is a camp made in the course of a climb using only materials that can easily be carried in a rucksack. For long ascents bivouacs are often planned and their rigors lessened by down clothing, a special bivouac sack, cagoule, or perhaps merely a tarp and extra clothing. Since a planned bivouac ordinarily occurs only on a difficult climb the weight of special equipment must be kept small, but a pound or two extra per man is worthwhile for safety and additional comfort.

Shelter from wind and/or rain is most essential. Every climber should carry an emergency shelter consisting of a lightweight plastic tube (or two very large plastic trash bags). Better yet for a planned bivouac is either a cagoule, which is large enough to cover the whole body when the knees are drawn up to the chest, or a *bivouac sack* — a large, tent-like envelope of tightly-woven fabric, just large enough to accommodate one or two persons, needing no poles or stakes but equipped with strong loops for anchoring to rocks or pitons. For insulation in cold weather a half-length down bag weighing about 1 pound can be used with a down jacket. Another alternative is fitting a *bivouac sleeve* inside the pack; the climber puts his feet in the pack and pulls the sleeve up over his legs and hips, protecting his upper torso and extremities with waterproof parka or poncho. Body heat should always be utilized and the entire party should huddle together as much as possible for warmth.

More common is the bivouac forced by such unanticipated delays as an accident or loss of route. At low altitudes extra clothing, a small (12- to 14-inch) square insulating pad (sit-upon) and a hot drink prepared over a stove or *small* fire will dispel most discomfort.

In organizing a bivouac on the peak anything or anyone liable to fall — packs, bivouac sack, and climbers — is anchored. Body heat is conserved by brushing snow from clothing, exchanging damp garments for dry, removing (and carefully anchoring) wet boots, placing feet with dry socks in the rucksack, loosening belt and items of clothing that impede circulation, and donning all warm clothing such as hats, scarf, and mitts.

In reasonably good weather a high-altitude bivouac can be a memorable experience, with physical miseries more than repaid by a sky that reveals a wealth of unsuspected stars, but in bad weather that same bivouac can be dangerous in itself and leave the party seriously debilitated by morning.

A bivouac can be made any place with minimum equipment and time and extracts the maximum possible comfort from terrain and materials available. Every climber in planning every camp should begin thinking in terms of a bivouac, very cautiously and only grudgingly adding items to this skeletal list.

Supplementary Reading:

Manning, Harvey. *Backpacking: One Step at a Time.* Seattle: Recreational Equipment, Inc., 1972.

4 *

ALPINE CUISINE

THE CLIMBER eats primarily to provide fuel for reaching summits. In theory, therefore, some standard menu could be devised, such as cube sugar, margarine, dried beef, powdered milk, prunes, and vitamin tablets, which would serve for every excursion, short or long. It is even possible that these ingredients or their chemical equivalents could be homogenized and pressed into compact, durable bars imprinted with the recommended daily dosage.

However, the mountain experience is considerably more complex than a track meet, and includes not only victories on peaks but such small joys as a nice cup of tea. Good food gives a festive touch to summit celebrations, improves the scenery, and keeps up spirits during days of storm and fog. Bad food makes trails steeper, beds lumpier, sunsets paler, and friends harder to get along with.

Nonetheless, few people go into the wilderness primarily to eat. If quickly and simply fueling the body is the first aim of alpine cuisine, the greatest pleasure consistent with time and energy available is the second.

THE FIRE

At some point in the last several tens of thousands of years man developed a liking for hot food. Little or no physiological basis has been found for this addiction, but psychologically the habit is hard to kick for much more than a weekend. Most climbers therefore heat some of their food, usually with a stove, sometimes with a wood fire; the alternative is no fire at all, often a forced choice but one preferred by many a lazy old sandwich-eating peakbagger.

Aside from the role of fire in cooking, the warmth of flames or hot food can be lifesaving in a survival situation. The Complete Wilderness Man is always prepared for every eventuality. He carries adequate clothing, knows heat-conserving survival techniques, and has a reserve of foods that need no fire at all. But he also has a canny ability to make wood burn and is never caught without dry matches and an emergency supply of chemical fuel; if lost in a forest or timberline meadow, a wood fire may save his life, as may chemical fire when he is trapped on glacier or cliff by weather, darkness, or accident.

Stoves

Above timberline and on glaciers there is no wood; in the meadow camps of popular areas all the easy fuel is long gone and what remains is scenery and should be left unmolested; even in a forest a party may not have the time or desire to gather damp sticks and nurse a flame. Typically, therefore, the contemporary mountaineer cooks his meals over a chemical fire, gaining the advantages of speed and simplicity at the cost of a relatively small amount of extra weight in the pack.

Solid fuels carried primarily as firestarters are light and cheap, but serve only for limited cooking, such as providing hot drinks on a bivouac. A stove with a pressure tank, burning kerosene, gasoline, or liquefied gas is indispensable for a normal amount of cooking, or if the only available water is melted snow.

A number of ingenious, inexpensive, lightweight, and reliable stoves are available. Each has advantages, each has special tricks. The climber should make first acquaintance with his stove at home to achieve mastery

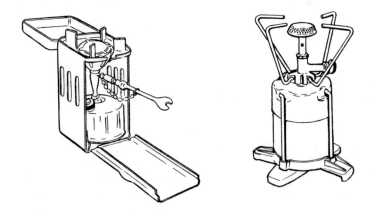

Fig. 13. Stoves. *Left,* gasoline. *Right,* pressurized gas.

and then escalate the relationship through steadily less ideal conditions. Kept in good working order these stoves last for years.

A typical small *gasoline* stove weighs a little over 1 pound empty, burns for about an hour on ½ pint of fuel, and boils a quart of water in less than 10 minutes. Gasoline stoves generally do not have pumps: initial pressure is built up by burning a small amount of fuel in the priming cup on the top of the tank; once ignited, pressure is maintained by heat from the burner. White, that is, unleaded gasoline is mandatory and that especially prepared for pressurized stoves is preferred as being less likely to clog jets; automotive gas clogs jets, may build up excessive pressure, and emits toxic fumes. *Kerosene* produces about the same heat per pound as gasoline, but is less volatile; kerosene-burning stoves are pressurized with a pump, in addition to being primed with alcohol or gasoline. Stoves with a pump are heavier but have higher heat output and can be set directly on snow.

Stoves fueled with disposable cartridges of *liquid butane gas* are comparable to gasoline stoves in weight and heating capacity. They are much simpler to operate but low temperatures can reduce efficiency to the point of non-functioning unless the fuel is warmed. At higher elevations, because atmospheric pressure is less and the pressure of the gas within the cartridge relatively more, butane can be used at lower temperatures: at sea level the stove will not function below 32°F but at 5000 feet it will function as low as 22°F, at 10,000 feet at 13°F, and at 15,000 feet at 4°F.

The chief enemy of any stove is wind, since even a slight breeze makes performance highly erratic. Placement in a sheltered nook helps; walls of rocks, packs, or snow are often necessary reinforcement for the combination shield and pot-supporter found on many models. Aluminum foil can be used as a lightweight wind screen. Pot lids conserve heat. A stove works best in a tent where the flame can be closed down for efficiency — unprotected, the flame must be kept roaring to combat the wind, very wasteful of fuel (see Table 3).

When a self-pressurizing stove is set on snow it must be insulated to prevent tank pressure from falling. A 5- to 6-inch square of masonite or ensolite is adequate for insulation and stability.

On a long trip when fuel must be conserved, stove-cookery requires careful planning to ensure that something is always on the flame and that the flame is always kept low — never licking up the sides of the pot.

Table 3 illustrates that melting snow for all of one's water *or* cooking outside a tent requires *twice* as much fuel as cooking inside a tent. Extra fuel should be carried in a tightly closed container, such as an aluminum bottle with a screw top backed up by a rubber gasket, plainly marked to avoid confusion, and stowed in an outer pocket of the bag to avoid food contamination. Fuel stored in polyethelene containers gradually diffuses out through the plastic.

Table 3. Consumption of White Gas or Kerosene.*

	In Pints	
Cooking Conditions	one meal	two meals (one day)
Cooking in a wind (without snow melting)	½	1
Melting snow for all water (cooking inside tent)	½	1
Cooking inside tent (without melting snow)	¼	½

*Standard three-course meals of 3 to 4 quarts of water for a four-man party.

Wood Fire

The bough bed and the wood fire are both obsolete in alpine regions, replaced by the mattress and stove. Within valley forests the prodigality of nature is such that dead wood can be used with an easier conscience, and similarly in high basins where winter avalanches regularly prune the cliffs, bringing down a fresh supply of fuel for the following summer. But one should *never* take from the country without first questioning, whether the country can afford the loss, and one should *never* set out on a trip into an unfamiliar area irrevocably committed to cooking with wood in or above the timberline zone.

The dead wood produced by a struggling alpine ecosystem, perhaps over a half-century or more, may tempt even the pure in heart to haul silver logs and snags to the kitchen, or erode off branches with a folding saw, but if a log or snag is worth a photograph or even an admiring glance it is too valuable to be used for firewood. In the case of *every* fire the burden falls on the camper to prove to himself that the fire is really needed, and that it will not damage the view.

Still, a wood fire is the only variety suitable for sitting around and drying socks, warming cold bones, and singing folk songs. Opportunities for evening seminars are not common on trips with intensive schedules, but these often linger in the memory of participants far beyond more dramatic events of the day.

Building a Fire

In dry, calm weather firebuilding is often so easy that even a spent cigarette tossed into the brush starts a spectacular blaze that burns whole sections of timber. In a howling rainstorm the combined concentration of several experienced woodsmen, applied for hours, may achieve nothing better than an occasional wisp of smoke. In heavy timber a persistent craftsman can almost always succeed.

The primary requirement is a plentiful supply of dry matches carried in a waterproof container. Solid chemical fuels provide steady flame beneath kindling, and in wet conditions often make the difference between easy combustion and the fruitless expenditure of matches by the gross.

When the situation is at all difficult, the secret of success lies in an extended search for good wood; it may be pointless to attempt to start a fire until an hour or more has been spent assembling proper materials in sufficient quantity to sustain a chain reaction.

The first object of search is tinder, which in wet weather must be the driest available, such as dry moss, needles, or cones protected under large trees or logs. The next is armloads of kindling and "squaw wood" gathered with no tools but the hands and perhaps a pocket knife, and a supply of large material. The dead lower branches of standing trees, protected by the canopy of live cover, are the most dependable source, though seasoned twigs under large logs, or the flaking undersides of decaying logs are often better. Larger dry twigs or slabs can be slivered with a knife. Much searching may be necessary to find the driest of the dry — under a rock ledge or a peculiar bend of a tree.

Wet fuel can be dried and burned on the fire once a good blaze is going, though this invariably produces prodigious quantities of smoke. (Wood that appears dry in the winter is often loaded with frost; when warmed the frost melts and the wood becomes very wet and difficult to burn.)

The fire is carefully nourished from small to large, taking care never to stifle a hesitant flame with excess fuel, never sparing the bellows of the human lungs, and providing shelter from gusts of wind.

When the fire is large enough to be useful, there remains the decision of how large it should be allowed to grow. For cooking, a bed of hot coals is most efficient, and therefore the fire is kept small during meal preparation. A trench fire offers great efficiency as a small cooking fire. A trench 4 by 10 inches is dug down to mineral earth and the fire built in it. The size of fuel is necessarily limited to twigs and small sticks and most of the heat is directed up against the bottom of the pots. The traces of such a fire are easily obliterated.

The general rule among climbers is that the fire goes out immediately after preparation of the meal, either because it is time for bed or because scarce fuel must be conserved for future campers. When a seminar or drying-out seems in order, the fire may be expanded, but only when the ecosystem can tolerate exorbitant wastage of resources.

Fire Control

After determining that the landscape can afford the wood, the responsible traveler builds his fire with care to do the least possible damage. A new firepit in forest or meadow unavoidably leaves a scar, so he always prefers to *use an established one.* He never leaves a fire without drowning it with water or snow until the last ash is cold to the fingers. He guards against later underground creep (since an apparently dead fire may be smoldering beneath the surface) by digging a circular trench with the ice ax; if the humus is so much as warm within this trench, he digs others with increasing diameter until the limit of creep is found, and then stirs and saturates every inch of enclosed soil. Unfortunately in alpine meadows the struggling tangle of roots severed by fire or cutting will often remain scarred for many years. Where such precautions are unnecessary, as in sand or gravel, he scatters ashes and charred sticks.

Sometimes a party with a very leisurely schedule encounters a meadow scarred by a senseless proliferation of firepits; in such case members may expiate some past sin by taking the time and trouble to obliterate one or several.

Cooking Setups

A *wire or tubing grate* weighing about 3 ounces, propped up on rocks or logs, is the easiest way to support pots over a wood fire.

A pot set on a flat rock beside the flames can absorb sufficient heat to boil its contents though only a fraction of its bottom plus one side are exposed to fire. This method is often used to supplement a grate, the serious cooking being done directly over the flames while other pots set on rocks keep the soup simmering and the dishwater warming.

HOUSEKEEPING

Cooking and Eating Utensils

Aluminum cooking pots have nearly replaced the various sizes of tin cans once found at every campsite. Bails are desirable for handling and carrying and pot lids to keep in heat and steam.

Typically a meal is cooked with two pots: one 3-quart size for the main-dish "stew" for four people and a smaller 1½-quart size for tea and other drinks. The large pot is the "grease pot" and the smaller is kept grease-free, seldom requiring cleaning. For two people the 1½-quart size is adequate for the main course; for a party of six a 4-quart size is best.

The simplest eating utensils are a single large cup (or small pot) and a spoon. Some people like to use a bowl in addition.

Dishwashing

On weekend trips it is easiest to carry dishes and pots home dirty; the city kitchen makes quick work of a chore that is rarely better than inconvenient in the hills. On longer trips where utensils are used more than once they must be kept reasonably clean. Cooking pots should be filled with water as soon as emptied and left to soak, or cleaned immediately. Teflon coated pots considerably simplify the cleaning chore. Paper towels are handy for removing initial layers of goo, the job completed with a scour pad of woven metal, plastic, or nylon. Cleaning pots with sand, gravel, grass, or heather leaves unsightly bits of food solids around lakes and streams to attract flies and rodents. Uneaten foods are a problem if a fire is not available to burn them; they should be carried out or disposed of distant from the water supply. Too much food indicates poor planning.

Soaps or biodegradable detergents are used cautiously if at all. Parties commonly remain healthy on week-long trips without so much as a pinch of soap by taking moderate care in cleaning pots with hot water after each meal. Utensils on which soap has been used must be thoroughly rinsed to avoid unpleasant symptoms in the lower digestive tract — better a bit of grease. The soapy water must not be disposed of near stream or lake but added to the ground where it will do the least harm.

Kitchen Organization

Organization of a backpacking kitchen properly begins long before loads are shouldered: months before in the case of expeditions; at home for 1- to 2-week "semi-expeditions"; at the trailhead for weekend outings. For long trips with many meals, foods are packed in logical groupings to save time and trouble in camp; for shorter trips they are merely divided among the party for carrying and the components of each meal assembled as needed.

Transparent poly bags allow each food to be separately protected yet easily identified, and the commissary to be logically and conveniently grouped. Tough poly bottles and jars with screw-on or snap-on lids store any liquid or dry food.

Frustrating Animals

Hungry rodents and bears will gnaw through plastic bags, packs, and even tents to get an easy meal. A food sack or pack hung from a tree or suspended from a pole must be farther from the trunk and higher from the ground than a bear can reach, and recent generations of bears seem to have evolved telescoping forearms. Considerable ingenuity is needed also to keep food safe from mice, which can walk a tight line and drop from astonishing heights.

Food caches are generally not acceptable in the wilderness except as officially designated and maintained for emergencies. Animals' discovery of a cache improperly protected merely results in a large mess and brings them back again and again with all their relatives.

Other animals present other problems. In areas frequented only by climbers, properly secured caches are quite dependable, but they are of little value in country traveled by campers who "live off the land." Here, the main consideration is skillfully concealing the cache. A note left with the supplies, explaining their importance, may shame some thieves into stealing only the tasty and expensive foods, but will only delight the deliberate vandal. Most people who go into the mountains, whether to climb, hike, fish, hunt, or whatever, respect the country and their fellow out-doorsmen, but in heavily-traveled alpine land the only sure way to protect a cache is to sit on it.

Garbage Control

The respectful traveler has a garbage sack in his automobile for banana peels and sandwich wrappers. The responsible hiker or climber maintains a garbage sack at camp, and on the trail stows every particle of paper, glass, plastic, or metal in his pack for later disposal.

And so the rule: *If you can carry it into the wilderness full, you can carry it out empty.* The rule applies universally to trips lasting one day or several weeks; the garbage, burned or unburned, is carried home in a heavy-duty plastic bag brought along for the purpose. On long trips a fire usually can be built occasionally to burn waste food, paper, and plastic.

The older ethic of burn, bash, and bury served well, when observed, until the population explosion began. Then mountaineers began to find that in popular areas wherever they tried to bury new garbage they were merely digging up old garbage.

Leaving a clean camp, and cleaning up a filthy camp, may have the effect of stimulating subsequent visitors to think it over before tossing cans into the brush. In theory, at least, many a person who will leave garbage where he finds existing garbage will not initiate the desecration of a field of flourishing flowers.

Water Pollution and Human Wastes

Not long ago, travelers of wilderness mountains in North America (contrasted to the non-wilderness Himalaya and Alps) drank any and all water found along the way with no more thought about its purity than a glance around to see what the animals might have been up to. Nowadays, however, with the growing back-country population, the traditionally inviolate springs and rills are not always to be trusted, particularly in camps favored by the cavalry, but also wherever walkers are numerous, not to mention areas undergoing "multiple use" by herds of sheep or cattle.

It is becoming apparent that much supposedly virgin wilderness water, however clear and cold, may be so contaminated by thoughtless humans and their uncontrolled domestic animals that it could be as dangerous as any city sewer. For personal protection, therefore, each traveler must now and increasingly in the future inspect carefully the water he proposes to use, and when in doubt give it preliminary treatment (with water purification tablets or by boiling 10 minutes — longer at higher altitudes) as if it came from the Hudson or Ganges.

The rules of good wilderness sanitation are simple and absolute. Use the facilities provided by the managing agency for the use intended (*never, never,* put cans and garbage in latrines). If no latrines exist, use the system of "biological disposers" nature has provided in the topsoil to decompose organic materials: dig a hole 8 to 10 inches in diameter, and no deeper than 6 to 8 inches, and at least 100 feet — farther if possible — from any open water, allowing for maximum water level around lakes. After use, fill the hole with loose soil and tamp the sod back in place. Used non-biodegradable items of personal hygiene, such as sanitary napkins, should be carried out in sealed, air-tight containers, unless a fire is available which will reduce them completely, finally, and absolutely to ashes.

SHORT-HAUL EATING: WEEKENDS

On trips of 2 or 3 days, or even longer if basecamp is close to the road, weight is not a major factor in planning meals. Any food on the grocery store shelves, tinned, fresh, or frozen, is a candidate for consideration; the modern abundance of processed foods allows great scope for the imagination.

Supper

When it is known in advance that time will be plentiful, gourmets (and exhibitionists) plan sensational suppers, such as a tossed salad of fresh lettuce, tomatoes, and cucumbers, imported egg drop soup, corn on the cob, broiled sirloin steaks with fresh mushrooms and onions, a shortcake made of hot brown-and-serve biscuits and frozen strawberries, and for beverages, fresh milk, or perhaps liebfraumilch, followed by coffee and liqueur. However, the climber frequently arrives in camp at 6 or 7 p.m. and must be in bed by 8 if he is to be cheerfully away at 3 a.m. or earlier. Remembering the old adage that "though the food is cold, the inner man is hot," he often contents himself with a supper of sandwiches and fruit juice.

Between menus·of steak and salad on one hand and sandwiches and juice on the other lie many meals both nourishing and delicious yet easily and rapidly prepared. The *supermaket stew* is concocted from various cans selected at random or by intuition. A safe but pedestrian example is a can of beef and gravy mixed with a can of whole kernel corn. More daring but quite edible are chow mein and shrimp, ravioli and turkey, beans and chopped ham. In any combination a dash of grated cheese or a chunk of margarine may enormously improve flavor. Bread, a hot drink, and a dessert of pastry or instant pudding round out a satisfying meal. Another simple supper is built around *hot sandwiches*: hamburgers, hot dogs, or minute steaks fried or broiled, combined with salad greens or relish, supplemented by drinks and dessert.

Cup cookery is particularly suitable for one-man meals, especially in cold and windy camps. Having at hand a stove, two large cups, and a pot of water, the climber crawls into his sleeping bag and heats each course in sequence: a cup of soup from an envelope of dehydrated soup mix, a cup of meatballs eaten with bread and butter, finally a nice cup of tea and a Danish roll and off to sleep. An alternative is the freeze-dried entree, to which only a cup of boiling water need be added.

Breakfast

When time is crucial, breakfast is merely the first installment of lunch. A tiny can of fruit cocktail, or a doughnut and a swallow of milk, are typical menus. Some persons are convinced their legs won't work without hot food; their neurosis can be quickly pampered with instant cereal or cocoa cooked on a stove.

Lunch

As soon as breakfast is completed the mountaineer commences lunch, which he continues to eat as long as he is awake, stopping briefly for supper. He has food in his rucksack and nibblies in his pockets, main courses for the summit lunch, morsels for rest-stops, and sweets to suck while walking.

Few trips are conducted so austerely that one cannot eat for pleasure as well as physiological efficiency. The confirmed athlete may operate solely on glucose tablets, but the average hiker or climber eats whatever delicacies suit him personally and which he is clever enough to carry. Differing physiological needs can result in endless debates over the types of food to carry. Some people require a high-carbohydrate diet with many candy bars; others thrive best on a high protein/fat intake including cheese, sausage, and nuts. Smaller amounts of food eaten several times during a long day are the rule, since a feast followed by violent exertion sets up a competition between the digestive and muscular functions of the blood that leads to indigestion or weakness or both.

The range of alternatives for lunches can be much greater on shorthauls than the semi-expedition lunches discussed later in this chapter. Sandwiches made before leaving town, wrapped first in plastic and then in foil, remain fresh and tasty through a weekend. Apples, oranges, bananas, grapes, cherry tomatoes, cucumbers, celery — fresh fruits and vegetables in general — are never quite so delicious as high on a hot, dry cliff. The choice, actually, is limited only by imagination and the time available before the trip for browsing through supermarkets and delicacy shops. A sound rule for short trips is to carry a variety of foods, even if this means

III. Bears Breast Mountain on crest of Cascade Range. Storm clouds are piled up on west side of crest. (Bob Gunning)

carrying home a surplus; the appetite often becomes tricky in a quick transition from city life and the beginner may not be able to predict in advance what will appeal to him during the climb, when he must take nourishment but may not be in the mood.

Water

The notion lingers that because it is a pleasure to drink when thirsty it must be harmful, and therefore one should resist the devil by sucking a stone, or perhaps a prune pit. Punishing the flesh through deliberate dehydration is an excellent way to prepare for a mystic experience, but a bad way to climb mountains. Water is as vital to life as oxygen; the body can lose as much as a gallon of water without lasting physical damage, but efficiency is substantially lowered well before this point. Authorities recommend an average daily intake of 2 quarts of water during active exertion — 4 quarts in hot weather. Salt lost by sweating must be replaced to avoid a deficiency and subsequent heat cramps; in addition to that gained from foods, about 2 grams of salt per quart of water drunk should be taken, most conveniently in the form of salt tablets.

The old superstition does, however, have some basis in fact; as beginners frequently learn the hard way, even when water is plentiful thirst should be slaked in moderation. Tossing a pound or so of liquid into the stomach slows a man down; if he is very hot and the water is very cold it can even knock him out. Drink little, drink often is the rule, and to this end mountaineers often carry loaded canteens even when they could, strictly speaking, survive from one creek to the next.

Plain water is always acceptable to the thirsty and is the best drink in the world when it comes from a torrent of white-frothing snowmelt, but for summits and other dry spots doctored-up water goes down better and also provides instant energy from simple sugars. A canteen supply of pure water should always be available in the party for first aid purposes, but powdered drink mixes added to the canteen are standard; on short trips cans of juice may be carried.

The same subterranean tradition that recommends sucking stones forbids eating snow. In contrary evidence, if all the tons of snow consumed by climbers over the years were heaped in a pile, the Greenland icecap would appear by comparison merely a heavy frost. The only caution is moderation, melting snow in the mouth before swallowing, just as a child learns to lick rather than chew an ice cream cone.

HIGH-ALTITUDE EATING

Water

Far above timberline water is often at a premium. As soon as the campsite is located one or more members of the party begin collecting a reservoir, since at sundown the high mountains generally freeze tight. Sometimes a tongue of snow dribbles a stream, but more often only dampens the rock or makes mud. In the latter case a depression may be dredged, the water allowed to clear, and the resulting spring channeled into a pot by a piton or tent stake. Another common source of water is overhanging eaves of snow. Their drips vary in volume; a number of pots under a number of drips may be required to fill party needs.

In the absence of streams or drips, "water machines" can be devised if the sun is shining or has been recently. A dark tarp spread thinly with snow makes great pools of water with little effort. Plastic bags filled with snow are slower but steady. Both produce an unpalatable, plastic flavored liquid that should not be called "water" but by its proper name "melted snow," suitable for cooking and hot beverages but a nauseous drink taken straight. A warm rock with a flat, tilted surface is fast but tedious. If there is no sunshine the only source of water is snow melted on a stove.

When a single night is to be spent at high camp and prospects for sunshine are poor, it is best to carry a large canteen supply from lower altitudes. In long stays at high altitude, dehydration is a major problem; there is evidence that some symptoms of altitude illness derive from dehydration and salt deficiency. An increase in salt intake along with increased water consumption decreases dehydration and helps the body retain moisture in the tissues.

The climber's last thoughts before bed are to protect his precious water supply from freezing, usually by storage next to or in the sleeping bag. There is no more cheerless beginning for a climb than a canteen of ice.

Food

In the gales characteristic of high camps cooking is difficult if not impossible. The most suitable foods are those that require only warming or may be eaten cold if worse comes to worst. Fuel must always be carried and its weight is another argument for simple menus. Boil cookery is a problem: for every 10-degree drop in boiling temperature, cooking time is approximately doubled. Table 5 shows the drastically inverse ratio between boiling point and altitude.

Table 5. Boiling Point of Water.

Altitude (feet)	Degrees (Fahrenheit)	Cooking Time (Sea level = 1)
Sea level	212	1
5,000	203	1.9
10,000	193	3.8
15,000	184	7.2
20,000	176	13.0

At low altitude a climber can make flagrant errors in diet without catastrophe; the same is not true at high altitude. The problems of prolonged stays in rarified air, specifically in the Himalaya and to some extent in the Andes, have received much study in the last few years, but lie beyond the scope of the treatment here. Short visits to high altitude are documented by more than a century of experience. A typical quick gain in elevation is the weekend ascent of Mount Rainier in the Cascades, where climbers normally spend Friday night near sea level, Saturday night at 10,000 feet, and perhaps only 20 hours after leaving tidewater reach the 14,410-foot summit. A majority feel symptoms of mountain sickness ranging from a slight malaise to violent vomiting and severe headaches. The eating habits proved successful on Mount Rainier by past generations are obviously valuable in all less demanding situations, and apply up to approximately the 20,000-foot level.

In the abrupt ascent to high altitude there is not time for physiological acclimatization and the entire circulatory system is laboring merely to supply oxygen to the body. Large meals and foods difficult to digest demand attention the system simply cannot spare, and illness results. The climber therefore eats light and often, never loading his stomach with a heavy meal. The menu stresses carbohydrates, which are easiest to digest, and scants fats and proteins, which are most difficult — though a good (*not* excessive) meal of fat and protein the night before the ascent is helpful in stoking the body later on.

Only trial and error can teach a person what foods his body can tolerate at high altitude. Some individuals seem unaffected and with great relish eat smoked oysters and pepperoni at 14,000 feet — partly, no doubt, for the benefit of their bilious companions. The climber in doubt should depend chiefly on carbohydrates, but at all costs and at whatever effort must continue to eat, lest the loss of energy reinforce the debilitating effect of oxygen lack; even when thoroughly ill, one often can take nourishment in the form of fruit juice.

LONG-HAUL EATING: THE SEMI-EXPEDITION

The "semi-expedition" is an extended outing with all food and equipment hauled on the party members' backs. The limit is about 2 weeks, since few people are capable of carrying, at any one time, the loads necessary for longer. Logistically at least, longer trips become true expeditions requiring relay packing, porters, or airplane drops. The person on a short vacation and a shorter budget may not be able to afford the expense of hired transport or the time of relay packing, and in such case plans the duration of his excursion to correspond to his carrying capacity.

Though even today there are wildernesses in Alaska, Canada, and the Antarctic large enough to require true expeditions, in Western America, where only relatively small enclaves of primitive nature remain, the semi-expedition is the most characteristic wilderness experience. One goal of contemporary preservationists can be defined as seeking to save for present and future generations the opportunity for semi-expeditions. For this reason roads, airplanes, air drops, helicopters, motorcycles, and all other mechanized devices are barred from lands included in the National Wilderness Preservation System of the United States.

The success of a semi-expedition depends on menu planning. Too much food means too much weight and too few peaks. Too little or improper food means not enough stamina and too few peaks. Unpalatable food in any quantity means low morale and unpleasant memories.

Planning and Packaging

Dividing the Group

Since meals are social events, many parties plan all food together. A common, carefully planned menu also requires the least weight. However, on other occasions tastes are so divergent that breakfast and lunch are left to the individual and only supper, the most complicated meal of the day, is a group effort.

The size of cooking units should rarely exceed six. Beyond that number the efficiency of group preparation is outweighed by complications of large fires, large pots, and hungry mobs milling about in discontent. Many factors influence the decision, such as closeness of social ties, type of fuel available, and the intensity of the schedule.

Selecting the Menu

Packs are not significantly heavier on short hauls if food quantities are estimated high, since excess weight may be only one or several pounds; also, if vital ingredients are overlooked there is no real hardship, since anyone can get by for a weekend without sugar in his oatmeal. Semi-expeditions, on the other hand, demand precise planning, both to save the unnecessary ounces that pyramid to staggering pounds and to ensure that right down to the last meal there is salt for the potatoes. The climber who groans as he shoulders an 80-pound pack on Day One feels justifiable bitterness when he arrives back at the road on Day Fourteen carrying an unused pound of margarine. And the climber who must endure bland tea night after night can never forgive the blundering fool who forgot the lemon crystals.

Meals are sometimes planned by the group sitting in committee, sometimes by an elected individual. In either case the same procedure is followed. First, menus are written down for each meal. From this is compiled an ingredients list with estimated quantities, and from this the shopping list. Estimation comes easily for the experienced semi-expeditioner who knows that a certain amount of a certain ingredient is just about right for so many companions of long-expressed tastes. The less experienced can benefit from study of Appendices 1 and 2.

The dietician must plan meals to remain within the maximum load limit the party can reasonably carry for the trip in question. A ration of 1½ to 2 pounds per man per day will fuel an active climber and feed him quite well if dehydrated products are used. A 1½ pound per man diet must be exceedingly well planned to provide enough calories; a careless planner can easily exceed 2 pounds without providing enough calories. Many climbers, particularly in Europe and America, have enough emergency food around their waists and hips to survive without eating for days or weeks, and therefore it is often possible to plan meals well below the 2-pound allotment, leaving enough leeway so that after all the essentials have been included there is room for a luxury tin of jam or peanut butter, or some other frivolity. It is much easier to plan on the low side and add extras than to think big and be forced to subtract a soup here, a dessert there.

Packaging

The elaborate packages of commercial foods are too bulky and heavy for the strained back of the semi-expeditioner; a supermarket cart piled high with cardboard-enclosed air can be, and must be, reduced to utilitarian containers.

After all foods have been gathered, they are repacked for carrying – a considerable but worthwhile chore. Many types of plastic sacks and sheets are available for the purpose, including some that offer air-tight seals, but the average semi-expeditioner gets by with freezer-type sacks of various sizes, tied or rubber-banded at the mouth. Food items, especially powdered ones, may be heat-sealed with an ordinary iron set at medium heat. Paper toweling is laid above and below the bag's mouth and the iron slowly and firmly moved across. As an additional refinement label and instructions for the contents may be sealed into the ironed portion at the top of the bag. Obviously bags thus sealed are not reusable. For finely powdered items, such as powdered potatoes or jello, double-sacking is wise and adds insignificant weight. Plastics have an odor that can permeate dehydrated foods, particularly dairy products, and make them unpalatable, but the effect is not noticeable until well after 2 weeks. Items such as honey and mustard can be safely stowed in plastic refillable tubes or flexible freezer containers with tight lids.

Though requiring considerable work at home, the greatest ease in camp comes from packaging individual meals before packs are ever hoisted. By doing so one can avoid the problems of too much rice at some meals and hardly enough for the last — as can happen when one has a single "rice sack" for the entire trip. A labeling system is also to the cook's advantage (felt pens mark efficiently on plastic). Smaller packages can be placed in larger ones of heavier-ply plastic, and lumped (and labeled) as "Breakfast," "Supper," "Drinks," "Desserts," "Soups," "Spices," "Candy," and so on. When planning is not so critical from the standpoint of weight, it may still be useful to gather foods into logical groupings.

Lunch

For the climber, unlike mountain travelers with more relaxed schedules, lunch is a critically important meal, beginning early and continuing late — and in the case of a bivouac, replacing suppers and breakfasts. Frequently, therefore, nearly half the daily ration is allotted to lunch — 12 to 16 ounces.

Lunching and munching preferences vary so widely that it is prudent for every party member to share in the planning; those who love their kippered herring or Italian salami may not be able to abide blue cheese and provoloni. A popular staple is "gorp," or "squirrel food," a mixture of nuts, candy, raisins, and other dehydrated fruits; one handful makes a snack, several make a meal; fastidious eaters may prefer the constituents served separately. The menu shown in Table 6 takes a bit more trouble to plan but usually pleases most palates day after day. The protein constituents should be included in every lunch; one or more of the others can be omitted on easy days. The "special delights" are a matter of personal taste. Appendix 2 suggests a variety of foods within each category.

Table 6. Basic Semi-Expedition Lunch.

Category	Amounts (Ounces per man-day)
meat	2
cheese	2
nuts or peanut butter	2
dried fruit	2
bread	3
(or crackers)	(2)
chocolate or candy bars	2
hard candy	1
dried mixes and special delights	2
	16

Supper

Main Course

With half the man-day ration of weight allotted to the nondehydrated foods of lunch, the other half makes up breakfasts and suppers consisting largely of dehydrated foods. Commercially prepared freeze-dried dinners offer tempting meals complete in one package — beef stew, chili con carne, and many others — at luxury prices. The industrious can concoct their own meals with substantial monetary savings and excellent results though at considerable expense in time.

In every climbing area of the world, parallel evolution has produced the same magnificent meal, variously called "one-pot-supper," "mulligan," "hoosh," or "glop." By any name its virtues are extraordinary. A large number of compatible ingredients are cooked in a single pot with a saving of equipment, time, and fuel. The blended components have a flavor greater than the sum of the parts; the result is a complete, satisfying, and memorable meal.

Every glop involves an act of unique creation and no two are ever exactly the same; the master chef steers by dead reckoning and insight.

Table 7. Meats for Semi-Expedition Glops.

Category	Amount (Ounces per man-serving)
Tinned	4
Chicken (boneless)	
Chopped meat ("spam")	
Corned beef	
Ham	
Roast beef	
Salmon	
Tuna	
Sausage	4
Chipped beef	2
Dried, compressed	1½-2
Meat bars	
Bacon bars	
Vacuum-dried meats	1-2
Freeze-dried	
Meat	1⅓-1½
Shrimp	½-1
Ham	½-⅔

Most glops have a simple-quick and a complex-long form, and thus can be adapted to the time available. For example, one that has proved lastingly popular requires in its simple form only warm water, instant potatoes, and Goteborg sausage and is ready to eat within minutes. In the complex form spices and dehydrated vegetables and maragarine are added and the mixture is allowed to simmer and blend.

The complete glop begins with a base of spicy flavor provided by a dehydrated soup or sauce mix placed in the pot along with the water. At appropriate later times, depending on the meal, starches and meats and various other things are added. Appendix 2 suggests some basic glops that offer unlimited opportunity for adaptation by individual imagination. Tables 7 and 8 give the principal alternatives available in meats and starches, and the amounts in each category.

Soups and Side-Dishes

A cup of soup is always a welcome prelude to the main course, and should be planned whenever considerations of time, weight, and fuel allow — always remembering, though, that whatever weight and fuel are expended on soup may be at the expense of the glop. Europe (and Israel and Japan) provide dozens of delicious dehydrated soups; America, lesser culinary achievements. One package, added to water at one cup per

Table 8. Starches for Semi-Expedition Glops.

Category	Amount (Ounces per man-serving)	Amount (Dry measure in cups)
Rice		
Pre-cooked (5-minute soak type)	2⅓	⅔
Quick-cooking (10-15- minute cooking type)	2	¼
Potatoes		
Mashed, powdered	1 to 2	¼
Mashed flakes		
(bulkier, easier mixing)	1 to 2	1, shaken down
Sliced, diced, cubed (slow cooking, may be soaked)	2	—
Wheat, processed ("Ala." Slow cooking— 15 minutes. Good change of pace.)	2	⅓
Pasta (macaroni, spaghetti, noodles. Choose thin varieties cooking in 7 minutes or less.)	2	—

person serves a party of three or four; with the addition of a bouillon cube, four or five.

If the weight of a genuine soup cannot be afforded, bouillon is an old favorite that weighs little, has minimal food value, but is helpful in replacing water and salt, warming cold bodies, and stimulating appetites of the exhausted.

Though bulky, dehydrated vegetables weigh little and cost little and become amazingly appealing to some people after a few days of potatoes and sausage. Freeze-dried vegetables and fruits are excellent but too expensive for frequent use. The food value of all these is mostly psychological, but it is not a bad plan to slip in a side-dish of vegetables once every several days; often they are greeted more enthusiastically than dessert.

Pre-cooked soy beans or processed soy products (in powder or textured forms) are excellent low cost protein additions to meals. For those more intimately concerned with nutrition and healthful foods many types of supplements and "organic" foods are easily incorporated in a backpack diet.

Bread or biscuit can rarely be planned for supper on a semi-expedition, but scraps left over from lunch are welcome.

Drinks and Desserts

Drinks and/or desserts are also added according to the weight allotment available. The total ration per man-day usually does not allow soup, vegetable side-dish, drink, and dessert for every supper. Planning one or two trimmings for each day provides a good balance; not all, and maybe none, are wanted each day and the extras can accumulate for the light days and rest days, including periods of storms when there is nothing to do but eat and sleep.

After a dry day on the peak or trail a cold flavorful drink is immensely delightful, and ideally the first order of business on reaching camp is mixing a pot of punch – lemonade, orange juice, grape juice, or whatever – from powdered mixes. The artifically sweetened drinks are inferior both in taste and aftertaste but are so light they can be used more liberally.

Tea is another no-weight item that can be planned for every supper, allowing one bag per man per day, or carrying bulk tea if preferred. Instant coffee can also be carried to allow addicts to maintain their habit. Where the weight mounts up in these drinks is the addition of sugar. Before the trip, count the members of the party who use sugar in their tea or coffee and figure about ½-⅓ ounce (a heaping teaspoon) per serving; on the trip, watch the sugar-users to make sure they don't consume the entire supply in a couple of days. Tea drinking can be varied by use of spiced varieties or a bit of dried mint or some lemon crystals; tea with brown sugar or honey is an abomination to purists but ambrosia to others. A powdered cream product should be included for those who can't endure black coffee, or even coffee with milk. Cocoa, and also coffee-cocoa, a half-and-half mixture of instant powders of the two, are as much desserts as drinks. The same is true of hot Jello.

Full-scale desserts — pudding being the standard — are usually planned only once every several days. The time and fuel required by cooked puddings have made them rather a rarity in mountain camps. Instants of many types are available and though most seem somewhat synthetic, some are quite acceptable and dependable. On a cold day any pudding — even instant — may be more appreciated served hot.

At camps where snow is available, and a good amount of salt for the freezing mixture, ice cream can be made from powdered mixes. Such an exotic dessert as Neapolitan ice cream should stun even the most chronic malcontent into awed silence.

Staples and Seasonings

Sugar is a matter of preference. Brown is one third again as heavy as white because of moisture, but much preferred by many for flavor.

Instant powdered *milks* are indispensable in the mountain diet for nutritional value.

Margarine (preferred to butter on long trips for its keeping qualities) makes every other food taste better — bread, potatoes, glops, oatmeal, even cocoa. It also has the most calories per pound of any food in the climbing larder; when weight is extremely critical and a party is trying to shave a few ounces from the 2-pound ration, the margarine allotment can be raised at the expense of other items.

Salt is essential to the body as well as the palate. Cooked cereals are virtually inedible without it, and individuals may want to salt their glop to taste. Relatively little is needed, since other foods (such as soup mix used as a base for glops and the salt tablets swallowed while sweating during the day) supply most of the physiological requirements.

As for *spices* — packages of dehydrated onions, tomatoes, peppers, and soups, and shakers of pepper and garlic salt and mixed condiments — their total weight is insignificant beside that of a piton but they can transform survival rations into banquets.

Breakfast

Breakfasts are a major semi-expedition problem. Cold-and-fast meals save time and fuel but are heavy and bulky; mush-and-cocoa meals take time but slip down easily in a freezing pre-dawn. The usual procedure is to plan fast breakfasts for the long days, hot for the medium days, roughly half-and-half, and add one or two luxury breakfasts for layover days of rain or recuperation. Another aspect of the problem is that most parties include a mixture of farm-type hearty-breakfasters and urbanized late-starters who can barely tolerate the thought of solid nourishment until the sun is high. The amounts suggested in the sample menus of Appendix 2 will strike the former as starvation and the latter as nausea; when there is any argument the farmers must give way in the interests of group efficiency, consoling themselves with the thought that lunch will begin shortly.

For the fast start, many mountaineers prepackage a standard meal before the trip, measuring a prepared cold cereal (such as granola) sugar, raisins or other fruit, and powdered milk into a "breakfast bag." Stir in water — cold for a cold meal, hot for a hot one — and breakfast is ready.

A hot drink is a pleasant addition to a cold meal and a standard element of a hot one. Common choices are cocoa, plain or chocolate Ovaltine, coffee-cocoa (mocha), instant breakfast drinks, plain or chocolate malted milk, all pre-mixed with powdered milk. Some favor hot Jello, and just plain milk isn't bad.

Mush — oatmeal, farina, or whatever — is the standard hot breakfast; the instant or quick varieties really take no time at all beyond heating water. Sugar, milk, margarine, and bacon bar can be mixed into the cooking pot or added by the individual to taste. Wheat germ can be added to the mush — or to cold cereals — for additional protein and B vitamins.

Powdered eggs, either pre-packaged or mixed with milk, cheese, and vegetables or condiments produce acceptable omelets, or a longer-lasting protein breakfast when combined with freeze-dried ham or compressed bacon bars. A less popular but comparable protein breakfast is dried chipped beef in cream or cheese sauce served on crackers. Either of these is more efficient than cereals in terms of calories per ounce.

Fruits, dried by sun or vacuum, can be soaked or cooked the previous night for quick reheating in the morning, then eaten separately or combined with mush. A powdered citrus drink, often warmed for a predawn start, adds variety; so, also, do the luscious freeze-dried fruits, which are the equivalent of eating pure money.

Into almost every rat-race a day of rain must fall and with it opportunity for the luxury breakfast — which actually need not weigh a great deal, the luxury lying in the time of preparation. Hotcakes can be delicious or execrable depending on the experience of the cook and the elapsed time since the party ate a civilized meal. A small, lightweight skillet that can double as someone's eating dish or a pot lid (as in some cooking sets) is almost a necessity; a small spatula is helpful. Syrup can be made from brown sugar, or lunch jam can be used.

Bacon is an old favorite with either hotcakes or scrambled eggs; canned sausages or Spam are magnificent. Whatever the main course, the ideal luxury breakfast includes cold orange juice for a start, stewed fruit, hot beverage, and bread or biscuit spread with margarine and jam or honey. When all this is eaten, it is noon or nearly so and time to take a short walk before lunch.

5 *

NAVIGATION

NAVIGATION is the technique of precisely determining one's present location, the location of the objective, and the direction of travel connecting these two points. Almost all wilderness navigation is done by inspection, that is, by looking at the surrounding country and relating what is seen to prior knowledge of the locality or to features described on a map. The area of navigational concern is small, seldom larger than can be seen from a vantage point. When resort to instruments is necessary or desirable, the only ones essential are simple, self-contained, easily mastered, and virtually foolproof; trigonometry, celestial observations, sophisticated electronics, and astrolabes are not required. When good maps are available, mountain navigation can be easy and exact; without good maps, it often takes on something of the character of a black art. Skill is very largely a function of experience, though the basic tools and procedures can be quickly mastered.

THE TOOLS

Nature offers more or less useful direction indicators. In the north temperate zone the summer sun rises somewhere between northeast and east, is due south at noon, and sets between west and northwest. South slopes are sunnier and thus drier than north, with vegetation sparser or of an entirely different type. North slopes are snowier and because of more intense glaciation in past ages often are steeper. A person stranded in the wilderness without equipment may be completely dependent on such information. However, so long as he is connected to his rucksack he can simplify orientation by always carrying among his personal gear an artificial direction-finder.

The Compass

A compass is a magnetized needle mounted so that it can respond freely to the earth's magnetism. It is by far the quickest and most accurate means of establishing direction since the needle always aligns itself with the magnetic field of the earth — almost always, that is. Hidden ore bodies and some innocent-appearing rocks may deflect the earth's gross magnetic field. In addition, items in the climber's outfit — ice axes, knives, belt buckles, and other metal — can attract the compass needle and must be kept away from the compass while it is being consulted.

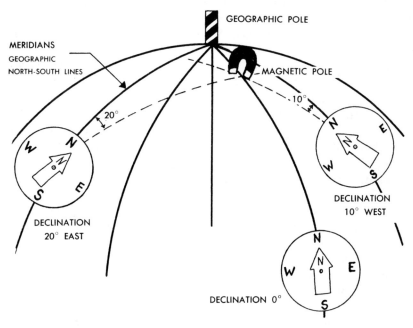

GEOGRAPHIC POLE

MERIDIANS
GEOGRAPHIC
NORTH-SOUTH LINES

MAGNETIC POLE

-10°

20°

DECLINATION
10° WEST

DECLINATION
20° EAST

DECLINATION 0°

Fig. 14. Compass declination, irregularities in earth's magnetic field are omitted.

The compass needle does not point to the geographic north pole, but to the magnetic north pole about a thousand miles to the south in Canada. The angle of difference between true (geographic) north and magnetic north is called *declination* and is different in various parts of the country.

The small, inexpensive pocket-watch-type compass marked only with the cardinal directions indicates little more than the general direction of sunset. A compass to be used for wilderness navigation should enable one to determine a bearing within 5 degrees, and the dial of the compass should be graduated in 1- or 2-degree increments in a clockwise direction. A 5-degree error in 1 mile of travel would lead the navigator about 460 feet astray from his intended destination. If no landmarks are visible, as in fog or dense timber, a more accurate reading is desirable. A liquid- or induction-dampened needle eliminates excessive oscillations and permits fast and accurate readings, or even continuous readings while walking. A transparent baseplate and a straight side or etched grid aids in aligning the compass with the map. A sight or direction arrow on the baseplate enables the user to determine the bearing to a distant object or to plot a course if the desired bearing is known.

Most maps are marked with various approximately north-south and east-west lines such as section lines, grid lines, meridians of longitude, and parallels of latitude. Using these lines and a compass (in this case functioning as a substitute for a protractor), the climber can measure bearings between two points. The most common practice is to state a *bearing* as an angle in degrees measured clockwise from true north of the observer to the desired destination. For instance, if he is looking directly toward the North Pole, he is said to be facing north, and the angle (bearing) is zero degrees. If he is looking in the direction of the rising sun, he is looking east, and the angle (bearing) between his line of sight to the North Pole and his line of sight to the sun is approximately 090 degrees. To "take a bearing" on something means to determine the angle between the line of sight to the North Pole and the line of sight toward the object. Thus the bearing from Forbidden Peak to Mount Torment (Fig. 16) is 275 degrees true. Bearings are numbered in a clockwise direction from north to east (090 degrees), south (180 degrees), west (270 degrees), and back to north (360 = 000 degrees). Bearings are written with three digits to avoid misinterpretations. East is, as stated, 090; 20 degrees is 020, not 20°, which might be confused with 200 when written with cold fingers.

Bearings can be read from the compass as either *magnetic bearings*, using the line of sight to magnetic north as the zero bearing, or *true bearings*, using the line of sight to true north as the zero bearing. It does not matter which way it is done so long as the distinction is kept clearly in mind and followed consistently. It is not necessary to remember some rule for converting magnetic bearings to true bearings or vice versa; inevitably the rule will be forgotten when it is needed most. It is safer to understand why there are two ways of stating bearings and observe the declination symbol — which appears on most topographic maps — to check the conversion between true and magnetic north.

For example, note how in the illustration of the Forbidden Peak map a compass has been superimposed with its edge in line with the true north of the declination symbol on the map, and the inner dial has been rotated to align true north on the inner dial (0 or 360°) with magnetic north on the map. (For the time being ignore the needle.) If the compass has a rotating ring with a mark to indicate the angle of declination, it can be set to correct for declination as shown on the map. If the compass does not have such an indicator, a piece of adhesive tape applied and marked as illustrated will do, but remember that the angle varies from area to area, and the indicator may have to be adjusted to the declination shown on the map if it is different from the one used previously.

Having set the declination in the compass, one can determine the course he wishes to follow from the map, using true bearings rather than adjusting to magnetic bearings. To travel a course, the compass dial is rotated until the desired true bearing taken from the map is at the mark on the compass at which the declination was originally set, or is at the mark on the tape, as the case may be. Point the compass so that the needle aligns with its engraved box and walk in the direction pointed to by the direction arrow on the compass baseplate.

To develop the ability to take compass bearings on visible objects, it is necessary to practice sighting various objects with a compass; this can be done even in the middle of a room. Many compasses are available with a variety of sighting devices designed to aid in precise reading of bearings. Whatever type of compass is used, the instructions should be read carefully and thoroughly and practiced in the home or yard until bearings can be quickly and accurately read.

Maps

Navigation is aided by verbal descriptions of an area from conversation or correspondence with previous visitors, or from published sources such as alpine journals and climbing guides. The value of photographs, especially those taken from airplanes, is obvious, though compared to the human eye a camera lens gives at best a distorted view of the world. Aerial photographs — even when available — are bulky, expensive, difficult to interpret, and difficult to keep in good condition, but are well worth the trouble and expense when extremely precise knowledge of the terrain is needed. For some regions there are aerial photographs but no detailed maps. Generally a climber depends chiefly for terrain description on a map, a symbolic picture of an area that by convenient shorthand conveys a wealth of information in a form easily carried and easily understood.

Types of Maps

Sketch maps are usually prepared for the special purpose of providing graphic notes of particular routes or features. They are not always drawn to scale, seldom show any surrounding detail, and may not indicate directions or elevations accurately. But do not sneer at sketches — all mountaineers use them. When used as supplements to proper navigational maps they are very useful as routefinding aids. There are still remote areas where sketch maps obtained from preceding climbers are the only detailed information available.

Forest Service maps and comparable ones issued by other government agencies are invaluable. The comprehensive "Forest Maps" and "Ranger District Maps" covering sections of the former are revised periodically in the light of news brought in by rangers walking over the country. Forest Service maps are the best guides to the current state of roads, trails, shelters, and other works of man. Drainage patterns and divides are carefully traced and some elevations are given. Nearly all Forest Service maps are *planimetric,* which is to say they do not show the vertical shape of the land. A few new ones are *topographic* (see below), but because they are not published to meet National Map Accuracy Standards can sometimes be rather confusing — for example, due to a slight mistake in printing, a trail that follows close beside a stream may be shown as going up the middle of the stream or on the other side. The maps can be obtained free of charge — or for a small fee — by writing to headquarters offices of the various National Forests or may be picked up at ranger stations. Similar maps transcribed more or less carefully from Forest Service and other sources are produced commercially for some areas. These are commonly called "county" or "sportsman" maps and are sold in stores catering to hunters and fishermen.

Hunters' maps distributed prior to each hunting season by several of the larger timber companies are revised yearly and are excellent for finding passable routes through the growing maze of logging roads. Careful perusal frequently reveals a new or shorter approach than those described in guidebooks or shown on other maps.

Pictorial relief maps covering parts of the Cascades and Olympics have their specific purposes and limitations. These are commercially produced, compiled from topographic and Forest Service maps, and present a somewhat happy medium between the two. In essence, an oblique, full-color view of the terrain is shown as it would be viewed from an extreme altitude. Though not three-dimensional, the illusion is given, but only in direct relation to the skill of the illustrator. Such maps are intended for general planning purposes and provide the trail mileages not shown on government maps. They cannot be used for compass navigation and in the back country must be employed solely as supplements to topographic maps.

It should be emphasized at this point that no one map tells the whole story, and that all sources should be thoroughly studied before entering unknown territory.

Topographic maps are the prime tool of the mountain navigator. Their name is derived from their depiction of topography, the shape of the earth's surface. On these maps the depiction of works of man is subordinated to terrain details. Topographic maps produced by the U.S. Geological Survey are published in four scales referred to as "series."

Maps on a *scale of 1:250000,* the *United States series,* are issued for all states including Alaska, for some portions of which they are the only maps. The scale, about ¼ inch to 1 mile, is of small use to the mountaineer afoot. However, these "quarter-million" sheets are superb for broad orientation, superior to highway maps in that with just a bit of practice one can soon name and describe hills and dales better than most local residents; from a summit they allow identification of peaks and ranges in the haze far beyond the boundaries of localized maps. Many are offered in three-dimensional molded-plastic editions, splendid for home study of mountain range structure and drainage patterns.

The oldest maps, some of which are still in print for remote regions, were published on a *scale of 1:125000* (roughly ½ inch to the mile) in the *30-minute series,* each sheet covering an area of 30 minutes or ½ degree of longitude and latitude, a ground distance in the northern United States of about 25 miles east and west and about 35 miles north and south. These maps usually interest the historian more than the climber.

Newer maps have enough detail for a *scale of 1:62500* (roughly 1 inch to the mile) in the *15-minute series,* each covering about 12 by 18 miles in the northern United States. For the mountaineer this series gives sufficient topographic information for route selection, and each sheet includes enough country to make orientation easy.

New mapping in the conterminous United States and much of the reissuing of older maps is proceeding on a *scale of 1:24000* (2½ inches to the mile) in the *7½-minute series,* each sheet covering an area 6 by 9 miles. The greater detail of these maps make them ideal for cross-country route planning; however, because more maps must be carried to cover the same area they may not be as desirable as others for field use.

Sometimes an area of interest lies near the corner or edge of more than one map. In such cases the pertinent area of each map can be cut out and the sections joined together with tape. More durable composites can be made by mounting the sections of maps on a lightweight cloth backing with photographers' dry mounting tissue. Such composites, when made up of two halves or four quarters from original maps, are no larger than one original sheet but they contain a wealth of information more closely related to the area of climbing interest.

Topographic maps of areas west of the Mississippi River can be purchased at mountain shops or ordered directly from the U.S. Geological Survey, Federal Center, Denver, Colorado 80225. For the east, maps should be ordered from the U.S. Geological Survey, Washington, D.C. 20242. Index maps for each state are free on request.

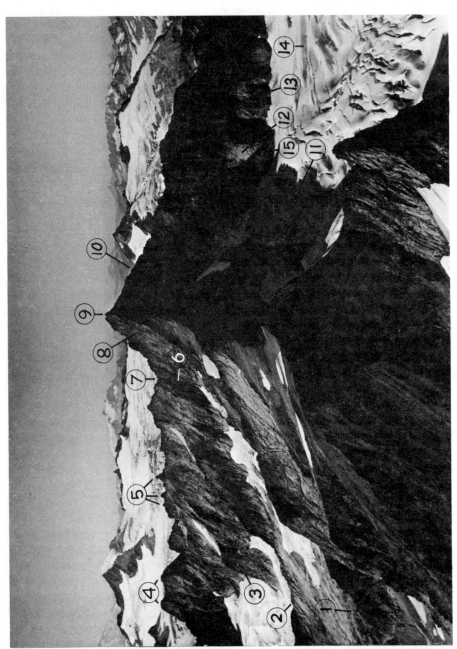

Fig. 15. Forbidden Peak with features keyed. (Tom Miller)

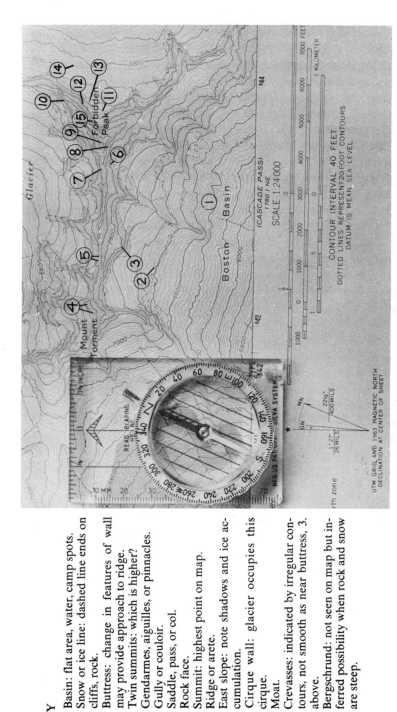

Fig. 16. Topographic map showing same features. Forbidden Peak Quadrangle, 7.5 minute series, U.S. Geological Survey.

KEY

1. Basin: flat area, water, camp spots.
2. Snow or ice line: dashed line ends on cliffs, rock.
3. Buttress: change in features of wall may provide approach to ridge.
4. Twin summits: which is higher?
5. Gendarmes, aiguilles, or pinnacles.
6. Gully or couloir.
7. Saddle, pass, or col.
8. Rock face.
9. Summit: highest point on map.
10. Ridge or arete.
11. East slope: note shadows and ice accumulation.
12. Cirque wall: glacier occupies this cirque.
13. Moat.
14. Crevasses: indicated by irregular contours, not smooth as near buttress, 3. above.
15. Bergschrund: not seen on map but inferred possibility when rock and snow are steep.

Similar topographic maps are available for much of Canada. Indexes to maps published by the federal government are free on request from the Map Distribution Office, 615 Booth Street, Ottawa, Ontario. Indexes to maps issued by the individual provinces may be obtained, at no cost, by writing the appropriate government office in each provincial capital. For British Columbia, write to the Surveys and Mapping Branch, Department of Lands, Forests, and Water Resources, Victoria, B.C.

Interpretation of Topographic Maps

Topographic maps show the shape of the terrain with contour lines, which are drawn to represent constant elevations above sea level on the surface of the earth.

The interval between contour lines always represents an equal number of vertical feet, generally from 20 to 250, depending on the scale of the map. For convenient reading, usually each fifth contour line is heavier and its elevation is printed periodically along its length. Interpretation of contour maps is quite simple. Widely-spaced lines indicate a gentle slope; lines that run close together, a cliff. A valley makes a pattern of V's pointing upstream. A ridge appears as downhill-pointing V's or U's depending on the sharpness of the crest. When the direction of travel crosses lines of succeedingly higher numbers it is going uphill; when it crosses lines of succeedingly lower numbers it is going downhill. If the line of travel does not cross contour lines, it is not going up or down, but *traversing* the slope with no more variation in elevation than one contour interval.

The value of topographic maps lies in the ability they give one to predict the main terrain features by looking at the general shape of groups of lines. Thinking of the contour lines as resembling stair steps, a hillside represented on the contour map has an appearance similar to that of a wide staircase viewed from above; a ridge, the appearance of two wide staircases back to back; and a very steep hillside, the appearance of a staircase with very narrow treads. A cliff is represented by contour lines very close together or on top of each other. A cirque, or head of a mountain valley, resembles the end of a football stadium. Finally, a mountain peak is represented as a circular-shaped staircase ascending in a series of closed contours to the innermost circle or point indicating the summit.

Contour maps offer much information about the landscape but do not tell all. In the older reconnaissance surveys contour lines were sketched more or less freehand. Even with modern maps it must be remembered that a 50-foot cliff will not be evident at all if it lies between lines at 100-foot intervals.

Map Protection and Modification

Inexpensive, easily-replaced maps are expendable, but not during the climb. Enclosure in a clear plastic bag is adequate protection and allows use without damage even in wet weather. Weight and trouble can be saved by transcribing Forest Service information and personal experience onto a topographic map, marking new roads and trails or routes, mileage and time between various points. Some topographic maps are confusing even to an expert; it is helpful to outline the ridge structure with pencil lines along the main crests. More laborious but even more valuable is shading a map to simulate shadows cast when the sun is low in the northwest. Such techniques speed development of the stereoptic vision characteristic of a practiced reader.

Altimeters

In addition to each member of the party carrying his own map and compass, it is wise for at least one member to have an *altimeter,* a variety of barometer which measures atmospheric pressure with a special scale. (Since atmospheric pressure decreases at a uniform rate with increased altitude, it is possible to use a standard barometer for measuring altitudes by fitting it with a scale labeled in feet or meters instead of pressure units.) Properly used, an altimeter can help verify one's location as determined by map and compass — or other means — and indeed may on occasion be the only means of knowing when a desired elevation or location has been reached, particularly in foggy weather or glacier travel. The altimeter should be set at a known elevation before starting a climb, and then checked and reset if necessary at any known points along the way.

The altimeter reading should be checked on arrival in camp, then checked and reset the next morning before leaving camp to correct for any barometric pressure changes that may have occurred overnight. Sudden and excessive changes may be interpreted as impending changes in the weather.

ORIENTATION

By orientation, the first step in navigation, a mountaineer finds where he is, of if he knows where he is, he determines bearings from his location to other landmarks. If a quick look around doesn't accomplish the job, he resorts to his map and compass. The compass, a deceptively simple instrument, performs one primary function: it determines bearings. Maps serve an equally basic purpose: they relate places to scale by distances and bearings. On such elementary principles rest the foundation of orientation and thus navigation.

One of the simplest methods of orienting map and compass is to place the map on a flat surface, with the compass on top of the map, its straight edge aligned with the north-south line on the map. Then rotate map and compass together until the compass needle is aligned with magnetic north as indicated by the declination symbol on the map. (Figure 16 shows the compass so aligned on the map.) There will now be a direct conformity between bearings (or lines of sight) read from the map and those observed in the area covered by the map.

With *point-position known* (summit, pass, lake outlet, river forks), any visible feature can be identified from the map and any feature shown on the map can be located. Assume the climber knows he is atop Forbidden Peak. To identify an unknown peak, he sights on its summit with his compass and determines the bearing of his line of sight. A quick plot on the map now shows that the compass bearing from Forbidden intersects an easily identified mountain. To find Mount Torment, he determines from the map the bearing from Forbidden to Torment (275 degrees). Using his compass, he sights on this bearing from Forbidden and discovers Mount Torment right where it belongs. By aligning his map as previously described he can identify whatever features of the landscape catch his eye.

With *line-position known* (ridge, trail, river) and one visible feature recognized, point-position can be found. Assume the climber knows he is on Unsavory Ridge and in the distance recognizes Mount Majestic. He uses his compass to determine the bearing from his position to Mount Majestic. He plots the line of this bearing through Majestic on his map and extends this line in the opposite direction to intersect Unsavory Ridge. The point of intersection tells the climber where he is.

With only *area-position known*, at least two visible features must be recognized to find point-position. Assume the climber knows only he is in the Fantastic Crags. Again he takes a bearing on Majestic, and this time pencils the bearing line on the map. He also recognizes Unsavory Spire, takes a second bearing, draws a second line. Where the two lines intersect, that's where the climber is. However, if he happens to be on top of a ridge and the lines intersect in the Fantastic River, something is wrong. Perhaps he now recognizes Imposing Peak and the third bearing line intersects one of the others at a more reasonable location. (The closer to a right angle is the angle between any two bearing lines, the more precisely their intersection shows position.) If several bearings agree on a location with no similarity to the terrain, then the climber suspects it's a crazy old map, he has read the compass incorrectly, or maybe those peaks aren't Unsavory and Imposing after all.

With only area-position known and only one visible feature recognized, only line-position (along the bearing line) can be found. However, assume the climber remains certain of good old Majestic, and also feels sure he is on a ridge, not in a river. He therefore knows he is at or near one of the several points where the Majestic bearing line intersects a Fantastic ridge. Perhaps, from comparison of map and terrain, he finds only one that fits the facts.

Since mountains are symbolized in three-dimensions on the topographic map, the altimeter is sometimes as helpful as the compass.

NAVIGATION

By *navigation* a mountaineer gets where he wants to go. Even while pounding a trail or following a leader, the navigator, unlike the passenger, does not orient purely by trail signs and summit registers, or navigate entirely by boot heels. At every step the look of the country changes a bit; at every step the navigator with his sharp and roving eye updates his last certain fix. At a pass, or around a bulge in the ridge, or through a sudden break in the clouds, whenever many new peaks and valleys appear, he pauses to connect them to the map.

The navigator knows how amazingly different the country looks backside from frontside. While the eager apprentice gazes to the summit, the sad old navigator constantly glances over his shoulder to camp, not so much because he wishes he'd never left as because he hopes to get back. Particularly at critical turns he fixes in his mind the *over-the-shoulder shape of the route,* such as: opposite a waterfall, at a moraine with an iron-stained boulder perched on the crest, the route busts through a cedar thicket and down a mossy slab to a gnarled snag.

When the route is complex, and especially when a late return is anticipated, the navigator finds a small *notebook* valuable for entering times, elevations, landmarks, and compass courses, as well as for writing his memoirs in later years.

When the way to an objective is blocked by cliffs, lakes, or other obstacles, navigation is accomplished by the use of intermediate objectives. If the intermediate objectives are not visible because of fog or dense forests there are several ways to travel a predetermined bearing: by walking in the direction of the desired bearing with continuous reference to the compass, by repeatedly sending a member of the party ahead to the limit of visibility on the correct bearing line and rejoining him with the rest of the party, or by sighting on a landmark within the limits of visibility and walking towards it.

When landmarks are lacking or obscured by fog or night, or may be on the return, the *route is marked.* On snow and glaciers wands are used, as described in Chapter 17. For most other terrain the best marker is bright-colored crepe paper in thin rolls, durable enough not to disintegrate in the first rain or wind, as does toilet paper, but perishable enough to vanish without a trace over the winter. Unless he can, and does, remove them during the return, the climber who decorates the hills with bright plastic strips should in all justice be condemned to spend eternity untying little bright plastic strips in whatever place is reserved for him and other despoilers of the wilderness.

In home hills or foreign ones, the navigator at all times keeps firmly in mind which way to go if completely baffled — the compass direction to some long unmistakable line, such as a highway or trail or lake or ridge, that forms one boundary of his climbing area. He knows the *baseline* always lies in the same compass direction wherever he is in the area, and whether or not it is a quick way out, it at least means an ultimate way out.

Navigators of ocean and air often travel great distances entirely by instrument to an exact destination. Mountain navigators also occasionally travel great distances blind, and sometimes even get where they want to go. Except when the objective is a baseline, a *compass course* cannot be set without an initial exact orientation. Once a course is set, a navigator can in clear weather hold to it visually, pointing his nose either at the objective or some intervening point on the bearing line. Assume a navigator on a broad glacier has been caught napping by a cloud, and just manages to whip out his compass for a bearing on Mount Scimitar before it vanishes. If Scimitar is the goal, the one bearing is enough; he doesn't know where he is but he knows which way to go. Since the better-grade liquid-dampened compasses hold an accurate course even when held in the hand while walking, the navigator can advance with confidence that Scimitar will be reached. The reliability of this technique is further improved when each member of the rope team travels compass in hand.

LOST

A good navigator is never lost, but having learned humility, he always carries enough food and clothing to survive hours or days of confusion. Moreover, his first act as an apprentice navigator is to master techniques for minimizing confusion.

The first rule is, *stop.* Exactly when caution is most vital, on the weary descent with night near, temptation is strongest to plunge hopefully forward, increasing any error with every step.

If orientation cannot be quickly regained even from a vantage point, using the principles outlined above, but was certain a short time earlier, retrace the route to the known point; an hour groaning upward may save a bitter night out. If the last certain orientation is hours away, and the present position can be approximately determined, it may be best to move cautiously ahead, alert for landmarks. On the other hand, the probable position may be so hopelessly off course it is time to bivouac.

Climbing history reveals the significant fact that a party of two or more, though the greenest novices or most complacent passengers, rarely gets dangerously lost. It is the lone human, abruptly aware how small and fragile he is, how immense and powerful the wilderness, who throws away his life. Terror in the face of nature is no sign of cowardice, but rather is the sane reaction; it is entirely proper, when alone, to treat every step as a life-or-death matter. However, it is essential not to try to take all the steps at once, in a hurry. Terror must be overcome by reason or it can kill.

Stop. Look around. Listen. Shout, and listen for answering shouts, but don't chase imaginary shouts. Instead, sit down, calm down. Look at the map. Look around. Resist panic, resist wishful thinking. Disregard the old, discredited rule of following a stream out of the wilderness. A stream may lead deeper into wilderness, and certainly will lead away from the search area and into dense timber. Relax. Once cool and collected, though still confused, mark the present position with a cairn or toilet paper. Scout in all directions, each time returning to the marked position. Well before dark, give up the scouting. Obtain water, collect firewood, if available. Find shelter from the weather, if bad. Spend the night keeping the fire going, and listening, and singing cheerful songs, and rehearsing out loud the funny story this will make someday.

If the lost climber behaves in this manner, and his companions are similarly sensible, they are invariably reunited in the morning. If they do not begin search next day, through some misunderstanding such as a divided party, the lost climber must once again fight down panic. He may decide, after a day or so, it is best to proceed cautiously to the baseline, but if the terrain is prohibitively dangerous for lone travel he concentrates on letting himself be found. It is easy to find a lost person who stays in one place out in the open, builds a fire, periodically shouts, or all of these. It is difficult to find a person who thrashes on in hysteric hope, steadily weakening.

FREEDOM OF THE HILLS

Navigation in the high country is not a science, but an art. Some travelers have the gift and some don't, but all must learn the tools and all can improve with practice. Under its other name, routefinding, navigation is the subject of several following chapters. Indeed, it is essentially the subject of this entire book.

In medieval times the greatest honor a visitor could receive was the rights of a citizen, the freedom of the city. The alpine navigator seeks to wander at will through valley jungles, green meadows, steep cliffs, and broad glaciers, to earn the rights of citizen in an alien land, to be fully at home in the high country, a mountaineer with freedom of the hills.

Supplementary Reading:
Kjellstrom, Bjorn. *Be Expert with Map and Compass.* Silva.

6 *

WILDERNESS TRAVEL

OVER THE CENTURIES civilization has gradually crept up the approaches to many mountain ranges. Armies and elephants have crossed the Alps, and the Himalaya is isolated more by politics than nature. In such ranges it is possible to be purely a climber, trusting a native guide or railway conductor to lead the way to the first rocks or ice.

There is another sort of mountain range that lies deep in wilderness. When a climbing party leaves its automobiles at a trailhead in a Cascade valley or is deposited on the beach of a British Columbia fjord it may face long hours or days of wilderness travel before enjoying alpine pleasures. The technique of muddling through brush is not as glamorous as Class Five rock climbing, but many a peak has been lost in thickets of slide alder. Indeed, the major defenses of a wilderness mountain frequently lie below snowline and the final scramble to the summit is anticlimactic after the epic approach.

ROUTES AND NON-ROUTES

No one set of immutable laws governs choice of wilderness route; each range has its own peculiarities of geology and climate. The Canadian Rockies mountaineer accustomed to broad, meadowed valleys and open forests is horrified when he encounters the narrow canyons, totally occupied by jungles and cataracts, of the Coast Range. The Cascades mountaineer used to deep snow in June everywhere above 4000 feet feels parched when he visits the Sierra Nevada and must climb thousands of feet higher to find more than scraps of snow.

Prolonged mountaineering in a single range fills one with the lore of routefinding in that range, but even the wiliest traveler should enter each new range humble in spirit. He is not utterly ignorant, for in knowing any mountains well he knows something of all mountains. This knowledge can be extrapolated, and supplemented by information from guidebooks, journals, maps, and acquaintances. None of these is a substitute for firsthand experience but all at least prepare him to be a good student.

Climate and geology make mountains what they are. Knowing that the west slope of the Olympics receives in excess of 150 inches of annual precipitation with a frost level that extends in winter to sea level prepares the experienced mountaineer for dense brush and a low snowline and miserable weather. Knowing that the Tetons are comparatively arid and hot prepares him for a relative absence of brush, snow, and water. Knowing that the Olympics are composed mostly of weak sediments leads him to anticipate wearisome scree and easy ridge-running. Knowing that the Sir Donald group of the Selkirks is quartzite gives advance confidence in the soundness of the rock, however steep. The mountaineer who knows the major outlines of a range's climate and geology can learn a great deal more by map study.

Whether the mountaineer's travels are in familiar or foreign territory, on trails or off, he must continuously be watching for the way back (viewed from the opposite direction a route may be remarkably unfamiliar), for changes that may occur during the day, such as a stream rising from snowmelt or rainstorm, and for emergency campsites, a water supply, and even for materials from which he could build an emergency fire in a downpour. These observations become second nature as the result of conscious practice.

Trails

A trail by definition is not wilderness even though it be a corridor of civilization barely a foot wide. Usually there is something of a trail between the roadhead and terra incognita, a track that starts bravely and dwindles to nothing. In many a present wilderness the traveler comes upon useful remnants of a past penetration by civilization, fragmentary trails of long-vanished miners or trappers.

Even in ranges with heavy traffic and well-posted with signs a moderate degree of alertness is required to find and keep on the correct trail. The beginning may be obliterated by logging operations or highway construction. Parties often stagnate mentally on a long monotonous walk and miss their proper turnoff. A good many more, awaiting an intersection with a prominent sign that has been flattened by winter snows or carried off by a souvenir hunter, find themselves at nightfall far up the wrong creek. Signs are poor substitutes for the methods of orientation discussed in Chapters 5 and 7.

The climber must remember that very few trails were engineered for his use. Miners build trails to ore, fishermen to the high lakes, trappers along valleys, pioneers over passes, and animals pursue their own special interests. Frequently the mine or the lake or the pass is a splendid basecamp, and any old remnant of track is worth following if it goes reasonably near the right destination. Inevitably, however, there comes the painful moment when a pleasant trail must be abandoned because it goes to a lake or a prospect hole many miles up the wrong valley.

A human trail is often blazed in the forests and indicated above timberline by rock cairns; some are, unfortunately, marked with the ultimate abomination — pressurized spray paint. Following a marked trail requires some skill and much care: the tree with the critical blaze grows old and topples, an avalanche carries away a cairn. Also many marks are made by confused climbers on the wrong route.

An important principle in choosing off-trail routes is always to follow the course that a trail would follow if there were one. Trail builders generally find the easiest going; by studying their work one can more quickly and wisely navigate the pure wilderness.

Brush

Wherever there is running water and/or sliding snow, brush thrives. The classic example is a low-altitude gully swept by avalanches in winter and a torrent in summer. Coniferous trees cannot mature but conditions are perfect for supple shrubs which flourish during the short summer season, usually bend undamaged under the snow, and even if stripped to the ground quickly sprout again from the roots. Coniferous forests, if allowed to mature, reach high and steal all the sunlight, eventually throttling deciduous trees; along river banks brush keeps a window on the sun and builds a narrow dense thicket. A river that changes course frequently prevents conifers from gaining control and has a wide belt of alder bottoms. At subalpine elevations the entire valley floor may be a tangle, winter avalanche snow lasting late into summer and thus preventing forests but encouraging brush.

Large conifers are on the side of justice and the traveler, but small ones are poor friends. The second-growth timber that springs densely up after a fire or windstorm or logging is at its worst when about 20 feet high, the branches completely filling the space between trees, the overhead cover not yet so thick that lack of sunlight has caused these lower limbs to die and fall away. Moreover, at this age deciduous brush is still very much in the contest. Even more difficult to negotiate are blowdowns, avalanche fans, and logging trash where the jumble is so chaotic that frequently a quarter-mile an hour is an heroic velocity. A single such obstacle only a few hundred feet wide may justify major modifications of route and schedule.

The scrub growth at timberline, where wind forces conifers to huddle next to the ground, usually stand alone or in small clumps, but occasionally they form a continuous belt. Another subalpine horror is scrub cedar that clings to bands of rocks and cliffs. These nearly impenetrable thickets of tough twisted trunks and branches are to be avoided entirely if possible by seeking breaks in the cliff bands.

If a skirmish with brush must be accepted there are a few techniques for getting through with a minimum of effort. Inspect the brushy area as much as possible on the approach and choose the shortest route across to a clear area beyond, using any fallen trees with long straight trunks as elevated walkways. Overlapping bushes may be parted vertically — wearing gloves if the vegetation is a type covered with thorns — to allow passage, and in some cases, such as slide alder, horizontally, stepping on some of the lower limbs and raising the higher ones to provide a passageway. In steep terrain some brush is helpful if it is well-anchored and strong enough to use for handholds and "vegetable belays."

Brush is not without its dangers. Downhill-slanting vine maple or alder gives slippery footing and if one is bouncing along many feet from the ground a lost hold can cause a bad fall. Brush obscures cliffs, boulders, and ravines, and more than once has led a traveler to mischief.

The best policy of all is to avoid brush. So bald a statement seems much like forthrightly condemning Hell, yet even in ranges where brush is a frightful menace an alert traveler often can thread an easy path. The following principles are helpful:

1. Use trail as much as possible. Five miles of trail may be less work than one mile of brush.
2. Travel above the brush on early season snowcover. Some valleys are easy going in May when the party walks on 10 feet of snow but are almost impossible in July when the party must burrow under 10 feet of brush.
3. In summer avoid avalanche tracks. When following a long valley the best route may be on slopes with a south or west exposure where the snow does not avalanche so ferociously as on the opposite side. When climbing a valley wall stick to the "timber cones" between avalanche paths.
4. Always aim for the heaviest timber.
5. The ridge spurs between creeks and the valley walls above rivers may be dry and brushless while the creek bottoms and valley floors are nightmares.
6. As a final alternative consider going right into the channel of the

stream. Gravel and boulder beds may provide a clear tunnel through
the brush, though wading may be the price. Streams flowing in deep
canyons, however, are usually either choked with fallen timber or
interrupted by waterfalls.

7. If the valley bottoms are hopeless and the valley sides scarred by
   myriad avalanche tracks, it may be worthwhile to climb as directly as
   possible to timberline and take a high route above the brush. The
   difficulties of the rocks and ice must of course be weighed against those
   below.

8. In alpine valleys travel on scree and remnants of snow rather than
   adjacent thickets.

9. Seek game trails. Animals dislike brush as much as man does. Their
   intelligence is less than human but their experience greater.

Talus

The rocks of the peaks constantly crumble and tumble and pile up in the
valley as talus. Most of the rubble emerges from gullies and spreads out
below in fan-shaped cones which often merge into one another, forming a
broad band of talus between the valley greenery and precipice. Talus fans
also often alternate with timber cones.

Talus slopes build gradually over the ages. In the oldest heaps, soil has
filled the interstices between boulders, making smooth pathways.
"Newer" rock piles without vegetation can be dependable where the
climber can leap about lightly, guarding against the occasional teetering
stone by his very momentum.

In volcanic and younger mountains talus can be dangerous. Rapid
disintegration of the rocks leaves even huge boulders delicately balanced,
and the traveler must always be ready to skip nimbly aside when his
foothold suddenly shifts. Occasionally a talus slope, and frequently
moraines, which are very recent piles of sand and rock, are so insecure that
kicking loose one key stone will destroy the precarious equilibrium, setting
off a disastrous rock avalanche. The slopes of smallest fragments, called
scree, may be securely anchored by vegetation or may be as loose as sand,
requiring great patience and energy to climb.

The most careful person on the stablest scree cannot avoid loosing an
occasional pebble or boulder and therefore routes are preferred which
allow each climber to avoid the fall line of climbers above and below.
When the choice of route is restricted, as in a narrow gully, each member
must tread gently and instantaneously give a warning shout should he start
a stone rolling. Frequently it is essential for a party to travel one at a time
or closely bunched up so that rocks cannot attain dangerous momentum
between members.

On descent, loose scree is sometimes sought rather than avoided, for the

IV. Glacier Basin; Monte Cristo area, Cascade Range. (T. M. Green)

sport of "screeing." The object is to start a minor slide of pebbles and then ride it down, in a standing glissade, shuffling the feet adroitly to keep them on the surface, avoiding large leg-breaker rocks, stepping to the side if things get out of hand. Screeing, however, is permissible only where vegetation is totally non-existent; the merits of the sport do not justify wiping out the tiniest struggling plant.

Snow

The techniques of snow climbing are the same whether the snow lies on a high spire or in the deep woods. If slopes are at all long and steep, safeguards such as ice ax and rope should be employed even if the party is walking along a trail — a trail buried under a dozen feet of snow.

Not to be overlooked are the advantages of snow in cross-country travel. Talus, brush, and logging slash are paved highways when covered by consolidated snow and for this reason many a peak is best bagged early in the season. During the same season snow bridges may provide quick passage over rushing streams, with the caveat that crossing snow bridges over streams is often much like crossing bridges over crevasses. As spring merges into summer and obstacles emerge, the route along a valley floor may be quite erratic, taking advantage of every remaining snow patch for the few yards or steps of easy walking it provides.

Despite the advantages of walking on the spring or early summer snow patches there are some potential hazards. Logs and boulders covered with snow often have adjacent hidden cavities which can give way under the foot of the unwary traveler. Probe or avoid likely spots, and step wide off logs or rocks.

Streams beneath the snow melt the underside of the snowcover until it can no longer support the weight of a traveler. A careless step may result in a sudden drop and wet feet, or worse, being carried under the snow by a swift stream. Watch for depressions or variations in color or texture of the snow and listen for sounds of running water underneath. The volume of water emerging at the foot of a snowfield may give a clue to the existence if not the size of the cavity beneath.

With experience a person is able to recognize and avoid the hidden dangers lurking under the surface of the snow and use the medium to his own advantage.

Streams

When a party enters wilderness without trail or bridge, water becomes a major impediment. In the Canadian Coast Range or Alaska, climbers may spend more time and energy crossing a perilous river than on their ultimate objective, the mountain.

Finding the Crossing

Whenever the peak lies beyond a respectable river the crossing is a major factor in route. A distant view — perhaps from a ridge before descent into the valley — is sometimes better than a hundred close views from a riverbank. When a distant view is unobtainable or unhelpful the party must balance one against the other the merits of going along close to the bank for the sake of finding a footlog or log jam, at the expense of suffering riverbottom brush, and walking high on open ridge slopes, then striking directly for the river.

In deep forest a party may find easy passage over even the widest river on a semipermanent log jam wedged together during some past flood. Higher in the mountains footlogs are harder to come by, particularly when the river changes course periodically, preventing the growth of large trees near its channel. If such footlogs are not available and wading is inevitable, one sound bit of not entirely obvious advice is to seek always the widest part of a river: the narrows of a watercourse, though seemingly offering the shortest duration of suffering, are the deepest and the swiftest, and hence the most dangerous.

Making the Crossing

Before attempting any stream crossing that would require swimming in case of a slip, unfasten the waist strap of the pack. Frequently it is possible to cross a stream by hopping from one boulder to another. The sequence should be closely studied beforehand and every stride and leap rehearsed mentally. Often safety lies in smooth and steady progress, the stones being too unsteady and slippery to allow balance for more than a moment in transit to the next. An ice ax or pole for an added point of support may be almost indispensable.

At low altitude footlogs are relatively plentiful and require a second thought only when slippery, awkwardly thin, or steeply inclined. Again an ice ax or pole, or a tightly stretched handline, is helpful in maintaining balance on an unstable log crossing.

The efforts of a wilderness traveler are directed toward finding a dry crossing by stone or log but the wet crossing must often be accepted. If the water is placid and the stones rounded, Spartan climbers carry boots and lower garments dry in the pack. In more severe conditions an excellent plan is to remove socks before wading and wear boots in the water; on the far side the boots can be drained and dry socks replaced. The climber must consider the advantages and disadvantages of removing trousers or other clothing in deeper crossings. Any loose clothing increases the drag from rapidly moving water, but clothing reduces the chilling factor of icy water and may permit a longer crossing before the legs or feet become numb.

The force of moving water is easy to underestimate. A swift stream flowing only shin-deep boils up against the knees. Knee-deep water may boil above the waist and give the traveler a disconcerting sensation of buoyancy. Whenever water boils above the knee it is dangerous – the rocks underfoot are also buoyant and easily dislodged, and one false step turns the brave climber into a frightened swimmer bounding in white water from boulder to boulder. It is well to remember that frothy water contains so much air that though wet enough to drown in, it may not be dense enough to float the human body. Water milky from glacier-milled rock flour presents the added difficulty that one cannot see the bottom but must probe blindly with the feet.

Sometimes if the stream is fairly deep but not too swift, a crossing can be made quite easily by angling downstream at about the same speed as the current. Usually, however, it is best to face upstream on the crossing, leaning into the current and stabbing the ice ax or a stout pole upstream for a third point of suspension. The leading foot probes for solid placement on the shifting bottom, the following foot advances, and then the ax or pole is thrust into a new position. Sometimes the crossing is best made in pairs, one person bracing the other while he advances to a secure stance. Team crossing with a pole is a method in common use in some parts of the world. Team members line up facing across the stream with the pole parallel to the stream. Each member grasps the pole securely. As the team advances across the stream the upstream member breaks the force of the current while the others help support him. If one person slips, the others can support him until he regains his footing.

On a very hazardous crossing it is only common sense for the leader to be belayed. Skill in belaying is essential, supplemented by visualization of a body caught in stream flow. Obviously it is best for the belay to be placed as far above the crossing as possible, for in a "fall" the leader will pendulum in the current to the near bank. The higher upstream the belay, the shorter the fall. Rescuers poised on the bank at the end of the pendulum swing can often save a life by swift action. Once the leader has attained the far shore his companions can be safeguarded by an anchored handline. They should stay on the downstream side of the handline and either move hand-over-hand or grasp a short sling clipped to a carabiner which slides along the line. When there is any doubt every member should be belayed, with due respect for potentially entangling snags.

Some rivers are quite perfectly impassable. If the headwaters are fed by snow, early morning is usually the time of minimum flow and a party may camp overnight awaiting lower water. Sometimes it is necessary to hike hours or days seeking a vulnerable point. Very rarely a Tyrolean traverse (see Chapter 13) can be rigged if one member is capable of swimming or wading the flood to fix a line on the far bank. For the widest and deepest rivers rafts are the only alternative short of hiking to the headwaters — which in the case of the Columbia would make a very long outing indeed.

EFFICIENT WALKING

In generations past, walking was so necessary a human activity that nearly everyone was expert. Nowadays, with the advance of mechanized transportation, walking has become so rare an art that usually a person taking up the sport of wilderness mountaineering must first learn to walk before he can climb. Though the technique is not at all complicated, and can be performed in a rough and ready fashion even by infants, a little study and practice are needed to become proficient.

Preparing to Walk

Conditioning

Any physical activity is most easily performed by a body in good condition from frequent exercise. Through a sustained high level of muscular exertion the capacity for exertion is increased, as discussed in Appendix 1. Mountaineering being predominantly a sport of those with sedentary occupations, most persons undergo the annual agonies of "getting in condition." On an extended trip conditioning comes naturally and easily. During the first days the heart pounds and the lungs gasp and the muscles ache, but the system steadily adjusts and eventually begins to attain that splendid and exhilarating state when extraordinary feats are possible and enjoyable. Weekend mountaineering is frustrating: the body "tunes up" during the weekend and on Monday — back in the office — is ready for marvelous things; by Thursday, disappointed, it begins to relax. Generally the early part of a season requires considerable mental resolve and some physical discomfort, for it takes several months of weekend outings to attain the physical fitness gained in one good week of hard walking. A schedule of training exercises helps immensely in developing endurance.

Going Light

If the fault of overloading were not so universal it would be banal to declare that one can walk faster with a lighter pack. Most novices quickly learn to do without pajamas, parasols, and cast-iron skillets but even the experienced sometimes fail to thoroughly analyze their gear. Each item should be considered: Is it absolutely necessary? Was it used on the previous trip? Is there any lighter substitute? Ruthless paring of ounces — always reserving safety and/or climbing essentials — saves pounds of weight and adds miles to the hiking range.

The Act of Walking

It is one thing to walk from the doorstep to the family automobile or from the bus stop to the office; on such short journeys it is not essential to walk efficiently. It is quite another matter to walk many miles through rough wilderness carrying heavy loads. The maximum capacity varies with individuals, depending upon conditioning and general physical size and strength. However, whatever the maximum capacity may be of a particular individual at a particular moment, it cannot be realized without careful attention to practices of good walking.

Pace and Rest

The proper pace is a complex equation between the body's strength, the load it is carrying, the distance to be traveled, and the time available. It is silly to specify 3 miles per hour as good average speed, or 1000 feet of altitude per hour, or 15 miles per day. There is too wide a range between flat sea level trail and steep alpine slopes, between 10-pound rucksacks and 100-pound expeditionary loads, for any average to be meaningful. There are several aspects to pace: first, the speed, or number of steps taken during an hour; second, the manner in which these steps should be taken to conserve energy; third, how frequently the party should cease taking steps — that is, rest.

The most common mistake of the beginner is walking too fast, thinking desperately of the great distance to be covered. It is pointless to travel 1 mile in 4 minutes — or 15 minutes — if the result is such utter exhaustion that the remaining 9 miles to basecamp are impossible. Nor do rational mountaineers keep books listing the "best time from Swamp Camp to Blowdown Camp as 3 hours 47 minutes 12.5 seconds." Sometimes it may be necessary to make all possible haste from Swamp Camp to Blowdown Camp, as when being pursued by a forest fire, but if an entire day is available for the journey it is far more meritorious to arrive relaxed at Blowdown with memories and photographs of the flora, fauna, and geology en route.

There is a simple test by which any individual at any time can determine if his pace is proper: if it cannot be sustained hour after hour it is too fast. Two departments of the body have separate control. A person can walk only as fast as his legs allow: when it becomes a mighty effort to drag the foot forward the pace is too fast. A person can walk only as fast as his lungs allow: when the lungs are desperately gasping for air the pace is too fast. Either symptom requires a slowdown. Along a flat trail the legs complain

V. Crossing Winthrop Glacier on Mt. Rainier during period in which ice axes were replacing alpenstocks. (Bob and Ira Spring)

while the lungs are still content. At high altitude the lungs are starving for air while the legs are growing stiff from lack of exercise.

Ambition and vanity usually ensure male chauvinists against going too slowly. Some hikers, particularly unliberated females, place excessive emphasis on the rule that a pace should be comfortable. The body complains long before it is hurt. The muscles may ache but still have 10 miles left in them; the lungs may gasp but be able to continue gasping another 3 hours. Indeed, the body improves its efficiency most rapidly when driven close to its limits of performance. A certain degree of suffering is inevitable if one is to become a good walker.

Speed fluctuates during the day. At the beginning of a walk, especially in the morning, it is well to go along slowly to let the body become gradually aware of the demands that will be made. With so courteous a start it is more enthusiastic about gearing up to full power. The phenomenon of "second wind" is familiar: after an initial period during which willpower must be exerted to keep going, suddenly the hiker finds himself striding along happy and strong, free to observe with pleasure the sights along the way. Physiologically this means the heart has taken a faster tempo, the blood is circulating more rapidly, the muscles have loosened.

Since the trail is seldom uniform the climber must adjust his pace. On a steep hill he plods slowly and methodically but as the grade lessens his speed increases until on a decline he may be fairly flying along. Late in the day speed decreases, for though adrenalin secretions allow short bursts of explosive exertion there is no "third wind." The body has already done its utmost and the accumulating poisons of fatigue steadily lower efficiency.

If one mountaineering technique had to be singled out as most important, honors would go to the *rest step,* used on any terrain whenever expenditure of energy is so great that either legs or lungs need an interval of recuperation between steps. The pace is slow, since for every step there is a pause. Breathing must be synchronized with the sequence. For example: inhale as rear foot advances to a new position; exhale as the unweighted advanced leg rests, the body entirely supported on the rear leg; repeat. When the air is thin it is the lungs that need a pause, sometimes for two or three or five breaths to each step. At high elevations climbers must make a conscious effort to breathe deeply and frequently. At lower altitude it is leg muscles that need extra time to accumulate energy.

An important element of the rest step is mental composure. When the summit seems to remain constantly distant for hours on end the individual must trust the rest step to slowly but steadily chew up the miles. When monotony impairs morale he must draw on his inner resources, his ability to lose time and place in reflection of other times and places.

A reasonable speed, with the rest step when needed, eliminates nearly all the collapse rests of the novice hiker, who sags in a heap at the slightest provocation. Still, some rests are required by the strongest and most expert walkers. Formulas are frequently proposed for the allowable number of rests per hour and their optimum duration. All such formulas presume uniform human beings with uniform packs walking along uniform trails and therefore they are all nonsense. Their one germ of truth is that "to rest is not to conquer." A party sprawled in the meadows is not getting any closer to its objective, unless its objective is sprawling in meadows. It is simple logic to ask always whether a rest is really necessary, and if not, whether there is time for luxury. A party holding to a tight schedule will not rest nearly so often as members would like. If there is no hurry it will rest whenever the mood seizes.

Mandatory for a large party and desirable for any is a *shakedown* rest during the first half-hour of the day: bootlaces must be loosened or tightened, packstraps adjusted, layers of clothing added or subtracted. In mixed groups party separations should be declared as a matter of course and/or as need and terrain dictate; their omission can cause almost debilitating distress to members too shy to express the need. (Wilderness etiquette and large numbers of weekend mountaineers dictate that the first party separation should if possible be near the trailhead at a service station or privy.) During the early part of a day, while the body is fresh, rests should be infrequent and short; for such *breathers* it is best to rest in a standing or semi-reclining position, leaning against a tree or hillside to remove packweight from the shoulders, taking deep breaths and a bite to eat. Later on the body demands more complete relaxation and about every hour or two the party staggers into a *sackout* rest. When it is nearing time for a stop members begin watching for some point with special advantages, such as convenient slopes for unslinging packs, a water supply, a view, or pretty flowers. It is all too easy to prolong such moments, but when the camp or summit is still far away climbers should remember how agonizing is the resumption of a march once muscles become cold and stiff. Experienced walkers, knowing the day's itinerary and whether it is easy or rough, automatically include the proper number of breathers and sackouts. They know moreover that at the end of a long hard haul the body, despite all reason and rest-stepping, begins to defy will and demand the *collapse* rest, toppling into snow or mud and lying there utterly inert and content.

Downhill and Sidehill

Downhill walking is nowhere nearly so fatiguing as uphill walking but the blessings of gravity are not unmixed. It is on the downtrail that blisters are raised and knee cartilage displaced, for weight drops abruptly and roughly on legs and feet. Jolts traveling up the spine so shock and jar the entire body that after a long descent the very head may begin to ache. Far sooner the hiker feels his knees coming loose at the hinges and expects them to begin working both ways like those of a rag doll. Even more serious, at every step the toes jam forward in the boot and hot spots develop on the feet.

The first preparation for the downtrail is to stuff the boots full of socks and tie the laces tight to reduce movement of foot within boot. The downhill pace is kept much more moderate than the one urged by gravity. The leg lands on each step with bent knee to cushion the jar and the feet are placed as lightly as possible, as if they were already sore. Such restraint is extremely tiring to muscles of the upper leg, which may begin to quiver under the strain of holding back the weight of body and pack; in loose pumice or scree a stiff-legged glissade provides welcome relief. Rests on the downtrail are just as essential as on the uptrail.

Sidehill-gouging is one of the ultimate evils of the mountain world; when it cannot be avoided there is no alternative to suffering the agonies of bent ankles and contorted hips. If there is a choice between struggling along a sidehill and dropping into a flat valley — barring valley bottom brush — the altitude loss is often more than compensated for by the saving of legs and ankles. Similarly, if the top of the ridge is rounded the walking may be much easier in the long run even though there are many ups and downs. On a long sidehill gouge it may be possible to switchback occasionally to alternate muscle strain. Any available flat spots such as imbedded rocks, grass or heather clumps, animal trails, and the like offer relief.

Etiquette

Walking is more often than not a social sport and demands a regard for certain social amenities, a trail etiquette which is really no more than commonsense thoughtfulness. On the trail it is very bad form to follow the man ahead so closely that he feels pressed; besides, he may respond with equally bad form by bending back the branches of a tree like a catapult and loosing them full in the face of the follower. If one wishes to tie a shoelace or adjust a pack, it is simple courtesy to step aside and not block traffic. In passing another member of the party, social amenities are better served by expressing this desire rather than crowding past, especially on narrow trails or the edges of cliffs. If a member or members of the party cannot keep up with the pace set by the leader, the speed should be reduced. Wilderness is characterized by a small population density, and ill will fostered by stumbling over one another is decidedly unnecessary.

Use of the Ice Ax

Although introduction of the flip-top beverage container has largely relieved the ice ax of its function as a can opener, the climber and hiker still find it an invaluable all-purpose tool. On open trails many climbers strap the ax on the pack, using the ice ax carrier provided or tying it to the frame. In rough country the ax is so useful in the hands, and in the pack snags so frequently on brush and tree limbs, it is better brought out into the open.

Ice axes, when purchased, are often sharpened to fine points on the pick and spike and to a razor edge on the adze. If the intent is to start immediately with high-angle ice climbing or to commit homicide, this sharpness might be desirable. For more modest mountaineering efforts, however, it is prudent to dull the adze by filing and/or to install an ax guard and a spike protector.

Even so the ice ax is probably the most dangerous implement of mountaineering. Carrying an ax without the skill to use it properly provides a false sense of security, as well as high risk of injury should the alpine traveler fall on his own ax and impale himself. All too frequently climbers have slipped on hard snow only to discover that the principles of ice ax arrest only vaguely recalled from the pages of a climbing text were not adequate to stop the fall. It is imperative that alpine travelers be skilled in arrest techniques *before* venturing onto hard or crusty snow. The way to acquire this skill is by practice on slopes with safe runout in case of failure to arrest (see Chapter 16).

When the ax is carried in the hand on good trail the shaft is grasped at the balance point, the spike forward and the head to the rear with the pick down. Thus the man behind is safeguarded against accidentally running

Fig. 17. Carrying ice ax on easy terrain.

into the spike, and the pick is less likely to do the owner harm in a stumble. When a climber is weary or footing is poor he can use the ax for a cane, grasped by the head with the pick to the rear. On steep slippery terrain, whether mud, needles, grass, or snow, the ax is grasped by the head with the guard removed and the pick to the rear, in position for a quick arrest in event of a slip.

On any terrain other than a flat and beaten trail the climber may find numerous unsuspected uses of the ax. In stream fording it provides a third leg among the shifting stones. When hopping over talus it gives many a slight touch-and-go balance point. On steep hillsides, just as on steep snow, the ax held diagonally across the body, spike touching the slope, helps hold a stable, vertical stance. Though the ice ax self-arrest is treated in Chapter 16 as a technique for snow, many a climber has been most happy to use it to stop himself in steep meadows and forest.

 PART TWO

Climbing Fundamentals

VI. Mt. Fury from above Luna Lake; Northern Pickets, North Cascades National Park. (Lee Mann)

7 *

ROUTEFINDING

ROUTEFINDING, an art not to be confused with the science of navigation, basically involves finding a route that "goes," from the point of leaving the cars to the summit of the peak. The neophyte mountaineer can, by a little practice at home with a map and compass, acquire enough skill to navigate a course from point A to point B across glaciers and subalpine meadows (barring, of course, physical obstacles beyond his ability to surmount). But while the principles of routefinding can also be studied at home, only by applying them in actual practice in the mountains can one develop any significant skill, and only then do the principles become meaningful. As with other climbing skills, the best way for an aspiring climber to learn is by climbing with experienced mountaineers, observing their technique and asking questions.

PREPARATION

Successful routefinding begins at home with assembly and study of as much information as possible. Route descriptions found in guidebooks or climbing journals are helpful whether the objective is to repeat a previous climb, to avoid it, or to establish a new route.

Photographs can be used to work out possible routes or identify peaks; liberal use of the camera on a previous trip often is appreciated when planning to return to an area. Guidebooks and journals may supplement route descriptions with drawings or photos, but even nonclimbing references — hiking guides, picture books, geological reports — can yield useful photos.

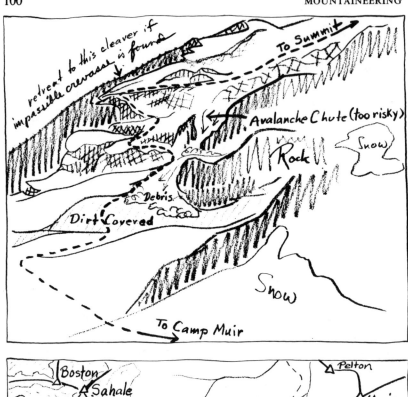

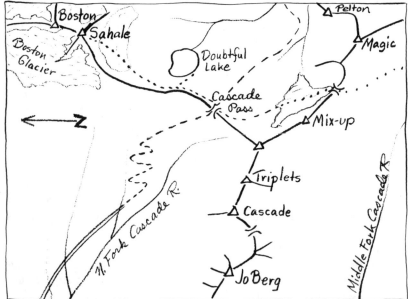

Fig 18. Sketch maps. *Top,* notes to help find route, made from distance; Nisqually Glacier. *Bottom,* climbers' map for showing location of peaks.

Maps should be collected, reviewed, and interpreted for as much route information as possible. The latest Forest Service map will show the deepest penetration by civilization and thus the start of routefinding problems. United States Geological Survey (USGS) topographic maps, which should be studied for possible routes and campsites, reveal the locations of peaks, ridges, avalanche gullies, glaciers, and other important features, but must not receive a climber's unqualified trust: a major climbing problem may lurk between 100-foot contour lines. Climbers' maps, whether sketched in a guidebook, or on a candy bar wrapper, are especially useful since they reveal features significant to a climber — difficult moves, belay stances, bivouac ledges; however, if drawn from memory such sketches are likely to be in error on distances and other details. Maps are discussed in greater detail in Chapter 5.

Few indeed are the wilderness areas not frequently visited by someone these days, and local authorities, including park or forest rangers, geologists, and other climbers, can frequently give valuable advice on routes or local conditions. Climbers' trails, undisclosed by any official map but well-known to locals, can immeasurably expedite the approach. Climbers visiting an unfamiliar area often find a brief visit with a forest or park ranger saves substantial time.

APPROACHING THE PEAK

Lower Elevation and Seasonal Problems

Although selection of approach roads and trails is a factor, the real art of routefinding begins where the road or trail ends, or at least when their direction and that of the climbing party become incompatible.

Getting to the mountain is the first critical problem of routefinding and errors in solving it have frequently resulted in loss of summits long before any technical climbing was encountered. Approaches may involve use of navigational knowledge and skills (Chapter 5), techniques of wilderness travel (Chapter 6), and recognition and understanding of avalanche and cornice hazards (Chapters 16 and 24).

Approach Observations

Throughout the approach the peak is constantly studied for details of possible climbing routes, since the distant view reveals gross patterns of ridges, cliffs, snowfields, and glaciers as well as average angle of inclination. As the party closes in on the peak, details of fault lines, bands of cliffs, and crevasse fields become apparent. It generally holds that gross patterns seen from afar are repeated in fine detail when viewed closer. Ledges revealed by snow or shrubs from a distance often turn out to be "sidewalks" with numerous smaller ledges interspersed between. The

VII. Cloud Cap Peak in Nooksack Cirque; North Cascades National Park. (Tom Miller)

Fig. 19. Features of rock are obscured by flat lighting on an overcast day as on Cloud Cap, *above.* Fresh snow and sunlight bring out form of rock, *opposite.*

major fault lines, or weaknesses, of the mountain visible at a distance, are usually accompanied by finer, less obvious repetitions.

If the party's approach skirts the base of the mountain, the peak can be viewed from various perspectives, sometimes revealing piece by piece portions of a climbing route not apparent from any single direction. A system of ledges not highlighted by snow or shrubs, and indistinguishable against background cliffs, may be seen with startling clarity from another angle with the sky behind.

Changing lighting as the sun traverses the sky often creates revealing shadows across a mountain face even when viewed straight on. Just a few minutes of studying lengthening or shortening shadows may be sufficient to disclose that apparently sheer cliffs are only moderately angled slopes.

The presence of snow, except perhaps during or immediately after a storm, discloses an angle of inclination permitting easy climbing, for snow will not long remain on slopes exceeding 40 degrees. Beware nature's tricks, though: rime adhering to vertical or even overhanging cliffs can at first appear to be snow, and deep high-angle gulleys often retain snow or ice year around, especially when shaded. Snow may glisten and sparkle, but does not shine: brilliant, shining snowfields high on the mountain are sheathed in ice and will no doubt call for the party's best ice climbing technique.

Crevasse fields are indicated at a distance by the larger fissures but closer inspection almost always discloses numerous smaller but not necessarily less significant holes. Pertinent inferences can be drawn from the fact that crevasses are the result of the motion of ice flowing down the mountain: on concave slopes crevasses tend to close up, becoming relatively narrow, perhaps even "stepping over" width. On convex slopes, crevasses open up, presenting major obstacles — wide fissures and steep walls. On an especially steep slope the glacier tumbles down the mountain as an icefall, always an impressive sight when viewed head on, and a whole new challenge to the routefinder.

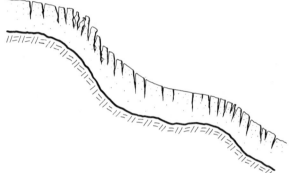

Fig. 20. Longitudinal section of glacier. Note that crevasses open over a convex slope and close over concave slope.

As the party nears the peak, keys to its defenses are sought: ridges with lower average inclination than the faces they divide; cracks, ledges, and chimneys leading up or across the faces; snowfields or glaciers offering easier or predictable pitches. Not only are possible routes identified, but climbing hazards are noted. Snowfields and icefalls are observed for avalanche activity. Rock faces are studied for signs of rockfall — snowfields readily reveal any recent activity on cliffs above by rock-filled "shell craters." If the route must go through such hazards, it may be better done in the cold hours of night or very early morning, before the warmth of the rising sun begins to melt the icy mortar bonding precariously perched boulders or seracs, setting off the daily bombardment of slopes below.

Throughout the approach the skilled routefinder repeatedly *"climbs with his eyes," seeking continuous routes and evaluating difficulties and hazards.* When the routes become so lengthy or complex as to tax the memory, quick sketches may be taken during rest stops. Such memory aids sometimes prove invaluable later in the climb when the critical exit gulley is lost from view.

ON THE PEAK

Routefinding on Rock

A classic lesson in routefinding is given by Edward Whymper's experience on the Matterhorn in 1865. After failing to climb the mountain in several attempts from the Italian side, he discovered that the difficult downtilting slabs that had so long defeated him formed an easily climbed staircase on the opposite or Swiss side.

This is but one example of the important effect of the *lay of the strata* in sedimentary structures. Flat-lying strata generally offer step-like irregularities which are easily ascended. If the strata are tilted downward into the peak the resulting *upslab* is so much the better; holds are abundant and even loose rocks tend to hold firmly in place. On *downslab* not only are the holds upside down from the climber's viewpoint but loose rocks tend to slide from position with little provocation.

Fig. 21. Lay of strata in rock.

The lay often leads to *ledge-running* routes, particularly common in certain parts of the Canadian Rockies. Some layers form good ledge systems while others form cliffs, and the party traverses along one ledge seeking a break by which access may be gained to the next higher ledge. If the strata are tilted, a single ledge may be followed on a long angling ascent, possibly all the way to the summit ridge. *Differential erosion* is the process responsible, strong bands of rock becoming cliffs while the weaker ones become ledges. The effect is very striking when the strata have wide variations in strength, as on the banded mountainsides of the Canadian Rockies where the ascent alternates between loose scree and steep cliffs. If the contrast between two strata is extreme, the cliff overhangs.

Another aspect of a mountain's internal structure which influences route selection is the *jointing* present to some extent in all rocks. Sometimes the jointing is so pronounced it produces a system of ledges and gullies similar to those of strata. Smaller joints lend themselves to various climbing techniques described in Chapters 12 and 13. *Faults* are of more questionable value since a fault zone usually consists of crushed and shattered fragments. When a fault plane is vertical it tends to be eroded into a deep gully of loose rock that is best avoided. If it is horizontal a very decent ledge may result. A *sill* or *dike* of igneous rock forms a cliff or a rib if stronger than the surrounding rocks, a ledge or gully if weaker.

A *ridge* is often the route of choice, the climbing angle tending to be less and the route generally free of rockfall and avalanches, though intensive weathering of ridges often causes unstable rock. A problem sometimes encountered is too much up and down — energy and time consumed skirting or climbing over gendarmes or traversing false summits. Snow cornices can be a hazard and when a ridge is snowcovered their presence should be assumed. On lengthy climbs a particular advantage of a ridge route is the better view of approaching weather.

A *face* tends to be challenging and is likely to require more frequent belaying and placing of protection. The route is not always apparent for its entire length, and a crack terminating on a blank wall may require a rappel or pendulum traverse to a lower, more climbable route. Rockfall hazard may be considerable. It is generally considered poor form to place bolts as a substitute for routefinding ability.

Routefinding on Snow and Ice

Couloirs

Deeply shaded couloirs, or gullies, are more often lined with ice than snow. Even in springtime when all open inclines are deep slush the couloirs may be hard ice from frost or avalanche-scouring.

Whether on a glacier or snaking upward into a rock precipice, ice gullies are often the key to passage, having a lesser angle from bottom to top than the cliffs they breach. However, the inviting aspect of a couloir in morning, contrasted with the forbidding menace of its enclosing cliffs, frequently proves in afternoon to have been a crocodile smile. Gullies are the garbage chutes of mountains, and however quiet they may be during night begin with the sun to transport toward sea level such rubbish as avalanching snow, rocks loosened by frost-wedging, and ice blocks weakened by melting. The climber strives to be out of the couloir before the sun arrives, which means an early start to accomplish a round trip, an alternate route for the descent, or a bivouac. Most, but not all, the debris comes down the center; but even when keeping to the sides it is well to cock a sharp ear for suspicious sounds coming from above and to have one member of the team watching for quiet slides and silent missiles.

In a steep couloir avalanches often erode a system of deeply incised ruts that usually are either avoided or crossed with all possible haste. However, early in the year rut floors offer the soundest snow available and in cold weather may be quite safe — particularly for a fast descent.

Couloirs can become increasingly nasty the higher they are ascended, presenting such nuisances as extreme steepness, verglas, moats, rubble strewn loosely over smooth rock slabs, and cornices. Many lead into traps, or cul-de-sacs, the gentle angle at the bottom compensated for by culmination in a frosty chimney. The rule is by no means invariable; when the couloir heads at a col it can well afford to offer a lower average angle than the face.

Despite negative aspects many ice routes follow gullies. Generally the techniques are simple cramponing and cutting, but crevasses, moats, and suncups, or blocks of fallen rock and ice, make rock-climbing techniques useful. Some of these irregularities are welcome for the sake of their belay potential.

When the bed of the gully is uncompromisingly steep, *moat-crawling* along the side of the gully is often more secure. Moats can sometimes be rather deep, requiring stemming between the snow and the rock wall; they also tend to be of irregular width, occasionally presenting alternately a tight squeeze and a gap too wide to stem. During the morning ascent cramponing or stepcutting may be faster; in afternoon a nervewracking descent on steep ice is hardly tempting compared to descending a moat with its lessened exposure and increased protection from rockfall.

Ridges

Routes along or near the crests of ridges are characterized by freedom from rockfall and avalanche hazards, but are exposed to wind and weather. Ridges may be composed of partly-rotten ice in the vicinity of rock outcrops and are frequently topped with dangerous cornices (see Chapters 16 and 24); if these are suspected — when, for example any sharp ridge approached from windward appears flattened — the safest line of progress lies below the crest on the side away from the overhang.

In regions of heavy snowfall ridges may prove the only wise choice when the ascent is at all lengthy. Routefinding is generally less critical than on other portions of a mountain and a safe retreat is usually open if proper equipment has been installed on the ascent. Ridge routes are less sensitive than others to the time factor, ordinarily not being threatened by avalanches and falling debris resulting from sunlight and warming conditions occurring late in the day.

Glaciers and Icefalls

Glaciers present their own peculiar routefinding problems, most frequently that of identifying and skirting crevasses. The lowest angle of ascent on a glacier is generally up the center, so this is the best route, crevasses permitting.

Too much emphasis cannot be placed on the *distant view*, taking into account all the many features of a glacier discussed in Chapter 23. As one approaches a glacier the long angle from the valley frequently tells more about the surface than the foreshortened perspective from the surface itself. A downward or cross-valley view is even more valuable. From a distance the route may be perfectly obvious, while once amid icefalls and crevasse fields finding passage may be a matter of blind luck. Often it is worthwhile to make a quick pencil sketch of significant features that can be seen from the intended route and the relative positions of major crevasses and other barriers. A distinctive block of ice may mark a gully that penetrates an icefall, or a bump on a moraine a narrow lane through a crevasse field. The distant view is no panacea, for closer inspection reveals much new information, but at the very least the main outlines of the route can be blocked out. The sketch should be referred to frequently and revised while working through a problem.

On large glaciers *routemarking* is essential for a safe return. It is easy to become confused in the bewildering monotony of the great white world of ice even in bright sunshine, not to mention fog; footprints are far too perishable to be trusted. The traditional marker was the willow wand cut from thickets near the glacier, but parties nowadays carry wands that are neither willow nor merely wands. Most commonly used are bamboo garden stakes about the diameter of a pencil and about 3 feet long, the ends split and cloth flags inserted and securely glued; the split is then banded, top and bottom, with tape. Fluorescent orange or dark red cloth is most visible at a distance and in all conditions of light. Square flags 3 by 5 inches or larger are better than long rectangular streamers, which tangle together while being carried in a bundle and once placed shred in the wind. Wands are placed on the ascent whenever the descent might be confusing, very much like blazes in a forest: several hundred feet apart when the route is a straight line, a rope-length apart for a twisting path, in pairs to mark turns or crevasses.

Icefalls offer interesting climbing routes that often are not so steep as they first appear. Good routefinding through the confused jumble can often reduce an apparently steep wall to a series of short 40- to 50-degree pitches.

The advisability of an icefall route depends on the stability of the icefall in question; fresh debris, or the lack of it, may indicate what can be expected. Icefalls are often protected from avalanches by the broken nature of the terrain, but it is most important to be aware of any snow or ice masses poised above. Routefinding can be tricky, with progress suddenly and abruptly halted by an enormous crevasse or a blank wall. Once in the icefall, the view may be restricted to the array of seracs and crevasses in the immediate vicinity. For this reason one should get a distant look before entering the icefall, and where practical select in advance each portion of the route and each avenue of escape, taking special pains to memorize salient landmarks, particularly those adjacent to unstable areas that must be climbed as rapidly as possible and at the optimum time of day. Appearance or disappearance of the sun can cause thawing or freezing, and in both cases avalanches. Exits or refuges, such as cleavers, should be noted for use in case of need, and on warm days or with a south exposure the risk of seracs becoming unglued and crashing down on the party will preclude climbing particular icefall routes altogether.

CLIMBING CLASSIFICATIONS

Climbers have found it desirable to be able to convey the difficulty of a climb by referring to a standard rating system. The several classification systems developed all have the same objective: evaluation of climbing routes by simple, universally recognized ratings. That none of these systems is perfect is evidenced by a continuing effort to improve them. On infrequently climbed routes the ratings tend to reflect the skill or ego of only a few climbers, or perhaps weather conditions or season at the time of the climb. Any climb classification is, at best, an approximation.

The Mountaineers use a modification of the Sierra Club system wherein there are six *classes* numbered from 1 to 5 plus A for aid. Class 5 (free, roped climbing) has been subdivided into decimals from 5.0, 5.1 to 5.11 to more precisely define the difficulty of free climbing. Class A likewise has been subdivided, but only from 1 to 5 (A1, A2, etc.). By this rating system a value is assigned to a climb based on the most difficult move. If the single most difficult move on a climb is 5.6 on only one pitch, it is a Class 5.6 climb. If it also has an A2 aid move, the climb is Class 5.6-A2.

These climb ratings are described briefly as follows:

CLASS 1 — *Cross-country hiking*, hands not needed.

CLASS 2 — *Scrambling*, hands helpful, rope not needed but probably carried to assure party safety.

CLASS 3 —*Easy climbing*, scrambling with use of hands, elementary climbing technique helpful. Rope should be available and may be desired by an inexperienced climber.

CLASS 4 —*Roped climbing with belaying*. Belays may be anchored using either natural anchors or climbing hardware. Some moves may be difficult and could be Class 5 except for the security of short pitches, or natural protection such as trees, shrubs, and rock horns.

CLASS 5 — *Roped climbing* requiring protection such as runners, artificial chocks, and pitons, as well as belays.

CLASS A — *Roped climbing* with an artificial assist, such as stepping on a piton or climbing a chain of slings or pre-tied stirrups.

Climbs are also rated by *grades* from I to VI to express a combination of factors determining the required level of general mountaineering skill and commitment. *Grade* should not be confused with *class,* which evaluates only the technical climbing difficulty. It should be appreciated that mastering the art of Class 5.8 moves on lowland boulders is not sufficient to assure success on a difficult alpine ascent. For instance, a Class 5.7 or 5.8 practice climb on boulders or cliffs next to the highway might be only Grade I, while on a remote alpine crag the same technical difficulty, if frequently encountered during 20 rope leads of sustained Class 4 and 5, may be Grade IV or even V.

Long difficult climbs are strenuous and present routefinding problems as well as objective hazards of rockfall or icefall. Local weather patterns or exceptional effects of bad weather on the climbing route may increase the grade rating as it does the technical climbing difficulty. The duration of exposure to these problems is itself a factor. While these factors contribute in varying degrees to the grade rating of a climb, the six grades can be loosely described by the following approximate guidelines. Only the technical portion of the climb is graded, without regard to approach, however long and arduous or short and inconsequential.

GRADE I — Technical portions can be done in several hours.

GRADE II — Technical portions require half a day.

GRADE III — Technical portions require most of a day; a minimum pitch difficulty need not be specified for Grades I, II, and III.

GRADE IV — Requires one long day; the hardest pitch is rarely less than Class 5.7.

GRADE V — Requires 1½ to 2½ days; the hardest pitch is rarely less than Class 5.8.

GRADE VI — Usually requires 2 or more days with considerable difficult free and aid climbing.

Climbers should be alert to the variation in significance of the several factors of grade from one climb to another. Successful completion of one Grade III climb does not assure competence for all Grade III climbs. Grade is only an approximate yardstick and does not relieve the climber of the responsibility of evaluating all factors of each climb against his own demonstrated ability.

While climb classifications may be subject to frequent debate and prone to human error, most climbers find them helpful in selecting routes within their known range of interest and ability, and this kind of information has become a standard part of the route descriptions in climbing guidebooks.

ROUTEFINDING AS AN ART

Some climbers delight in a free move done well or an overhanging aid pitch. Some aggressive types prefer to test their endurance by spending several days scaling a vertical face. But those who prefer to avoid the privation of exposed bivouacs when climbing a big mountain must try to keep the climbing difficulty down to more manageable levels. This requires an eye for weak points in the mountain's defenses and enough experience to sense when a route will "go."

When selecting a route, beware the possible latitude in guidebook descriptions. Standards tend to vary from one climbing area to another and particularly among climbers of varying skills and experience. A guidebook description can sometimes make the route seem an easy warm-up pitch when, in fact, major difficulties and appalling exposure may abound. With constant upgrading of equipment and standards the converse is more often true; a difficult climb in the days of tricouni-nailed boots may be rather easy with 12-point crampons and short-handled ice ax. Also, skill in crack climbing on granite relates rather poorly to a sandstone slab: a climber accustomed to the relative security of fingers and toes jammed in a crack may draw little comfort from the assurances of his partner that the super friction of a coarse-grained high-angle slab offers abundant security. Climbing problems must always be evaluated on a local basis. Geographic location, season, type of rock, present weather, and local weather patterns all combine to create problems peculiar to each region. A veteran of years of climbing solid Sierra granite may feel grave misgivings on the fragmented sedimentary rock characteristic of much of the Olympics. He may find his fine piton selection of dubious value on a mountain where artificial chocks offer better security because the only available placements are behind loose flakes.

In selecting the best route, *perhaps the most useful rule is to "look around the corner."* When a climber is clinging nose-to-quartz-crystal on a cliff, toes and fingers jammed in a crack, his view tends to be limited; his tactics, moreover, are restricted by a pressing need to relieve his immediate and precarious situation. If the route presents an undesirable degree of difficulty, or seems to be leading to a poorly defined position, it is time to look around the corner. A few minutes devoted to investigating other ways frequently pays dividends in time saved, and when retreat is necessary, an alternate will already be in mind. Particularly when the objective is an ascent of a very difficult route, an easier descent should be sought.

The neophyte fortunate to be introduced to the mountains by experienced climbers has an excellent opportunity to observe good route-finding in practice. Beyond this, additional experience may be gained by visiting the popular local practice areas, guidebook in hand, to seek out and climb the favorite routes. Before long, full of acquired confidence, the new climber will begin to seek the unclimbed route and the virgin peak, the ultimate test of routefinding skill.

Supplementary Reading:

Beckey, Fred. *Cascade Alpine Guide.* Seattle: The Mountaineers, 1973.

Shipton, Eric. *Mountain Conquest.* New York: American Heritage, 1966.

Young, Geoffrey Winthrop. *Mountain Craft.* London: Methuen, 1920, 7th ed. revised, 1946.

8 *

ROPES AND KNOTS

MANY EXCELLENT CLIMBERS began their careers prancing naively among the crags linked together by a length of clothesline. That those careers did not end while still budding was in many cases due purely to dumb luck; because of the false sense of security it conveys, an inadequate rope usually is worse than no rope at all.

The main purpose of a rope is to protect a climber when his strength, judgment, or the terrain let him down. Climbers therefore should devote much thought to its selection, care, and use.

THE CLIMBING ROPE

Selecting a Rope

Climbing ropes of natural fibers, mainly manila, were used until the development of synthetics. Because of low strength and limited shock-absorbing properties, manila has no place left in climbing except as expendable training ropes, and then only in situations where the inadequacies cannot lead to injury.

In order to select the rope to which he will trust his life, a climber must know which qualities are essential and which merely desirable. The two essential qualities are *strength* and *shock-absorbency:* the rope must be strong enough to withstand a fall, even after considerable use, and it must stretch to absorb the kinetic energy generated by a fall, but should neither stretch far enough to allow the falling climber to sustain additional unnecessary injuries nor be so elastic that it stretches noticeably under static body weight.

In addition to these essential properties, a climbing rope should be relatively light in weight and resistant to abrasion and kinking, hold knots well, produce low friction when passing over rock or through carabiners, offer a good grip to the hands, soak up little or no water, and have a reasonably long life-expectancy.

While the nature of the synthetic fiber used largely determines the handling properties of a rope, design is also a factor. The traditional laid or twisted ropes are usually composed of three main strands twisted around each other, each strand consisting of many individual fibers which are also twisted around each other. Such ropes are usually strong and offer adequate shock absorbency. Satisfactory in most respects, they are, as a bonus, ordinarily the least expensive. Their principal disadvantages are a readiness to kink, a tendency to unwind and spin a free-hanging climber, and greater friction on rock.

Fig. 22. Climbing ropes. *Left,* laid. *Right,* kernmantel.

Kernmantel, or core-and-sheath ropes, developed in Europe and introduced in America in the 1960s, are made of a core of twisted, braided, or parallel strands enclosed in a tightly woven outer sheath. Though costing more, these ropes have become very popular because of superior handling qualities. Most European ropes of this type, manufactured specifically for climbing, have been subjected to the test of the UIAA (Union Internationale des Associations d'Alpinisme), an organization whose membership includes climbers, climbing organizations, and equipment manufacturers. The UIAA test focuses on the rope's ability to withstand shock-loading yet continue to reduce impact to the falling climber. To pass the tests, a rope must sustain two falls of an 80-kilogram (176-pound) weight falling 5 meters (16 feet) with an *impact force* (amount of impact transmitted to the falling climber by the rope) not exceeding 1200 kiloponds or kilograms-force (2650 pounds) on the first fall.

Any rope meeting UIAA standards is satisfactory for climbing. Minor variations in tensile strength or impact force are usually ignored when selecting a rope, the final decision frequently being based on such intangibles as "feel" and appearance.

When choosing a rope, the diameter and length should be considered. Ropes of 11 mm or 7/16-inch diameter, occasionally called *single* or *full-weight,* are the preferred choice, especially for the one-rope climber.

Though heavier and more expensive than thinner lines, they last longer, offer a better grip for the hands, and often encourage the leader to great things by their wider safety margin.

For all-around use the 150-foot length is most satisfactory. Rock-climbing enthusiasts may prefer longer ropes and snow climbers shorter ones. A 120-foot rope is generally considered the shortest useful length and 165 or 180 feet about as long as practical, especially in full-weight ropes. Backpackers may carry an 80-foot rope for emergency use only, if not intending any roped climbing.

The European practice of climbing "double-strand" on very long (240- to 300-foot) 9 mm or ⅜-inch diameter ropes and clipping each strand into alternate protection points has never gained wide acceptance in America because of the bother of climbing and belaying with two ropes at once. Note that this technique may result in a full-force fall on a single strand and subsequent sequential failure of both strands.

Care of the Rope

As with any other piece of fine equipment, a rope deserves care in storage and use to avoid damage. Novices are frequently taken aback by the outraged screams they hear when a foot carelessly lands on a rope. They may even fear for the life of the offender if the foot wears crampons! While such vehemence may seem unwarranted at first, thought of oneself dangling in an exposed situation from a partly perforated rope may lead to a greater understanding of the experienced climber's attitude. In general climbers take great care NOT to step on the rope, to avoid snagging it on sharp rocks, and to keep it out of the way while chopping steps. Even when the greatest care has been exercised, the rope should be checked over its entire length for cuts and abrasions after each use.

During periods between use, the rope should be stored in a clean, cool place, out of the rays of the sun. All knots should be removed and the rope coiled loosely. It should not be stretched or left under tension during storage and at no time should it be brought into contact with battery acid or other potentially harmful chemicals. The ends should be fused in a flame and taped or whipped to prevent unravelling and only manufacturer-recommended preparations or procedures should be used for marking the mid-point.

Over a period of time, dirt and tiny rock particles work their way between fibers of the rope and cut them, so the rope should be washed periodically. Use mild soap and the "delicate fabrics" setting on an automatic washer, rinse well to remove soap, then drip dry.

Even with the best of tender, loving care, a rope eventually wears out. When its strength is in doubt, for whatever reason, retire it. A cut in the rope is always grounds for retirement, as is a hard fall (defined by many climbers to be any free, vertical fall over a distance equal to twice the length of rope from the climber to his belay; the distance of the fall is not a factor except as compared to the length of rope involved: a fall of 6 feet on 3 feet of rope is a hard fall just as is a fall of 40 feet on 20 feet of rope). Many circumstances can modify a fall, such as a pendulum swing after climbing upward at an angle, or bumping and sliding down a slab, but a conservative evaluation is called for; attempts to rationalize continued use of a doubtful rope after a fall may lead to a fatal failure on the next fall.

Various organizations concerned with mountain safety offer "days of usage" estimates of climbing rope life; however, any such figure is merely an educated guess. A rope may be considered overdue for retirement when the hand can no longer feel the separate strands while sliding along a laid rope or when the outer sheath of a kernmantel rope is worn or cut through, anywhere. A safe rule of thumb is to retire a rope when 50 per cent of the surface strands are worn to fuzz.

KNOTS AND COILS

Some climbers, infatuated with technique for its own sake, have an almost endless repertoire of knots. While each knot may answer a specific purpose admirably and a display of knots furnishes an evening's entertainment around the campfire, most climbers use a rather limited selection. The knots described below have survived the test of time and are recognized as safe and dependable.

Most knots should be "backed up" as a safeguard against accidental loosening or untying; to do so, the free end is left long enough to tie an overhand knot or two half-hitches next to the main knot. Even with this precaution the climber should still check his knots from time to time.

Knots for Tying In

Any knot used for connecting the climber to his rope should be strong, easy to tie and adjust, and should not convert into a slip knot. The one knot which has gained universal acceptance for this purpose is the *bowline-on-a-coil*. It may be tied with a single rope (for endmen) or on a doubled rope (for the middleman). This basic knot should be learned thoroughly by every climber. Note that three or four wraps are taken around the climber's waist to distribute the impact of a fall and that the free end is backed up by overhand knots.

The bowline-on-a-coil uses about 15 feet of line, which means two climbers on a 150-foot rope have no more than 120 feet of usable length. To increase the usable length and distribution of impact, the *swami belt* was invented. In its simplest form a swami belt consists of five or six wraps of 1-inch tublar nylon webbing or three or four wraps of 2-inch webbing.

It is wrapped snugly around the waist and the ends tied with a *water knot* (see Fig. 27).

A hazard of tying in with a bowline-on-a-coil or to a waistloop is suffocation by restriction of the diaphragm while hanging on the rope after a fall. This difficulty can be overcome by transferring the body

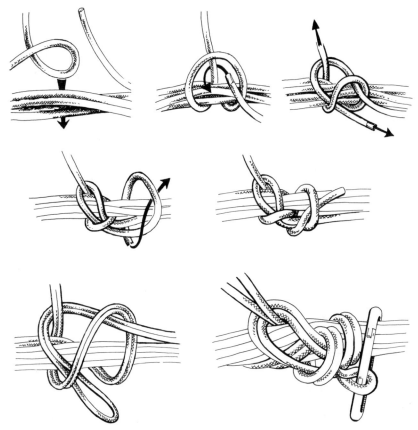

Fig. 23. Bowline on a coil. Using single rope for endman and double rope with carabiner jam for middleman.

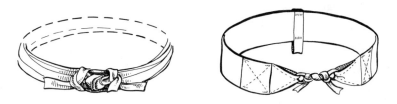

Fig. 24. Swami belt. *Left*, improvised. *Right*, commercial.

weight with a *baboon hang* (see Chapter 9), by having *prusik slings* readily accessible for rigging quickly, or better still, by using a *seat harness* (see below). Many home-tied seat harness arrangements of varying complexity exist, as well as elaborate commercially manufactured ones. Simplicity, comfort, and safety must be considered when choosing among the alternatives.

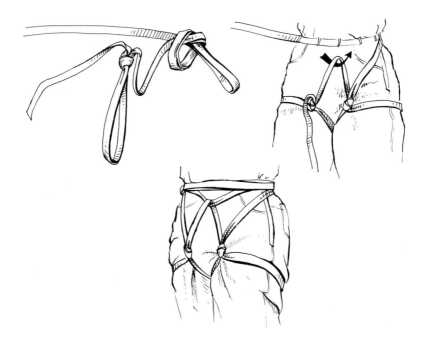

Fig. 25. Example of seat harness with tying sequence.

One thing all swami belts and seat harnesses have in common: the climbing rope must be tied directly to them. *Never* clip one to the other with carabiners; failure at the carabiner gate can be fatal. An endman ties in using a figure-8 loop; the middleman may tie in with a bowline around his waistloop or seat harness.

Knots for Joining Ends of Ropes, Slings, and Webbing

Nylon webbing is used for an amazing variety of purposes. Tubular webbing is generally used for rigging belay and rappel anchors, the 1-inch size being preferred for belay anchors and runners for Class 5 protection. Smaller sizes are limited to lower-strength needs.

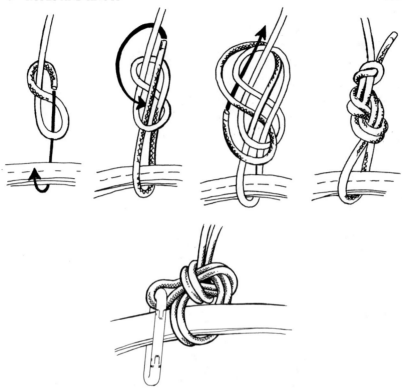

Fig. 26. Tying into swami belt. *Upper,* figure-8 for endman. *Lower,* bowline on doubled rope with carabiner jam for middleman.

The *water knot* is commonly used for joining the ends of webbing to make continuous loop runners or for tying the ends of a swami belt. Although the water knot is strong when tightly tied, it tends to loosen in use and should be inspected frequently. When tying runners from webbing where the knots must stay indefinitely, tighten the knots by hanging the runners from a cross bar and bouncing full body weight on them while pulling the two short ends at the same time (pliers help). Leave 1 or 2 inches of free end on these knots and, even after tightening, check them from time to time.

For tying runners from kernmantel rope or for joining two ropes of dissimilar construction together for a rappel, the *double fisherman's knot* is superior in strength and security to most other knots. It locks tightly when tied in rope or webbing — so tightly in webbing, indeed, that it may be nearly impossible to untie when the webbing is needed for some other purpose.

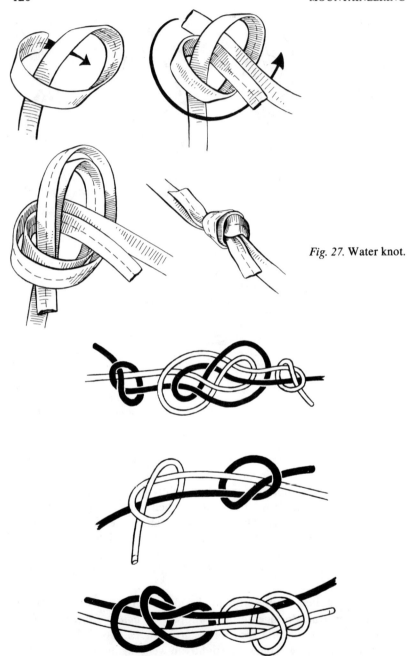

Fig. 27. Water knot.

Fig. 28. Knots for joining ropes. *Top,* double figure-8 backed up with overhand. *Middle,* fisherman's knot. *Bottom,* double fisherman's knot.

Miscellaneous Knots

Other knots a climber should master are the *figure-8 loop,* used to tie climbers to anchors, and the *double figure-8,* used to join the ends of two ropes for rappels. The figure-8 loop, also used to tie swami belts to ropes, is formed by tying an ordinary figure-8 knot in the rope, passing the running end around the waistloop, and weaving it back through the original knot.

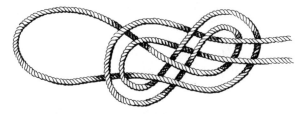

Fig. 29. Figure-8 loop tied in center of rope.

The *prusik knot* will slide on another rope when there is no tension on the knot; when tension is applied, it locks. On kernmantel ropes three wraps are needed to make it hold, and if slings are made of webbing, four wraps may be necessary. Prusiking, or climbing the rope using prusik slings, is described in Chapter 17 under crevasse-rescue methods. Two knots for "tying off" pitons are the *girth hitch* and *overhand slip knot.*

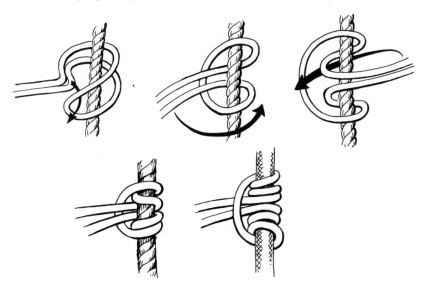

Fig. 30. Prusik knot. Tying sequence and three-wrap prusik for kernmantel rope, viewed from the back.

The *clove hitch* is also used to tie off pitons in aid climbing and in addition to secure fixed lines at intermediate points and to make rope stretchers.

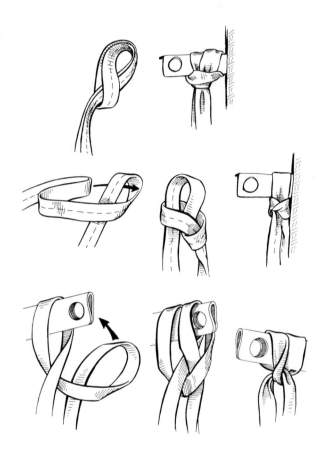

Fig. 31. Top, girth hitch. *Center,* overhand slip knot. *Bottom* clove hitch.

Coils

Of the several ways to coil a climbing rope the two methods illustrated are recommended as fast and easy to uncoil. While coiling the rope, allow it to form its own natural loops. Forcing it into neat, orderly coils will perpetuate kinks.

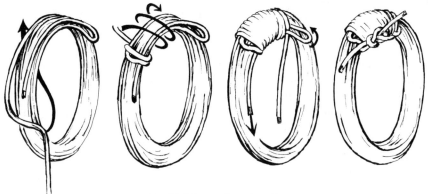

Fig. 32. Mountaineer's coil.

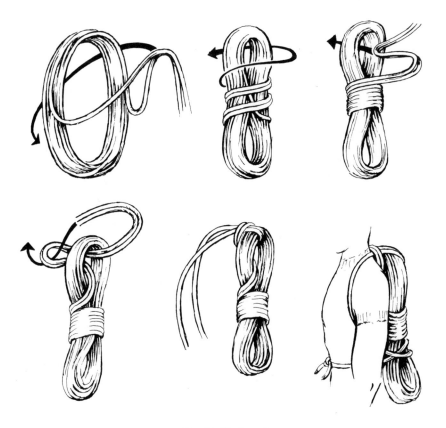

Fig. 33. Skein coil.

ROPES AND WHATKNOTS

The risk in using worn or doubtful rope was demonstrated tragically years ago on the first ascent of the Matterhorn. Unfortunately this lesson has not been learned by everyone and almost every year there are victims of rope failure. With the high quality and long-use life of today's synthetics, no mountaineer can afford to skimp on this basic piece of equipment.

While a climber can walk out of his favorite mountain shop with years of research and technological development wound up in a 150-foot coil, the effectiveness of his rope is still limited by his skill in using it. The strongest, most shock-absorbent line available will not prevent a tragedy if it is secured with an inadequate knot. Knotcraft and belaying technique cannot be purchased at the mountain shop, but must be learned and practiced to perfection. The rope, more than any other piece of equipment, symbolizes climbing; skillful rope-handling is basic to safe climbing.

Supplementary Reading:

Wheelock, Walter. *Ropes, Knots, and Slings for Climbers.* Glendale, California: La Siesta Press, 2nd edition, 1967.

9 *

BELAYING

Climbing is essentially a team sport, and the rope which joins the team is not only a symbol of its unity but also insurance for safe travel on steep rock, ice, and snow. The very act of roping up may instill confidence in an unsteady climber, but to have any value the rope must be used in such a way as to provide genuine security for all members of the team. The technique of providing this security is called *belaying* and its purpose is to reduce the length of a fall and minimize its consequences.

In its simplest form, belaying is wrapping the rope around a snubbing post — a climber's body, a tree, or whatever is available and sufficiently sturdy. The belayer controls the rope to keep it from developing unwanted slack between belay and climber, absorbs the impact of a fall, and limits the distance fallen.

WHEN TO ROPE UP AND BELAY

The decision on when to rope up will depend on a combination of factors: exposure, difficulty of the climb, and experience of the party. However, roping up is mandatory, and without argument, whenever any member so requests, and for all party members for all glacier travel — except where avalanches may present a greater hazard than crevasses (see Chapter 16). A belay is also given whenever any member of the party so requests. (Since the party will rope up in exposed areas, belays are generally implied by that act.)

Roping up one-handed, clinging to small holds, is at best unnerving, and thus is better done before being committed to steep, exposed, or difficult climbing.

VIII. Climbing on Cathedral Peak; Cascade Range. (Bob and Ira Spring)

The rope often creates its own hazard on rubble-strewn slopes where a dragging line may dislodge death-dealing rockfall. It also may be more hazard than help on steep, loose walls with few ledges, on terrain offering no adequate belay stances or reliable anchors, and in areas subject to rockfall or avalanche. A party encountering such problems may have to decide between climbing without protection of the rope or retreating.

ORDER OF ROPING

Two- and three-man rope teams both are standard, with two-man teams preferred for speed and efficiency (generally on rock), and three-man teams for greater strength (generally on glaciers). Teams of four or more are slow and unwieldly.

Each position on a rope team carries quite different responsibilities. The first person up a rock pitch, the leader, makes most of the routefinding decisions and takes the greatest risk, since he has the farthest to fall in case of a slip. The second man can help select the route but mainly is concerned with providing the leader a sound belay. On a three-man team the third climber ordinarily has nothing to do but take care of himself, since he has the security of an overhead belay and no one to belay; sometimes he can pay his way by carrying the heaviest rucksack or standing watch for rockfall.

In descent the first man down usually must find the route, guarded by a belay from above. The second man down a rope of three (or the first on a rope of two) must belay the last or uppermost climber, who again has the least protection. On a traverse the endmen both may chance long falls, with only the middleman held by belays from both sides.

When all members of a party are approximately equal in ability, positions on the rope are chosen on a basis of personal preference, and it is customary to trade positions to distribute the fun and workload. A rope of two equally skilled climbers ordinarily uses the pleasant and rapid leapfrog method, each climber alternately belaying and leading. Even in an experienced party individuals usually differ in skill: one person may be happy to allow a partner to lead the long insecure artificial pitches, claiming in compensation the exhilarating free sections. On climbs over mixed terrain, the rock expert leads difficult rock pitches, while the ice expert takes over on steep ice.

When members are markedly unequal in skill and experience, the order on ascent is best climber first, second-best second, third-best third. On descent the best climber remains in the uppermost and most exposed position, and thus is last down. The second-best climber ideally still should be second down to provide a sound belay, but if the route is obscure or tricky, it may be wiser for him to go first to find the way; the least-skilled climber, usually at the bottom end of the team, in this case comes second.

On a traverse the weakest member is given the most protected position, the middle of the rope. Such absolute distinctions between individuals are rather rare and special cases are innumerable. Sometimes the least experienced member is put in the lead on suitable terrain in order to develop his skills. Sometimes one member is an avid photographer and requests the freedom of the third position. Finally, weariness or illness changes the situation. Rope order must be assigned always with careful consideration of the pitch just ahead and the current strength of team members, and must be changed to meet changing conditions.

HOW TO BELAY

The Belay Chain

The belay chain consists of everything protecting the climber, from the belayer's anchor to the climber's body. In sequence the components are: the belay anchor, the belayer, the rope and any knots in it, intermediate points of protection (natural, artificial chocks, pitons, and the like), and the climber. The rope, knots, and intermediate protection equipment are covered in other chapters; the discussion here is confined to the anchor and the belayer.

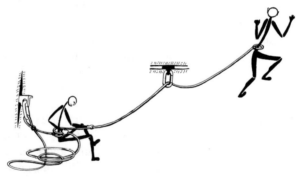

Fig. 34. Belaying chain includes climber, climbing rope, intermediate points of protection, knots, belayer, and anchor.

The Belay Stance

The belay stance takes into consideration the terrain, the anchor, the belayer's position, and the direction of the belay. The stance must be on a solid part of the mountain and it must be protected from rockfall and avalanche. Once a safe stance has been found, secure anchors must be located. Finally, thought should be given to the belayer's comfort since he may be in position a long time. The experienced belayer realizes that no matter how well protected and anchored he may be, hours of continuous sitting on the same sharp lump will neither soften nor hatch it, and the result will be a weak belay. Therefore he must do everything possible to make his stance physically comfortable before settling down.

Some form of *padding* — rucksacks or rolled parkas or sweaters — to prevent deep rope burns on the hips provides additional comfort and safety, and use of *belaying gloves* is mandatory. Keeping the rope laid out or coiled neatly prevents sudden kinks or snarls in the rope from tearing it from the belayer's hands or flipping him out of position.

The Anchor

A secure anchor for the belay is absolutely essential — if everything else fails, two or three climbers may end up hanging from it. Whenever possible, a large tree or solid horn of rock should be used; however, such welcome objects are not always available and thus the climber frequently must devise his own anchors where nature has failed to provide.

Two anchor points are preferred over one but some common sense should be applied: one large solid tree is far better than two shaky pitons. Each point of the anchor should be rigged independently of the other so that failure at one point will not cause a total collapse of the system.

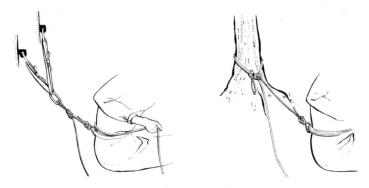

Fig. 35. Belay anchors.

There should be no slack whatsoever between the belayer and his anchor points. The anchor, in addition to providing ultimate support for the entire chain, should assist the belayer in maintaining his stance and should restrain him from being pulled out of position. Thus the belayer must predetermine the direction of pull (see Aiming the Belay) and place the anchor behind him and in line with the direction of pull. The distance between the belayer and his anchor should be kept as short as possible to minimize the distance he may be moved if he is pulled out of position by a hard fall.

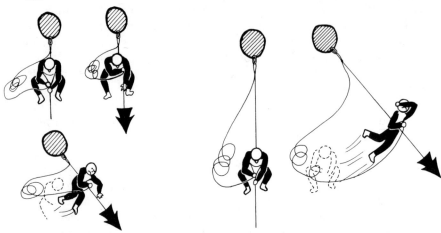

Fig. 36. Relationship between belayer and his anchor. *Left,* short anchor in line of pull is best; even if pulled to side, belayer is moved only a short distance. *Right,* long anchor is poor; belayer can be pulled far to side.

Tying into the anchor, or at least into one of the anchor points, with the climbing rope is strongly recommended. Not only does it provide one of the strongest attachments of the belayer to the anchor, but also has the climber on a "pre-tie-off" if, as a result of a fall, the belayer has completely run out of rope.

Hip Belays

Over the years many belay positions have been tried and tested; in North America the *hip belay,* in its various forms, remains the favorite.

The *sitting hip belay,* in which the belayer sits, his legs straight and spread apart and his feet firmly braced if possible, provides the belayer with an ideal means of protecting his fellow climbers under most circumstances, keeping the belayer's center of gravity low and providing a strong, solid position. In a variation of the sitting hip belay, the belayer's legs dangle over the edge of an in-sloping lèdge; if available, a tree or knob of rock between his legs adds to the security of the position. This variation is extremely useful when belaying the second man up a pitch. The sitting hip belay is also the best and most secure on snow. The stance is prepared by stamping out a depression to sit in and troughs for each leg terminating in compacted-snow foot braces. When anchored with a snow fluke or deadman anchor (see Chapter 15) the security of such a belay can encourage a climber to attempt impressive feats and can greatly reduce the risk on a doubtful snow bridge.

The *standing hip belay* lacks the solid foot-bracing advantage of the sitting position. The belayer's center of gravity is high and his position

Fig. 37. Sitting hip belays — the ideal on rock, snow, brush, anywhere. *Left,* standard position. *Right,* using rock projection.

quite unstable. Sound anchors are essential when this position is used, as indeed it may have to be on small ledges or steep ice.

The most versatile of positions is the *modified sitting hip belay,* which like the standing belay can be used where space is limited. The belayer braces his feet against whatever support is available and leans back in a half-sitting position, tied securely to his anchor. The stance can be used on ledges of all sizes, or even while hanging in stirrups or supported by a belay seat or harness.

Once again, the climber is urged to use common sense: a standing belay from a moat, with the rope running over the lip at chest height, is generally as solid as the most securely anchored sitting hip belay.

Aiming the Belay

Ideally the pull exerted on the belayer by a fall should be between his braced legs and in direct line with his anchor, pulling him into his platform. If the stance faces the direction of pull and the anchors can be placed behind it, this natural stance is the belayer's preference.

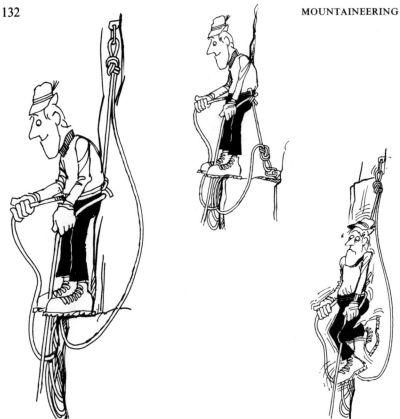

Fig. 38. Standing belays — used when terrain too steep for more stable positions. *Left,* high anchor supports position. *Center,* anchor is low, belayer can be jerked off as shown on *right.*

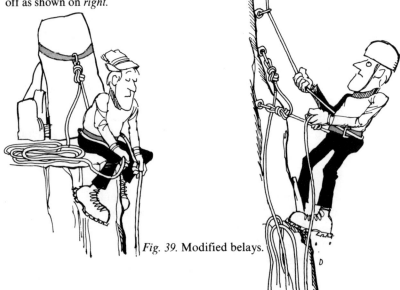

Fig. 39. Modified belays.

Fig. 40. Aiming belays. *Top,* naturally aimed belay; belayer faces direction of pull. *Center,* unaimed belay; belayer not facing directon of pull, which would twist him around; he might lose control. *Bottom,* artificially aimed belay; direction of force remains constant.

As might be expected, circumstances usually are less than ideal. Ordinarily the belayer cannot simply aim his belay at the climber but instead must choose an *aiming point* — any natural feature such as a rock or tree, or such a climbing device as a piton or ice screw — to insure that the pull of a fall will come from the direction he is best prepared to handle. The rope runs from the belayer to the aiming point and on to the climber.

In all belays discussed so far, the rope is passed around the belayer's hips and his hands grip the rope. The rope must be kept on the muscle/fat/bone part of the anatomy and not allowed to ride up to the unprotected spinal area. To keep the rope in place and prevent losing it if a fall occurs, the belayer may clip a carabiner to the braking hand side of his waistloop and pass the belay rope through it.

Fig. 41. Retaining carabiner on braking hand side of waistloop.

The hand on the portion of the climbing rope between the belayer and climber is called the *feeling hand*; its function is to sense the amount of tension or slack in the rope. The other hand is the *braking hand* — the one that does the work of stopping a falling climber. UNDER NO CIRCUMSTANCES MAY THE BRAKING HAND BE REMOVED FROM THE CLIMBING ROPE UNTIL THE CLIMBER SAYS "OFF BELAY." The feeling hand (or braking hand) may be either left or right, depending on anticipated direction of pull, "handedness," or belayer preference.

As long as the climber is stationary neither hand does much except hold onto the rope. When the climber is moving away from the belayer, slack is fed to him by the feeling hand pulling rope through the braking hand. The braking hand stays on the rope and shakes any kinks or snarls out of it.

The sequence of hand movements when the climber is approaching the belayer is carefully synchronized. The two hands, working together, take up rope, removing slack as it develops. At the end of each sequence the feeling hand usually is closer to the belayer's body than the braking hand. To begin the next sequence the feeling hand slides out along the rope (meanwhile not moving the braking hand) until both arms are fairly straight and the hands side-by-side. The braking hand lays the rope beyond it across the palm of the feeling hand. The feeling hand grips *both*

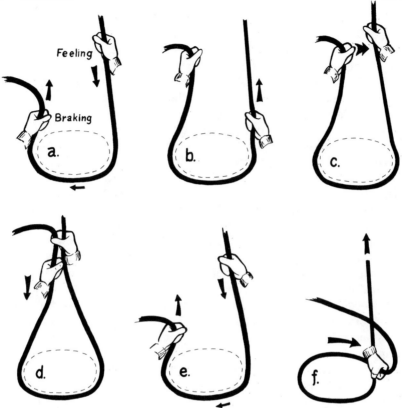

Fig. 42. Taking up rope — left hand is braking hand, right hand is feeling hand.

a. Pull in rope with both hands on rope until braking hand is fully extended.

b. Hold rope with braking hand and slide feeling hand out.

c. Bring hands together.

d. Hold both parts of rope with feeling hand, slide braking hand towards body, keeping it ready in case of a fall.

e. Repeat cycle.

f. Holding a fall: braking hand wraps rope around body and tightens grip to hold fall, feeling hand is off rope, helping to brace belayer.

strands of rope and the braking hand slides back along the rope toward the hip, but not too far back or it may be pulled behind the back if the climber falls. The feeling hand releases the strand of rope running from the braking hand and the process is repeated until the climber has joined the belayer. The movements are not entirely instinctive and novices must practice them until the sequence is quick and automatic with either hand serving either function.

Holding a Fall

In a fall, potential energy is converted to kinetic energy which must be absorbed by the entire belaying chain — rope, intermediate points of protection, and the resilient bodies of both belayer and climber.

The farther a climber falls the more likely he is to strike projections which can cause injury. Action to check the fall must be taken promptly to stop it in the shortest possible distance.

When a fall occurs everything is up to the belayer. The climber can do little to help himself except make futile grabs at ledges and vegetation. The belayer must promptly assume the *arrest position*, bracing his body with his feeling hand and wrapping the rope around his body with his braking hand. It is important that the rope be wrapped around the hips first, *before* the braking hand clamps down. When the belayer is holding a fall in this manner he becomes a sort of animated snubbing post.

For years climbers used manila and other ropes of low breaking strength and little shock absorbency. To absorb the energy of a fall without breaking either climber or rope the belayer had to check the fall gradually by allowing the rope to slide — a dynamic belay. With the introduction of synthetic ropes, and especially the newer dynamic ropes, much of the necessity for such dynamic belaying no longer exists. Short falls can be held "statically" by the belayer taking the arrest position and gripping the rope firmly.

On longer falls, where greater forces develop, it is not possible to stop a falling climber quite as quickly. Try as he might, the rope slides through the belayer's grasp and, like it or not, the belay is dynamic. When the rope starts whizzing through his hands the belayer must stay calm and remain confident that his technique *will* work. He must realize the sliding of the rope is the result of forces he cannot control instantaneously. The rope will run, but if he perseveres, the energy will be dissipated and he will hold the fall. (The value of the retaining carabiner on the belayer's waistloop is especially obvious on such long falls as insurance against losing control of the rope.)

Belaying on Snow and Ice

The two belays most commonly used on snow, a modification of the sitting hip belay mentioned earlier and the boot-ax belay, are discussed in Chapter 16.

On ice the standing hip belay often is employed if a cave or moat is not available for a sitting belay. When the terrain permits, rock-climbing anchors are preferred; for example, pitons placed in couloir walls. Otherwise one of the types of anchors discussed in Chapter 15 is used.

Climbing Signals

Effective communication between climber and belayer is essential for safety and efficiency. Over the years climbers have developed a set of universally accepted rope signals, each with a different sound so that even wind-garbled words can be interpreted correctly. After the signals have been learned they must be used properly, clearly, and loudly enough to be heard. This may involve bellowing on windy days and/or when the climber is out of sight; such conditions may also demand shorter leads. In crowded practice areas, belayer and climber should use each other's names to avoid confusion. Misunderstandings can be prevented by echoing the other person's signal.

Table 9. Climbing Signals

Belayer	Climber	Meaning
	"On Belay?"	I want to go. Aren't you ready yet?
"Belay On"		All set; the belay is ready.
	"Climbing"	Here I come (or Off I go).
"Climb"		Come ahead (or Off you go).
	"Slack"	I can't move without some slack in the rope.
Give slack. No verbal answer required.		
	"Up Rope"	There is slack in the rope. Take up all loose rope.
Take up rope. No verbal answer required.		
	"Off Belay"	I am in a secure position and do not need a belay any longer.
"Belay Off"		Echoed to insure there is no misunderstanding.

Special or Emergency Signals

Belayer	Climber	Meaning
	"Tension"	Hold the rope tight (used infrequently).
The belayer uses braking position and holds the rope tight.		
	"Falling"	Catch me—I'm falling.
The belayer uses braking position to stop the fall.		
"Rock" ⟶⟵ "Rock"		This signal must be echoed by all climbers in the area to warn of a falling rock.

These signals are verbal. Sometimes it is necessary to prearrange a set of silent signals, using tugs on the rope. Since no standardized set exists climbers generally work one out on the spot. The main requirements are simplicity and agreement between members of the team.

After the Fall

When a climber has fallen and the belayer has stopped the fall, procedures are as follows, depending on the situation.

If the climber is uninjured, he will probably swing back onto the rock, expressing annoyance freely, and try again, or move to a resting spot to collect his wits. Terrain and available rope permitting, the belayer may lower him to a ledge. However, if hanging free from a waistloop the climber must somehow relieve its pressure from his lower rib cage before his diaphragm is compressed, causing suffocation, unconsciousness, and eventually death; hanging free in a seat harness creates no such problems. For fallen climbers who cannot reach the security and comfort of a ledge the *baboon hang* converts a standard-length runner into an emergency seat. (Incidentally, for whatever small comfort it is worth, falling out of a properly tied waistloop when hanging upside-down is virtually impossible.)

If the fallen climber is unconscious or injured, the belayer must lower him to a ledge, providing one is available. In any event he must "tie off" the climber before rescue efforts can be initiated. The simplest means of so doing requires a short sling of ¼-inch or 7 mm sling rope or ¾ to 1-inch webbing. A standard runner is almost ideal for the purpose.

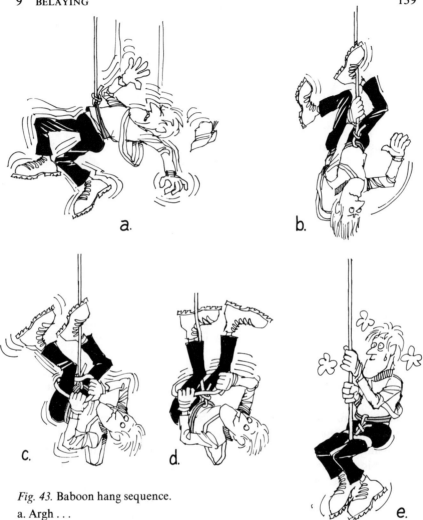

Fig. 43. Baboon hang sequence.

a. Argh . . .

b. Tip upside down, hook foot around rope.

c. and d. Slide runner over feet in front of rope — no need to twist runner.

e. Sit up.

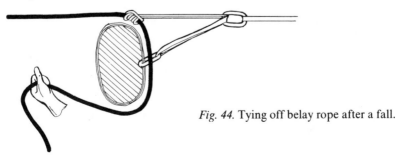

Fig. 44. Tying off belay rope after a fall.

After tying a prusik knot around the belay rope with the sling or runner, the belayer clips the tie-off to his anchor with a carabiner. He slowly releases his grip and, if the sling holds firmly, comes out of his position and reinforces the anchor securing the fallen climber. This accomplished, he may summon additional help and/or start rescue measures himself.

Mechanical Belaying

The restless mind of man ever seeks to insure greater ease and security for himself, in climbing as in all other endeavors. In recent years, special pieces of equipment have been manufactured and techniques developed to make the belayer's job easier. Working with varying degrees of effectiveness — and some have been well received —they all suffer from the same important disadvantages: they all add at least one more link to the belaying chain, one more chance for error or failure; they all involve at least one more piece of equipment that must be carried or another special technique that must be learned, adding complexity to the climbing process; they encourage dependence upon gadgetry and may cause climbers to leave gaps in their training, gaps which may have fatal results if the special tool or technique is lost or forgotten. While such devices may have some value, many experienced climbers prefer to keep things simple and therefore shun them.

In years gone by, climbers practiced belaying in teams. One climber would belay and two, three, or four others would grab the end of the rope and run down a hill or steep slab while the belayer tried to stop the simulated fall. Other groups built towers and brave members took turns jumping from them, thus adding a bit of realism to the practice.

Most recently, belay towers using expendable weights and hauling lines have been designed. The weight-lifting power is furnished by a group of climbers, or lacking a large enough group, perhaps a car. A 100-pound weight falling from a well-oiled pulley is surprisingly difficult to arrest, especially if it goes through a few feet of free fall — a truly sobering experience. Besides, very few climbers weigh as little as 100 pounds and leads of 10 feet or more are common when the climbing is easy. But one slip and a 10-foot lead becomes a 20-foot fall — before the belayer even feels a tug on the rope. Even under such ideal practice conditions the need for belay practice *before* the first climb becomes suddenly and graphically evident.

SUMMARY

Good belaying is what makes roped climbing safe. Every climber must understand the belay chain, its strength and weaknesses. The following points summarize the important factors in competent belaying:

Fig. 45. Belay practice on tower
and parallel in mountains.

1. A climbing route is generally divided into pitches according to the location of good belay stances; the full length of the climbing rope need not be used.
2. *Anchor the belay,* preferably with two anchor points. The climbing rope should be used for this purpose and the anchor should be kept as close as possible to the belayer. The line between belayer and anchor *must be snug.*
3. *Aim the belay* so that the force of a fall will pull the belayer against his anchor and braced limbs. A "manufactured" aiming point prevents unexpected changes of direction of pull.
4. Be alert to changes in direction of pull, if no aiming point is used.
5. *Never, never, never* take the braking hand off the rope during a belay.
6. Learn the climbing signals thoroughly and use them correctly.
7. After anchoring and assuming the belay position, haul in all the slack *before* passing the rope around the hips and beginning the belay. The slack should be laid out or coiled as neatly as possible.
8. Wrap the rope around the hips as far as possible when assuming the arrest position, and before gripping the rope tight.
9. Practice whenever and wherever possible.

10 *

RAPPELLING

WHEN THE CLIMBING PARTY is descending, a choice must sometimes be made between climbing down and rappelling — a means of descent in which the climber makes a controlled slide down the rope. The choice is based on many considerations: safety, speed, convenience, nature of terrain, weather, time available, and condition of the party. Properly done, rappelling may be the fastest and safest means to descend a given pitch; done incorrectly, it may slow the party and add to hazards already present. Safe rappels require sound anchors, good equipment, and correct technique.

SETTING UP THE RAPPEL

The first step in setting up a rappel is locating a sound, dependable anchor — ideally a large tree or solid rock projection around which a sling or runner can be placed. Good natural anchors are not always available and the climber must use less desirable ones — bushes, small trees, or large boulders — and frequently, artificial anchors. When less-than-ideal anchors are used two or more are preferable; however, on a series of rappels down a long mountainside, one well-placed and thoroughly tested anchor may have to suffice on each pitch. Rappel anchors encountered on established descent routes should be inspected and reinforced as necessary.

After anchor point(s) are located or placed, loops of sling rope or webbing are tied around or through each point to reduce wear on the rope during pulldown and to ease its retrieval. Parties usually carry 20 to 30 feet of ¾-inch webbing or other sling material for this purpose.

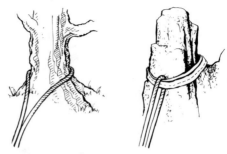

Fig. 46. Rappel anchors.

   Two or three independently tied loops on each anchor obviously are safer than one, but on long climbs a shortage of material often permits only a single loop. In any event, sufficient material should be used to allow secure knotting of the slings. To prevent accidental cutting of the rope, piton and bolt-hanger eyes should be padded, often easily done by leaving one end of the sling long enough for the purpose. If the anchor sling must be placed around a sharp rock corner, judicious padding of sharp edges reduces chances of its being cut. Reduced wear on the rope and easier retrieval are gained by tying a *descending ring* into the anchor sling.

   In most mountaineering situations rappels are fairly short and one climbing rope, doubled, gets the party past a brief steep or slippery section. Where a long rappel is necessary, two climbing ropes frequently are tied together. After anchor slings have been tied, one end of the rappel rope is passed through the descending ring (or through the sling, if no descending ring is used) to the midpoint. A figure-8 loop or other bulky knot tied into each free end of the rappel rope is a safeguard against rappelling off the end.

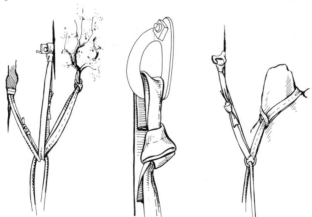

Fig. 47. Sling use. *Left to right:* independently tied loops; "tail" of knot to pad eye of bolt hanger; and descending ring on rappel sling.

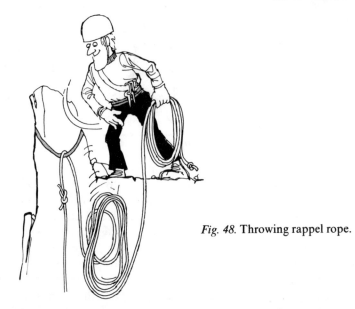

Fig. 48. Throwing rappel rope.

Beginning with the rope ends, each half of the rope is coiled separately to form two coils, one on each side of the anchor sling. The coils are each thrown down the pitch, one at a time, and in the following manner: first about half of one of the coils (the half nearest the sling), then the remainder. The sequence is repeated with the other coil. Throwing first the "center" and then the end reduces rope snags and tangling and makes rappelling and rope retrieval easier and safer.

The anchor should be tested before anyone rappels from it. If space does not permit proper testing, the main anchor may be reinforced with several back-up anchors connected to the main anchor with slings. If the back-ups are adequate the first climber down bounces at the bottom of the rappel, safely subjecting the anchor to high loading. If the main anchor is secure, the last man down removes the back-ups and rappels on the main anchor only.

Fig. 49. Main anchor with back-up anchor.

Despite care taken in rigging and testing, the system does not pass its acid test until the first person completes his rappel. If there are enough ropes, he may be belayed; indeed, a conservative leader may have all members of his party belayed on steep, exposed rappels. Belays are imperative for sick or injured climbers descending *en rappel.*

RAPPEL SYSTEMS

Of the many different rappel techniques, the following have the most general acceptance in the Pacific Northwest. Each should be practiced until it can be done correctly without fumbling: under the best of conditions there is little margin for error in rappelling; under poor conditions, none.

The *arm rappel* is useful for negotiating short, low-angle slopes. The climber steps into an arm rappel by laying the rappel rope over his shoulder, then wrapping it once around both extended arms. Rate of descent is controlled by hand grip and by friction on shoulders and arms. Stability is improved by facing downhill and keeping the legs spread; however security is minimal at best, and the arm rappel is best reserved for easy, low-angle pitches and rappels directly down the fall line.

Fig. 50. Arm rappel.

The simplest all-purpose rappel is the *dulfersitz,* which requires no special equipment and should be mastered by every climber. Friction of the rope around the leg and across the shoulder makes padding and careful control advisable. The climber steps into the dulfersitz by straddling the rope while facing the anchor, bringing the rope forward around one hip, up across the chest and over the *opposite* shoulder, then

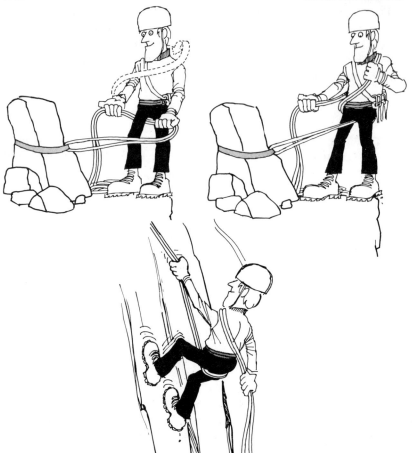

Fig. 51. Dulfersitz rappel: straddle rope facing anchor, pass rope diagonally across chest and over shoulder (braking hand is on same side as hip over which rope passes).

down the back to be held by the *braking hand on the same side as the wrapped hip.* A hazard with the dulfersitz, especially on high-angle rappels, is unwrapping the leg; this possibility is reduced by keeping the wrapped leg slightly lower than the other.

Brake rappels are comfortable and easy to control. Free rappels (below overhangs), rappels with bulky or heavy packs, and rappels on single or small-diameter ropes are much easier when using brake systems. If it is necessary for a disabled person to rappel, a companion stationed at the bottom of the slope can control his descent by putting tension on the rope. The principal disadvantage of brake rappels is that they introduce additional pieces of equipment into the rappel system, each of which becomes a point of potentail failure. While most experienced climbers have adopted brake rappels, their use requires great care.

All brake rappels require a seat sling or a swami belt. Although commercially manufactured swami belts and legloop harnesses are available, many climbers prefer to carry diaper slings or improvise figure-8 rappel seats.

The *figure-8 seat* is fashioned from a standard length of runner or any other suitable length of webbing or small-diameter rope. This seat must be clipped to a waistloop to help maintain stability.

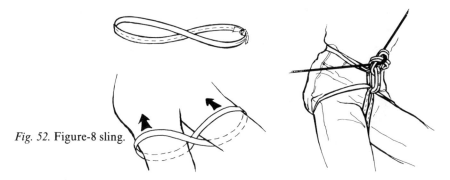

Fig. 52. Figure-8 sling.

The *diaper sling* requires about 10 feet of webbing or sling rope tied into a large loop. Starting with the loop behind the back, one end is pulled to the front from each side and a third end from between the legs. The three loops are clipped together in front with carabiners. This sling may also be clipped to a waistloop or swami belt, if one is worn.

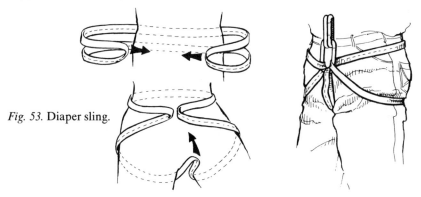

Fig. 53. Diaper sling.

The brake system is attached to the rappel seat and waistloop with two carabiners. The gates of these carabiners are reversed or opposed to prevent accidental failure of the system (see diagram). Either of two braking systems may now be attached.

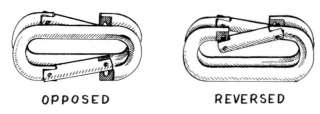

OPPOSED   REVERSED

Fig. 54. Doubled carabiners. *Left,* gates opposed. *Right,* gates reversed.

The simplest brake system is another carabiner with a brake bar attached. The rope should be fed through the carabiner so it *locks the brake bar in place.* If more friction is needed, another carabiner and brake bar can be added.

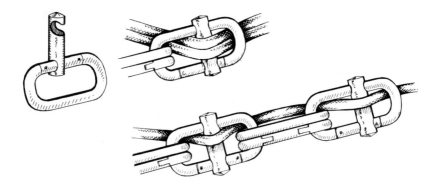

Fig. 55. Brake bars: on carabiner, single bar used for double rope rappel; and multiple brake bars for single rope rappel.

A brake system improvised completely from carabiners — three, or for more friction, when needed, even four — is commonly used. Although more complex and time-consuming to set up, it has the advantage of not requiring any special equipment other than carabiners. While the diagram illustrates the rigging method, two precautions must be carefully observed:

1. The second pair of carabiners, clipped to the pair of carabiners attached to the rappel seat, must have their gates opposed, or at least reversed.
2. The rappel rope must run over the *solid side* of *both* braking carabiners; *never, under any circumstances,* should the rope be allowed to run across the gates.

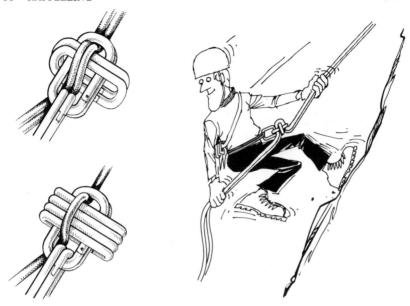

Fig. 56. Carabiner brakes: for normal double-rope rappel; with added carabiners for greater friction with single rope or small-diameter rope; and in use.

RAPPEL TECHNIQUE

Starting may be the most nerve-racking part of the rappel. To obtain any degree of stability it is necessary for the legs to be nearly perpendicular to the slope. Thus, at the very top the rappeller must force himself to lean out; where this would be awkward or dangerously unstable, it may be possible to climb down several feet before leaning and sliding. With a brake-bar system it may be easier, safer, and less worrisome to rig the rappel, sit on the edge of the rappel ledge, and slide gently off, simultaneously turning inward to face the slope. A rappel should never be commenced with a wild leap into space; such acrobatics not only place a heavy load on the anchor but may leave the rappeller in a dangerously unstable position.

Once started, the rappeller should "walk" backwards *smoothly* down the slope, the rate of descent about that of a fast walking pace, *without bouncing or placing other sudden strains on the anchor.* "Movie rappels," long, wide-swinging bounces followed by sudden braking, can triple the load on an anchor and cause its abrupt, total failure.

The body position should be semi-sitting, knees flexed to allow comfortable, relaxed movement, feet slightly apart for stability. Stiffening the body or leaning too far backwards creates unstable positions and can

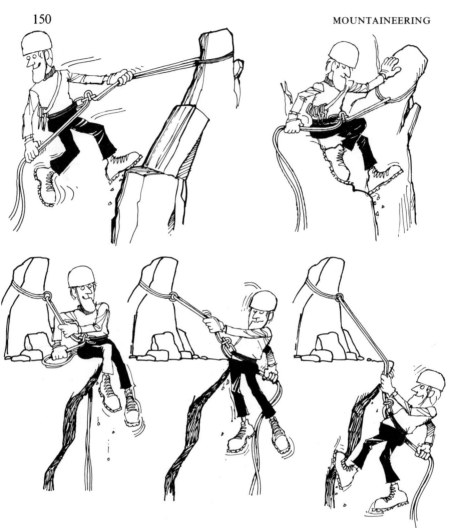

Fig. 57. Getting started on the rappel. *Top*, starting directly from high anchor, and climbing below a low anchor to start. *Bottom*, sitting down and squirming past overhang.

cause the rappeller to turn upside-down. A better view of the rappel slope can be gained by facing about 45 degrees toward the braking hand. This allows the rappeller to avoid snagging the rope around brush or rock and knocking off loose rocks.

The braking hand controls the rate of descent by controlling the amount of rope wrapped around the body — never let the rope out of the braking hand. The guiding (uphill) hand merely slides along the rope to help maintain balance. Beginners should first practice on a comfortably angled 50- to 60-degree slab and should always be belayed.

On multi-rappel descents the first man down should carry enough hardware and sling material to anchor himself before freeing the rope for the others to descend. While they are rappelling, he establishes the next rappel. If the slope is not entirely visible from the top or if there is a possibility he may end up hanging free and/or unable to pendulum-swing to the next rappel point and thus be forced to retreat, the first man should carry easily accessible prusik slings. Some climbers like the security of a prusik in place while rappelling, sliding the knot along as they descend. The loop is attached to the swami belt and the knot is in place above the brake assembly. Care should be taken to keep the prusik from locking unexpectedly; a short prusik loop will keep the knot within reach if this occurs so the climber can unjam it fairly easily.

At the bottom of the rappel, those who have descended move to the side, away from the impact of falling debris.

A commonly encountered problem is inability to retrieve the rappel rope due to one of two reasons: either the knot joining the two ropes is caught on the edge of the cliff or excessive friction results from the ropes sliding around each other or against the rock. This is at best embarrassing, and when encountered during retreat in the face of a storm or nightfall, downright hazardous. To avoid this, the first man down should always untangle the rappel ropes as he descends and those following him should make an effort to keep them clear. Before the last man comes down, one end of the rope should be pulled to make certain the rope can be retrieved easily. After test-pulling, the last man down must be certain that if a knot joins two ropes it is free of the anchor and cliff edge. As he rappels, he keeps a finger or carabiner between the two strands of the rappel rope to remove twists and tries to keep the rope out of places where it could jam. When he arrives at the bottom, the safety knots in the rope ends *must* be untied before pulling down the rope. If two ropes were used, he must be sure to pull on the correct one, that is, the one with the knot on the downhill side of the descending ring.

The rope usually pulls down fairly easily if the above procedures have been followed. A direct pull may not start the rope moving, but stepping to one side or the other or away from the slope may change the angle enough to permit it to slide. The rope should be pulled steadily, without jerks or stops, so the free end will not whip and wrap around anything.

When the rope has been pulled most of its length through the anchor sling, its weight usually provides enough "pull-down force" to keep it coming. If friction prevents this, the steady pull usually frees the rope, at which point all should be alert — as the falling rope can deal a solid blow.

Tying Off

Occasionally it may be necessary to stop partway down a rappel. With either the dulfersitz or brake system two or three wraps of the rope around the leg (plus the weight of the rope) generally provides enough friction to hold.

When using the brake system, an alternate method is to pass the rope around the waist and tie two or three half-hitches around the rappel rope above the brake system. This can be released easily when the rappel is to be continued.

Fig. 58. Stopping in mid-rappel with rope wrapped around leg, and tied off around body.

Rappelling on Snow and Ice

Rappels are rare on snow because the angle is usually low enough to walk or glissade down. Even on steep slopes, less time may be wasted by climbing down, belaying where necessary. Rappels are done only on very steep, hard snow or ice or to bypass bergschrunds too high for jumping and such obstacles as seracs and ice walls.

The rappel techniques discussed above are suitable for snow or ice with little modification. The main problem is that of providing sound anchors on terrain of widely variable consistency. Where possible, anchors of the types discussed above should be used; for example, trees may be used on descents from winter climbs or anchors may be placed in the rocky walls of icy couloirs.

The simplest anchor that can be constructed on snow is the *bollard*. If snow is firm enough a bollard is adequate; if the snow is soft, probably no bollard will be safe, but it may be reinforced by stamping the snow down hard and lining the sides with rocks, sticks, or other load-distributing objects.

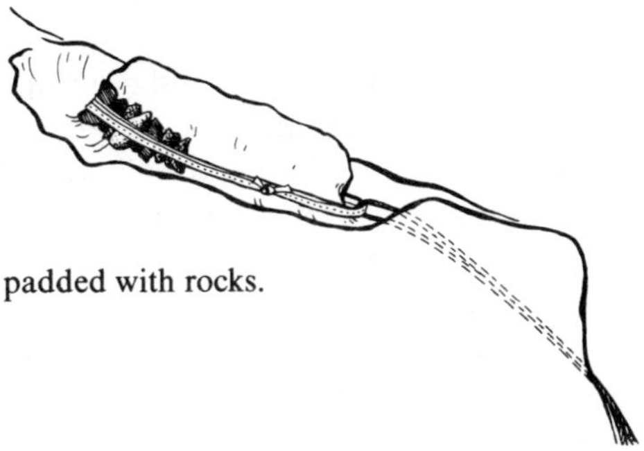

Fig. 59. Bollard as rappel anchor, padded with rocks.

Pickets and *snow flukes (deadman anchors)*, discussed in Chapter 15, are preferred over bollards. Their holding power is more uniform over a wide variety of snow conditions and they can be placed more rapidly than bollards can be built.

Ice is firmer and obviously offers more security as an anchor than snow. *Ice screws* and *pitons,* discussed in Chapter 15, can be placed rapidly and generally are safe. They cannot be retrieved from below, so a series of rappels may result in the loss of quite a bit of equipment. Unlike anchors in rock, they melt out under pressure and parties of more than three or four climbers may have to replace rappel anchors at least once before all members have descended.

SUMMARY

Rappelling is deceptive: it appears easy but has led many incautious climbers into trouble. Most of the many accidents which have occurred on rappels may be attributed to carelessness and/or poor judgment. The following suggestions are offered to assure the climber's next rappel is not his last:

1. Use new slings or webbing on the rappel anchor.
2. Use two anchors and, if necessary, even more.
3. Test anchors thoroughly before rappelling.
4. If wearing a heavy or frame pack, rappel in a more upright position than usual to avoid being turned upside-down. This is a very real possibility when negotiating the lip of an overhang. Unfastening the waistband before rappelling, so the pack can be jettisoned, can prevent being trapped head-down.

5. Secure all clothing, hair, and equipment so they do not get caught in a brake system.
6. As in any other phase of climbing, belay anyone on request and all beginners.
7. Check and double-check *every* part of the rappel system before starting down.
8. Rappel smoothly — without bouncing or sudden stops.
9. If, despite all precautions, something jams in the brake system, remain calm and work it loose carefully. Have a sling rope available; it may be necessary to stand in a prusik sling tied on the rappel rope above the brake system to relieve tension so the obstruction can be cleared.
10. Before the last man descends, test to assure that the rappel rope can be retrieved.
11. At the bottom of a rappel, move aside, away from the impact area of falling debris which may be knocked off by the next rappeller.

 PART THREE

Rock Climbing

IX. Free climbing. (Steve Marts)

11 *

ROCK CLIMBING EQUIPMENT

THE EQUIPMENT described in this chapter forms the majority of items in a rock climber's arsenal. Some items, such as carabiners and runners, are also used in general mountaineering and by ice climbers. Other items of specialized purpose or limited utility have been deliberately omitted as being beyond the scope of the present treatment. While RURPs, cliffhangers, mechanical ascenders, and other specialized tools have their place in mountaineering (see Chapter 13), most climbers can do most of their ascents without them, and while still learning the fundamentals should have little need for them.

EQUIPMENT – DESCRIPTION AND USES

Runners

One of the simplest and most useful all-purpose mountaineering devices is the runner, a loop of 1-inch tubular nylon webbing or rope of ⅜-inch or 9 mm diameter. Though runners may be used to improvise chest harnesses for glacier travel or rappel seat slings, or to mend broken pack straps, their two principal uses are as points of protection or aid and as a means of reducing rope drag on long Class 5 or direct aid pitches. As protection or aid devices, they may be looped or tied around trees, bushes, natural chockstones, rock spikes and flakes, or anything else the climber's ingenuity may suggest. After a runner is placed, a carabiner is clipped to it and the climbing rope put through the carabiner.

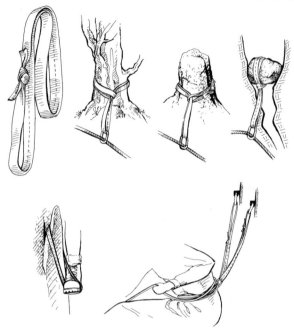

Fig. 60. Tied runner and its uses.

The "single" or standard runner is usually tied from a 5- to 6-foot length of webbing or rope. Double or triple-length runners, fashioned from 10- and 14-foot lengths of material, are also frequently useful. After the runner material is cut to the desired length, both ends are fused in a flame before tying. Although the double fisherman's knot (see Chapter 8) is probably the safest knot in both webbing and rope, it should be checked regularly, like any other knot, to make certain it has not "crept" or partially untied. Material of different colors may be chosen to identify runners of different lengths.

While technical rock climbers may find it necessary to carry a dozen or more runners, six or eight are enough for most climbs. Half-a-dozen single length runners should be satisfactory as an initial selection.

Rope drag, the friction of the rope passing through several carabiners and across intervening surfaces of rock (or ice), may be reduced by clipping a runner to a piton, ice screw, or other anchor and clipping the rope into the runner with a second carabiner. The runner allows the rope to run more freely since it is not held closely against the rock.

Under the general heading of runners are certain specialized items intended for more limited purposes. Among these are hardware racks, hero loops, and aid stirrups.

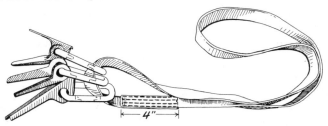

Fig. 61. Sewn hardware rack.

Hardware racks are used for carrying carabiners, nuts, pitons, and the other paraphernalia of rock climbing during the climb. They may be made from 1-inch solid nylon webbing which resists rolling and is less likely to hang up in a carabiner gate while the climber is frantically trying to free a carabiner to clip in to a protection point. As might be expected, various mountaineering-equipment manufacturers have designed and market specially stitched racks.

A hardware rack should fit the climber: it should be neither so long that the equipment pendulums wildly about nor so short that it is uncomfortable and renders the hardware impossible to reach. When making their own racks, most climbers prefer to overlap the two ends about 4 inches and stitch them together.

Hero loops are small runners made from 24- to 30-inch lengths of ½- to 9/16-inch tubular nylon webbing. Made just like standard runners, they are used primarily to tie off partially driven aid pitons.

Aid stirrups are used for direct aid climbing in place of footholds on the rock. They may be improvised from runners, or for extended artificial climbs specialized stirrups may be fashioned. Chapter 13 discusses stirrups in detail.

There are indications that webbing runners wear more rapidly than rope and should be watched more closely. Hero loops and runners should probably be retired after a year's use, after having held a relatively hard fall, or if cut or abraded. In general, all rules for the care of the climbing rope apply to runners. Stirrups and hardware racks may be used until nearly worn out.

Carabiners

Next to runners, carabiners are probably the most versatile tool climbers carry. Their principal purpose in climbing is connecting the climbing rope to the intermediate point of protection or direct aid device. The demands made on carabiners in Class 5 and aid climbing have strongly influenced their design and strength characteristics.

Since, when a fall occurs, the climbing rope usually is passing through a carabiner attached to an intermediate point of protection, it should be obvious that any carabiner used should be strong enough to hold a fall. But how strong is "strong enough?" Referring to the impact force (see kernmantel ropes, Chapter 8), 1200 kiloponds or kilograms-force (2650 pounds) is the maximum force allowed in a UIAA test fall. Due to the braking effect of the rope running over the carabiner, the *maximum* load which can come on the carabiner in a UIAA fall is about 1⅓ times this figure, or about 3500 pounds. Thus, for maximum security on the most severe falls, a carabiner must be able to withstand at least this load.

Steel carabiners offer great strength (indeed, some will withstand loads in excess of 10,000 pounds), but their weight makes it impractical to carry very many of them. Fortunately, aluminum alloys are lighter and adequately strong, especially in the D- and modified D-shapes.

Aid climbing requires another feature in carabiners: the gates must open under body weight so the rope can be manipulated. Here, material strength, shape, and gate design all play important and interrelated roles to allow ease of operation and a high degree of safety.

While rescue personnel may use locking or safety carabiners, most climbers no longer do so because the gate occasionally unlocks when it should be closed or locks closed when it should open. To avoid carrying a special limited-use item, most climbers now use two regular carabiners with gates reversed or opposed whenever additional security is desired.

The shape of the carabiner is of little concern until one's preference has been established through experience. The weakest part of a carabiner usually is the gate, although the sharp bends in some D-shaped carabiners also provide points of potential failure. In general, D-shaped carabiners are stronger than ovals because their shape permits nearly all of any load to come upon the longer solid side, opposite the gate.

Oval carabiners rack pitons better than most Ds and are easier to use as carabiner brakes on rappels; in aid climbing, they allow the rope and stirrup carabiners to move freely rather than slide together in one corner and occasionally shift, or "pop." Some ovals are so designed that their gates will open while body weight is suspended from them; however, under the impact of a fall, the load comes equally on both sides of the carabiner and ultimately on the two small pins (hinge and locking) on the gate. Failure of these pins and the possible subsequent failure of the entire carabiner generally occurs at a significantly lower load than that at which total failure occurs in D-shaped carabiners. Despite their generally lower strength, oval-shaped carabiners have retained popularity for all-around use.

Carabiners should be checked closely for cracks and flaws in the metal and to be certain the gates open and close smoothly and without binding.

The gate must open when the body weight is being supported by the carabiner. Note that the locking notch slants downward so the gate will lock shut under the impact of a fall.

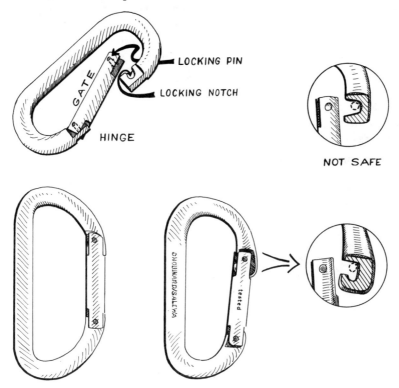

Fig. 62. Carabiners: oval with parts named; *lower left,* "D" carabiner; *center,* modified "D" with gate detail; *upper right,* gate which has developed flared notch is unsafe.

In technical climbing many carabiners are used. For example, on long difficult leads climbers may carry 50 or even more; however novices on easier beginning climbs generally find six carabiners—enough to rappel using the carabiner-brake system—sufficient. When a climber ventures into Class 5 climbing, 12 to 18 carabiners are needed, and, unless supplemented with a partner's equipment, may still prove too few. If it is anticipated that equipment will be shared, carabiners can be marked for identification with colored tape, paint, or a vibrating engraver. (Engraving devices may be applied to the gate *only*; under no circumstances should the solid load-bearing side be subjected to stamping, engraving, or filing.)

If the gate sticks after having been in use a while, the cause may be a burr on the gate or locking hook, dirt in the hinge or spring, or a bent gate. Burrs can be removed by careful filing. Corroded and dirty gates can be cleaned by applying oil, kerosene, solvent, or white gas to the hinge spring slot and working until smooth, then dipping the carabiner in boiling water for 20 to 30 seconds to remove the cleaning agent so more grit will not adhere to the newly cleaned area. Carabiners with bent gates should be retired — thrown away or relegated to use as a "cleaner-biner"— a carabiner clipped to a driven piton so an outward pull can be exerted on the piton while it is hammered about during removal.

The use of carabiners is simple — clip them to a protection or aid device and put the rope in them — but some general suggestions may increase the novice's efficiency and safety:

1. The gates should open either *down and out* or *down and towards the belayer*.
2. The rope should run from the climber through the carabiner(s) to the belayer without twists or kinks.

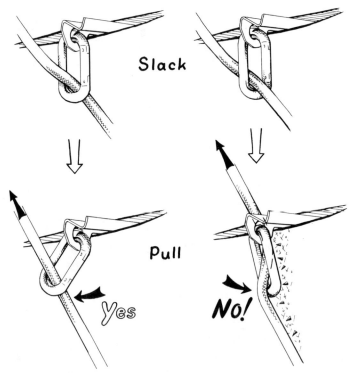

Fig. 63. Clip rope into carabiner so that rope runs freely as shown at *left. Right,* unsafe; under tension rope pulls carabiner against rock, rope binds and is held against rock.

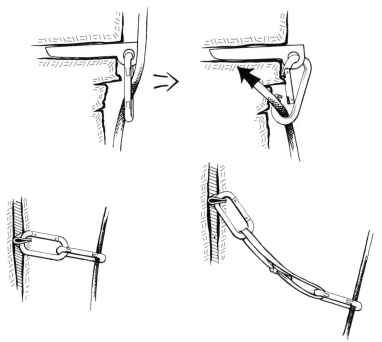

Fig. 64. Clipping into pitons. *Top,* unsafe; gate forced open by rock. *Bottom,* "chaining" to reduce rope drag.

3. To reduce friction of rope against stone and to prevent kinking, use two carabiners or a carabiner-runner-carabiner combination. Chains of three or more carabiners should not be used because they can twist and detach themselves.

Artificial Chockstones ("Jam-nuts" or "Chocks")

In the early days of English rock climbing, courageous leaders used natural chockstones for leader protection. Upon finding a rock wedged in a crack, the leader would untie from the rope, thread it behind the chockstone and re-tie in. As carabiners became more prevalent, climbers abandoned the untying-retying struggle for the procedure of looping a runner around the chockstone and clipping in to it, thus eliminating rope drag.

This technique worked well as long as natural chockstones could be found; however, their presence could not be depended upon, especially on new, unsurveyed climbs. The next step was to help nature by placing chockstones in strategic spots along the route. Indeed, pebble selection at the parking lot and along the trail to the cliffs became part of the climbing ritual.

Technology, in the form of hexagonal machine nuts, inevitably entered the scene. At first they were picked up from the ground beside railroad grades and behind factories; later, they were purchased at hardware stores. Their introduction eliminated the delay of pebble hunting, their shape and variety of sizes allowed them to be placed and removed quickly and easily in all sizes of cracks, and the hole in the center seemed just made for inserting runners, especially with the sharp threads bored out.

Soon it became apparent that an artificial chockstone superior to improvised "stones" could be designed and manufactured specifically for climbing. Entrepreneurs acted on the opportunity, and there are now a number of manufactured artificial chockstones, or "jam nuts," available, several types of which are illustrated.

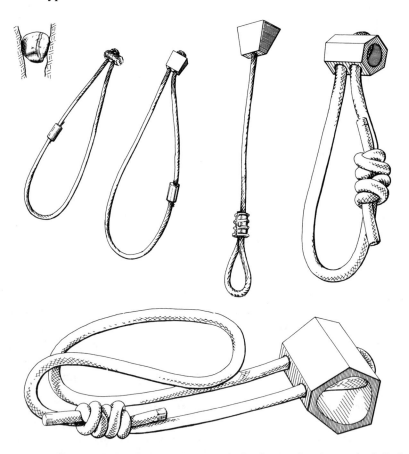

Fig. 65. Chockstones. *Left* to *right*: natural chockstone in place, wired Peck cracker, wired Chouinard stopper, wired Forest foxhead, Clog hexagonal nut, and *bottom,* Chouinard "Hexcentric."

Chocks have been enthusiastically accepted in America for many reasons: lighter and faster to place and remove than pitons, they do not chip or scar the rock, can be placed where pitons would be of doubtful value, and may eventually eliminate the need for carrying a hammer. On the other hand, not all rock is well-suited to their use and a good deal of practice may be necessary to locate good placements. Where they can be used, their advantages outweigh their disadvantages and in many areas they are replacing pitons as the main protection device. Their use has had a profound impact on climbing ethics and appears to have ushered in the concept of "clean climbing" (see Chapter 14).

Chock Loops

Some climbers prefer wired chocks, some use webbing, and others perlon cord or rope. No single way is recognized as best for all situations; thus, the following comments are offered as guidelines rather than hard-and-fast rules.

Wired chocks are easier to place and remove than those on webbing or rope loops, especially if the chock is epoxied to the loop. The wire acts as a handle to guide the chock in or out of place; however the short stiff wire loop may transmit the movement of the climbing rope and lever the chock out of place. This problem is dealt with in free climbing by "chaining" with a carabiner-runner-carabiner combination to absorb the vibration; in aid climbing the problem does not exist because movement is slower and usually in a more direct line. *At no time* should a runner be tied directly to the wire loop because, under the tension of a fall, the nylon can be cut by the small-diameter wire.

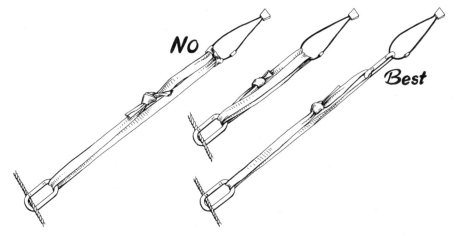

Fig. 66. Attaching runner to wired nut. *Left,* unsafe. *Center,* better than at *left* but still not good. *Right,* safe.

Though these comments might cause one to feel somewhat hesitant about using wired (or cable) chocks, reluctance is not warranted because the wire is stronger, size for size, than perlon or nylon and not significantly heavier in the smaller diameters. As a general rule chocks which do not allow use of perlon in diameters of 5 mm or larger should be wired, especially if they are to be used for free climbing.

Perlon cord and rope appear to last longer and be safer than nylon webbing, though both are used as chock loops. Whatever the material, the largest size which can be squeezed through the hole in the chock should be chosen. The loop should be tied with a double fisherman's knot and pulled tight by suspending one's full body weight from it. The climber learning to lead using chocks for protection should make himself aware of the "fail strengths" of the various types of loops and avoid putting himself in positions where a fall would exceed their strengths.

The length of the loop depends on the purpose of the chock and the climber's personal preference. Generally, short loops are preferred for aid climbing because they enable the climber to move higher and closer to the chock; they also are more commonly used on small-size chocks. Longer loops, which typically go with larger chocks, are probably better for free climbing protection because they may eliminate the need for the extra runner and carabiner; in addition they allow the climber to carry the chocks around his neck. Obviously, long loops can be shortened with a knot and short loops lengthened with a runner. Once again, the specific advice of experienced climbers in each locale should be sought when purchasing and preparing equipment. Reading climbing periodicals and catalogs keeps one abreast of developments.

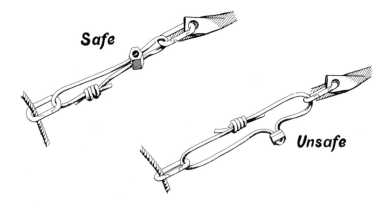

Fig. 67. Chock slings used as runners; to avoid sharp bends in rope, slide chock towards center.

Placing Chocks

To place a chock, find a locally wider portion of a crack. Select a chock which fits closely to the widest portion of the crack and insert it above the point where the crack "bottlenecks." It should be placed deep enough so a load will come on the entire nut and so it will not rotate out of position, but not so deep it becomes impossible to retrieve. Especially with small chocks, care must be taken to avoid jamming against a small crystal which will break off when a load is applied. Maximum surface area should be in contact with the rock and, ideally, the chock should fit closely enough that it has to be worked into position. When the chock is placed, jerk hard on the loop in the direction of pull, that is, in the direction a fall would pull on the chock, to seat it firmly.

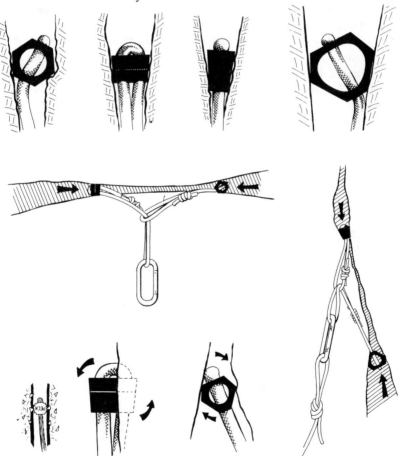

Fig. 68. Chock placements. *Top,* good. *Bottom,* bad. Counterforce placements are also shown; the vertical crack placement, which is used primarily as a belay anchor, must be kept under load at all times to prevent failure.

While chocks are especially well-suited to placement in vertical cracks, it may be possible to place them in horizontal cracks whose interiors are wider than their lips. To do this, find a spot wide enough for the entire chock to be inserted deeply, then slide it towards the desired placement and pull outwards.

Chocks can also be placed in horizontal or vertical cracks in a counter-force attitude. For example, in a horizontal crack two chocks may be placed so they are seated toward each other. The runner from one is passed through the loop on the other. A force exerted downward will pull the two chocks toward each other along the long axis of the crack. When used to anchor a belay, this same technique may be used in a vertical crack – one chock placed right side up to support the belayer if he is pulled downward and the other placed upside down to protect against an upward pull.

Artificial chockstones usually can be removed by jerking them upward or opposite to the intended direction of pull. Well-placed chocks may require some jiggling to loosen, and sometimes a long-bladed piton, stick, or "nut pick" may be needed to guide them out of placement. A stiff piece of ⅛-inch steel wire, such as a skewer-type tent peg, makes a light, inexpensive pick.

Hammers

Piton hammers, essential for driving and removing pitons and, occasionally, removing chocks, receive a lot of hard use and should be of good quality. When selecting a hammer, the climber should consider the amount and type of rock climbing he expects to do. A light (16- to 20-ounce) hammer generally suffices for those who place no more than half-a-dozen pitons per season. A climber who specializes in rock should choose a heavier (22- to 27-ounce) hammer.

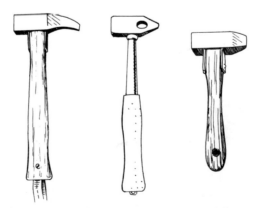

Fig. 69. Piton hammers. *Left to right:* Chouinard, Salewa, and mediocre.

One end of the hammer head should have a good-sized striking surface for driving pitons; the other end should taper to a pick. A short blunt pick enables the user to direct blows very precisely to a small area — useful, for example, when removing a piton from an awkward placement. A longer, thinner pick can be used to clear moss and dirt from cracks or to pry chocks out. If the pick is slightly hooked or has two or three notches, it can also be used to pry out pitons. The battering and prying cause hammer heads to loosen if not securely fastened, so when selecting a hammer, check it closely to make certain the head is fastened tightly and in such a manner that it will survive hard use.

Grip, shaft size, and balance are a matter of personal preference. A longer shaft aids in delivering more force to the hammer blow and more leverage when prying; however it may be awkward and certainly adds weight. The shaft may be wood, fiberglass, or metal, and there seems little reason to advocate one material over another. Wooden handles, though they do get chewed near the head can be protected by tape.

The hammer must be attached to the climber to prevent loss. Most climbers use a one- or two-piece sling made from lightweight nylon cord or webbing. Check the sling from time to time to make certain it has not been cut or abraded. In sizing it, remember it must be long enough that the hammer can be used at arm's length.

The hammer may be carried in a pants pocket or stuck through the climber's waistloop on a climb, but neither arrangement is very satisfactory and a hammer holster is recommended. Before buying one, make sure the hammer which will be carried in it, with carrying sling, fits, can be easily removed, and is held firmly enough not to accidentally fall out.

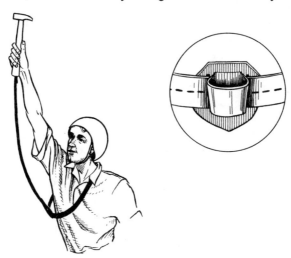

Fig. 70. Hammer sling correctly sized with insert of hammer holster.

Pitons

Pitons may be crudely described as metal spikes which are pounded into cracks in the rock as intermediate points of protection or as a means of ascent. The blade is the part driven into the rock and the eye is the point of attachment for a carabiner.

Until 1960 most pitons were made of soft iron or other ductile metal which would bend to fit the crack into which it was driven. Holding power rarely exceeded 1000 pounds and quality control in manufacture was nil.

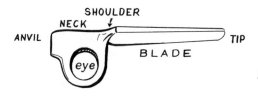

Fig. 71. Piton with parts named.

Soft-iron pitons now have been relegated mainly to use as "fixed pitons" on popular routes and as expendable anchors, having been replaced for nearly all purposes by the newer, stronger chrome-molybdenum alloy pitons. Chrome-moly "pins" depend on stiffness for holding power; when driven, their blades bend very little but are gripped along their length by protrusions within the crack. Without doubt, chrome-moly pitons are the safest and strongest for leader protection on virtually every kind of rock.

Pitons may be divided into two general types: *blades,* whose holding power results from their being wedged into tightly-fitting cracks, and *angles,* whose holding power is derived from both wedging and blade compression.

Blade pitons are described in terms of length and thickness. They may be either long or short and their thicknesses range from "knifeblades" through thin and medium to thick.

Between the medium blades and the small angle pitons, the Leeper Z-shaped pitons and "shallow angle" pitons are preferred by some over extra-thick blades and wedges because they are lighter and, because of their shapes, give greater holding power.

Angle pitons are made in sizes from ½ inch to 2½ inch. Larger-sized angles, usually aluminum and ranging to 4 inches, are onomatopoetically called "bong-bongs."

The when and where of placing pitons are discussed in Chapters 12 and 13; techniques of placement are covered here.

Basically the use of pitons is simple: locate a crack, drive a piton that fits, clip in and climb. The last man up usually removes the pitons as he climbs. Since the pull on a piton is almost always downward, horizontal cracks are preferred over vertical ones. The piton should be driven in a

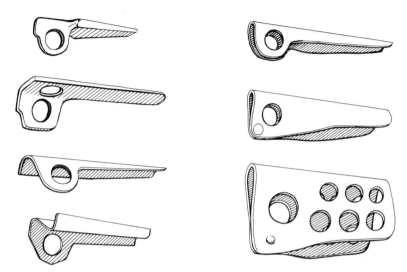

Fig. 72. Pitons. *Left* — top to bottom: Lost Arrow, Bugaboo, shallow angle, Leeper "Z" shape; *right* — top to bottom: regular angle, wide angle, and bong-bong.

locally wider portion of the crack to reduce the likelihood of failure due to shifting or rotation under load. If possible, the eye should point in the direction of pull.

First, look at the crack to select the best place to drive the piton. Try to visualize the particular piton on your rack which will fit the crack; if that one fits, drive and use it, and if not, try another. Selecting a piton and then trying to find a crack to fit it is a waste of time.

Before driving, the piton should be inserted finger-tight at one-half to two-thirds of its blade length. Drive it with the hammer until only the eye protrudes. Soundness of placement may be gauged by feel and sound: it should feel as though the piton were being driven against increasingly firm resistance and the pitch should rise with successive blows of the hammer. Inspect each piton to make sure that as much of the blade as possible is in contact with solid rock — a piton placed between two closely set points could easily rotate and pull out. Pitons driven in vertical cracks *must* be tested by tapping lightly on the head in a downward direction. Similar testing of pitons driven in horizontal or diagonal cracks is, perhaps, less essential but strongly recommended, nevertheless. If the piton shifts or displays other signs of potential failure, it may be necessary to try elsewhere, use a longer or thicker piton in the same place, or resort to some of the tactics described below, especially stacking or nesting.

On long climbs, overdriving pitons takes valuable time in placing and, especially, in removing them, shortens their lives and badly defaces the

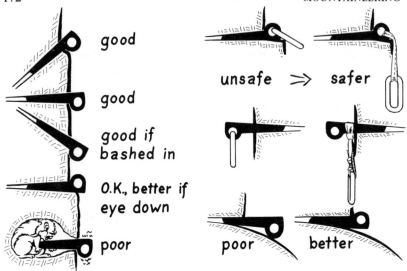

good

good

good if
bashed in

O.K., better if
eye down

poor

unsafe ⟹ safer

poor   better

Angle pitons must be placed with both edges and back
bearing on the rock.
        this ◹   not this ⊻

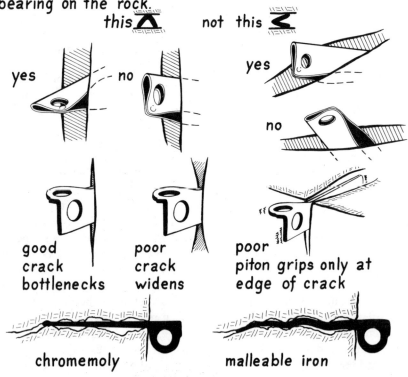

yes   no   yes

no

good
crack
bottlenecks

poor
crack
widens

poor
piton grips only at
edge of crack

chromemoly   malleable iron

Fig. 73. Piton placement.

rock. While solidly placed pitons are necessary to preserve the composure — and life! —of a climber, excessive battering is usually futile and may even weaken an adequate placement.

Pitons placed too solidly or awkwardly for removal should be redriven if necessary and left as "fixed pins." Pins found in place should not be bashed or subjected to thoughtless hammering, especially if made of soft iron, but tested by tapping lightly and redriven firmly if loose.

Sooner or later the best-equipped climber will reach a spot where nothing fits or where those pitons that can be driven fail to inspire confidence. In such situations the following tactics are basic; refinements are limited only by the climber's ingenuity. If there is any basic rule, it is "use whatever works."

When pitons cannot be driven fully because the crack "bottoms," they may be tied off with hero loops or runners, using the slip knot, girth hitch or clove hitch. Hero loops are used mostly on aid pitons because they will probably not be called upon to hold a severe fall; runners are preferred on tied-off protection pitons for free climbing because of their greater strength. The carabiner should be clipped to the hero loop or runner, not into the eye of the piton. A second hero loop may be tied to the eye of the piton and clipped around the load-bearing loop or runner to avoid losing the piton if it pulls out.

Fig. 74. Partially driven piton tied off.

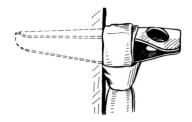

If the only crack available is larger than the smaller pitons on the climber's rack and too small for his larger pitons, he may use two or three pitons together. Blades are "nested," one on top of the other. Angles are "stacked," again one on top of the other, but back-to-back and at right angles. Under the general guideline of "whatever works," any combination may be used. The main effort should be directed toward obtaining the most solid and stable placement, but one should remember the holding power of such combinations is limited. In some very poor cracks it may even be necessary to place two or three pitons, none of which individually will support the climber, but when joined by runners may collectively hold his weight.

If the crack is wide and shallow, a combination of pitons may be stacked or nested and then tied off. When combining two pitons, drive them as a single piton and really smear them in. If using three or more, drive the final piton between others that have been inserted by hand.

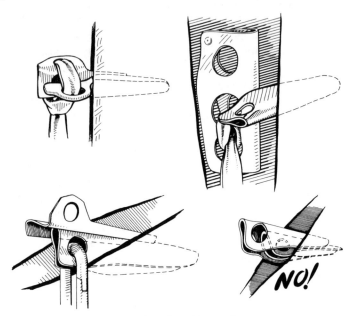

Fig. 75. Examples of stacking and nesting.

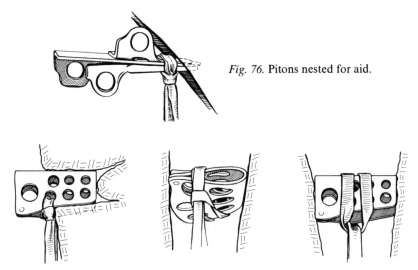

Fig. 76. Pitons nested for aid.

Fig. 77. Bong-bongs. *Left* to *right:* tied off through lightening holes; sling around entire piton; and bong-bong used as chockstone.

Angle pitons of 2 inches or larger may be used as artificial chockstones. Runners can be tied through the lightening holes of partially driven large-angle pitons; however the best method of tying off large angles is to tie the runner around the entire piton. This latter procedure is frequently used with bong-bongs even in ideal placements.

Piton removal is facilitated by avoiding awkward and inaccessible placements, such as off-set corners. Generally, beating back and forth along the long axis of the crack works out the most solidly driven piton. Blades should be driven in one direction until they stop moving, hit hard two or three more times in the same direction, and then removed back in the other direction. With angles less piton movement is needed — just enough to create a "removal groove." Bong-bongs are most easily removed by reaching inside the crack and driving them out.

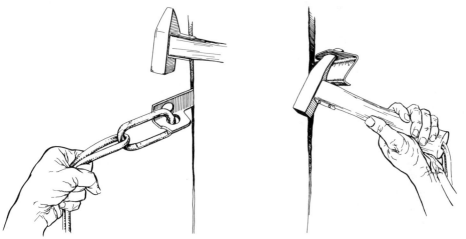

Fig. 78. Piton removal. Use of cleaner-biner, and hammer used to pry.

An old carabiner and runner may be used to apply outward pressure while hammering on a stubborn piton or to jerk a loosened piton free. A slightly drooped or notched pick on the hammer aids in prying pins from tight placements.

Expansion Bolts

Expansion bolts are used to provide anchors in otherwise flawless rock, primarily for fixed anchors on established routes and on otherwise unclimbable or unprotected sections of rock. Their placement requires that a hole be drilled in the rock deep enough that the bolt does not hit bottom; the bolt is then inserted and a hanger with an eye for clipping in a carabiner is attached.

On climbs bolts may be encountered with or without hangers. In areas where hangers customarily are removed by the second man, climbers must carry their own plus a supply of ¼-inch and ⅜-inch nuts to fit the bolts. In the Northwest the common practice is to leave hangers on bolts once placed.

Bolts generally may be considered at least as safe as fixed pitons. Inspect the rock around the bolt for evidence of crumbling or cratering and test it by clipping in and jerking, but NEVER hammer on a bolt found in place to test or "improve" it; repeated hammering, in fact, loosens bolts which would otherwise be reliable. A further discussion of bolt use is in Chapter 14.

Fig. 79. Bolt and hanger in place.

Racking Hardware

However the individual climber racks, or carries, hardware, his method should meet four criteria: all equipment should be easily accessible, it should not get in his way, it should be reasonably comfortable, and on longer climbs where the hardware rack will be exchanged with the lead, the racking method should be similar to that used by the other climber(s).

Fig. 80. A method of racking hardware.

The rack, or hardware loop, described earlier in this chapter, generally is worn with the hardware on the climber's side opposite the hammer and on top of the hammer sling. Thus, most right-handed climbers prefer the hammer on their right side and hardware on their left.

Artificial chockstones on short loops and pitons are carried on carabiners whose gates are "down and out." The smallest pitons are at the front and the largest at the rear. As a general rule, no more than three pitons should be carried per carabiner. Chocks are racked in the same manner, generally in front of the pitons. Extra, or "free," carabiners may be carried at the climber's preference in front of everything, behind everything, between the pitons and chocks, or even on a separate rack.

Chocks and runners may also be carried around the neck or over the neck and shoulder. On climbs where only a few chocks and runners are carried, and all are slung around the neck, a carabiner may be carried on each to eliminate the time-wasting motion of taking a carabiner off a separate rack and clipping it to the chock sling or runner.

Hard Hats

Though wearing a *hard hat* while climbing is an individual decision, no one can dispute the number of serious injuries and fatalities that have resulted from accidents where hard hats were *not* worn or where they came off. In recognition of their importance, many climbing organizations have made their use mandatory on club-sponsored rock climbs and recommended for all climbs.

The hard hat offers protection in two general types of accidents: falling objects striking the climber, and the climber falling and striking objects. No specific standards presently exist for mountaineering helmets but the following points should be taken into consideration when buying one.

The hat should have a hard shell to prevent penetration by sharp objects. Equally important is a suspension system that holds the head clear of the shell, absorbing a portion of the blow to the top of the helmet and reducing to a survivable level the amount of force transmitted to the wearer's head. Protection from blows to the side of the head (such as in a tumbling fall) appears to be provided best by thick (½-inch or greater) styrofoam pads lining the shell interior. The hat must have no sharp edges or internal protrusions which could injure the wearer. The shell material must not soften in warm weather nor become brittle in cold. Bills and brims are to be avoided since they tend to obstruct vision and catch on rock projections. Finally, the hat must not impede hearing, as excessive protection for the head, neck, or ears certainly does.

To be of any value a hard hat must stay on the wearer's head during rolling, tumbling falls, protecting as much of the skull as feasible from battering and rockfall. For this reason the chin strap design is especially important. A single chin strap is not sufficient to prevent tipping or loss of the hat. A Y-strap design is better but fails to hold the hat on some persons' heads if the attachment points are too close together, the rear attachment not far enough to the rear, or the arms of the Y not long enough. The chin strap, or forward arm of the Y, must be fairly far forward to prevent the hat from tipping back, but if too far forward may obstruct vision. Another attachment system uses a chin strap plus nape straps attaching at the center back of the head. The straps should not be elastic but of ½- to ¾-inch nylon or other durable webbing. Snaps are not satisfactory for fastening; positive locking buckles or double D-ring attachments are preferable.

Any helmet must meet certain comfort and convenience requirements or it will more than likely be left at home. It must be comfortable under a wide variety of conditions: ventilated for use in hot weather, adjustable or large enough to accommodate a wool hat or parka hood during cold or wet. The weight must not be excessive and the lining and suspension must be comfortable. The hat must never fit so tight that any part of the head is in direct contact with the shell.

A final point: the finest hard hat notwithstanding, the human head and neck have limitations. To expect "bomb shelter" protection from any helmet is to be in for a rude surprise. While no one can deny the benefits of a good hard hat, liberal use of common sense and judgment do more to ensure longevity than any helmet one can buy.

Rock Shoes

A person who develops an interest in rock climbing eventually becomes aware that specialized rock shoes offer advantages over mountain boots. Of several styles and brands available each has its own characteristics of fit, sizing, comfort, performance, life and price; before purchasing a pair, one is wise to talk to climbers experienced in the area in which he plans to climb.

A rock shoe must fit snugly so it acts as an extension of the foot and permits no sliding about within. The welt must be extremely narrow to allow body weight to press the foot firmly to the rock and not let sole material flex and thus slide off a small hold.

Brake Bars

The use of *brake bars* is slowly being superseded by carabiner brake systems described in Chapter 10, primarily to avoid carrying an extra piece of single-purpose equipment which could be lost, dropped, or forgotten. Despite this trend, many climbers still believe brake bars are fast to set up and simple to use; certainly they are valuable in rescue work.

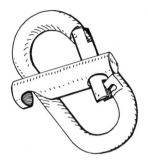

Fig. 81. Brake bar on carabiner.

Since a brake bar must fit the carabiner with which it will be used, it should be checked against one's carabiners at time of purchase. Brake bars made of tubular metal eventually wear through, with the possibility of sharp edges sliding along the rope in the middle of a rappel; therefore although heavier, solid-bar stock is far safer for brake bars than tubular. Finally, the brake bar must be long and thick enough to sustain hard use. If it is so thin it can be bent, either deliberately or accidentally, it is not safe.

Descending Rings

Descending rings, usually welded steel or aluminum rings about 2 inches in diameter, are employed to reduce rope wear and ease rope retrieval on rappels. Rings of solid, non-welded construction are preferred over the more common welded variety but are more expensive and almost impossible to find. The strength of descending rings varies widely, the common weak spot being the weld. While only a metallurgical X-ray examination can be positive, scrutinize the weld when purchasing; any signs of cracks or weak welding should arouse suspicion. Paint can obscure poor workmanship, so purchase only unpainted rings. Similarly, rings found on peaks must be checked most carefully — heavier rusting at the weld may indicate a poor joint; any such unsafe rings should be removed and carried out of the mountains.

SHOPPING WISELY

Though nearly all contemporary equipment is of fairly high quality — and correspondingly high cost — it is in the interests of persons making their first equipment purchases to obtain as much information as possible from this and other texts, catalogs, climbing periodicals, and other climbers before investing large sums in equipment which may prove not to be necessary or satisfactory.

Next to ascents they have done and want to do next, probably no other subject is so near and dear to the climber's heart as his gear, and the inquirer will find himself deluged with excellent, albeit highly opinionated, advice. Novices especially are wise to limit purchases to high quality, multi-purpose items rather than to spread themselves and their finances thin by trying to buy all the exciting gadgets available in mountain shops.

When the decision is made to purchase a certain item, the wisest course is to shun the cheap and the shoddy and to acquire the best quality available. An investment in the best suitable equipment yields the greatest returns in safety, pleasure, and longevity. Finally, once the selection is made and the equipment purchased, the climber must learn its performance and strength limitations and climb within them.

12 *

FREE CLIMBING

IN FREE CLIMBING only naturally occurring features of the rock are used for progress. The "rules" may permit the climber to clutch conveniently placed vegetation; however, he may not stand on a piton placed for protection nor grab hold of a runner.

Climbing is a joyous, instinctive activity; unless restrained, most children will scurry up trees, garden walls, building facades, and anything else steep and enticing. While society, in the form of parents, teachers, and the law, discourages these activities, some determined individuals persist and eventually find their way to the peaks. Those, on the other hand, who have submitted to social pressure and forsaken the steep and airy pathways should, and usually will, content themselves with hiking and leave rock faces for those who are comfortable and happy there.

Despite any natural inclinations toward climbing, the human body is more adapted to plodding along on the level than swinging through trees. Skill, or technique, must be developed to make up for inadequate musculature and to allow the climber to move competently and confidently. So while one might obey the suggestion of one climber "to remember our arboreal ancestors, retreat intellectually a couple of million years and make like monkeys, defying gravity with our own impetus," it must be remembered that instincts must be supplemented with skillful, planned effort, or bodies will quickly weary and fall short of the goal.

FUNDAMENTALS

Balance

Efficiency of movement and rhythm are intimately associated with a sense of balance. In walking, the eyes are focused on a distant point as a sort of "third leg" to help keep the body upright; in climbing, the horizon may be limited to a point just beyond the nose, so the hands must serve as the "third leg."

In *balance climbing* the climber stands up straight with body weight directly over his feet and uses his hands only to maintain balance. The beginner's tendency to lean in and "hug the rock" gradually disappears as he learns, through practice, to stand erect, allowing himself to be supported by his skeleton. As confidence grows, he discovers this upright stance actually improves footing by allowing him to make the most of friction between boot sole and rock and by pressing unstable holds into place.

Controlled Motion

Controlled motion means climbing in balance, or in strenuous situations, moving with an economy of effort to avoid undue fatigue. It is more efficient to push the body upward with the legs than to haul it up by the arms. This is not to say that arms are never used, but the more upright the stance and the greater the reliance on feet and legs, the longer arms and fingers last when their strength is really needed. Keeping hands at about head height produces a good stance and helps conserve arm strength by maintaining a supply of blood to the arms.

Holds should be spaced as comfortably as possible, without excessively high steps or long reaches; intermediate holds, even small ones, should be used. On the other hand, do not dither looking for tiny intermediate holds when one big step will do the job safely and more efficiently. Jumping or lunging to reach a hold can have disastrous results if it is missed, or if it turns out to be loose or illusory; movement should be controlled and deliberate, with the possibility in mind of having to reverse a series of moves.

The type of movement should be varied, spreading the work of raising the body among different sets of muscles, always trying to press downward rather than pulling up. Natural body positions should be sought, rather than cramped, awkward, or strained stances which promote fatigue. On difficult rock all tactics are combined: a sequence of moves is worked out from resting spot to resting spot, then executed, moving with determination, speed, and precision, the climber finally resting when the next secure position is reached.

Climbing with the Eyes

Generally, the eyes should climb the pitch first, so look ahead! Study the general line to be followed, then look for specific holds. Alternative holds and resting spots should be noted, if possible, before starting to climb.

Three-Point Suspension

Stability and security, especially on unsound rock, are promoted by maintaining three points of support at all times (that is, two feet and one hand or one foot and two hands) while the remaining limb moves to the next hold. Using holds on either side of the direct line of advance helps provide a firmer base and greater mobility.

Attitude

The universal fears of falling and being injured, or appearing weak, frightened, or ridiculous in front of companions leads many novices to "tighten up" both mentally and physically. Although a degree of self-confrontation is inevitable, concentrating on the act of climbing rather than on its most horrible potential consequences helps reduce tension. A valid bit of advice is "Don't worry — you're only climbing rocks, a few feet at a time. Think just in terms of those few feet, rather than of the mountain (or pitch) as a whole, and climb as calmly and carefully as you can."

HOLDS

Handholds and footholds should be chosen for firmness, convenience, and size, tested with a blow from the heel of the hand or a kick of the foot and a perpendicular push or pull. If the hold is loose it should not be dropped (think of the people below); furthermore, it may be secure enough to use, for example, in a downward direction though it might fail in an outward or sideways direction. Kneeholds should generally be avoided since knees are susceptible to injury and offer little stability; nevertheless, even the best climbers occasionally use a kneehold to avoid an especially high step. The main considerations are avoiding injury (look out for pebbles and sharp crystals and not becoming trapped and unable to rise to the feet.

Footholds

In rock climbing as in all active sports, deft footwork is a sign of skill. Feet should be placed on holds and left there, not blindly thrashed about in hopes something will stick. With marginal footholds it is important that once placed in a hold, the foot not be moved; even a small change of position can cause the boot to slip off.

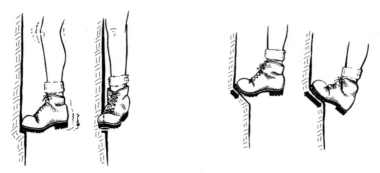

Fig. 82. Footholds. *Left:* small footholds; toeing in is tiring, edging is more secure. *Right,* sloping holds; bend in ankle increases contact with hold.

"Toeing in" on small holds can result in great strain on the leg muscles, which, in turn, leads to "sewing machine leg." Less leg strain results from turning the foot sideways to get the big toe or ball of the foot over the hold, especially if the climber is wearing flexible shoes. The more flexible the shoe, the less help they give the foot in supporting the climber, so more sole area must be "smeared" on the rock to bring body weight more directly over the point of support.

Flexing the ankle allows the sole to be flat on the rock and to push down firmly, whether the hold is incut, flat, or outward sloping. If handholds are adequate, additional security on slippery, steeply inclined, or extremely small footholds can be obtained by leaning away from the rock and thus creating an inward as well as downward pressure on the hold. Practice develops one's ability to lean out just enough to wedge the feet firmly on holds without unnecessarily tiring hands and arms.

Large footholds, called "buckets," are never scorned, but only as much of the foot as necessary to stay in balance is placed therein, for sticking the foot too far underneath a bulge can force the shin and knee outwards.

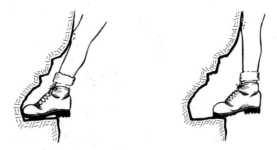

Fig. 83. Bucket hold. *Left,* body forced out of balance. *Right,* retaining balance.

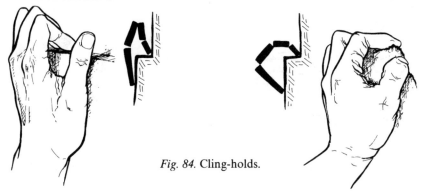

Fig. 84. Cling-holds.

Handholds

The cling hold, in its many variations, is the most commonly sought handhold; however, its overuse can lead to a "chin your way up the mountain" style of climbing and to fatigued hands and arms. A very useful variation is the "vertical cling" in which the climber grasps the edge of a crack, corner, or knob and leans slightly away from the hold as he steps upward. On small cling holds, the fingertips form to fit the rock.

A larger fingertip hold becomes a true handhold — for the entire hand — and, hopefully, slopes inwards. The best and most comfortable of all such holds are nicknamed "jug handles" or, when appearing at the end of a hairy lead, "Thank God holds."

Fig. 85. "Thank God hold."

Downpressure

As the climber moves above a cling hold he may be able to continue using it by placing the palm, heel, or outer edge of the hand on it and pushing down. Downpressure holds may be used by themselves, or in combination with other types. The heel of the hand may be pointed in either direction, depending on which way the climber wants to go. Once the arm has been extended and the elbow locked, the climber can balance one-handed on it — long enough, perhaps, to move the other hand to a higher hold.

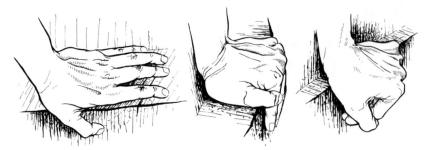

Fig. 86. Downpressure. *Left* to *right,* whole hand, heel of hand, edge of hand.

SPECIAL APPLICATIONS

Slab Climbing

Practice climbing on the relatively smooth, hold-less rock pitches known as *slabs* is an excellent way to learn the limit of boot sole friction and at the same time to develop footwork and balance, however, slab climbing is a highly developed art in itself. When the angle is low enough, no handholds are needed and the friction of the boots, placed to get maximum sole area on the rock, provides the adherence needed to climb. Somewhat steeper slabs demand the use of hands, palms pressed flat on the rock; however, almost all the weight is still directly over the feet.

As the slab becomes very steep, the climber seeks out natural undulations of less slope than the average gradient for holds. Tiny cling holds become more and more important, as do neat footwork, slow, smooth movement, and calculated tactics. Slab climbing is a very precise, deliberate craft, requiring poise, confidence, and balance.

Fig. 87. Slab climbing.

Mantleshelving

Mantleshelving, or mantling, uses downpressure holds and is a means of gaining a ledge or set of wide holds where there are no holds above — like climbing onto a fireplace mantle, using only the mantle for support. For the simplest mantels, the hands are placed about a foot apart, palms down

Fig. 88. Mantleshelf sequence.

and fingers pointing towards each other, on a chest-high flat ledge; the body is raised by straightening the arms (a spring with the legs makes this easier). Supported on straight arms, the climber may then raise either foot to the ledge and stand up. If the ledge is above his head, he grabs hold of it, leans back a bit, and walks the feet up the face as far as practical. A quick movement is necessary to change from a cling hold to a downpressure hold, elbows up, fingers in towards the body — one hand at a time. He then presses up (exercises to loosen shoulder muscles may make this easier). The judicious use of any available footholds or even scrabbling with the feet facilitates the move.

Balanced on his hands in mid-mantle, the climber may find a bulge in the rock does not allow him to stand up easily on the ledge; however, by mantling only partway he may be able to reach another handhold that was previously out of reach.

Mantling on very small or sloping ledges or onto good ledges above sharply cut overhangs calls for much strength and gymnastic skill. Sharply undercut mantels seem best maneuvered by a swinging technique — first hanging from the ledge, swinging under, then pulling up on the outward swing. Arm strength and a good deal of bouldering practice are necessary to become proficient in mantleshelving.

Hand Traversing

By clinging to a series of holds above his head, and with feet dangling free, the climber can "hand over hand" across an otherwise blank section of rock. Such "hand traverses" are very strenuous, especially if the traverse ascends, and fortunately are rather rare. If forced to make a hand traverse, the climber uses his feet as much as possible, moves as rapidly as care will permit, and avoids prolonged hanging on a partly flexed arm.

COUNTERFORCE AND LAYBACKING

Very often a person can climb securely by using a combination of opposed forces. Some techniques involve only one or two points of sup-

Fig. 89. Pinch grip.

port, others involve the entire body. For example, a firm pinch-grip on a flake or knob of rock is an elementary form of *counterforce*.

Counterforce holds are frequently used in conjunction with cracks. If the fingers can be inserted up to the knuckles in a small crack, the thumb can be pressed, in opposition, on the opposite side, or the hands can "pull apart" in opposition to generate enough force to stay on the rock. Closely

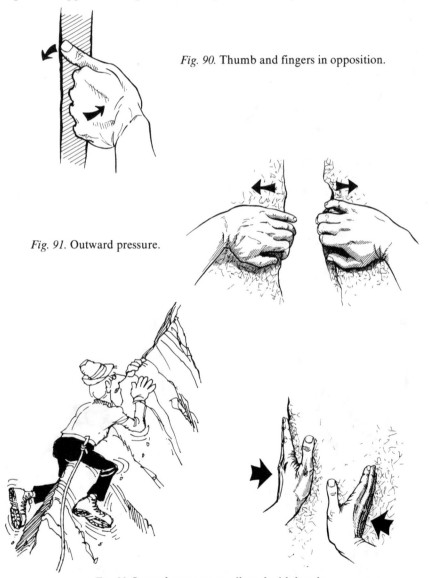

Fig. 90. Thumb and fingers in opposition.

Fig. 91. Outward pressure.

Fig. 92. Inward pressure on rib and with hands.

spaced double cracks may be climbed with an outward pull, as above, or by pressing inward with the hands. Inward pressure with the hands is not as secure as pressure with the knees when straddling a very narrow, knife-edge ridge. Widely spaced double cracks give a feeling of security when used in a "pull together" manner. The climber can lean out a bit to force his feet onto the rock and probably must shift weight a little to one side or the other in order to move his hands.

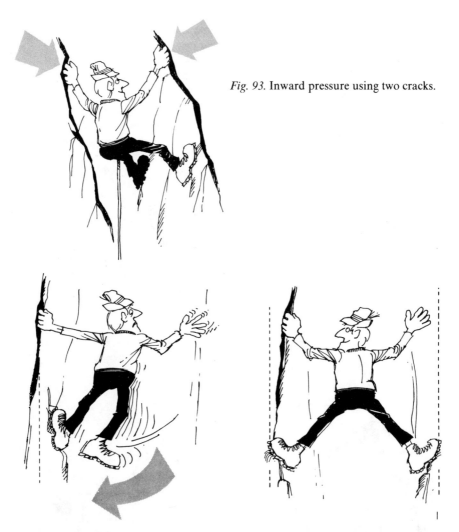

Fig. 93. Inward pressure using two cracks.

Fig. 94. Relationship of hands to feet on very steep rock. *Left,* hands beyond feet: if one hand moves body can pendulum from remaining hand. *Right,* more stable; movement will not cause loss of balance.

As can be seen, these holds do not offer a great deal of grip on the rock if the body starts to tip over and away from the rock. On very steep rock — nearly vertical and beyond — the hands should be kept within a vertical line above the feet to prevent swinging like a badly hung door. This is applicable to widely spaced double crack systems described above and to free climbing in general.

When the entire body is involved in counterforce climbing, good holds are vital for a strong push-pull or push-push combination. Undercling holds formed by solid flakes or undercut ledges provide good upward

Fig. 95. Undercling.

Fig. 96. Climbing sequence using both up and downpressure handholds.

pulls for the hands while the body leans out, "pushing" the feet against the rock. As another example, in a small recess or cave, one might stay in balance by pushing down with the feet on the floor and pushing up with the hands on the ceiling.

Combinations of these holds can be developed; for example, an overhead flake can be pinched while the feet are moved higher; then, provided the flake is securely attached to the mountain, it can be utilized for an undercling hold while the climber leans out with his feet braced and moves to the next hold.

Laybacking is the classic form of counterforce, the hands and feet pulling and pushing in opposition and the climber moving up in a series of shuffling movements. It can be done where two rock faces meet with a crack in the corner (an "open book") or where one side of a crack offsets the other and provides space for the feet. A flake also can be laybacked.

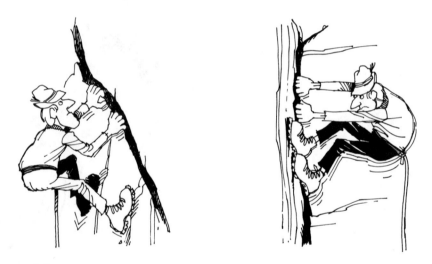

Fig. 97. Layback. *Left,* up a flake. *Right,* in a corner.

Laybacking is so strenuous it is necessary to move rapidly, though deliberately. Keeping the arms extended as much as possible puts the strain on bones and ligaments rather than on tensed, flexed muscles. Feet are kept high enough to maintain purchase on the rock but not so high as to unnecessarily tire the arms. Frequently the feet can be placed on small holds or a hand or foot jammed, allowing the body to assume a more vertical, less tiring stance. Depending on steepness of the rock, the position should be adjusted to be as comfortable and relaxed as possible under the circumstances.

CRACK CLIMBING

Crack climbing is less instinctive yet often more secure than maneuvers heretofore discussed. Some methods are obvious, as for example, using the edge of a crack as a cling hold, pulling downwards on a horizontal crack, or sideways against a vertical crack.

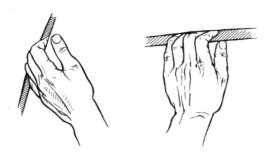

Fig. 98. Cracks used as cling holds.

Less obvious and of great value is the technique of jamming. In theory, jamming is straightforward: fingers, hands, arms, legs, feet, knees, and/or any other usable portion of the body are wedged into cracks and hopefully lodged securely enough to bear weight. The process may be summarized:

1. Insert a hand, foot, or other body member into a crack, preferably at a locally wider point.
2. Lock it by flexing or twisting so it pushes or "jams" against both sides of the crack and resists a downward pull.
3. Do the same with other members as required.
4. Raise body, pushing with legs as much as possible.
5. Repeat sequence.

Each movement should be deliberate and useful. Thrashing about, groping, and desperate pawing at the rock are useless and tiring. Learn to look ahead, selecting a prospective placement, before moving a hand or foot; *then* move hand or foot to the new jam and lock it in place.

Hand Jams

Fingers may be jammed in narrow cracks and small solution holds. After they are inserted as far as possible, a twisting or torqueing action of the hand provides the necessary expansion to lock fingers in place. In vertical cracks bottlenecks may be found which improve the jam.

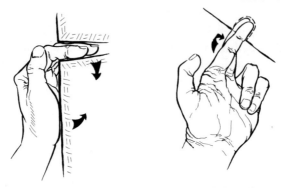

Fig. 99. Finger jams. *Left,* in crack. *Right,* in former RURP crack (see Chapter 14).

As a crack gets wider, the entire hand can be inserted and pressure exerted between the back and heel/fingertips. In ideally sized cracks, expansion is provided by tucking the thumb across the palm; somewhat larger cracks require that the hand be "cupped" to lodge it in place. Once again, a twisting action can improve the jam, and placement just above a bottleneck gives maximum security. The preferred attitude for hand jams is "thumbs up" (palms facing each other) because this position gives

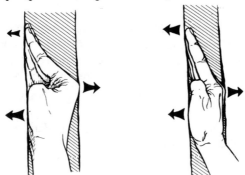

Fig. 100. Hand jams. *Left,* thumb tucked across palm. *Right,* "cupped" hand.

Fig. 101. Hand position in diagonal crack.

greater freedom to the arms. However, in diagonal cracks or because of oddities in the crack's formation, it may be preferable to jam both hands "thumbs down" (palms facing the outside) or jam the upper hand "thumbs down" and the lower "thumbs up."

The fist can be jammed in a variety of ways, with the thumb tucked inside or out to make the fist. Fists are best jammed in the manner that one places an artificial chockstone — inserted in a locally wider section of the crack and pulled downward to jam. Some expansion can be provided by flexing muscles in the fist and by pressing against the side of the crack with the back of the thumb. Fist jams are generally dependent on bottlenecks in the crack for most of their holding power, the human fist having relatively little expansive capability.

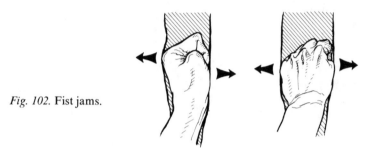

Fig. 102. Fist jams.

Jamming the Feet

In a corner the toe tip may be jammed using a technique best described as "smearing" — flexing the boot, with the heel at a lower level than the toe, and applying pressure *down* and *in* to wedge the toe in place.

The toe may be jammed in a crack either vertically or horizontally by inserting the shoe with its sole parallel to the side walls of the crack and twisting to jam it. Since the twist on the ankle can become painful this is not a good "resting" jam. Similarly the entire foot can be jammed, either vertically or horizontally.

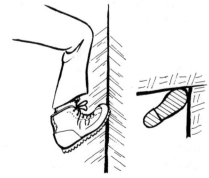

Fig. 103. Toe jam in corner.

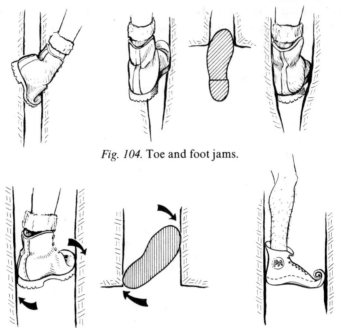

Fig. 104. Toe and foot jams.

Fig. 105. Heel-toe jams.

The entire foot may be jammed end-to-end, either "heel-toe" or with the ankle flexed. If the crack is not wide enough to admit the full length of the foot, it may be jammed diagonally, with twisting force exerted by the anke and leg. Pressing the knee against the rock may improve the jam.

Elbows, Arms, Shoulders, Knees, and Hips

Cracks too large for hands and fcet to jam yet too small to admit the entire body must be climbed using jams of the arms, legs, hips, and shoulders. The same sequence is followed: insert small, expand to jam, move up. The *arm lock* uses the elbow pressed against one side of the crack, the heel of the hand pressed against the other side, and as much of the shoulder squished into the crack as possible. Similarly a leg jam may be devised between the knee and heel/toe of the foot; occasionally the leg and/or knee can be jammed without benefit of the foot. The outside arm may be placed in front of the chest, pushing away from the body on the other side of the crack. The outside foot can sometimes be jammed, heel-toe; often it just scrapes on the face outside the crack, gaining purchase on such footholds as may exist. The combinations and possibilities in climbing wide cracks are endless; each individual climber must experiment to find the techniques which work best for him.

Fig. 106. Arm locks in cracks.

Application of Jams

Narrow cracks — ½ to 1½ inches — require finger and toe-tip jams, hopefully provided with an occasional foothold on which to rest.

Medium cracks — 1½ to 4 inches in width — call for hand, fist and foot jams as described above.

Wide cracks — from 4 inches in width up to a size in which the whole body will fit — are affectionately dubbed "off-width cracks" by some because no part of the body fits perfectly. Progress in such cracks is obtained by using techniques already described. Ingenuity, strength, and aggressiveness are necessary, as well as a high degree of personal commitment because it is often not possible to place protection for the leader. Some cracks narrow towards their interior, so the climber may be struggling awkwardly with a 5-inch nasty with his "outside" hand and foot, but jamming comfortably with his "inside" ones.

A crack which is wide enough to admit the body as a whole becomes a chimney (see below).

Fig. 107. Climber partly into wide crack.

Finally: each climber should leave his ruler behind and crack climb *his* way, with whatever methods work best for him.

CHIMNEYS

The term *chimney* defines a size range of cracks between those which barely admit the body ("squeeze chimneys") and those so wide a climber's length does not span them. Whatever the width, the principle of climbing them is the same: the climber pushes outwards on both walls of the chimney simultaneously to remain in place. To move up he relaxes this tension in one part of his body, moves it up, reapplies tension, relaxes the other part of his body, and moves *it* up. Depending on width, this pressure in the upper body is generally between back and hands, elbows and hands, or hand and hand. In the lower body, this cross-pressure is most often between heel and toe or foot; knee, buttocks, and foot, buttocks and foot; or between foot and foot.

In very narrow "squeeze chimneys" the body is forced into an almost vertical position and movement so restricted that it is difficult to exert cross-pressure on either side of the chimney. In the narrowest of such chimneys, sufficient cross-pressure can sometimes be created by merely inhaling deeply! Progress is by a shuffling, squirming action. If the chimney is deep enough, somewhat more rapid progress is possible using a "diagonal inchworm" method: the lower body is shuffled up and to one side, then the upper body is shuffled until the body is again in a vertical position.

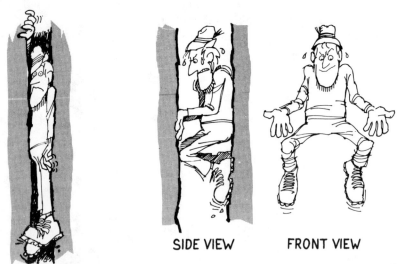

SIDE VIEW   FRONT VIEW

Fig. 108. Climber in chimney. *Left,* squeeze chimney. *Right,* side and front view in narrow chimney.

Somewhat wider chimneys, which the entire body can easily enter, are climbed with the back, shoulders, and feet pushing against one wall, and the knees and hands (palms against the rock, fingers pointing down) against the other. To ascend, use either a one-thing-at-a-time squirming action, or a system of wedging the upper body while raising the knees and feet, then wedging them while the rest of the body moves up.

Probably the easiest chimney to climb is one about 3 feet wide. The arms and legs work alternately, as shown, pushing against opposite walls.

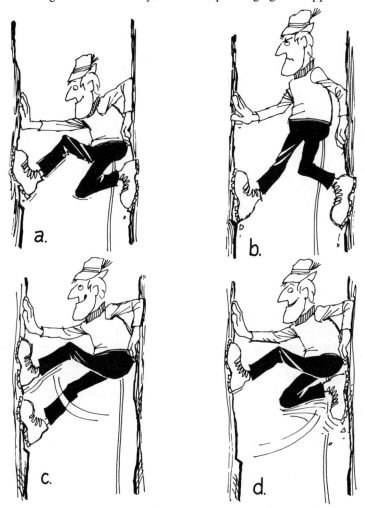

Fig. 109. Chimney climbing sequence.

a. Legs drawn up.   b. Legs straightened.

c. Left leg across.   d. Right leg back, then repeat.

As chimneys grow wider the climber's position changes from that of facing across the chimney to that of facing in or out, with arms and legs pushing sideways against the walls. Progress is similar to that above: arms and legs alternately move, or both legs then both arms. The final absurdity, a chimney too wide for the body to span in a vertical position, can occasionally be climbed with the body in a horizontal position. This type of chimney is quite rare, and climbers with an interest in such hi-jinks even more so.

Fig. 110. Wide chimney, use downpressure with hands.

Although very smooth-walled chimneys may be climbed using only outward pressure against the walls, no hand or footholds should be scorned if they make the climbing easier. In narrow chimneys which taper towards the back, a hand or foot can sometimes be jammed. The hands should almost always be kept low rather than raised high where they cannot help wedge the climber in position if his feet slip. Far from being of use only in chimneys, chimneying technique can be used wherever it is possibly to push on surfaces of the rock in opposite directions. For example, stemming technique may sometimes be used to climb right-angle corners, using face holds on either side of the corner. This may afford an easier means of climbing and holds the body away from the rock for better visibility of the route ahead; however, it offers the psychological disadvantage of a magnificent view of the route below, which is probably exposed. Very often, though, climbers find that getting out in the exposure offers easier and safer progress than hugging the rock or struggling in the interior of a dark, slimy chimney.

OTHER CLIMBING TECHNIQUES

Traversing

Every so often the route deviates from a direct upward line and traverses across the face. While traversing is no more difficult than moving in any other direction, attention to a few points may make the going easier.

Walking across a series of small holds, with the feet pointing in the direction of travel, offers good visibility of the route but puts the body off balance and increases the amount of hand strength needed. Facing in, toes pointing away from each other may, on occasion, be awkward; however it holds the body close to the rock and enables the climber to change direction easily. Generally shuffling the feet is preferred over stepping through because less of the climber's body gets between him and the rock, enabling him to stay in better balance. Hop steps, to change feet on a small hold, should be kept to a minimum and hopefully done only when good handholds are available.

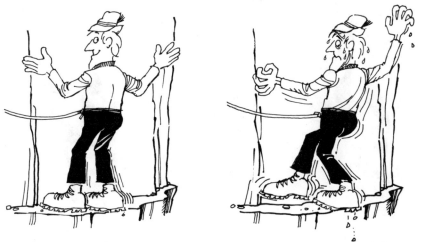

Fig. 111. Traversing. *Left,* shuffling. *Right,* stepping through (more awkward).

Down Climbing

While climbing down is, in actuality, no more difficult than climbing up, it often seems so. This is because one cannot see the holds as easily as when climbing up and feet and bodies feel heavier and clumsier on the descent than they did when lightly bounding upwards.

On easy and low-angled rock, the climber faces outward as he descends. He may crouch slightly, feet flat on slabby areas, heels planted on holds in broken areas. As a general rule, hands should be kept low and ready to support the climber using either downpressure or cling holds. The buttocks may be used for support when facing out.

As the angle or difficulty increase, it becomes necessary to face sideways, leaning out at intervals to see what lies ahead. This position still permits a view of the route, and allows good freedom of movement.

Finally, when descending very steep or difficult rock, the climber must face in. As he descends, he moves as carefully as on the ascent, maintaining three-point support where possible, and occasionally leaning away from the rock to see where he is going.

Despite the seeming "unnaturalness" of down climbing, it is a valuable technique well worth developing. Besides being necessary for getting off a mountain, it is also invaluable for retreating when routefinding errors have led one astray.

Fig. 112. Down climbing. *Left* to *right:* easy, face out; moderate, face sideways; more difficult, face in.

PROTECTING THE LEADER

While the second and any subsequent climbers on a pitch usually may climb in safety, so well-belayed from above that a slip cannot turn into a real live fall, the leader must obviously take a dreadful chance, at least according to the pundits of mass literature. In reality, the shopworn cliche that "the leader must not fall" (oft accompanied by drum roll and fanfare) has given way to the more practical "the leader probably will fall (sooner

or later), and when he does, minimize the possibility of a serious injury."
At this point, belaying techniques and the various protective climbing
tools described in Chapter 11 come into play as means of protecting the
leader.

Unless protected along the way, a leader will fall twice the vertical
distance from him to his belayer — plus a little more, due to slack in the
system and rope stretch. For example, in the diagram, a leader 90 feet
above his belayer will fall somewhat more than 180 feet. This could hurt,
so the climber, in essence, "takes his belay with him" by clipping the rope
to runners, chocks, pitons, or, infrequently, bolts placed along the way.

In the second diagram, the leader on the same pitch has placed protection: a runner on a tree 20 feet above his belayer, a chock 25 feet farther,
and a piton 15 feet below himself. Since the rope is clipped to each
protection point (see Chapter 11), and assuming that the protective
devices are well placed, the leader cannot fall farther than about twice the
distance between him and his last point of protection. In this case, should
the leader slip, he will fall slightly more than 30 feet, a big improvement
over 180 feet.

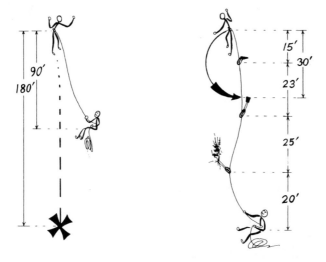

Fig. 113. Distance of leader falls. *Left,* unprotected lead. *Right,* protected lead.

The techniques of hardware placement are discussed in Chapter 11. The
next question after "how to place," is "when to place." The quick answer
is to place protection *before* it is needed. By this is meant that the climber
must continually appraise the situation ahead and place protection before
a hard move or series of moves.

The leader usually finds he has enough to occupy his thoughts while placing protection without the additional strain of dangling one-handed from poor holds in an insecure position. Therefore he prefers a comfortable stance from which to work if it is available. On the other hand he should refrain from standing on a comfortable ledge and mashing in a piton at arm's reach — the second man usually finds said piton quite difficult to remove without a series of tension-supported moves which unduly consume time and energy.

With the protection in place, the usual sequence is to clip a runner to it with a carabiner, then clip a second carabiner to the runner and clip the climbing rope to the latter. This "chaining" procedure is one of the best methods of reducing rope drag.

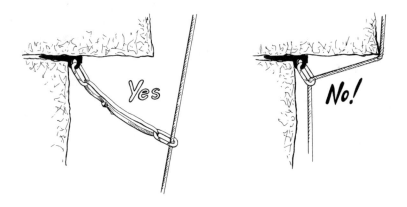

Fig. 114. Chaining to eliminate rope drag.

Near the end of a long 5th Class pitch the drag caused by friction of the rope running in a zigzag through several carabiners and over intervening surfaces of rock can be horrendous, magnifying the effort needed to move, pulling the climber off balance, and infuriating when he is trying to clip the rope, one-handed, to a hard-to-reach anchor. Chaining, forethought in selecting placements, and clipping in properly minimize rope drag. The leader must make every effort to keep his rope running in the straightest possible line and clear of friction-producing corners, bulges, and overhangs. He may use similar procedures to ensure that the rope does not jam in a crack or cross a sharp edge of rock where it could be cut in a fall.

Rope drag can be a problem on Class 4 pitches also. A leader can solve this problem with pitons, chocks, or runners placed to keep the rope from jamming or from dragging across a ledge strewn with loose rocks.

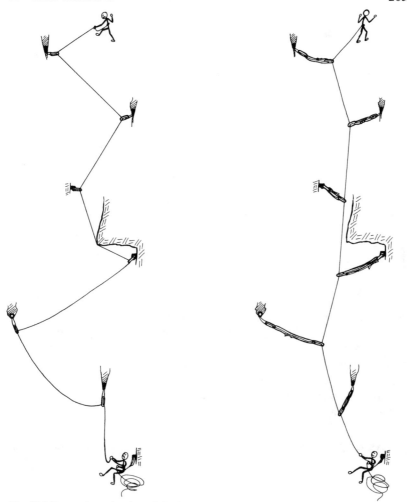

Fig. 115. Protecting a lead. *Left,* bad. *Right,* good. Rope should run in as straight a line as possible.

Protecting Traverses

Especially on traverses the leader must remember he is placing protection for his second as well as for himself. Inexperienced leaders often protect themselves well on a hard traverse, but fail to place protection for the second man after completing the difficult portion. This forces the second man to climb the same difficult area without the same protection the leader so carefully placed for himself. A slip then results in the second penduluming wildly across the face, careening off assorted obstacles along the way.

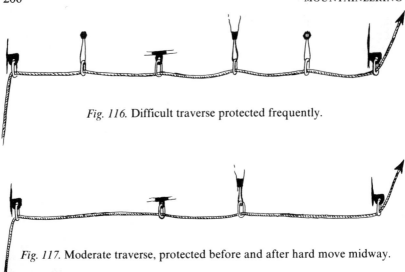

Fig. 116. Difficult traverse protected frequently.

Fig. 117. Moderate traverse, protected before and after hard move midway.

Placement of protection after the start of a traverse depends upon the climbing encountered. On a difficult traverse, adequate protection is placed before and after each hard move along the way, while on an easy-to-moderate traverse with an occasional hard move, the leader protects himself before the move and his second after it. On the other hand, the leader should wait until he has climbed several feet above the end of an easy traverse before placing protection, to shorten the second's pendulum if he falls.

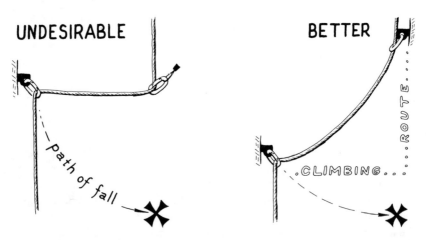

Fig. 118. Protecting easy traverse for second man. *Right,* second still pendulums, but drops a shorter distance, gaining less speed than at *left.*

Of course the situations are not always clear-cut, for one can belay:

1. At the beginning of a traverse.
2. At the end of a traverse if there is hard climbing beyond it.
3. The second man with a second rope (using the hauling line or that part of the rope already taken in).
4. The second man with a back rope technique.

Traversing pitches, especially unprotectable ones, is considered by many climbers to be the most "sporting" because the second man generally runs at least as high a risk as the leader in case of a fall.

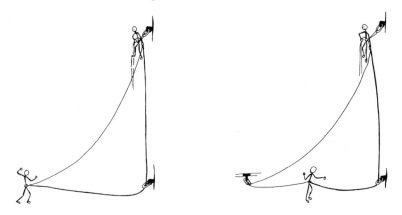

Fig. 119. Back ropes. Two ways of belaying with a back rope to protect second on a traverse.

Protection on Ridges

Many alpine routes lead along ridgelines – some on the very crest. Methods of protection here depend on the location of the climber. If he is climbing along the side of a ridge, he must remember, as in traversing, to place protection for his second *after* a hard spot. If climbing along a broad ridge crest, ordinary face climbing protection methods are used. Anecdotes abound of climbers on very narrow, knife-edge ridges telling their partners to "jump off the other side if I slip." Since no one seems to have actually tried this technique, there is some doubt about its usefulness; fortunately such ridges commonly bristle with opportunities for runners over horns and around small pinnacles.

OTHER GOOD ADVICE

All the detail of this chapter notwithstanding, there is no cut-and-dried method for climbing any given pitch. Individual differences in physique, strength, confidence, footgear, and ability as well as a climber's own preferences in technique make each pitch a unique experience. He may find that all his skills are needed on a particular pitch and that he may have to invent something to get past a particularly difficult crux move. Experience, gained through practice and actual climbing, is the only way a climber will ever be able to climb without losing time experimenting with each move.

Practice climbing can be done on boulders, buildings, artificial rocks and climbing walls, trees, doorways, and any other feature offering a chance to move upward in a climbing fashion. Exercises such as stepping up and down on a high table, running over uneven ground, and skiing improve a climber's balance, agility, and endurance. Chinning on doorways, weightlifting, gymnastics, yoga, and any frequent and vigorous exercise can contribute to one's fitness. In *practice situations* — bouldering, top-roping (that is, climbing with an overhead belay), practice pitches, following a leader on a climb, or on well-protected leads — one should climb until he falls. If on the point of falling, try harder — *fall trying*! This is the only way to learn and extend limits.

Free climbing on sound rock can be one of the most exhilarating facets of mountaineering. Like anything worthwhile, it demands personal commitment and at least *some* practice to achieve anything but the most mundane results. As one gradually develops his own style of climbing, he discovers that textbooks, lectures, and demonstrations by others are very poor substitutes for actually getting hold of the rock and trying. As skill grows, early failures give way to successes; but without those first faltering efforts, skill can never develop beyond mere potential.

Supplementary Reading:

Aleith, R. C. *Bergsteigen.* Scottsdale, Arizona: R. C. Aleith, 1971.

Blackshaw, Alan. *Mountaineering.* England: Penguin, 3rd edition, 1970.

Rebuffat, Gaston. *On Ice and Snow and Rock.* New York: Oxford University Press, 1971.

Robbins, Royal. *Basic Rockcraft.* Glendale, California: La Siesta Press, 1971.

Robbins, Royal. *Advanced Rockcraft.* Glendale, California: La Siesta Press, 1973.

13 *

AID CLIMBING

ARTIFICIAL, or direct aid climbing, is defined in the United States as the use of anything other than the rock's natural features for support or rest while climbing. Aid techniques vary from the leader's use of his second's shoulder — or head — as a foothold or the impromptu grab of a runner on an otherwise free pitch to the continuous use of stirrups and the many types of rock climbing hardware.

At one time, aid climbing was literally tension climbing: the leader was held in position by his belayer while he placed his next piton. Hanging one-handed from a piton, he would pull in slack rope, clip it to his next higher anchor, and haul himself up by his own efforts and the pull of the tight belay rope. The addition of a second rope made things easier on the leader, but required good coordination on the belayer's part, or a second belayer. Stirrups, which offered the leader a place to stand, were the next innovation. Frequently of ¼-inch manila rope, they served adequately but were terribly uncomfortable when used with soft shoes. Sometimes rope ladders with metal steps were used for comfort, but these jammed in cracks and were awkward to carry. Since the end of World War II, chiefly as the result of pioneering efforts in Yosemite Valley, revolutionary changes have taken place, elevating aid climbing to the level of an art.

AID CLIMBING EQUIPMENT

Although aid climbing requires all the items used in Class 5 climbing as well as some specialized tools described below, the main difference between the equipment needed for Class 5 and aid climbing is quantity: because hardware is so much more closely spaced on aid pitches, more of everything, especially carabiners, is essential.

Stirrups, sometimes called *etriers,* are short ladders used as the principal means of movement in aid climbing. On routes involving only
occasional bits of aid or in remote areas where weight and bulk in the pack
are critical, stirrups may be improvised from runners or tied from ½- to
9/16-inch webbing; however, for the extended use on any route where aid
climbing predominates, the preferred practice is to tie them from 1-inch
width flat nylon webbing.

Twelve to 20 feet of webbing are required for each stirrup, depending
on the climber's height and the number of steps desired. A guide to sizing
is shown in the accompanying figure. In general, stirrups should be long
enough that the climber can easily step from the top step of one to the
bottom step of another that is clipped to a piton placed at arm's reach. The
number of steps in each stirrup — usually three, four, or five — depends
upon the height of step the climber can make comfortably.

Whatever the method used for tying stirrups, that illustrated or any
other, the top step is always positioned in each so that when the climber is
standing in it, the piton or chock to which it is clipped is about midway
between his waist and knees. This permits him to stand in the top step
nearly all the time when placing his next anchor. Corresponding steps of
individual stirrups should be at the same level for comfort and stability.

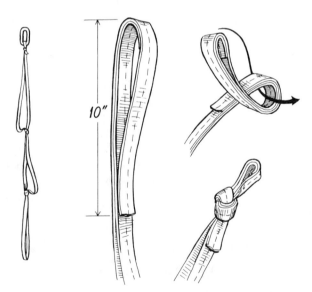

Fig. 120. Stirrups. Completed stirrup and tying sequence for Frost knot. The
amount of webbing needed to make this stirrup is twice the finished length plus 10
inches for each step plus 8 inches extra for Frost knot. A 60-inch stirrup with three
steps takes 2 x 60″ + 3 x 10″ + 8″ or 158″.

After the stirrups have been tied and tightened, a carabiner is clipped into the carabiner loop of each stirrup and left there to be moved with it from placement to placement. On less-than-vertical aid climbs, a hero loop can be clipped into this "stirrup carabiner" to provide an extra high step for the climber.

In addition to pitons, chocks, and other items discussed in Chapter 11, the following specialized tools are essential for the more difficult aid routes:

RURP (*R*ealized *U*ltimate *R*eality *P*itons) — hatchet-shaped pitons about the size of postage stamps which are designed to chop their way into incipient cracks.

Bashies — soft aluminum blocks which are bashed into shallow grooves or even piton holes.

Cliffhangers — often referred to as skyhooks; can be hooked over tiny nubbins, ledges, or flakes.

Belay seats — small contrivances of nylon webbing and fabric in which the climber sits when there is no handy ledge from which to belay.

Mechanical ascenders — substitutes for the prusik knot which facilitate cleaning and hauling on aid routes.

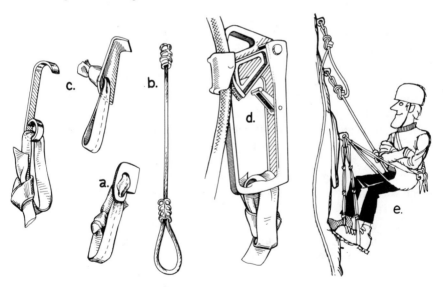

Fig. 121. Climbing aids.

a. RURP.   d. Jumar ascender.

b. Bashie.   e. Belay seat in use.

c. Skyhooks.

TECHNIQUES

Climbing

In the following sequence of the "Yosemite Technique" of aid climbing, the assumption is made that pitons are being used exclusively. The same sequence is followed, without modification, when any other anchor is used.

1. Place piton.
2. Clip in a "free" carabiner.
3. Clip in a stirrup to the "free" carabiner.
4. Test the piton, first by tapping with the hammer, then by subjecting it to greater than body weight; a small hop in the stirrup suffices. If the best pin placement obtainable is obviously insecure, most climbers forego the hop and ooze, heart-in-mouth, into the stirrup.
5. Standing in the stirrup, clip a second stirrup to the free carabiner, and, before moving up, reduce rope drag at the lower piton as necessary.
6. Move up; when the piton is at waist level, clip the climbing rope to the free carabiner.
7. Repeat procedure.

The leader does not clip into his anchor until it is at waist level, thus eliminating the need for the belayer to pay out slack and pull it back in as the leader moves up, and also reducing the length of fall should the new piton fail while the leader is standing on it.

The novice on his first direct aid climbs is frequently dismayed by the seeming insecurity of his stance in stirrups; however, he should stand or climb in stirrups the same way he would on the footholds they replace — that is, his legs should lift him from step to step with his hands used mainly for balance, not as a means of hauling himself up.

The sequence for following is similar except the second should unclip the rope from each piton before clipping in his stirrups. Standing in his slings, the climber may find he cannot reach the piton below him to remove it. In this case, he may either clip two stirrups together or use one or two runners to lengthen his regular stirrups.

There are two ways by which the climber can free both hands, or rest on a steep aid pitch, without calling on the belayer for tension. The quickest way involves tucking one foot under his buttocks and "sitting" on it. The other method uses a short sling, called a cow's tail, tied to the swami belt and provided with a carabiner. The sling is clipped to the free carabiner and supports the climber while he leans back.

Normal piton and chock placements are illustrated in Chapter 11. However, some aid climbs follow cracks behind relatively thin flakes or behind large semi-detached blocks. The danger in such situations is that

Fig. 122. Resting on foot.

the pressure created by the hardware and/or the leader's weight may expand the crack behind him, allowing his pitons or chocks to drop out below him, or may pry the rock off the mountain, dropping rock, leader, hardware, and all into the belayer's lap. (Artificial chockstones are less likely to cause such a crack to expand and should be used wherever possible.) If successive pitons are placed in the same crack, a carabiner and aid sling should be clipped to the highest piton as soon as it has been driven far enough to give some promise of security; the climber then shifts his weight gradually onto the aid sling, hoping it will hold his weight should the piton he has been relying on for support fail as a result of expansion of the crack. Driving the piton at an angle to the direction of pull may permit it to rotate slightly and re-lodge itself rather than pulling completely out under load.

Traversing

Pendulums and Tension Traverses

Pendulums and tension traverses offer means of reaching cracks, ledges, or other features off to one side of the original climbing route and inaccessible except by bolting. Tension traverses are generally used for short distances: the climber leans sideways against the rope and "walks" across, using friction and the few holds that may be available. The belayer pays the rope out slowly against the climber's pull.

To pendulum, the climber is lowered from a securely placed anchor point and runs back and forth across the face until able to reach his goal.

After he has completed the pendulum and resumed climbing, the leader usually does not clip into any aid or protection anchor until he is level with or above the pendulum anchor. This reduces rope drag, shortens the length of a possible fall, and makes following easier for the second.

If the pendulum pitch ends below the pendulum anchor — an unusually long pitch — the second generally follows by rappelling down, and across, to the leader. More commonly, the second must lower himself or swing over from the pendulum anchor using the climbing rope, a spare rope, or the hauling line. In any event, the anchor and a runner or carabiner are left behind.

Tyrolean Traverses

Tyrolean traverses have been made to less accessible pinnacles by lassoing them, anchoring the near end of the rope securely, and prusiking or sliding across the intervening chasm. With the advent of modern techniques and climbing philosophy, Tyrolean traverses have assumed an insignificant role in the climber's repertoire, though they continue to be of importance to rescuers, expedition climbers, and others needing to move men and equipment efficiently across rivers, gorges, crevasses, and similar obstacles.

Use of Mechanical Ascenders

When the climbing is predominantly direct aid and on long climbs where a heavy pack must be hauled, it is generally faster and more efficient for the second to clean the pitch using mechanical ascenders while the leader hauls the pack. Jumar, the most widely used brand of mechanical ascenders at present, has become the generic term for all mechanical ascenders and the process ("jumaring") of using them.

At the end of a pitch, the leader ties the climbing rope securely to two or three bombproof anchors. The second ties both his jumars to his waistloop with runners and clips a stirrup to each jumar. As an additional convenience, he may attach a belay seat to the lower jumar, enabling him to sit comfortably while removing hardware. The annoyance of feet slipping from stirrups while jumaring may be eliminated by tying them around the feet with girth hitches or by securing them with large rubber bands.

Still tied to the lower end of the climbing rope, the second jumars up and cleans the pitch as he goes. As he reaches each point of aid or protection placed by the leader, he generally finds it necessary to remove one ascender and re-attach it above the anchor in order to unclip the rope from the chock or piton.

In theory, using jumars is as safe as using prusik knots or climbing with an overhead belay. Most, if not all, accidents which have occurred in-

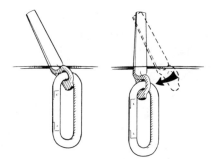

Fig. 123. Piton placed at angle to direction of pull. Before and after pull.

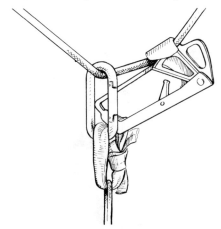

Fig. 124. Using carabiner to stabilize jumar in traversing.

volving their use can be attributed to human error. To be sure, doing everything correctly will not ensure immortality; however, it does significantly lessen the chances of being killed through procedural error.

To summarize:

1. The anchors must be *absolutely bombproof,* inasmuch as the *minimum* load they are called upon to hold is that of two people and a heavy pack.
2. The climber should be tied to *both* ascenders *and* the end of the rope; thus, three points of security exist. Climbers lacking confidence in mechanical devices may gain additional assurance by tying a small figure-8 loop in the rope below the jumars and clipping it to their waistloop. By replacing the figure-8 loop with a new one every 20 feet or so, the length of a possible fall, should both jumars fail, is limited.
3. When attaching the jumar to the rope, the safety trigger must be fully closed or the jumar may pop off the rope. If the trigger is closed, the

jumar cannot come off a rope of 7 mm or greater diameter. Failure of this nature occurs most often on diagonal ascents. To reduce rotation of the jumar on a diagonal rope and thus its likelihood of "popping off," clip a carabiner around the rope to which the jumar is attached and then through the base of the jumar.

4. When following complicated traversing or overhanging pitches, it may be safer, faster, and easier for the second to climb the pitch belayed. Since he is protected by an overhead belay furnished by the leader, he may stand in his stirrups or, on occasion, take tension while he removes the hardware in relative security.

Fig. 125. Climber jumaring.

Sack Hauling

On long technical ascents a party must carry many pounds of food, bivouac gear, and water in addition to climbing equipment. Normally, one does not joyously contemplate leading steep, difficult rock with a heavy pack on his back, so means must be found to transport gear. Early "big wall" climbers either hauled loads hand-over-hand or prusiked with packs hanging from their waistloops. During the early 1960s the following technique was devised for hauling on long and difficult climbs. It has the great advantage over earlier methods of employing leg power and body weight rather than the weaker, more easily fatigued arms. An additional benefit is the cheery diversion it provides the leader while the second man jumars and cleans the pitch.

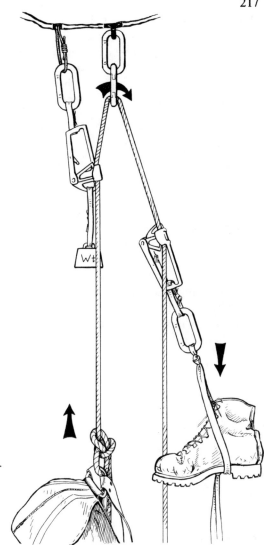

Fig. 126. Pack-hauling setup.

The party climbs using two ropes – the climbing rope and a separate hauling line – and each climber carries a pair of jumars. After anchoring the climbing rope so the second man can ascend and clean the pitch, the leader attaches one jumar, upside-down, to an anchor and weights it with his hardware rack. A pulley is attached to the same anchor, above the jumar, and after pulling up all slack the hauling line is inserted in both. The second jumar, with a stirrup attached, is clipped to the hauling line, right-side up. To raise the pack, the leader simply jumars "up" the hauling line. The upside-down jumar acts as a ratchet to prevent the sack from sliding back down between pulls.

The efficiency of this technique is reduced if the rock is of low angle or very broken up. It may be necessary for the second man to help the pack over overhangs or other obstructions. On traversing pitches, it is wise to have a very light third rope which is used to lower the bag across and prevent damage to it and its contents.

TO CONCLUDE

To the beginner on his first aid pitch, artificial climbing may seem the perfect illustration of the law of maximum perversity: "anything which can possibly go wrong will." He soon learns to organize his equipment carefully and to follow the same sequence of movements every time. He cultivates the ability to select the correct size piton or chock with a minimum of trial and error. With practice he finds he can place hardware securely enough to be safe without mashing it in so hard that time is wasted removing it, and learns to place anchors as far apart as practical without wasting time and effort stretching for "that extra inch." Especially while learning, each movement should be thought out and performed carefully and deliberately. Experience develops the necessary efficiency of movement which enables the proficient aid climber to move steadily, smoothly, and confidently.

Supplementary Reading:

Aleith, R. C. *Bergsteigen.* Scottsdale, Arizona: R. C. Aleith, 1971.

Blackshaw, Alan. *Mountaineering.* England: Penguin, 3rd edition, 1970.

Rebuffat, Gaston. *On Ice and Snow and Rock.* New York: Oxford University Press, 1971.

Robbins, Royal. *Basic Rockcraft.* Glendale, California: La Siesta Press, 1971.

Robbins, Royal. *Advanced Rockcraft.* Glendale, California: La Siesta Press, 1973.

14 *

ROCK CLIMBING ETHICS AND STYLE

ETHICS AND STYLE or, more accurately, courtesy and good climbing behavior have only recently become of widespread concern to mountaineers. Earlier there were so few climbers in the mountains that their impact on the environment was negligible. Further, since the equipment of the sport was basically a rope and perhaps an ice ax, there was little likelihood of damage to the mountain.

Today, increased leisure time and a romanticized view of climbing bring more people to the mountains in a single season than previously came in a decade. The challenge to do bigger, more sensational climbs has quite predictably led to an unprecedented wave of technology. New kinds of equipment means the ability to substitute mechanical protection for climbing skill — the ability to ascend by mechanical devices routes which seemed denied to man's natural ability. This, coupled with an attitude which diminishes the sport of climbing by placing all value in the achievement of the summit at any price, has brought about the necessity of a new climbing ethic. The self-centered approach to climbing is viewed with deep concern by climbers who have developed a true appreciation of and love for mountains.

Rock climbing poses an exceptional requirement for a code of climbing ethics. The increase in the number of rock climbers coupled with the idea that "enough hardware will get me to the top" causes a serious problem in popular rock climbing areas: the amount of rock good for climbing in any area is limited, and nature's rocks are literally being destroyed. Climbers are now aware — or should be — that the rock which seems so solid and enduring is, after all, a rather fragile, easily marred, and non-healing climbing medium.

Ethics are related to "purer" motives for climbing, that is, the active participation in, and enjoyment of, the alpine environment. Competition between climbers and selfish motives of "me first," and "the summit at any cost," reflect little concern with ethics.

Any statement of ethics must realistically face the fact that the most "pure" climber has a strong competitive streak, is highly motivated toward achievement of his personal goals, and will make any rationalizations necessary to achieve those goals, and explain his actions to others afterwards. Thus, a realistic expression of climbing ethics must arise from and encourage the pure ideals of "doing well," "taking pride in a craftsman-like job," and "following natural lines in a natural manner," and yet be tolerant of the human-ness of teenagers emulating their heroes by repeating extraordinary climbs (making up in equipment what they lack in skill), middle-aged novices fumbling valiantly on climbs somewhat over their heads (making up in equipment what they lack in youthful qualities), and slightly over-the-hill super-climbers trying desperately to leave a high-mark that will survive at least one season's challenges by younger, better climbers.

At this point, also consider esthetics — the field of philosophical thought concerning art and beauty. Climbers find beauty in the climbing environment and derive great pleasure from pursuing the various arts of climbing. The pleasure and beauty derive from the creative act of fashioning one's own three-dimensional path over the climbing medium. Intrusions into this creative act change the climb from its original state and affect its spontaneity — fixed anchors, "gardened" cracks and ledges, loosened flakes, ledges used as sewers and garbage dumps, and boot- and piton-scarred rock — each robs the climber of at least a little of his most meaningful personal involvement in his climb.

One possible way to keep the rock "new" is for climbers to limit themselves to only those climbs which have not previously been ascended, to climb them as "cleanly" as possible, and to refrain from discussing their climb. Another possibility is simply for climbers to quit climbing and stay away from the cliffs and peaks because of man's ultimate destructive effect on nature. Both "answers" are absurd — man is as much a part of nature as any other being and destruction too, is a natural process. But there is a difference: a flower crushed beneath a boot is neither more nor less a "loss" than the same flower being eaten by a small rodent or that rodent being in turn eaten by a predator. The difference lies in life's ability to replace itself — rock cannot. Holes drilled in rock do not heal; flakes

X. Mt. Goode from the north; North Cascades National Park. (Austin Post, University of Washington)

broken off do not grow back; cracks chewed by hundreds of repeated piton placements cannot mend themselves.

Thus climbing ethics must have their basis in preservation of the climbing environment, both its beauty and its utilitarian features which make possible the sport of climbing. The following rules are proposed as a foundation to "ethical rock climbing," to help preserve the climbing environment, and to promote high personal standards of climbing:

1. Preserve the climbing medium.
2. Adhere to the "first ascent principle."
3. Climb in "good style."

Preserve the Climbing Medium

To preserve the rock, the route, and surrounding terrain:

1. Find out the traditions of the area and individual routes as to accepted means of protection and method of climbing *before* climbing there.
2. In *descending order of preference* use: runners on natural formations (horns, trees, chockstones), artificial chockstones, pitons, and, as a last resort, expansion bolts.

Do *not* use any potentially permanent aid or protection device, other than those named above, which scars or defaces the rock unless it affords the same long-term security for other climbers as a well-placed piton or expansion bolt.

Use of expansion bolts "as a last resort" does not imply a reflex grab for the bolt kit when opportunities for using runners, chocks, pitons, and cliffhangers no longer appear to exist. A climber should deliberate before arriving at a conscious decision to alter the rock permanently by placing a bolt. Some questions he might ask himself are "must this route 'go'," "could a better climber than I lead this section without a bolt," and "is there another way"? There is no disgrace in recognizing one's limits and demonstrating personal integrity by withdrawing when those limits have been reached. Not every route is for every climber; perhaps some routes are not for any climber.

3. Never remove an obviously fixed piton, whether it is one's own or another's.
4. Never place a bolt on an existing route. If the need is felt to do so the person is climbing above his standard.
5. Never "chop" a bolt.
6. Never carve a hold and never remove one.
7. Leave no litter or trash on the route and clean up at the base after the climb.
8. Leave the climb in its natural state, as much as possible.

Adhere to the "First Ascent Principle"

No one should bring a climb down to his standards. If he cannot climb it at least at the level of the first ascent party, he should do other climbs until he *can* meet the standards and, in the meantime, leave the route to those who can. It may be possible for someone to climb *above* the level of the first ascent party, but in so doing, he must not deface the route.

As an extension of the first ascent principle, the climber should learn to place pitons and learn aid climbing in out-of-the-way places reserved for the beginner to hammer away. While learning, he must make certain he is not destroying free-climbing cracks or boulder problems in the process.

Climb in "Good Style"

By this is meant use of the best techniques available at the time of the climb, taking advantage of natural anchors wherever possible, and making the fewest changes possible in the climbing medium.

Climbing in "good style" also involves using tactics most appropriate to the climb. For example, fixed lines and intermediate camps would always be inappropriate for routine ascents of easy local peaks whereas they might be appropriate for climbs of major Alaskan or Himalayan summits.

Climbing standards, ideals, and ethics are continually changing and so are climbers' opinions of what, specifically, constitutes "good style." For example, in the Northwest, when an aid climb goes free, it is an improper application of the first ascent principle to continue to climb it artificially or in any manner which may deface the rock. As another example, expansion bolts may justifiably be placed as anchors on popular climbs where chocks or runners cannot be placed and/or where repeated piton placement would seriously deface cracks.

The "ultimate experience," if there is such a thing, is to make the first ascent of a major natural line using only natural means of protection. Since first ascents are becoming less frequent, repeat climbs should be in at least as good style as the first ascent and, in view of the continuing improvements to equipment and technique, in better style wherever possible.

The bulk of this chapter has dealt with rock-climbing ethics. However, the principle of climbing in good style might well be applied to climbs of an expeditionary nature. Until recently it has been generally accepted that the long difficult climbs found in Alaska, the Himalaya, and the Andes cannot be accomplished without many thousands of feet of fixed rope and the general expeditionary extravaganza. While quite true at the time of this writing, one need only look back to 1950 to see that climbs once thought to be impossible, or possible only with seige tactics, are now routinely done in alpine style. In the not-too-distant future it may be possible to do climbs such as the South Face of Annapurna in alpine style. Therefore, in view of the finite nature of mountains it would be admirable if expeditionary climbers of today would exercise restraint, leaving those climbs which cannot now be done in alpine style to some future generation with that capability.

An Invitation to Forge a New Ethic

Ethics do not demand the sacrifice of safety in climbing; rather, they demand viewing the act of climbing within the context of man's personal integrity and his stewardship of a finite planet. A climber's safety begins and ends with his efforts to avoid, control, and cope with climbing hazards. His safety being a personal matter, he must accept responsibility for himself when he climbs. He must know his limits and climb within them or accept the results when he goes beyond them. A climber's ethics begin with his realization that the climbing medium is the only one we will ever have, his understanding that he need not be a two-legged geological catastrophe, and acceptance of his rightful place within the functioning of the alpine environment. Ethics find their ultimate warrant for "thou shall" and "thou shall not" in the ideals of the individual and these ideals, as personal as his safety, must find their expression in the individual's acceptance of his own limitations and sense of responsibility to the climbing community of today and tomorrow.

Some writers who have dealt with this subject recently have approached it either belligerently or apologetically. This chapter is primarily for the benefit of the novice who has no frame of reference from which to form his own opinions and chart his own course in the mountains; however, many "old-timers" and experienced climbers can benefit from the discussion. If some climbers take issue with the ideas expressed, so be it. The topic can produce many hours of challenging debate.

The Mountaineers are legitimately concerned with the future of planet Earth and with the preservation of the entire alpine environment. There is no need for anyone to apologize for broaching this subject nor should any individual or group be expected to apologize for uninformed, thoughtless, or expedient actions of the past. The message of this chapter is that every individual and every group must accept their responsibility to think and act to ensure the preservation of all those qualities of the alpine scene which we treasure. Established practices must be examined and modified or discarded where necessary, and new, suitable procedures adopted. It is no longer enough to say "we didn't know" or "we didn't think"; in the context of rock climbing ethics, the club climber following the well-worn path up a popular climb and the rugged individualist blazing his own trail on a virgin wall *must* know and, more important, *must* think.

Supplementary Reading:

Aleith, R. C. *Bergsteigen*. Scottsdale, Arizona: R. C. Aleith, 1971.

Robbins, Royal. *Basic Rockcraft*. Glendale, California: La Siesta Press, 1971.

Robbins, Royal. *Advanced Rockcraft*. Glendale, California: La Siesta Press, 1973.

XI. Descending the Ingraham Glacier on Mt. Rainier. (Bob and Ira Spring)

PART FOUR

Snow and Ice Climbing

XII. Looking south across Névé Glacier and Snowfield Peak; North Cascades National Park. (Austin Post, University of Washington)

15 *

SNOW AND ICE
CLIMBING EQUIPMENT

SINCE THE MIDDLE 1960s the equipment and techniques of snow and ice climbing have been undergoing almost continuous improvement. New designs in crampons, ice axes, ice hammers, ice screws, and belaying aids all have contributed to better leader protection and more efficient climbing.

Ascents of difficult ice routes which once involved considerable risk now can be made with a significantly greater margin of safety — indeed ice climbing may be said to be at about the stage of development of rock climbing in the late 1950s, when today's standards were being evolved in Yosemite and one or two other centers. The principal difference is that ice climbing developments are occurring everywhere; no small select group and no geographical area has a monopoly.

While this chapter concentrates on equipment in current use, climbers must be aware that testing and modification are continually taking place and that it is in their own best interests to stay abreast of advances.

ICE AXES

Anywhere a climber encounters snow or ice the ice ax is his most valuable tool. With it he may probe for crevasses, belay, fashion an anchor, chop steps, or arrest a fall. Although not intended for use as a cane, axes are often used as such, to prop up weary climbers on trails and off and as an extra support while walking logs or fording streams. In the Pacific Northwest, even the hiker/backpacker finds an ax useful if not essential. This discussion concerns primarily the general-purpose ice ax most climbers and hikers select.

Parts of the Ax

Ice axes are basically simple tools, consisting of a *head* having a *pick* on one end and an *adze* on the other, and attached to the *shaft,* or handle, which terminates at the *spike*. The climber may attach the ax to himself with the *wristloop* to prevent its loss.

Head

In recent years a great deal of research has been done in ice ax design. Much of it has centered around the head, especially the pick. Generally the pick should be about 7 to 8 inches in length measured from the center of the head (or shaft); longer picks are unwieldly and shorter ones provide too little penetration for dependable self-arrest in all types of snow. Width of the pick makes very little difference as long as it is wide enough to withstand forces placed on it without buckling or bending.

The height of the pick makes little difference *except* when trying to arrest on hard snow. Then excessive height causes the pick to twist, or "rudder" out of the snow, especially when arresting from a sideward slide. There is no need for the pick to exceed 1 inch in height.

Teeth on the pick, usually cut within 2 or 3 inches of the tip, are useful for climbers who may use the ax as a hold (see Chapter 18) and to improve the arresting capabilities of a straight-picked ax. When placed nearer to the shaft, teeth are of limited value. Their purpose is to give greater holding power to the ax when the full length of the pick cannot be lodged in snow or ice; however, they can "bite" any time the pick is used and may make step-chopping frustrating and laborious.

A *chisel-tipped pick* is of much greater general use than a *pointed* one. The pointed pick may be useful to an ice climber because it penetrates ice and hard snow easily; however, it is far less efficient for cutting steps than the chisel-tip. Further, positive clearance (see Fig. 127) enables a chisel-tip to obtain the same penetration almost as easily and allows the climber to chop steps easily.

Positive clearance refers to the way in which the pick tip meets the slope (see diagram). The purpose is to provide a sharp point which meets the slope at an acute angle so the tip can claw its way through the surface. *Negative —* and *neutral clearance* picks tend to "skate" on hard, icy surfaces and do not penetrate them reliably during arrest attempts. Any sharply pointed pick, unless worn down, has this feature; chisel-tipped picks must be examined to be sure they do. Positive clearance should not exceed 10 degrees; if it does, the ax becomes too pointed to cut steps efficiently. If, on the other hand, it is less than 5 degrees, it becomes, in effect, a neutral-clearance tip. Clearance may be measured by placing the tip of the pick on a flat surface and holding the shaft parallel to the surface. The "top" of the tip should be about 1/16 (but no more) off the surface when the "bottom" is just touching. Although this feature is highly desirable, few manufacturers (at date of writing) have incorporated it in their axes; fortunately a file (NOT a grinding wheel) and a few minutes work will add this feature to any ax.

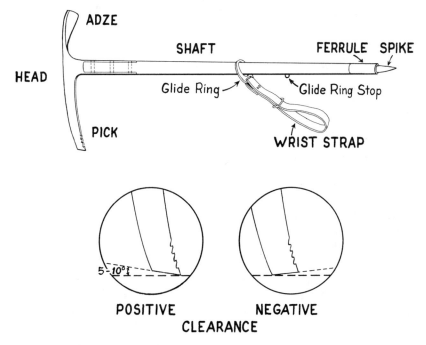

Fig. 127. Ice ax with parts named and inserts of pick clearance. Reference line for measuring pick clearance is parallel to shaft of ax.

The tip of the pick *must* be sharp and kept that way. This is true whether it is chisel-shaped or pointed. In days gone by (and better so) a concern with the appearance of safety, not matched with an understanding of what is really essential in safety, led many climbers to grind the tips of their axes into blunt, rounded points. Such axes became, in effect, neutrally-cleared and skated futilely on hard crusts or ice during arrest attempts. This practice is no longer followed and climbers whose axes have been mistreated in this manner are well advised to re-sharpen them.

Until the late 1960s, picks were made in one shape only — straight. Recognition of the advantages of curved or inclined ("drooped") picks dates back to the mid-1800s; however, until the recent upsurge of interest in ice climbing led to a rediscovery of these advantages, no axes were made this way. The pick is drooped to give it a "hooking" action in snow or ice which increases the ax's holding power when used as a handhold in steep ice climbing and causes it to dig in faster while arresting. Since the droop is matched fairly closely to the radius of swing of the ax, it is also considered an aid in stepchopping. This feature is desirable in anyone's ax; however, hikers and climbers not intending to go beyond the easiest terrain would probably not find it of sufficient benefit to warrant retiring their old axes and buying new ones with drooped picks.

Fig. 128. Ice ax head shapes. *Left* to *right;* straight pick and adze, "drooped" pick and curved adze, and inclined pick and adze.

Because the combination of positive clearance and drooping greatly increases the penetration and holding power of the ax, caution in applying an arrest may be advisable: the pick can dig in so quickly that a climber in a weak arrest position may be pulled out of position or even have the ax torn from his grasp. Good arrest technique and a firm grip on the ax prevent this; climbers who have been accustomed to older-style axes are advised to practice arrests when and if they acquire a modern ax.

Ax adzes appear in many configurations — flat, curved or deeply curved, straight-edged or scalloped, and straight-out or inclined. Few of these variations really offer any significant advantage to the user and the trend is generally back to a straight-edged, flat adze. Most important is making sure that the edge and corners have been dulled and rounded so they will not cut or gouge clothing and flesh.

One ax currently available features an inclined adze. This is a specialist's feature and of little value to a hiker or average climber. The inclined adze may, in fact, cause bruising or fracturing of the collarbone while arresting on a bumpy surface; however, it is excellent for cutting steps in hard snow.

The *carabiner hole* in the ax head is there to provide a handy way of carrying the ax when dealing with a short bit of rock; it should *never* be used for belaying. In any event, the presence or absence of a carabiner hole should not be a deciding factor when purchasing an ax.

Shaft

Until about 1970 nearly all ice ax shafts were made of wood. Dense, straight-grained hickory was considered to be best because it combined high strength with light weight. Ash, a lighter, cheaper wood, saw increasing use in the late 1950s and throughout the 1960s; however, as its use increased, so did reports of broken axes. Today more and more shafts are being made of metal, although many wood and laminated-wood shafts are still on the market.

The strength of the shaft is most important to boot-ax belays: the stronger the shaft, the greater the reliability of the belay, other things being equal. Any ax meeting UIAA standards of 880 pounds (applied to the midpoint of the shaft when the ax is suspended in two loops of rope 20 inches apart) is strong enough to handle almost any fall which will reasonably come on it when used in a boot-ax belay.

Ash shafts vary widely in strength, but even at best are still the weakest. Laminated-wood-shafts are about halfway between ash and hickory in strength — their principal advantage is that lamination results in shafts of uniform strength rather than in the widely varying strengths of natural materials. Good hickory shafts are surprisingly strong and compare favorably with some metal shafts. No wooden shaft, however, meets the the UIAA standards; metal is the surest way to guarantee a uniformly high-strength shaft for belays and arrests. Meeting this standard does not guarantee an ax will always perform perfectly under all conditions nor will failure to meet it guarantee one's early demise through failure of a too-weak ax. Nevertheless, a strong ax shaft cannot be a hazard and may well earn its way by providing the extra margin of safety where needed.

Fiberglassing ax shafts in general raises the strength of an ash shaft to about that of a good hickory shaft, but seems to offer no significant increase in strength to hickory shafts and has no real value when applied to metal ones. Since it may also lead to dry rot in the shaft of any wooden ax so treated, the practice is now considered obsolete.

On metal axes the spike is generally crimped, riveted, epoxied, or affixed to the shaft in a combination of these ways. In wooden axes the spike is inserted into the shaft and compressed in place by the ferrule. The spike is the "ground" end of the ax and, as such, receives the full brunt of the wear from use as a cane. Since the ax is intended to assist a climber on snow or ice, and a sharp spike does this better than a dull one, most climbers prefer to avoid using their axes as canes on rocky trails. Shape and length of the spike actually make little difference in the function of the ax, and like the carabiner hole, should not be considered important when choosing an ax.

Wristloops

One of the last things a climber wishes to see is his ax glissading out of sight down a long, steep snow slope or into a crevasse. He therefore uses some means of attaching it to himself. The traditional method is a short *wristloop* on a *glide ring*. The ring slides along the shaft between the head and the *glide ring stop* and allows the climber to hold either end of the ax without removing the loop from his wrist. When properly sized, this type of loop is satisfactory for most climbing and hiking. The glide ring stop may pose a hazard if it juts out too far: when attempting an arrest, the stop may snag in clothing or in mittens and delay application a little too long.

The "longthong" wristloop has become popular among climbers whose goal is the steeper, longer climbs and very difficult ice ascents. It consists of a loop of 5 mm perlon or light webbing reaching from the carabiner hole in the head of the ax almost to the bottom of the shaft. When the wrist is in the loop, the hand should just be able to reach the lowest point on the shaft to allow the climber to swing the ax for cutting steps. As an additional benefit, it avoids the need to weaken the shaft with a glide ring stop screw.

Selecting an Ax

Essentially, the selection of an ice ax reduces to two decisions: the features it should have and how long it should be. The individual should decide what type of hiking or climbing he intends to do, consider the features discussed above — perhaps listing those features he needs — and then start looking at catalogs or in local mountain shops. One recommendation for a good all-purpose ax would be one with a metal shaft, flat adze, and drooped, chisel-tipped pick with positive clearance.

The length of the ax has long been a subject of dispute. For years the ideal length was thought to be one which would reach from the heel of the hand to the ground beside the climber and allow a slight bend in the elbow. Though most climbers prefer shorter, less cumbersome axes, this advice is probably still valid for the hiker or backpacker, and an ax of this length is a particularly good choice when much crevasse probing is anticipated.

The most urgent use of an ice ax is in self-arrest and the ax should be sized to the individual to allow the most effective arresting technique. With either the pick or adze resting on the point of one shoulder, the spike should reach about 2 to 4 inches beyond the prominent bone on the opposite hip, and no farther. An ax thus sized is ideal for arrests, adequately long for belays, and convenient for stepcutting on all but very steep terrain; unfortunately, it makes downhill crevasse probing a misery.

Shorter axes (55 cm and less) are specialists' tools. Far more useful on steep slopes, they are tricky to arrest with anywhere. Most climbers find them good as second axes to supplement their all-around ice axes.

If selecting a wooden-shafted ax, make certain the grain is straight, dense, and runs parallel to the long axis of the shaft. There should be no knots in the wood and no signs of splintering whatever. Any ax not meeting these criteria is unsafe for any climber or hiker since it will probably fail the first time any significant load is placed on it.

Care of the Ax

While metal-shafted axes require almost no special care or treatment, wooden shafts need protection. Boiled linseed oil or a 50/50 mixture of linseed oil and turpentine should be rubbed into the wood and allowed to soak into the endgrain around the spike. To protect the interface between the metal spike and the lower portion of the shaft from rock, ice, and crampon damage, it should be wrapped with adhesive tape; if extended stepcutting in ice is anticipated, tape should also be wrapped around the upper part of the shaft, just under the head.

Any hole through an ax shaft, such as for the rivets which hold the head on the shaft or the screw holes for attaching the glide ring stop, are points of potential failure. A deep dent or gouge (not to be confused with the minor nicks which accumulate on any ax shaft and which are relatively harmless) may lead to collapse of the shaft under load. To avoid trouble, inspect the shaft of the ax, especially at these points, before every climb. On metal-shafted axes, check that the threads holding the glide ring stop screw have not been stripped out of the soft aluminum shaft.

Clean any mud or dirt off the ax after each use and rub off any rust which may accumulate. If the ax is to be stored for some time, a light coat of oil should be applied. Wooden-shafted axes should be either hung by their heads or laid flat to prevent bowing of the shaft.

Management of the Ax

Useful as it is, the ax can still become an awkward, encumbering nuisance when travel alternates between snow and steep brushy or rocky terrain which calls for the use of both hands. The practice of dangling the ax from the wrist by the loop is awkward, but suffices for short stretches. Somewhat better is hanging the ax from the waistloop by a carabiner, either clipped through the carabiner hole or by passing the shaft down through a carabiner on the waistloop, spike first. Many axes, especially the shorter ones, can be carried conveniently in a piton hammer holster.

It is often too time-consuming to place the ax inside the pack or to attach it to the pack by the ice ax carrier, unless the ax will not be needed for some time. A quick alternative is to pass the shaft down between the packstraps, holding the ax between the back and sack. Angling the shaft to one side keeps it from being pushed against the back by the pack and is much more comfortable.

Properly maintained axes are sharp, potentially hazardous implements and must be handled with this in mind. Guards should *always* be used on sharpened picks, spikes, and adzes when use is not imminent. When carrying the ax without guards, these points should be away from the body and, where practical, towards the ground. In transport the sharp points should be protected from damage (and from inflicting damage) by rubber or leather protectors. This is essential when shipping axes, especially by air.

CRAMPONS

Numerous designs of crampons have been used in the past and many remain on the market, but those most generally accepted nowadays are 10-point models with vertical toe points and 12-point styles with slanting or horizontal points. Crampons with fewer than 10 points, such as the instep type, do not provide sufficient security in most situations.

Vertical toe points are excellent for easier climbs and adequate if the party is willing and has the time to cut steps on steeper portions. Vertical toe points are easier to handle in self-arrest and are also less likely to slice open a leg or snag clothing.

For any technical ice climbing requiring front-pointing, 12-point crampons are essential. Arriving with 10-point crampons for a climb on which everyone else is planning to front-point, thus causing the party to cut steps, is a short route to unpopularity.

Forward-slanting 10-points were thought for a while to be a good compromise; however this has proved not to be the case since this style not only fails to work as well as 12-points but has the same tendency to catch on the surface in self-arrest and to snag clothing and slash legs.

Besides point configuration there are three other considerations when buying crampons, all of which affect their cost. First, heavyweight models made of mild steel are usually less expensive and not as strong as the lighter steel alloys. Second, some of the older adjustable crampons are not very strong and should be avoided; however, the newer models are as strong as the nonadjustable. Their main disadvantage now is the price, which may range from a few dollars more per pair for the partially adjustable models to twice as much for totally adjustable ones, but this can be easily justified if the same pair of crampons will have to fit more than one pair of boots. The third consideration, whether to purchase rigid or flexible crampons, should be decided on the basis of the type of climbing intended; if one does not plan to do much front-pointing it is not necessary to buy rigid crampons, but if considerable front-pointing is anticipated, rigid crampons are a better choice as they give greater support, putting less strain on calf muscles and allowing more front-pointing without fatigue. They are, however, considerably more expensive than flexible crampons and have a tendency to break *unless used on very rigid climbing boots*; this fault has to some extent been remedied in the newer models by strengthening possible flex points.

Proper fit is essential. When crampons are purchased they must be tried with the boots on which they will be worn. Attachment prongs should contact the boot snugly without significant "bending to fit." (Follow the manufacturer's suggestions as to which parts can be bent without weakening the structure.) When the boot is lifted from the floor, the prongs should hold the crampon to the boot without assistance from the straps. About one-half to two-thirds of the front points of 12-point crampons should protrude beyond the toe of the boot and all others should be close to the side of the sole. All points should be close to the side of the sole in 10-point models.

The method of attachment is as important as style. Best of all is a buckle harness of neoprene-coated nylon: it is strong, does not absorb water,

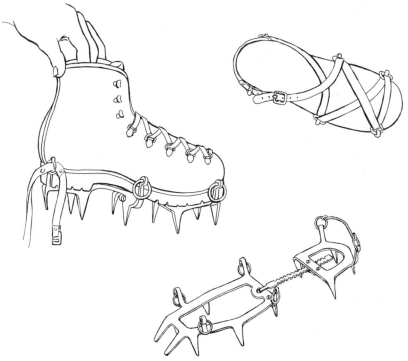

Fig. 129. Crampons. *Upper left,* ten-point crampons showing proper fit. *Upper right,* strapping crampon to boot. *Lower,* twelve-point adjustable crampon (Salewa).

collect snow, or stretch, is almost totally unbreakable, and can be moved
from one pair of crampons to another, thereby somewhat overcoming the
objection of high purchase price. Almost as good is chrome-tanned
leather; however, leather stretches and may eventually rot and break.
Nylon cord is inexpensive, easily removed, and easily replaced in an
emergency. Nylon strapping is about equal in strength to nylon cord but
faster to put on; however, abrasion can be a serious problem. Cotton
webbing is least desirable since it readily picks up snow and frequently
freezes at the buckles, sometimes making it necessary to cut the straps to
remove the crampons. Slip-type buckles are to be avoided since they tend
to break more easily than regular buckles.

When attaching the harness the buckles should be positioned to cinch
on the outward side of the boots. Special care must be taken to strap the
crampons tightly to the boots, running the strap through each attachment
prong or ring and tying off the end with a double knot. If crampons do not
have heel loops, ankle straps should be long enough to be crossed behind
the boot before being secured to prevent boots from sliding backward out
of the crampons; many crampons have been lost and some exciting situations have developed because this precaution was not taken. With
single strap crampon attachment another possible hazard is failure of the
strap on a steep climb, resulting in loss of a crampon. This can be
prevented by passing a nylon string through the two heel attachments and
tying them over the instep. When trimming new straps, allowance must be
made for gaiters, which sometimes cover the instep of the boot.

The novice is well advised to become thoroughly familiar with his
crampons and their straps before going on his first climb with them,
because he may have to put them on by feel or flashlight. The best method
is to lay each crampon on the snow or ice with all rings and straps outward,
then place the boot on the crampon and tighten the straps. Even modern
neoprene-coated nylon straps should be checked from time to time to
make sure they are tight, have not been cut, and are not trailing loops or
loose strap ends which could trip the unwary climber.

Crampon maintenance demands close attention, both to metal parts
and straps, which must be checked regularly for abrasion. For maximum
effectiveness points must be kept reasonably sharp, despite the increased
hazard of slicing legs; dull spikes give a false illusion of security and
demand greater effort to drive into the slope. Exactly parallel alignment is
important to minimize leg slashing by splayed points. Many ice routes are
interrupted by short passages over rock; crampons are expected to take
such punishment without falling apart, but over a period of time the points
are inevitably dulled or splayed. Sharpening should be done with a file
and never with a grinding wheel, which might overheat the metal, thereby
destroying the temper so necessary for hardness and rigidity. It is also

ill-advised to straighten bent points or frames by hammering: if the weakened metal does not break in the straightening process it may do so under some future stress. In fact there seems to be no satisfactory method for straightening points except by taking them to a qualified metal worker.

Crampons are dangerous. When they are worn every step must be taken with care to avoid snagging trousers, gashing legs, or stepping on ropes. When carried, some way of disarming the spikes is mandatory; sad experience has proven the extreme hazard of loose, sharp iron dancing about during a fall. A good method is to cover the points with rubber-spider crampon-point protectors and carry the crampons inside the pack, or strapped firmly to the outside with the covered points inward. Some climbers cut lengths of surgical tubing into 1-inch pieces which are placed on each individual point.

SNOW FLUKES AND PICKETS

Belaying on steep snow has always been a critical problem. It is difficult to anchor the belayer using any of the conventional methods employed in rock climbing. As a result, specialized belays which use the ice ax in various ways has been developed, as described in Chapter 16. These techniques, however, still give only limited security.

The first attempts, in the early 1940s, to create secure anchors resulted in *snow pickets* which are still in use today. When these 3- to 4-foot-long aluminum tubes (or T-sections, about 1 inch in diameter or width) are to be used as belay or rappel anchors, they are driven into the snow in pairs, one anchoring the other. Pickets are also used for anchoring fixed ropes in expedition climbing. However, for alpine-style climbing they are prohibitively cumbersome and in addition subject to failure because of narrow cross section.

Recent attempts to find more suitable anchors have led to development of *"deadmen"* or *snow flukes.* In their simplest form a 12-inch-long piece of metal is merely buried with a runner coming to the surface; this can pull out if snow conditions are not just right. Better resistance to pull-out is gained with a large flat piece of metal driven into the snow surface at an angle, acting in the same manner as the fluke of an old-fashioned anchor. With the attachment of a wire cable there is no danger of the runner being cut or weakened by continual wetting. The softer the snow the larger the size of the plate needed. Stability can often be increased by bending the plate slightly. When using flukes it is very important that the proper angle with the surface be maintained — otherwise, instead of going deeper when pulled, they come to the surface.

A second danger — that of the cable acting as a lever arm on hard snow, causing the fluke to pop out — can be prevented by carefully cutting a channel in the snow for cables so that the pull comes directly at the plate.

If attention is paid to placement, great security can be obtained from snow flukes as belay and rappel anchors. Used in conjunction with a properly emplaced fluke a sitting or standing hip belay on snow is very secure.

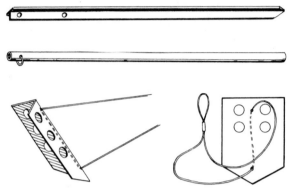

Fig. 130. Pickets, *upper.* Snow fluke, *lower.*

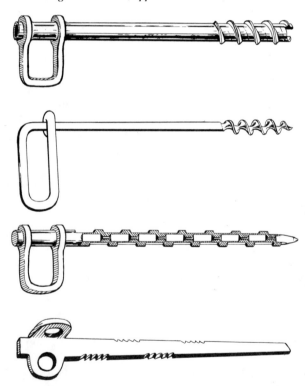

Fig. 131. Ice screws and pitons. *Top* to *bottom:* tubular screw, coathanger type, Wart Hog, and T-shaped ice piton.

ICE SCREWS

The first ice pitons were extra long, blade-type, rock pitons with holes, notches, or bulges to give a better grip on ice. After World War II climbers experimented with new designs, T- or X-shaped or tubular in cross section, with greater shaft area to decrease the load-per-square-inch on the ice and with holes to help the shaft freeze into the slope. Ice screws developed by the Russians first appeared in the early 1960s. Enthusiasts claimed that ice screws would revolutionize climbing, bringing security to the slopes where previously the only rule was "the leader must not fall, and nobody else, either." Critics, however, felt the screws were not all that superior to older ice pitons; this was particularly true of the older, lightweight "coathanger," which has little use today except for direct aid. Ice screws were improved during the late 1960s and early 1970s and today are considered to provide reliable protection for the leader.

Tubular screws are very strong and are the most reliable. They are, however, difficult to place in hard or water ice since they tend to clog and have a large cross section. Their main advantage is that they minimize "spalling" (a crater-like splintering of the ice around the shaft of the screw) by allowing the displaced ice to work itself out through the core of the screw. If the core of ice remaining in the screw is frozen in place, it jams the screw in subsequent placements; it may be removed by pushing with a length of stiff wire or by heating with a cigarette lighter. This type of screw requires both hands for placement; however, once it is started, the pick of an ice hammer or ax inserted in the eye allows the climber to gain the advantage of considerable leverage. Removal is quite easy and melt-out slow due to the large cross section.

Heavier *"coathanger"-type screws* are a tremendous advance over the original Marwas since they can actually be relied upon to stop a fall. They are easier to start in hard ice than tubular screws and can often be placed with one hand, although it may be necessary to tap them while twisting as they are started. Their holding power is less than tubular screws, they tend to fracture hard ice and, under heavy load, tend to shear through the ice because of their small cross section.

Developed as an attempt to make an easy-to-place and easy-to-remove screw, the *solid screws* are driven in like a piton and screwed out. They offer excellent protection in water ice but are less effective in other forms. Melt-out is sometimes rapid because of limited thread displacement and, under load, they tend to shear through the ice, as do coathanger screws.

Before placement of ice screws or pitons, any soft snow or loose ice should be scraped or chopped away until a hard and trustworthy surface is reached. A small starting hole punched out with the pick or spike of the ax or hammer facilitates a good grip for the starting threads or teeth. The screw is pressed firmly into the ice and twisted in at the same time, angled slightly uphill against the anticipated direction of pull. Ice pitons are, of course, driven straight in but must also be angled against the pull that would result from a fall.

Any spalling or splintering of the ice that occurs weakens the placement, rendering the anchor useless. When this occurs, the screw should be

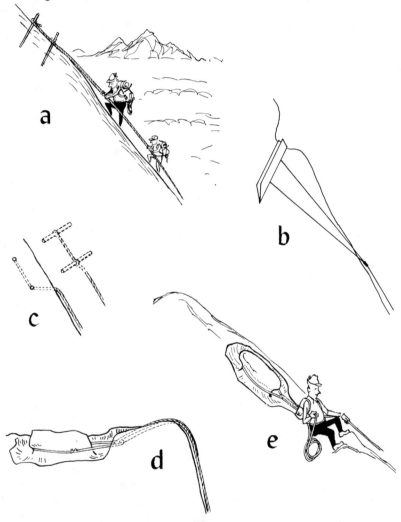

Fig. 132. Use of snow anchors.

a. pickets to anchor fixed rope
b. snow fluke in place
c. deadman anchors in place
d. bollard
e. bollard as belay anchor

removed and another placement tried 1 or 2 feet away. Some glacier ice will spall near the surface but, by continuing to place the screw and gently chopping out the shattered ice, a deep, safe placement may be obtained. As a general rule, short screws or pitons should be used in hard ice and long ones in soft(er) ice. They should *always* be placed all the way in to the eye.

When removing ice hardware, take care not to bend it since this diminishes its effectiveness in future use.

ICE HAMMERS

As happened with rock climbing a generation earlier, new equipment and techniques have advanced ice climbing to the point of being a sport in its own right as well as a technique used in climbing mountains.

During this evolution it was found that when ice is steep enough to front-point, an ice ax alone does not give enough balance and security. To remedy this, an ice screw was sometimes carried in the free hand; this helped to some extent but the screw did not penetrate ice very well or provide much stability. Ice daggers, basically thick ice picks, were developed but were tiring to use and pulled out easily if a proper angle with the ice was not maintained.

A major development was the combination of piton hammer and ice ax, called ice hammer, alpine hammer, or North Wall hammer (an ice or alpine hammer is about the length of a piton hammer, while a North Wall hammer is as long as some of the very short ice axes). The head consists of the pick part of an ice ax, heavily drooped, and the pounding part of a piton hammer; a wrist loop is added to give support and greater security. With a short ax in one hand and an ice hammer in the other, it is possible to move quite rapidly and safely up very steep ice. In addition a hammer gives leverage to twist ice screws into hard ice or to bash in ice pitons.

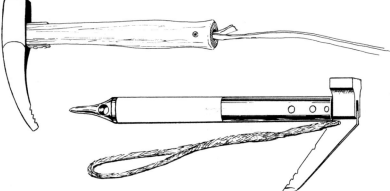

Fig. 133. Ice hammers. *Top,* Chouinard alpine hammer. *Bottom,* Terrordactyl (British).

Another variation, an ice ax with a shaft only slightly longer than a piton hammer, is used on extremely steep slopes where even a 55 cm ax would be cumbersome. These are, however, of limited use for standard alpine climbs.

The British have introduced changes in the picks of some very short axes and ice hammers. Instead of curved picks, these have a sharp angle (of 55 degrees) with the shaft. Requiring a slight downward pull as it hits the ice, the pick usually takes two or three blows to set, but gives very good security. It seems at this time that choice of the British design or the conventional drooped pick is a matter of personal preference. Both these designs now make obsolete the older North Wall hammer with its straight pick and longer shaft.

16 *

SNOW TRAVEL AND ARREST TECHNIQUES

IT IS NOT POSSIBLE to become a competent snow mountaineer in one season, no matter how intensive the climbing schedule. One quickly learns that the snow of April is but a distant cousin to the snow of August, that the grim flutings of a northern precipice bear not the vaguest resemblance to the slushy crystals on the southern benches, that the same snowfield may be transformed from a fine frozen highway at dawn to a bottomless bog in the afternoon and to a sheet of ice moments after sunset. In one season a climber can learn much, and be conditioned to learn more, but he cannot learn all; the repertoire of snow is too large for all its tricks to be encountered in one year — or in ten.

Fundamental to the understanding of snow is Chapter 24, with its laboratory outlook; another way to consider snow is from the rough empirical standpoint of climbing technique. For easy presentation the term *snow* is reserved in the present context for slopes that are neither very hard nor very steep. *Ice* climbing, treated in Chapter 18, encompasses slopes that are hard and/or steep and thus demand a more complex approach. *Glaciers*, the subject of Chapter 17, are almost entirely composed of snow and ice but have some peculiar characteristics, most notably crevasses.

SELECTING THE ROUTE

The wise mountaineer begins routefinding long before approaching the peak, starting indeed with observations made during winter. For instance, a prolonged thaw in late winter followed by a cold snowy spring indicates need for caution; weeks or months later the thaw's thick crust may hold a heavy load of spring snow poised to avalanche. More immediately, the weather and temperature during the ascent and in the period preceding are of the greatest importance.

Routefinding on snow is complicated by the quest for easy walking on one hand, and on the other, the desire to avoid avalanches and collapsing cornices. Choice is particularly excruciating when ease and security are mutually exclusive.

Good Walking

Spring

Snow is considered excellent if the climber can stand on or near the surface, only fair if he sinks to his calves; when immersion is knee-deep or greater it is good only for building character. The *crusts* discussed in Chapter 24 have a major influence on route selection in winter and spring. *Differential consolidation* is equally important. South and west slopes, bearing the full heat of afternoon sun, consolidate earlier in the season and quicker after storms, offering hard surfaces when east and north slopes are still soft and unstable. Similarly, dirty snow absorbs more heat than clean; slopes darkened by rocks, dust, or uprooted vegetation usually provide relatively solid footing.

The principles that apply in large apply also to *micro-exposures.* The walking on one side of a ridge or gully, or even on one side of a clump of trees or a large boulder, is often more solid than the other. When the going is very bad it is well to detour toward any surface with a different appearance and possibly better support. Sometimes unstable and stable crust may be only a foot or two apart, and deep slush only a step from hard ice.

Location of the best and easiest route varies from day to day and hour to hour. In cloudy weather snow conditions are unlikely to change significantly around the clock, but a clear cold night after a hot day suggests an early start to take full advantage of the strong crusts on open slopes. As the sun rises higher, the search shifts for shadows where remnants of crust linger, or alternatively, for dirty snow. Late on a hot afternoon all crusts deteriorate and the deep shade of trees and steep cliffs offer the best slopes of a bad lot.

Early-season snowcover is scattered with pitfalls; particular caution is needed in the zone between deep snow and clear ground. As soon as snow falls on a hillside it begins a slow protracted settling called *creep*, moving away from trees and rocks, forming a fissure below each. New snow may fill the holes, called *moats* — or it may merely camouflage them. Later in the season the moat below a large rock or cliff may be as wide and deep and difficult as a crevasse. *Differential melting* both initiates and emphasizes fissures; snow adjacent to objects such as logs, brush, or rocks is likely to be hollow. When the temperature of the ground is at or above freezing, extensive melting occurs at the ground-snow interface. The route should follow either solid snow or solid ground, avoiding margins; when they must be crossed, catlike steps avert wrenched ankles and broken legs.

Summer

As the months progress into summer, walking conditions become so nearly uniform that the major difference is between the hard surfaces of early morning and the morasses of hot afternoons. The Cascades, by July in an average year, present summer snow conditions. By August — again on the average — consolidation is so complete that snow conditions do not change significantly with time of day. However, new vexations develop. *Suncups* may grow into *nieve penitentes* through which travel is a relentless, exhausting grind. Moreover, consolidation is not an unmixed blessing, for on the hard slopes of autumn every foot of the route may require crampons or step-chopping, and the climber remembers fondly the yielding surfaces of spring in which mere swings of the boot made such superb steps.

Avalanche Hazard

Snow avalanches occur by the thousands every winter and spring in mountainous country. Although these avalanches generate tremendous forces and are a serious threat to a traveler, knowledge of their characteristics can help him avoid being caught by one, and to survive if buried. Experts do not fully understand all the causes of these complex phenomena, nor can avalanche conditions be predicted with certainty. However, the guidelines given here will aid the alpine traveler in developing judgment about the presence and degree of avalanche danger. Further information is given in the section on "Stability of the Snow Cover" in Chapter 24.

Avalanche Conditions

A high percentage (about 80) of all avalanches occur during and shortly after storms: snow falling at the rate of 1 inch per hour, or more, or snowfall accumulating to a depth of a foot or more, increases avalanche danger rapidly. Storms starting with low temperature and dry snow, followed by rising temperatures, are even more likely to cause avalanches, because the dry snow at the lower level forms a poor bond and has insufficient strength to support the heavier snow deposited later in the storm. Rainstorms or spring weather with warm winds and cloudy nights can warm the snowcover; the resulting free and percolating water may cause wet snow avalanches. Many other factors — temperature, wind, and even the shape of the snow crystals — can also affect or create avalanche conditions. Rapid changes in temperature and wind — particularly if sustained at 15 miles per hour and over — cause adjustments in the snowpack and affect its stability. Small snow crystals — needles and pellets — result in more dangerous conditions than the usual star-shaped forms.

Location can be as important a factor as internal conditions: snow on north-facing slopes is more likely to slide in midwinter, while south-facing slopes are dangerous in spring and on sunny days. Because wind-deposited snows add depth and create hard, hollow-sounding wind slabs, leeward slopes are more dangerous than windward slopes, which generally have better compacted snow of lesser depth.

Signs and Tests

New avalanches in the vicinity indicate dangerous conditions. Little *sunballs* or cartwheels roll spontaneously down a slope during the warming of loose snow and frequently indicate deep instability. A slope actively sunballing, or streaked with tracks, may be dangerous. *Spontaneous surface slides* can also occur on fundamentally sound slopes, the degree of danger depending on the depth of snow involved. *Surface slides which start from the climber's tracks* cause alarm unnecessarily unless they tend to deepen, involving lower snow layers. If any of these symptoms of instability are encountered and the route leads onto slopes that have had even greater exposure to the sun or are steeper than those being negotiated, the need for increased caution is apparent.

Throwing rocks onto a slope is too localized a test to be sensitive, but allows at least some rough conjectures; if a rock can start even a small avalanche a man can do much better. Indeed, short of mortar bombardment the *best test is the climber himself.* A well-belayed person can find out a good deal by deliberate attempts to avalanche a suspected slope; the belay must obviously be so placed that it cannot be involved if the attempt is successful. It must also be kept in mind that danger can vary within the slope. Only a few feet away from a point proven safe, increased steepness or greater exposure to sun or some unknown local condition may be just enough to trigger a slide.

Avoiding the Hazard

According to the classic law of avalanches there is least danger on ridges, more on the valley floor, and most on inclined slopes. Even when the entire alpine world is shuddering from the roar of sliding snow the ridges may be safe, though perhaps presenting serrate profiles or cornices that cancel their usefulness. A valley floor is the catchment basin for avalanches. In narrow-floored canyons the danger is obvious, but often equally great on a broad plain surrounded by mountains; there are recorded instances of avalanches sweeping over the flat for more than a mile, and even climbing the opposite side of a valley. Avalanches are most common on slopes of 30 to 45 degrees but large avalanches do occur on slopes ranging from 25 to 60 degrees.

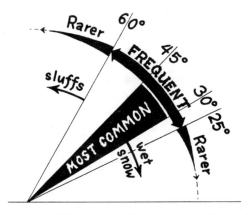

Fig. 134. Avalanche probability as a function of slope angle. Angles are shown in degrees.

Slides rarely start in dense forest or closely spaced rock projections on slopes, but such obstructions are little protection when a large avalanche comes from above, witness borne by the shattered trees in avalanche fans and the wide swaths cut through old timber. Downslanting brush and small trees tell plainly their slope is so frequently swept that timber has no chance to grow.

Avalanches usually follow existing channels. Gullies are many times more dangerous than adjacent slopes, their existence proclaiming them as natural chutes. Furthermore, a slide on any one slope within a gully's drainage system can sweep the entire main channel, and by undercutting every tributary on its descent may either pick up bigger loads or leave the tributaries poised and ready to discharge their volleys at the slightest disturbance.

The climber should glance upward frequently along the way. He will thus avoid routes exposed to cornices, snow perched precariously on rock ledges, or masses of icicles. Their collapse could cause a fall which, even if it did not immediately overwhelm the party, might disturb an otherwise stable slope.

Passage through Danger

Since passage through dangerous terrain is sometimes necessary, there remains to be considered how the hazards can be minimized for a party forced to cross a questionable slope. Although avalanches have been considered thus far as a menace sweeping down on the climber from above, relatively few victims are claimed by such slides. Most avalanches that involve a climber are triggered by the climber himself, posing the twofold problem of attempting not to disturb a slope, and if unsuccessful in this, of minimizing the consequences.

Whenever possible the party should *keep above the avalanche danger*. If a ridge route is not feasible and sidehills must be crossed, a doubtful traverse is taken high, at the very top of the slope, leaving most of the dangerous snow below the party. It should be remembered that snow is tautly stretched over protuberances and firmly compressed in hollows — convex slopes are thus more prone to avalanche than concave ones. For instance, the outer lip of a hillside bench may be perfectly sound while the steep slopes below it are weak with tension. Short slopes may be as dangerous as long ones.

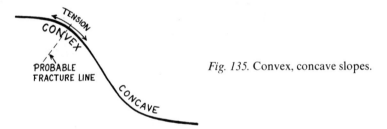

Fig. 135. Convex, concave slopes.

When the route lies up a questionable slope, general stepkicking practice is modified from the switchbacking described later in the chapter, which undercuts snow, to a path *straight up the fall line*. Only one person moves at a time, the others watching from safe places, ready to warn him if a slide starts or to rescue him if he is caught. If the slope is very narrow a firmly anchored belayer can safeguard each climber, the belay rope acting in the same manner as an avalanche cord in event the climber is caught in a severe avalanche. A belayer should not tie himself to the rope, for once a climber has been engulfed in a wet, heavy avalanche, his belayer might as well try to snub an express train, and risks being snatched into the slide himself.

Before venturing onto a suspected slope each person should put on warm clothing and mittens. All equipment should be loose and free to be thrown away, not only so it will not drag him down, but also because loose articles provide clues to the location of a buried person. The rucksack may be carried in the hands, ready to throw away or to clutch in front of the face to gain breathing space. During winter mountaineering where many of the slopes traveled are of dubious stability each person should trail from his waist about 100 feet of bright-colored avalanche cord.

The crossing is made gingerly on foot, only one person at a time, with long smooth strides, taking care not to cut a trench across the slope, such as is efficiently done by skis. Persons following the leader step carefully in the same footprints. The party is silent, the better to hear the start of an avalanche and sound the alarm.

Trying to outrun an avalanche is futile; the climber should dash for the side of the slope or at least for a rock or tree to which he can cling. As a last resort, he should throw aside all equipment, jam his ax deeply into the underlying snow, and hang on. If carried away he should fight to keep on the surface, swimming on his back with head uphill, flailing his arms and legs. If buried, he must inhale deeply before the snow stops to expand his ribs and raise his arms or hands over his face to make a breathing space.

Dry, powdery snow poses slight danger of quick suffocation, containing trapped air and being loose enough to allow respiration. In heavy, wet snow immediate suffocation is probable, even if a person's face is above the surface. A cubic foot of wet snow weighs as much as 55 pounds; packed solidly after the slide stops, it holds the climber like a vise, compressing his ribs and preventing respiration. Thus he must obtain breathing room while in motion. Rescue must come quickly, for wet snow contains little air and his breath will soon glaze and seal the surface around his face. Once the avalanche stops and struggling appears futile, he must conserve his energy and oxygen by waiting quietly for help, listening for the sound of rescuers, shouting only when there is some chance of being heard.

The techniques of avalanche rescue are covered in Chapter 22. However, a hasty search can be immediately initiated by the rest of the party provided that they carefully observe, first, the *point on the slope where the victim was caught*; second, the *point where he disappeared*; and third, the *point on the moving surface of the avalanche where he disappeared*, noting these with respect to fixed objects nearby — trees or rocks.

Avalanches are not to be trifled with. Any safe alternate route, however much longer, more tiring, and difficult, is preferable to one in doubt. When no safe route of ascent can be found the only sensible procedure is to turn back. If, on the return, descent is cut off by imminent avalanching, the party should sit down and wait for afternoon or evening cold to stabilize the slopes. After shadows cover the snow, time must be allowed for it to freeze and consolidate, since freezing itself sometimes starts a slide. During periods of general danger all travel should be in the morning or evening — or even at night.

Two fallacies are worth noting. One is the belief that established tracks are safe; conditions change quickly and climbers have been killed in footsteps made the day before. The other is the belief that clearing loose snow before the descent reduces the threat; though safe and practicable on small slopes where the descending party will spend but a very few minutes, this common practice can result in further slides from undercutting.

There is no expert in the world who can precisely calculate avalanche risk. Any climber who repeatedly approaches the limits of safety is certain to make occasional trespasses into danger zones. The way to become an old experienced climber in the due course of time rather than prematurely is to limit oneself to conservative estimates and to allow a comfortable margin for error.

Cornice Hazard

The shape of the ridge crest determines the extent of cornice-building. Generally speaking, a ridge that slopes on one side and breaks into an abrupt cliff on the other develops gigantic cornices, whereas a knife-edge ridge or one gentle on both sides has only a tiny cornice, if any at all. When the physical features are right for cornice-building, wind direction decides their exact location, and since storm winds have definite patterns in any given mountain range, most cornices in the same area face in the same direction. In the mountains of Washington State, for example, most storms blow from the southwest and the majority of cornices therefore overhang on the north and east. Since these same exposures were steepened by past glaciation the ridges are ideally shaped for the purpose. It must be remembered that temporary or local wind deflection can contradict the general pattern. In rare instances cornices are even built one atop the other, facing in opposite directions, the lower one partially destroyed and hidden by later formations.

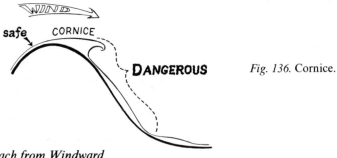

Fig. 136. Cornice.

Approach from Windward

From windward a cornice gives little indication of its presence, appearing as a smooth slope that runs out to meet the sky. Observation of surrounding ridges tells a great deal about the probable frequency, location, and size of cornices in the immediate area, not only on the high divides but on subsidiary ridges, knolls, and boulders. Fracture lines from partial collapse are sometimes visible, either as deep cracks or as slight indentations.

Not every snowy ridge conceals a cornice, but great care must be exercised in finding out whether any particular one does or not. If at all possible a safe vantage point should be found — a rock promontory or tree jutting through the crest — from which the lee side of the ridge is clearly visible. Otherwise the belayed leader approaches the ridge at right angles, probing with his ax and testing with his weight. Only when the extent of the overhang has been clearly established should other members of the party join him.

To insure a sufficient margin of safety the party must follow a course along a corniced crest well behind the probable fracture line, which is sometimes difficult to determine, since the line of fracture may extend 30 feet or more back from the lip of the cornice. Moreover, though rocks or trees projecting from the snow suggest safety, if they are the tops of buttresses the ridge joining them may curve far back into bays supporting wide cornices. Many a party has looked back along a ridge and shuddered at the sight of its tracks poised over a chasm.

Approach from Leeward

From leeward a cornice is readily apparent, resembling a wave frozen in the act of breaking. At close range the overhang is an awesome spectacle, but if the weather is cold enough the climber may forge ahead without fear, trusting the cornice to be a strongly engineered structure. It is even possible, and often necessary, to force a direct passage while crossing a pass or seeking a summit route on the far side of the ridge. A late-season cornice that is almost completely broken down need cause little concern, but earlier in the year the route of approach should be chosen with care, keeping as much as possible among trees or along crests of spurs, away from the line of fall. It is easiest to penetrate an overhang where a rock spur leads toward the summit or where a partial collapse has occurred.

Cutting through a healthy cornice is a task only to be undertaken if the structure is judged strong and solid. First the leader must bring up his second so that he will be belayed close to the problem at hand. The point of least overhang is attacked, with a belayer positioned beyond danger. The leader cuts straight uphill, undermining as little of the mass as possible, preferably standing to one side of the path he is cutting. Once he has surmounted the crest his immediate task is to install a sound belay behind the fracture zone before attempting to bring up his companions.

CLIMBING

Pace

On long snow slopes the depressing sensation that no progress is being made often tempts beginners to adopt a "dash-and-gasp" pace, trying to rush the objective. This inevitably fails, requiring frequent halts for recuperation. The only sure way to gain the summit is to find a suitable pace that can be maintained, then maintain it.

The rest step, described in Chapter 6, is one of the most important techniques of a snow climber, and its relaxed, machinelike regularity must be practiced to perfection. The upward step, the rest, the breath — these follow a regular sequence, at a tempo that can be maintained without excessive tiring of the legs or shortness of breath, in a rhythm that ideally could be paced by a metronome. Meanwhile, and often equally important, the climber foils the despair born of monotony and weariness by such spiritual resources as he may possess, but not failing, in his mental wanderings, to stay alert to any new potential danger.

Stepkicking

In soft snow on steeper slopes, pits must be stamped for solid footing. On hard snow the surface is solid enough, but slippery, and level platforms must be kicked. In both cases the step is made by swinging the leg — not by pushing the foot alone. In hard snow when one or two blows do not suffice, crampons should be used.

Steps *spaced evenly and rather close together* are easiest to make and easiest to follow in good balance. Often the spacing must be closer than the step-maker needs for himself, since those following may have shorter legs.

Climbing parties travel in *single file*, when ascending, letting one man at a time do the work. The physical exertion of the leader is greater than that of any other member of the party, and he is meanwhile constantly on the alert to safeguard those behind him and to choose the best route. The lead should therefore be changed regularly, whenever practical, so that no one climber remains in front until exhausted.

The rest of the party members use the same leg-swing as the first man, improving the steps as they climb. The cardinal rule is that the *foot must be kicked into the step*; simply walking on the existing platform does not set the boot securely in position. In compact snow the kick should be somewhat low, skimming off the floor and thus enlarging the step by deepening. In very soft snow it is usually easier to bring the boot down from above, shearing off a layer of snow which strengthens the step.

Etiquette

Climbing can be tiring and sometimes dangerous. A thoughtless climber adds to the weariness, to the exasperation that accompanies weariness, and to the danger. Even when unroped each member of a party is dependent on the consideration of all the other members, and everyone should observe certain simple rules of courtesy.

The leader who has exceptionally long legs and kicks steps useful only for himself does the party little service, since the followers have to strain to reach the steps, or must kick new steps, in either case resulting in a greater expenditure of energy and consequently a slower speed. The fellow who breaks out an excessive number of steps should mend his technique, if not to conserve his energy then at least to placate his wrathful friends. When a step is broken repairs are, for the sake of party rhythm, left to the next man. The stepbreaker should, however, take care to use proper foot-sequence in re-entering the line; those behind do not relish following a person with two left feet. It is unwise to walk in close-order drill; not only does the man ahead have the unpleasant sensation of hot pursuit; but he lacks room to control slips. *Another climber's fall line should always be avoided.* If it is necessary to pass it is done *below* the man ahead. Passing on the uphill side may endanger others in case of a fall and usually fills the steps with snow. Unless each climber maintains a regular pace he breaks the party rhythm. The erratic walker is a nuisance, alternately breathing down the neck of the man ahead and blocking the man behind.

Switchbacking Uphill

Ascending by traverses, which allows body weight to be supported by the entire foot rather than merely the toe, gives the most altitude for the least effort. Therefore on steep slopes when the goal is directly above the climber it is customary to make a zigzag or switchbacking path, which has the additional advantage of alternating strain on the feet, ankle, legs, and arms.

The critical phase of switchbacking is at the point of *changing direction.* If the slope is steep, the *pivot is made on the outside foot.* A climber with the upper slope on his right kicks the left (outside) foot directly into the slope. Weight is then transferred entirely onto this toes-in turning step, and the first step is kicked in the opposite direction. The upper slope is now on the left and the right foot has the outside position. The *turning step,* particularly critical since the pivot puts the body temporarily out of balance, is made deeper and wider than others.

Sidehill Gouging

The human body is so constructed as to make stepkicking easier when gaining altitude, but quite often it is necessary to make a long sidehill traverse without any rise in elevation. In this case a different kicking procedure is in order, with the heels rather than the toes taking the lead.

During the stride the climber twists his leading leg so that the boot heel strikes the slope first, carrying most of the weight, the toe pointing up and out. As in the plunge step described later in the chapter, the heel makes the platform secure by compacting the snow, which it can do much more efficiently than the toe.

Balance: Use of the Ice Ax

Though all elements of balance climbing are as important on snow as on rock, vertical stance is particularly so since snow can be made solid only by compression. The temptation to lean into the slope is almost irresistible at high angles, yet results only in tearing out steps and pushing the feet off their holds. Methods of holding the ax vary with the terrain. Along trails or gentle slopes it makes a splendid walking stick (see Chapter 6); on steep slopes the ax aids balance and is held ready to check slips and for instant arrest (as described later in this chapter).

Balance with the Ax

In ordinary snow climbing only three suspension points are convenient: the two feet and the ax. The ax is used either as a cane or in the cross-body position, depending largely on individual preference. A slip can be checked by leaning on the ax and pressing the spike into the slope. On steep, soft snow the ax is the best possible anchor since the shaft can

Fig. 137. Use of ice ax on slopes of increasing steepness.

penetrate deeper than the feet. If the shaft can be rammed in up to the hilt more support is obtained by grasping the axhead with both hands; if it is only half-buried, one hand grasps the axhead and the other holds onto the shaft next to the surface.

Hanging Onto the Ax

In some mountaineering circles the wrist loop is regarded with derision as an accessory for tourists who have not learned the first commandment of snow climbing: *hang onto the ax.* Other climbers have no quarrel with this commandment but recognize certain legitimate uses of the loop. All schools of thought agree most emphatically that a climber must learn to hang onto the ax, and not depend on the loop to insure that the ax will hang onto him. Even in a short fall an ax dangling uncontrolled from the wrist can seriously injure the climber. Those who have taken a long ride down a snow slope attached by a short length of strap to a flailing ax are not inclined to repeat the experience, even if able to do so.

The loop has several important functions. On terrain where a dropped ax might be lost and when such a loss would be disastrous, as on long steep slopes and among crevasses, the loop is excellent insurance. It serves as a wrist support in step-chopping, minimizing fatigue and preventing the loss of the ax from cold and tired hands. It also frees the hands for other uses, as on a brief rock pitch amidst a snow climb. (Of course, in such a situation the ax can be slipped diagonally between the rucksack straps and the climber's back or hooked onto his thumb at the neck of the adze.)

DESCENDING

The route down is sometimes quite different from the route up. By afternoon the upward path may be so subject to avalanching that a steep or circuitous way down on rock is best. Terrain suitable for uphill climbing is often poor for descending, such as icy surfaces that make for good cramponing but poor glissading. Route variations may range from going down a different side of the mountain, which may be hazardous if the terrain is unfamiliar, to moving a few feet from icy shadow onto sun-softened slopes. Snow in good condition is almost the ideal medium for losing altitude rapidly, yielding comfortably under the foot without the jolting shocks that the body must absorb on rock. Far from increasing the risk, within reasonable limits speed and élan make the footing more secure. Because of these factors and the opportunity for glissades, snow descents are highly favored.

Climbing Down Step by Step

When the snow is very steep, speed is the last thing a climber wants. On nearly vertical walls it is necessary to face into the slope, cautiously lowering a foot to kick a step with the toes, meanwhile trusting the ax to prevent a slide during the delicate moment when the new step is first entrusted with the climber's full weight. On slopes more moderate but still too steep or exposed for sliding techniques, the superior facing-out position is adopted, giving better visibility and allowing step-kicking to be done by the heels.

Plunge Step

The most common use of the heels is in the plunge step, a fundamental technique applicable not only on snow but on any similar terrain, such as scree. The ideal plunging surface is a fall-line descent in fairly soft snow at a moderate angle. From the upper step the climber rolls onto the toe, swinging the stiffened lower leg well forward out into space. The heel of the descending foot strikes the slope with most of the climber's weight behind it, driving as much as several feet along the soft surface, and eventually, by compacting the snow into a hard step, effects a skidding stop. Immediately the body leans to the other side and the opposite leg stiffens for action. The ax held in cross-body position supplies a third balance point when needed. When performed properly the plunge step is a comfortable, rapid means of descent, and certainly faster and pleasanter than jolting down on hard platforms step by step.

Lunging outward and landing on the heel are essential features of plunge-stepping. The angle at which the heel should enter the slope varies with the hardness of the snow: on very soft slopes almost any angle suffices, although if the climber leans too far forward he risks having his leg lodged in a deep well and may sustain a fracture in the next plunge. On hard snow, exactly where one tends to become more conservative, greater abandon is desirable, for the heel will not penetrate the surface unless it

Fig. 138. Plunge-step.

has sufficient weight behind it. Cringing from the outward lunge and leaning back into the slope cause the heels to become instruments of cutting rather than of compaction. Striking the slope at an acute angle, they slice through the surface and glance out into space, dumping the climber into an unpremeditated sitting glissade.

As long as a climber keeps his footing using this technique, the quickest way to check a slip is a reflexive shift of weight on to the heels, or, once a slide has started, by making several short, stiff-legged stomps with the heels. This method is not intended to supersede the ice ax arrest, which must be mastered before a climber can be anything but a liability to himself and the party. However, a flip onto the stomach is not always the best reaction to a slip — the heels can be quicker.

The plunge step must be used with discretion under certain conditions. On hard, steep snow the climber should be familiar with the entire slope and confident he can arrest a fall should it occur. Plunging carelessly in thawing spring snow may well result in compound fractures and difficult rescues. Plunging when roped requires teamwork and awareness of companions' progress; speed of the team must necessarily be limited to the speed of the slowest member. Plunge-stepping is unsatisfactory when wearing crampons due to the tendency of the snow to compact and stick to them.

Glissade

Standing Glissade

One of the more graceful methods of alpine travel is the standing glissade. The basic position, similar to that of skiing, is a semi-crouch, with the knees bent as if sitting in a chair. The legs are spread somewhat for lateral stability and one foot is advanced slightly to anticipate bumps and ruts. For additional stability the spike of the ax can be skimmed along the slope, the shaft held alongside the knee in the arrest grasp, the pick pointing down or to the outside, away from the body.

Stability is increased by widening the spread of the legs, deepening the crouch, and putting more weight on the spike. Unfortunately all these decrease speed and increase muscular strain, and the technique becomes awkward, less graceful, and tiring — though safe.

Speed is increased by bringing the feet close together, leaning forward until boot soles are running flat along the surface like short skis, and reducing weight on the spike; if gravity gives insufficient impetus a long *skating* stride helps. Unfortunately all these variations enable a tiny chunk of ice or rock to cause a spectacular headlong tumble.

To stop, the climber may dig in his heels while throwing most of his weight back on the spike, or as is more commonly done, swinging sideways and edging both boots while riding hard on the spike. On steep slopes just barely within the safe limits of the standing glissade this "stop" position, or *sideslipping,* is preferred for the entire descent since the climber is only a split-second from an arrest.

Another way to check speed is by making a series of linked turns, keeping the boots parallel and shifting weight smoothly from side to side as direction varies. Balance is easy on the traverse where the climber is moving along in "stop" position, but difficult and delicate on the opposite tack, since either the spike has to be brought entirely out of the slope or contact maintained by an awkward stretch of the arms.

Sitting Glissade

When snow is not hard or steep enough to allow sliding on the feet, the sitting glissade is the easiest and often the most pleasant way down. There is about as much technique involved as riding a rollercoaster: the climber simply sits in the snow and slides, holding the ax in arrest position. Any tendency of the body to pivot head-downwards may be thwarted by running the spike of the ax, rudder-fashion, along the surface of the snow.

On soft snow, speed is increased by lying on the back to spread the body weight over a greater area and by lifting the feet in the air. Sitting back up and lowering the feet to the surface of the snow reduces speed. On snow that is crusted or firmly consolidated, pitted with icy ruts or small suncups or punctuated with occasional rocks or shrubs, stability and control are greater, a better view of the slope obtained, and damage to softer portions of the anatomy minimized by sitting fairly erect, heels drawn up against the buttocks and boot soles planing along the surface.

Fig. 139. Glissading. *Left* to *right:* sitting, standing, and side slipping to a stop.

In either position speed is decreased by dragging the spike and applying increasing pressure to it. After momentum has been checked by the spike, the heels are dug in for the final halt — but not while going along at a good rate or the result is likely to be a somersault. Emergency stops at high speed are made by arrest.

Turns are almost impossible in a sitting glissade. The spike, dragged as a rudder and assisted by body contortions, can effect a change in direction of several degrees at most. Obstructions in the slope are best avoided with a right-angled pattern of straight-down slides and straight-across traverses rather than trying to steer past them at high speeds. On fast snow an experienced glissader can perform with more craftsmanship, rising while moving into a standing glissade for the turn, then reverting to a sitting position.

Glissade Precautions

A glissade should be made *only when there is a safe runout* — remembering that a runout is not in itself a sound guarantee if the slope is so long and steep that a climber could be abraded and fractured beyond repair during the slide. Unless a *view of the entire run* can be obtained beforehand the first man down must exercise extreme caution and stop frequently to study what lies ahead.

Equipment is adjusted before beginning the descent. Crampons and other lethal hardware are stowed within the rucksack. *Never attempt to glissade while wearing crampons*; it is too easy to catch a crampon in the snow and go cart-wheeling down the slope. Mittens are donned, snow being so cold and abrasive it can chill and flay the hands until they lose control of the ax. Finally, and most important, if by any chance the ice ax wrist loop is around the wrist it must be removed: glissades should never be attempted in terrain where the wrist loop is needed and the hazards of a flailing ice ax should never be risked during a glissade.

Under some soft-snow conditions, the glissader initiates movement of a mass of snow which continues down the slope with him. These *avalanche cushions must be used with caution*, the climber being always ready to roll clear. Rather considerable avalanche cushions can be ridden in perfect safety and incomparable comfort but the novice must keep in mind that their momentum can be enough to carry him across rocks or hurtle him over a cliff.

ARREST TECHNIQUE AND BELAYS

To repeat a point which scarcely needs emphasis, it is better for a climber never to fall, but when he does he should stop without delay. On snow and ice there are three divisions of the technique of stopping: the *self-arrest* by an individual, *team arrest* of a roped party, and the *belays* with which a moving climber is protected by a stationary companion.

Self-Arrest

On any slope where a slip could lead to a fast, rough slide the climber travels in constant readiness to make arrest. An *eye for consequences*, continual awareness of what lies around him wherever he walks, is as characteristic of the experienced mountaineer as an eye for weather. Always in his mind are the chances of a slip and the dangers of a fall — the length and steepness of the slope, the rocks or cliffs or crevasses below.

Physically the climber rigs for arrest by rolling down shirtsleeves, putting on mittens, securing loose gear, and most important of all, by making certain the ax is held correctly. Mentally he prepares by recognizing the importance of *instantaneous application*. A sloppy but quick arrest often has a better chance of success than a stylish but leisurely one.

Position

1. One hand on head of ax with thumb under adze and fingers over pick; the other hand on the shaft next to the spike; both hands with firm grip.
2. Pick is pressed into the slope just above the shoulder so that the adze is near the angle formed by neck and shoulder; shaft crosses chest diagonally; spike held firmly close to the opposite hip. A short ax is held in the same position, although the spike will not reach the opposite hip.
3. Chest and shoulder pressed strongly on shaft; spine arched slightly to distribute weight chiefly at shoulders and toes.
4. Legs stiff and spread apart, toes digging in (if wearing crampons, keep the toes off the surface until almost stopped).
5. *Hang onto the ax!*

The firm grip on the head of the ax holds the pick close to the shoulder and neck. The other hand must be *at the very end* of the shaft lest it act as a pivot around which the spike can swing into the thigh, inflicting a nasty wound.

The pick and the toes (when not wearing crampons) are the most effective brakes. A slight arch of the spine concentrates body weight on the toes and on the chest-and-shoulder region which presses on the shaft, driving the pick in. With a limp backbone much of the abdominal mass lies wasted on the snow. However, the slight arch must not be confused with the ineffective and unstable very high arch of novices unwilling to get chest and face down into the rough, cold snow.

Particularly in soft snow the stiff, outspread legs with digging toes give the pick important help and also add stability. However, when arresting on hard snow or ice while wearing crampons, the knees must do the job

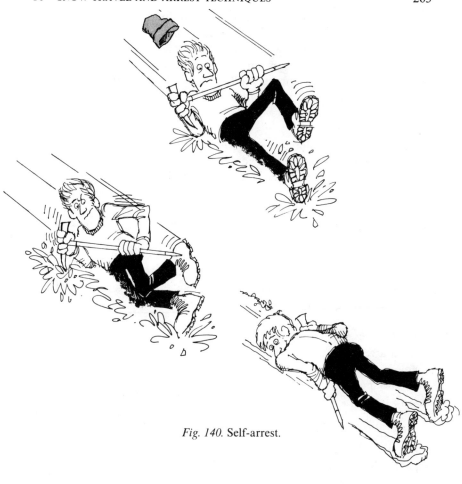

Fig. 140. Self-arrest.

Fig. 141. Wrong way to do self-arrest — do not roll toward spike.

described above for the feet. Under these conditions the feet must be held away from the slope until speed is reduced, so that crampons do not catch and flip the climber backwards. The knees help stabilize the sliding climber but do not help stop him on hard snow or ice, especially if he happens to be wearing slippery wind pants. Again the emphasis is on the urgency of driving in the pick as *hard* and as *quickly* as possible.

On hard surfaces, an ax with slightly drooped pick and/or positive clearance (see Chapter 15) bites into the snow more readily than one without. Owners of older axes may wish to file their picks to provide this positive clearance. The more rapid deceleration caused by these features necessitates an even firmer grasp on the ax to prevent its being carried out of position or lost. For all axes, and particularly the shorter ones, it is very important that the hands *never, never* be allowed to get above the line of the shoulders — there is then no body pressure to keep the pick in the snow.

One of the prime laws of snow is that it takes an ax to turn a hiker into a climber. When the ax is lost in a fall there is no longer a climber but only a hiker attempting with fingernails and teeth the pick's proper job. In other words, *hang onto the ax.*

Arrest in Wild Flight

Most arrests are applied to check a slip resulting from a stumble or a simple breaking-out of a step. Even a half-hearted arrest can usually stop such low-speed slides, if indeed hopskipping of the feet is not enough to restore balance. The smaller proportion of arrests is also the more critical — those applied while the climber is flying blindly and wildly, half in the air and half in the snow, whirling, spinning, and bounding until he quite literally cannot distinguish up from down. Such falls quickly separate the good arrests from the bad.

The first step in making arrest is gaining the ideal position — sliding on the stomach with the feet downhill. The climber *sliding on his back rolls onto his stomach toward the head of the ax.* If his axhead is on his right shoulder he rolls to his right. Rolling left might jam the spike into the slope before the pick, wrenching the ax from the climber's grasp.

To *pivot into an arrest from an on-back head-downhill* position the best method is the *tuck pivot,* in which the falling climber, while still head downhill on his back, jams the pick into the slope beside his hip, with the ax shaft held across his body. If the axhead happens to be in the left hand, the pick is driven into the slope by the left hip; in the right hand, by the right hip. With the pick as a pivot, the body flips from back onto the hips and side and then onto the stomach while feet swing around into the lead. In the flip, which can be expedited by a downhill kick of the legs, the body falls onto the ax in correct arrest position.

Arrest Variations

In loose snow of winter and early spring the pick cannot reach compact strata and the usual self-arrest is useless. The falling climber being nearly submerged, his most effective braking instruments are feet, knees, and elbows, all widely spread and deeply pressed. The greatest drag potential

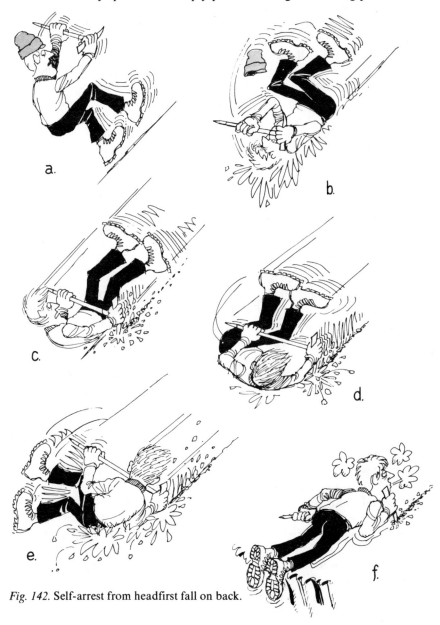

Fig. 142. Self-arrest from headfirst fall on back.

of the ax lies not in the pick but in the shaft — thrust vertically into the slope, exactly as the alpenstock was used by an earlier mountaineering generation. Pivots are usually unnecessary, the fall often being stopped while the climber is still head-down.

Under any snow conditions, the speed with which the arrest position is attained is the key to success. In soft snow the reflexive speed of ramming in pick and toes brings the quick stop. On hard snow a quick stab at the slope with the pick or spike — or even boot heels — may stop a fall before it gets started. On the other hand acceleration is so terrific that the first instant of fall is often the whole story. Once underway on hard snow the climber commonly rockets into the air and crashes back to the unyielding surface with stunning impact, completely losing uphill-downhill orientation.

The arrest on ice is very difficult if not impossible, but should always be applied whether or not a belay is also set up. Occasionally in the first instant of fall the pick lodges in a crevice or behind a hump and effects a stop even on a very steep slope. As mentioned before, crampons must be managed with extreme care during a fall. Presumably a party on steep ice will belay unless the slope is short with a snow runout below, in which case if the arrest is begun on ice it can more easily be completed on the snow.

Limits of the Arrest

The arrest stops a fall by friction of ax and body against the snow. When the slope is too steep or slippery — too "fast" — not even the most skillful technique can reduce acceleration. Moreover, even successful arrests require at least a little time, during which the climber slides some distance. Therefore the value of the self-arrest is *limited by the climber's speed of reaction and the steepness and length of the slope.* Also, though a climber may be confident that under a particular set of conditions he can stop within 100 feet of slide, his faith in the arrest is misplaced if the slope terminates in a cliff 75 feet below him.

Even when friction potentially available from the slope-climber contact is plentiful, still the arrest is limited by strength and skill. The athlete with perfect timing and bulging muscles may be able to arrest a bounding fall down a cliff of ice while the tourist slides helplessly to disaster on a gentle snowfield. However, the *learned skill* is more significant than physical ability. Arrest with an ax is not instinctive; only thorough practice can provide reflexes to do the right thing at the right time. Practicing arrests from head-first falls is especially important, these being the most commonly experienced as a result of slipping or stumbling.

A climber must *at all times be aware of his arrest limits.* If the slope seems too fast or too short, or if he is not sure of his strength and skill, the self-arrest should be supplemented by other protective techniques.

Team Arrest

The team arrest is intermediate between self-arrest and belays. When there is doubt that an individual could arrest his own fall — such as on crevassed glaciers and steep snowfields — and yet conditions are not so extreme as to make belaying necessary, the party ropes up and travels in unison. Should any member fall he is *arrested by two or three axes,* not one.

If it is to be a safety device rather than a hazard, the *rope between the climbers must be fully extended* except for a minimum amount of slack carried by the second and third men to allow them to flip the rope out of the track (steps). This also allows easy compensation for pace variations. However, slack is kept at a minimum to bring the second and third axes into action at the earliest possible moment of need.

When the roped climber falls he *immediately screams* "FALLING!" It is not advisable to delay the alarm to see how the self-arrest will come out; the partners may then hear the signal only after they have already begun their trajectories. *When a roped climber hears the cry* "FALLING!" *he reflexively drops into arrest.* Turning in slow amazement to watch the catastrophe wastes seconds that may prove precious.

Fig. 143. Sitting hip belay in snow.

Belays

Of the belay techniques available to the snow climber, the one favored is the *sitting hip belay,* in which the climber first stamps out a seat in the snow and then stomps down with outstretched siffened legs, thereby cutting troughs in the snow and consolidating platforms for his feet. Additional security can be gained by using a snow fluke or deadman anchor. A piece of ensolite foam pad or some other form of insulation to sit upon is an appreciated touch.

Though less secure than an anchored sitting hip belay, a *boot-ax belay* is much faster to set up and thus can be used when a team is moving together and belaying is required only at a few spots. The technique is awkward for most novices and should be practiced until a sweep and jab of the ice ax set up the stance within a couple of seconds, the ax providing an anchor to the slope and the boot a brace for the ax, and both giving a friction surface over which the run of rope is controlled. The elements of the stance are as follows:

1. A firm platform is stamped out in the snow, large enough for the ax and uphill boot.
2. The ice ax shaft is jammed into the snow at the rear of the platform as deeply as possible, tilted slightly uphill against the anticipated fall.
3. The pick is parallel to the fall line, pointing uphill, thus applying the strongest dimension of the shaft against the force of a fall; also, the length of the pick prevents the rope from escaping over the top of the shaft.
4. The belayer stands below the ax, facing at approximately a right angle to the fall line and *toward* the side on which the climber's route lies.
5. The uphill boot is stamped into the slope against the downhill side of the shaft at a right angle to the fall line, thus bracing the shaft against downhill pull.
6. The downhill boot is in a firmly compacted step sufficiently below the uphill boot so that the leg is straight, stiffly bracing the belayer.
7. The uphill hand is on the axhead in arrest grasp, bracing the shaft against downhill and lateral stress.
8. From below, the rope crosses the toe of the boot, preventing the rope from trenching into the snow.
9. The rope bends around the uphill side of the shaft, then down across the instep of the bracing boot, and is controlled by the downhill hand; to apply braking through greater friction, the downhill or braking hand brings the rope uphill around the heel, forming an "S" bend.

Not only is the boot-ax belay sensitive to careless technique, but excessive friction from a wet rope can result in catastrophic failure if the braking hand develops the S bend too rapidly. Poor placement of the shaft or weak or defective wood grain have led to numerous failures of wooden shafts during practice arrests. Taking up rope requires much dexterity of the belayer: the uphill hand must guard the ax, take up rope, scratch the nose, and in case of complete failure, grab the axhead in arrest grasp. The downhill — that is, the braking — hand, as with all belays, must never leave the rope. The switchbacking nature of snow climbing demands that every climber be equally adept at installing the boot-ax belay with either foot uphill, since above all it is essential that the belayer face his climber's

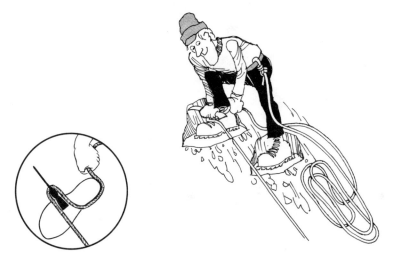

Fig. 144. Boot-ax belay with insert showing rope wrapped as to hold a fall.

fall line; if the climber falls behind the belay, obviously there is no belay.

Although the effectiveness of the boot-ax belay has been questioned in some quarters, it has proven to be a useful technique provided its limitations are understood, and more importantly, provided it is thoroughly practiced, both by setting it up and testing to find those limitations.

Whatever the method used, the belay must be close to the difficulties, and if the leader is belayed, the belay stance must be to one side of his fall line. On diagonal ascents the belay should be 2 or 3 feet outside the turning point, and on direct ascents 5 or 6 feet to one side or the other of the line of ascent. When climbing a ridge it may not always be possible to predict a fall line and plan a belay in advance, and in case of a teammate's slip the best course of action may be to roll off the opposite side.

Supplementary Reading:

LaChapelle, Edward R. *The ABC of Avalanche Safety.* Denver, Colorado: Colorado Outdoor Sports Co., 1970.

17 *

GLACIER TRAVEL

IF IT WERE NOT for crevasses, a separate consideration of glacier travel would seem superfluous, since nearly all the required techniques are treated in other chapters. But however myopic the article of faith "no glacier, no mountain" may seem, crevasses do create special problems for travel in glacier-clad mountains — ask the climber who has fallen into one.

TRAVEL AMONG CREVASSES

The hidden crevasse is the special problem of glacier travel, its distinction being that the more harmless the outward appearance the greater the threat. The most casual observer takes protective measures in the face of obvious chasms; the really hazardous holes are those that show on the surface as mere cracks or are completely invisible. It is easy to move from a snowfield onto a snowcovered glacier without recognizing the need for added protection. Also, even after much experience, a climber who has traveled under a lucky star may imagine himself able to negotiate glaciers without special precaution, confidently depending on his wisdom to predict when and where he will come upon a crevasse; an alarming percentage of such gifted seers, however, eventually lose either their second sight or their luck.

Protection: The Rope

The first law of traveling glaciers is to *rope up*. Whether stepping onto a known glacier or onto a snowfield of unknown status, whether or not crevasses are visible, whether or not crevasses ever have been reported as existing there in the past, the law with but one exception is: *rope up* — the exception being the occasion in which avalanches present a greater hazard than crevasses. Even though a fortunate climber makes hundreds of climbs during a score of seasons and never once steps into a crevasse, if he is as wise as he is lucky he has kept up the premiums on his climbing insurance by wearing a rope during all these climbs, realizing that too frequently a climber's first unroped fall into a crevasse is his last.

More is involved than merely roping, which can in fact be the visible declaration of a mutual suicide pact; it is well for each member to ponder for a moment the reasons the rope is used and to visualize in detail the consequences of a fall. If this is done no one will need urging to *keep the rope fully extended between members* to minimize the length of falls. Climbers who march in friendly proximity through crevasse fields, whether dragging long loops of slack or carrying neat coils, are liable to continue their close association as a rope team all the way to the bottom of the same crevasse.

On moderate climbs the *preferred number on a team for glacier travel is three* climbers to a rope 150 feet long; on severe climbs requiring belaying, a rope team of two using a 120-foot rope is more practical. With but two on a rope a crevasse fall must be arrested by a single ax; more than three on a rope so shortens intervals between climbers that if one man drops in a hole often another is dragged down before he has time to take any action. Due to the difficulty of crevasse rescue, *two rope teams are the recommended minimum for glacier travel,* since a single team is sometimes pinned down in arrest position, members unable to free themselves to begin rescue. Even if able to do so, a single rope team may be insufficient to effect rescue and in any event extra equipment and manpower expedite matters, many times having proven the margin between failure and success. If, however, the rope teams do not travel close enough together to render immediate assistance to one another, the principle is lost.

The traditional method of roping up is the bowline-on-a-coil. However, since the main hazard of glacier travel is falling into a crevasse, and hanging from a waistloop results in constriction of the diaphragm and eventual suffocation, many climbers prefer to use a seat harness of some kind. *Prusik slings* or mechanical ascenders are attached to the rope and a chest sling and carabiner are worn.

The iciness of crevasse interiors must be taken into account and *warm wool clothing* worn or carried; a climber can die of cold within easy speaking distance of companions who are sweltering in sunshine. All *equipment is secured* — pockets buttoned, loose gear safely stowed. The *ice ax wristloop is kept on the wrist at all times.* The climber holds the ax with the head in arrest position, ready to drop immediately into the self-arrest position if a rope companion falls. Finally, *competence in the rescue methods* detailed later in this chapter is an absolute prerequisite for glacier travel.

Rope team order on glaciers is sometimes slightly different from that described in Chapter 9. Usually the first man should be the one most experienced in crevasse detection and avoidance, but when crevasses are thoroughly masked an alternate policy is for the lightest member of the party to lead, followed by the climber most skillful at belays and arrests.

The basic aim of glacier travelers is to complete their trip without falling into crevasses. Should they fail in this, however, it is even more fundamental that members of a team must never fall into the same crevasse. Consequently, whenever possible the team *crosses the visible or suspected crevasse at right angles.* When the route precludes such a course *echelon* formation is used, somewhat awkward, but good insurance that if one climber plunges into a chasm his companions will not immediately join him; at the worst they will topple into neighboring chasms, a sufficiently unhappy situation but better than everyone landing in the same hole.

An alarmingly common blunder is for a party to cluster close together at rest stops. A number of alpine tragedies have resulted from this convivial instinct when a chosen rendezvous proved to be the bridge over an unseen crevasse, strong enough to support one or two climbers at most. If areas of indisputable safety cannot be found the rope must be kept extended during rests just as during travel. A party establishing camp on a snowcovered glacier similarly remains roped for a long period, stomping and probing the surface thoroughly before according any trust to the site.

During extended periods of glacier living, skis and snowshoes are often of inestimable value. The climber equipped with such footgear distributes his weight more widely than when clumping along on boots and by placing less strain on bridges falls into fewer crevasses. Neither skis nor snowshoes can be considered substitutes for the rope, but in semi-arctic ranges or winter mountaineering they may be needed for easy travel and if available give considerable protection as a bonus.

Ice Ax and Crampons

Glaciers being rivers of snow and ice, a climber's ice ax and crampons are as important tools as his rope; their use is fully discussed in Chapters 16 and 18.

Much glacier travel is on snow in which steps can be kicked as required, or the surface is of such a consistency and grade that lug-soled boots grip well enough to render crampons unnecessary. As the snow hardens and the slope increases (say to greater than 30 degrees) crampons come into use. Surface variations from snow to bare ice, and intervals of steepness, necessitate a decision between cutting occasional steps for assistance and security or wearing crampons continuously.

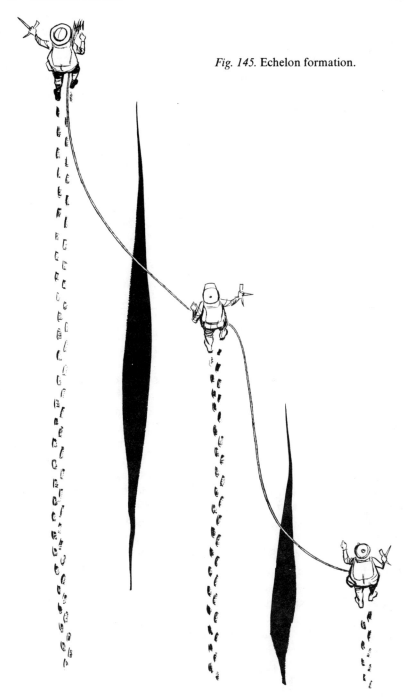

Fig. 145. Echelon formation.

Avoiding Crevasses

Except when photography is the object of the trip the best route is one that completely avoids all crevasses. Simple and self-evident as such strategy seems, the distant view may be misleading. Scale is difficult to estimate from far away and often a crevasse judged to be the merest crack turns out to be many feet wide. Moreover, if one crevasse can be seen from several miles off, odds are that on close approach it will prove to be merely the largest of a cluster. Finally, even if the climbers have a near view of the terrain to be traveled and can see every tiny break in the surface, hidden crevasses must always be suspected.

Familiarity with the mechanics of glacier motion, described in Chapter 23, is essential to wise routefinding. An understanding of where crevasses are most likely to form may allow a party to proceed rapidly and safely even in the extreme case of a glacier surface entirely free from visible breaks but honeycombed with chasms beneath the snowcover.

Detecting Hidden Crevasses

The climber should continually search the route ahead with a roving eye for suggestions of hidden holes. Suspicion increases in areas likely to be crevassed, such as the sides of the glacier, around nunataks (protuberances of rock through the glacier surface), and icefalls, and at any sharp bends or drops. Memory is sometimes useful, for on many glaciers crevasse patterns change little from year to year. A thin snowcover which masks crevasses without bridging them is particularly hazardous, and extreme caution is mandatory in late spring, after snowfalls, and near exposed ice. Once one crevasse is discovered the climber does well to keep in mind that crevasses usually form in parallel belts, and usually have hidden extensions.

When a crevasse is suspected the climber seeks visual clues, and all of these stem from the natural inclination of snow arching over emptiness to *sag* under the pull of gravity, creating a shallow trough with a linear form that distinguishes it from suncups, which tend to be circular. A sag smoothed over by a continuing succession of storms gives no surface indication of its existence, but any interval of good weather allows gravity to do its work; the sag may then give itself away by a slight difference in sheen, texture, or color. Snow in the trough may have a flat white look and a fine texture from being newer than the old névé, or be dirtier from collecting windblown particles of dust, or have the chalky appearance typical of a windslab, since the trough presents the wind with a lee slope. Proper light helps in spotting sags. In the dull illumination of fog and in the glare of midday sun details are blurred. With moderate light from a low angle, such as in early morning or late afternoon, differences in snow textures are distinctly revealed and shadows outline the characteristic linear form of the sag.

XIII. Mt. Rainier, east side at sunrise. (T. M. Green)

Very commonly there is not the slightest clue to the location, size, and direction of crevasses, and the party must *probe* the surface with an ice ax. Continuous probing is scarcely practical through a large suspected area but it is advisable at points of maximum probability; that is, on the lips and at the ends of open crevasses, across all sags and dubious bridges.

The axhead is held firmly in the arrest grasp and attached to the climber by the wristloop. The shaft is thrust into the surface well *in advance of the climber's weight, with a smooth sensitive motion,* the angle as *nearly vertical* as convenient, since otherwise the climber is merely skimming the surface rather than penetrating the underlayers. If resistance to the thrust is uniform it has been established that the snow is solid at least to the depth of the shaft. If resistance abruptly lessens, probably a hole has been found, and further thrusts are made to establish its extent. The value of probing depends largely on the climber's sensitivity to changes in resistance and his skill in interpreting the meaning of such changes. The shaft may seem suddenly to plunge into space when actually it has merely broken through a buried crust into a softer stratum. In the structure of the ax a smooth line from spike to shaft is essential for accuracy; a blunt-pointed spike or a jutting ferrule may give a false reading. The length of the shaft remains a limiting factor, since obviously all one can find out is whether a bridge is as thick as the shaft is long. In heavily crevassed areas, where the holes are smoothly surfaced with recently fallen snow, a shovel is a valuable addition to the leader's equipment. With it he can dig through the roof of a crevasse discovered by his probing and visually determine its width, length, and direction.

PASSING A CREVASSE

End Run

If a crevasse pinches out anywhere within reasonable distance the end run is much preferred over any other tactical maneuver; even though it may involve traveling half a mile to gain a dozen feet of forward progress, the time taken to walk around is generally much less than in forcing a direct crossing. Important to remember in an end run is the almost invariable hidden extension of a visible crevasse. A frequent error is aiming at the visible end; unless the true, or subsurface, end has been clearly seen during the approach it is wise to make a very wide swing around the corner. In late summer the visible end is often the true end of a crevasse, but early in the season even the tiniest surface crack may be a chink in the roof of an immense cold cavern.

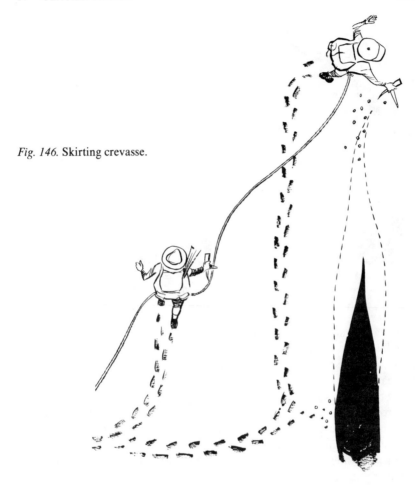

Fig. 146. Skirting crevasse.

Bridges

When end runs are impractical because of the distance involved or because the ends of the crevasse are adjacent to other crevasses, the party looks for bridges. One variety consists of remnant snowcover sagging over an inner vacuity. Another kind is less a bridge than an isthmus between two crevasses with a foundation that extends downward into the body of the glacier.

Ideally any bridge should be closely and completely examined before use. A side view may give a stamp of such unqualified approval that the party can stride across in perfect confidence. If overhanging snow obscures dimensions the leader must explore at closer range, probing the

Fig. 147. Crossing bridged crevasse.

depth and smashing at the sides, walking delicately all the while and equally ready for an arrest or a sudden drop. The second man gives a belay, anchored by the third man, who is also prepared to start rescue if the leader falls.

A bridge excessively narrow for walking or apparently quite weak may be crossed by straddling, or even slithering on the stomach, thereby lowering the center of gravity and distributing weight over a broader area. When the bridge is extremely dubious but still the only feasible route, the smallest climber in the party should be the first across, the followers walking with light feet and taking care to step exactly in the established tracks without the slightest deviation.

Bridges vary in strength with changes in temperature. In the cold of winter or early morning the thinnest and airiest of arches can have incredible structural strength; when crystals melt in the afternoon sun even the grandest bridge may suddenly collapse of its own weight. Each must be tested with care, being neither abandoned nor trusted until its worth is determined. Moreover, dependability in the morning does not mean that testing can be omitted in the afternoon.

Jumping

Narrow cracks can be stepped across, but increased width requires jumping, often faster than an end run and sometimes the only possible passage. Crevasse jumping, however, is one of the alpine techniques

Fig. 148. Crossing sunken bridge.

dramatized far beyond its importance, although distinction must be made between the routine hops of fact and the long desperate leaps customary in novels.

Care must be taken to find the precise edge of the crevasse, which often overhangs. The jumper holds his ax in the arrest position in case he falls short and must claw for purchase on the far side. The belayer leaves slack in the rope exceeding the width of the crevasse; at best harsh words may result if the jumper makes a splendid effort but while still in forward flight is suddenly snapped backward by a taut rope.

A running jump can carry somewhat farther than a standing one, but not so far as usually expected. With full gear it is difficult to get up much momentum, particularly since the dashing climber is likely to plunge deep into the snow, or perhaps even through the overhanging lip of the crevasse — an inglorious conclusion to a thrilling beginning. If the jump is so long that a run is required, the approach is first carefully packed. Before takeoff the lead man leaves his rucksack and other encumbrances with companions, rolls down shirt sleeves and puts on mittens, checks his waist knot and prusik slings. In point of fact, running jumps are not often practical; most are made from a standing start or with but two or three lead-up steps. Unlike the heroes of fiction the ordinary real-life mountaineer finds more than adequate challenge in leaps of 5 or 6 feet on a flat surface; if he falters in midflight he at least has a fighting chance to claw over the lip with ax and feet. A jump is obviously much less dangerous once one climber is across, for then the belay is on the landing side and if the second man falls short he has assistance from the rope in scrambling out of the hole.

Downhill jumping, such as from the overhanging wall of a bergschrund, is a different matter entirely. With momentum from a descending run a climber may perhaps clear prodigious horizontal distances. Such leaps, however, are made only in desperation. Danger can be minimized by a proper landing position, with the feet slightly apart for balance, knees relaxed to absorb shock, ax held ready for arrest, and the belayer alert. Still, the landing platform is an unknown quantity that may be so weak the climber plunges through into the crevasse, or so hard he breaks both legs. Moreover, the choice between jumping and slower methods of passage usually is made late in the day when weary climbers are apt to forget the brittleness of bones, the forces generated by a falling body, and the world record for the broad jump.

Fig. 149. Jumping a crevasse.

CREVASSE RESCUE

To an unroped climber a fall into a crevasse is almost certainly fatal, for even if he survives the tumble, death from hypothermia is only a matter of hours. Traveling roped, but with improper technique, the result can be the same. On a slack rope a person can plunge freely to the bottom, the rope being no more than a retrieving line; companions unskilled in self-arrest can be dragged in with him. Many people, although stopped by the rope, have died of suffocation because they were not able to relieve the pressure of the waistloop, or of hypothermia because companions did not know how to extricate them.

Today such fatalities are largely needless. Modern climbing and rope-handling techniques can virtually eliminate injuries in crevasse falls, and rescue methods have been devised which are successful under almost any circumstances. The knowledge is available, yet all too often climbers venture onto glaciers without learning these skills. In time of trouble, they must then rely on trial-and-error and blind luck, both of which are almost universally untrustworthy.

Preparation for Accidents

The success or failure of crevasse rescue depends very largely on advance preparations. Most glacier accidents occur while the whole team is moving, a plunge without warning into a hidden crevasse or an accidental slide on steep slopes being much more common than a fall protected by a belay at an obviously dangerous spot.

A small party may have to depend upon the ability of each member to prusik from a crevasse; hence in such cases each climber must travel with *two prusik slings and a chest sling and carabiner already in place.* The prusik slings are attached to the rope and the other ends are generally put down through the waistloop and tucked away where they can be easily reached. (The *middleman needs a sling ahead of him and one behind,* since in a fall he might be caught by either rope.) Stepping into one of these slings allows the fallen climber to relieve the strain on his waist. The chest sling is a nylon runner crossed on the climber's back and clipped together in front with the carabiner. After stepping into a prusik, clipping this carabiner to the rope allows the climber to more easily stand up without toppling over backwards. The technique of prusiking is described later in this chapter.

Some climbers (recently escaped from high-angle rock) prefer to carry mechanical ascenders and a set of their retired aid stirrups (see Chapter 13) stuffed into a handy pocket.

Besides prusik slings each party member carries a rescue pulley, several carabiners, and nylon runners to facilitate setting up a pulley system if needed.

Knowing he might be trapped for a long time in the ice, each climber must remain dressed for survival; clad in shorts and a thin shirt for a hot day he will not survive long in the depths of a glacier.

When a Climber Falls

Assuming a three-man team, the instant a fall occurs team members drop into the self-arrest position, and as soon as the fall is checked, use their prusik slings to escape from their prone arresting positions: with an endman in the crevasse, either of the two partners may be able to hold the load alone while the other attaches a prusik sling to the rope near the crevasse and loops it over his anchored ice ax; if the middleman has fallen and is held from both sides, one partner holds as much of the load as possible while the other rises and anchors his rope. The first man now relaxes and seeks some safe way to reach the other side of the crevasse so that rescue can begin. If one of a two-man team falls, assistance from another rope team is usually essential to rescue.

Organizing the Rescue

Hidden crevasses should always be assumed to exist in the work area, which is probed thoroughly and safe boundaries marked before anyone moves about unroped. Without fail, those who must work in dangerous spots are belayed.

The lip of the crevasse above the fallen climber is reconnoitered. If it is overhanging or thinly bridged, a new access hole is cut at least 10 feet to one side. *The hole directly above the victim must not be enlarged* — he might be smothered or injured by snow and ice dropped in the process. All communications and rescue activity are conducted through the access hole. A line with a carabiner can be lowered to bring up the victim's ice ax and pack, and warm clothing sent down in the same way. Once the ax has been retrieved it is placed at the edge of the crevasse to *prevent the rope from trenching into the snow.*

Often a little ingenuity makes the rescue easier. The victim may be hanging near the bottom or above a ledge to which he can be lowered to wait in comparative comfort. With a narrow place in the crevasse nearby he probably can traverse and climb out, or someone can stem down to him (stemming with crampons in a narrow crevasse is very like stemming in a rock chimney). If it appears that surmounting the lip will be difficult, the victim might be pendulumned along the crevasse to a better spot as described in Chapter 22. If the rescuers are working on a steep slope above the crevasse, they should, if possible, transfer operations to the lower edge to save time and reduce risk.

If someone must descend to render first aid he can rappel through the access hole and prusik out again. However, the party must make certain before he enters the crevasse that he can get out again and will not merely compound the problem.

In the Crevasse

When a climber has fallen into a crevasse, his first action (upon regaining his wits) is to step into his prusik slings. He does this even if wearing the most comfortable seat sling or harness. Next, he clips the climbing rope into his chest carabiner and slides the prusik knot up until his weight is back on his feet. If additional warm clothing can be donned, he does so; he also prepares to send up his pack and ax when the hauling line is lowered. He is now ready to either extricate himself by prusiking or to be hauled out by his comrades.

An unconscious or badly injured person must be raised by pulley. If possible he is immediately swung to a place where he can rest comfortably. A companion descends quickly to render first aid, add warm clothing, remove pack and ice ax, and rig a seat sling or rope stretcher. Sometimes these duties must be performed under extreme difficulties, even hanging in midair. Work completed, the helper may return to the surface, or he may guide the victim up if enough lifting power is available to raise their combined weight.

Raising Techniques

Prusik

With two prusik slings and a chest sling and carabiner a person can climb the length of a fixed rope, the slings attached with a prusik or similar knots that grip tightly when loaded yet slide when the load is removed. Prusiking is strenuous and requires the use of both hands and both feet; hence it is no system for a badly injured person.

Prusik slings are usually made from lengths of ¼-inch braided dacron or polypropylene rope. These materials stretch less than nylon and there is much less tendency for the knots to jam. Smaller diameter rope is less bulky and grips the climbing rope better but in practice the knots are very difficult to work with gloved hands and it is therefore not recommended.

To allow the climber to make maximum steps up with each foot in turn,

Fig. 150. Prusiking.

the longer foot sling should extend to about nose level and the other to several inches below the waistloop, both with loops just big enough for the foot, with crampons. The chest sling is just long enough to keep the climber from toppling backwards when rigged.

Standing upright with all his weight bearing on the foot slings, the climber lifts one foot and raises its unweighted knot. Now, stepping up and shifting his weight onto this sling, he repeats with the other foot. The climb is less tiring when the foot slings are of different lengths; he can then take equal steps with both feet. Some difficulty can be expected in sliding the knots when the rope is wet or the slings are made from laid rope; spinning also can be troublesome under overhangs where the wall cannot be touched to maintain stability, particularly when climbing a laid rope. Spinning is reduced by using braided rope for slings on a kernmantel rope.

While a fallen climber is ascending via the prusik method his companions have little to do except guard the anchors and prepare to lift him over the edge.

Pulley Systems

The previous method cannot be used when a fallen climber is incapacitated. Even so he can be lifted easily — along with an accompanying helper if necessary — by rigging a pulley system that increases the lifting capacity of the rescuers.

Any pulley system gains its mechanical advantage by multiplying the number of ropes lifting the load. If two ropes can be employed, then each carries half the weight but the rescuer has to haul in 2 feet of rope to gain 1 foot of elevation; three ropes reduce the pulling force to one-third, while the rescuer hauls in three times as much rope as the distance lifted. With several frictionless pulleys, very large weights can be hoisted by small forces — however, lightweight rescue pulleys are not frictionless and this fact imposes a definite limitation on the force multiplication of such systems.

The pulley systems illustrated use ice axes for anchors, but any of the methods described in Chapter 15 could be employed. If bollards are the main anchors, a trough must be dug beneath the rope so that pulleys and prusik knots slide easily.

If the victim is able to help himself to the extent of operating a carabiner, or if someone else can operate it for him, a quick evacuation can be made by a *single-pulley system*.

The lip of the crevasse must be prepared in the same manner as for any other rescue method; that is, an ice ax or something else must be placed at the crevasse edge to keep rescue ropes from cutting into the snow. The victim's climbing rope must be dug out of the crevasse lip, but this is easily done once the victim's weight is on the rescue rope. The climbing rope then serves as a safety belay and is hauled up through an anchored prusik sling as the victim is pulled out.

An extra rope is useful in performing a single-pulley rescue; however, if the victim is not in too far, the free portion of the climbing rope (that portion not being used to anchor the victim) may be used. One end of the extra rope is securely anchored and the other grasped firmly by one of the rescuers. A pulley is fitted around the center of the rope, secured by a carabiner. The center of the rope and the pulley are lowered to the victim, who clips the carabiner into his seat harness, if he is wearing one. If he is not wearing a seat harness he may rig a diaper seat or figure-8 sling or simply clip the carabiner to his waistloop. Lifting forces applied to the waistloop are very uncomfortable for the victim but certainly preferable to the alternative — staying in the crevasse. After attaching the pulley the victim then snaps the "up moving" rope into his chest carabiner to reduce the tendency to topple over backwards. He then tucks away all loose clothing and rope tails and signals the team above to haul away. If not

Fig. 151. Single-pulley system. Pulley is attached to seat harness of climber being raised. Note: more than one person would normally be required to effect the rescue.

dangling free he scrambles up the wall on all fours, using his feet to gain what purchase he can.

While the rope with the pulley and carabiner are being lowered to the victim, other members of the rescue team should be anchoring one end of the rescue rope, forming the loop. When the victim is clipped into the pulley, the rescue team pulls on the other end of the loop rope as directed. Simultaneously the climbing rope is raised and passed through the safety prusik sling to eliminate the possibility of suddenly dropping the victim into the crevasse again should the pulley system fail.

Advantages of the single-pulley method as compared to the Z-pulley method described next are that it is easy for rescuers to understand and quick to set up, and the victim can be hauled out quickly on one continuous motion without having to stop and reset prusik knots. Disadvantages are that the system has less actual mechanical advantage than the Z-pulley system and the victim (or helper) must be able to attach the rescue pulley to the victim. Furthermore, objects may become jammed in the pulley, in which case the rescuers may have to lower the victim slightly to clear the obstruction.

The *Z-pulley system* illustrated is one of two methods which enable a party on the surface to raise a fallen climber who cannot assist in his own rescue. A large party can pull one man out by sheer brute force; however, since a Z-system enables a party to raise a weight about 2½ times the pulling force (theoretically 3 times the force, but reduced by friction), it is a basic technique which should be learned thoroughly by every climber who intends to climb in parties of six or less. For simplicity, the illustration shows typical loads in the ropes in the absence of friction. Carabiners can be substituted for pulleys if the latter are not available, but add much friction.

In setting up the Z-pulley system, the main anchor is normally placed about 15 feet from the edge of the crevasse, and an anchor sling attached. The climbing rope is laid out in a "Z" pattern, one apex of which is snapped into a pulley located at the main anchor. A short sling, fastened with a prusik knot to the climbing rope near the crevasse edge, is snapped into a pulley to the other apex. As the rope is hauled in, the floating pulley on the short sling moves upward toward the main anchor pulley. Now the rope is anchored with the safety sling attached to the main anchor while the pullers slide the sling attaching the floating pulley down for a new grip. Too long a pull at one setting must not be attempted — if the two pulleys touch, the "Z" will snap out of the rope and the mechanical advantage will suddenly be lost, with a corresponding increase in effort required. Mechanical advantage is regained as soon as the pulleys move apart again. For greatest efficiency the main anchor should be well back from the crevasse, and all ropes should pull as nearly parallel as possible to the loaded rope. A long lift with each setting of the safety prusik knots speeds the operation.

Sometimes the terrain is cramped and a pull in the opposite direction may be necessary, toward the edge of the crevasse. Theoretically the same mechanical advantage with reversed pull can be obtained, with a system similar to the one illustrated, by rigging another pulley from an additional anchor located near the main anchor. In practice the added friction reduces the overall system's mechanical advantage to about 1.75. There is also great risk of pulling out the additional anchor, which must therefore be well guarded if this sytem is used.

For a long lift when two ropes are tied end to end there is a method of bypassing the joining knot around the pulleys. When the knot reaches the floating pulley, the prusik knots pass easily over it but the joining knot balks at the main anchor pulley. Now the safety prusik sling holds the load while the main anchor sling is lengthened slightly and its pulley relocated below the knot. The pull continues until the knot reaches the floating pulley; again the safety prusik sling holds while this pulley is changed to the other side of the knot. Finally the system is free to operate for another rope length.

Fig. 152. Z-pulley system.

Crevasse Lip Problems

With all rescue methods great difficulty can be encountered in bringing the victim the final few feet to the surface. The climbing rope tends to cut into the crevasse edge in stopping the fall; unless buffered with an ice ax the rope saws deeper still during the rescue and may utterly vanish into a deep groove, freezing there so that no amount of effort can budge it. A person thus stalled is in serious trouble.

One solution is to tunnel down along the rope, taking care not to drop debris on the victim. Failing that, rescuers can drop a spare rope to which the victim shifts his weight while the other is freed. Usually the rope can be peeled back out of the slot once the victim's weight is off it. If that fails it may be necessary to *carefully* chop the adjacent snow away.

If spare line is not available the stuck rope must be salvaged. In the prusik method a person usually, by the time he reaches the buried section of rope, is trailing enough slack to reach his rescuers. He ties in again to his climbing rope near his prusiks and then unties his original waist knot and sends up the end of a retrieving line. With this anchored he can retie his foot slings on the free rope and resume ascent.

Even when the rope has not gouged deeply into the lip there is always the problem of prusiking the last few feet; when the knots bear against the wall, the final stretch must be surmounted by a scramble or a hard upper haul. It is much easier for the climber to scramble over the lip when he remembers to *unclip his chest sling* from his prusik slings and/or climbing rope. In a pulley rescue the last bit over the lip may similarly require brute strength, though usually by the time the imbedded portion of the rope is reached enough slack has been hauled in for free ends to be lowered.

If the rope has gouged into the lip so deeply that the victim is pulled into the wall rather than over the edge, a sling can be attached to the rope behind the lip to use as a step to get up over the edge.

Supplementary Reading:

Post, Austin, and Edward R. LaChapelle. *Glacier Ice.* Seattle: The Mountaineers and University of Washington Press, 1971.

18 *

ICE CLIMBING

A NUMBER OF SUBSTANCES requiring similar climbing techniques are ordinarily grouped under the generic term "ice." Most common is *hard snow* or *firn*, which on warm days loosens into a coarse-grained snow but in shadows and cold weather freezes hard. Snow that lasts out a summer and is compressed under winter snowfalls may ultimately become *glacier ice*, varying from *white ice* with considerable entrapped air to *blue ice* with little or none. Snow in north-facing couloirs may undergo a similar transformation, primarily through melting and compaction. Impregnation of blue ice by sand and gravel results in *black ice*, abrasive and hard as concrete. The term ice may also be extended to the icy snow in avalanche channels, cornices, moats, and strong crusts. *Water ice*, or *verglas*, forms in layers over rock when mist or rain freezes to the surface or as a result of snow melting and refreezing. Despite the differences in structure and origin, these different forms of ice are all climbed using the same general techniques.

In ice climbing, snow techniques are used to their limits, then supplemented by others that increasingly resemble those used on rock. When steps can no longer be kicked, crampons provide traction; when the slope steepens, front-pointing techniques are used or steps and holds are cut with the ax; on the steepest slopes, the climber may have to resort to direct aid, using ice screws or pitons.

BALANCE AND HOLDS

Ice climbing is balance climbing; indeed, the elements of balance on rock presented in Chapter 12 are even more essential on ice with its low friction and complex, unreliable structure. To further complicate matters, the rock climber maintains three of his four points of support (hands and feet) while moving the fourth; on ice, the climber often has only three points available — his feet and his ax — and must move with only two points of support. On moderate slopes, either the spike or the pick touch the ice to help the climber maintain his balance, just as a rock climber's hands are used in balance climbing. On steeper slopes, the pick is lodged in the ice and the ax is used as a hold. On the steepest slopes, the ax may be supplemented with an ice hammer or another ax to provide an essential fourth point of support, or, alternatively, steps and handholds may be chopped.

CRAMPONS

Three points from Chapter 15 must be re-emphasized before further discussion of the role of crampons in ice climbing: (1) the crampons *must fit* the boots as snugly as possible, (2) the crampons *must be sharp*, and (3) they *must be suitable* for the climb being attempted. For example, 10-point crampons are entirely satisfactory for ascents of most (but NOT all) routes on the gently sloped volcanoes of the Pacific Northwest, but useless in midwinter climbs of verglas-clad gullies. Conversely, the ice-gully and frozen-waterfall specialist finds only 12-point, rigid-frame crampons suitable for his purposes, whereas the average climber finds them too specialized for his more general needs.

When to Put Crampons on

If there is any reasonable likelihood that crampons may be needed, they should be carried. Conditions change rapidly: an east-facing slope may be mushy enough for step-kicking during the morning's ascent but can become a sheet of smooth white ice in the afternoon's shade. Furthermore, cramponing may contribute directly to the party's safety by enabling it to negotiate stretches of ice more rapidly and with less fatigue than if steps were chopped.

The decision whether or not to wear crampons is too dependent upon the situation for any hard-and-fast rules to be given. Wearing crampons should not be considered mandatory for simply venturing onto a glacier; neither should a climber habitually "save time" by never wearing crampons on steep, exposed icy patches just because they are fairly short. As a general guideline, crampons should be used on any ice or frozen snow slope longer than one rope length if there is a possibility of a serious fall, and on rock climbs when they are "iced up." Another important guideline is to don crampons *before* they are needed to avoid the unhappy situation of trying to put them on while teetering in ice steps.

On mixed rock and ice climbs constant donning and removing of crampons consumes so much time that the summit may well be lost.

Alternatives which may be considered include (1) wearing crampons through the entire climb (a good solution if the terrain is 50 per cent or more suitable for crampons; however, crampons may skid or be broken on rock surfaces); (2) climbing without crampons and chopping steps where necessary (if the snow/ice patches are fairly short, good belays are available, and rock predominates); and (3) one climber wearing crampons throughout the entire climb to lead the ice pitches and one climber without crampons dealing with the rock. Again, it should be emphasized that these alternatives are suggestions and that the decision must be based on the conditions at hand.

Crampons should be taken off whenever the snow begins to ball up badly in them and no improvement in snow conditions is reasonably anticipated. On the ascent, it may be possible to clear away the soft surface snow and climb on the ice below, but this usually is impractical and utterly futile on the descent. Some balling usually occurs on even the hardest snow and the climber should occasionally kick his crampons free of accumulated snow. The time-worn practice of whacking the ice ax shaft against the crampons to knock out the snow works, but is hard on the ax (and perhaps the ankle). Alternatively, the crampon may be wrapped in plastic sheeting or coated nylon fabric, which is forced on over the points.

In those unhappy situations where the crampons must be worn even though the snow balls up in them, shuffling the feet through the snow instead of stepping along over the surface tends to force the accumulated snow through the back points. The normal kicking motion of the foot generally keeps the crampons snow-free on the ascent and while traversing. On the descent, the climber drives the toe of his boot under the surface of the snow ahead of the heel, literally walking on the ball of his foot; if he keeps his weight well forward and deliberately uses short skating steps, his foot slides forward to penetrate the harder sub-layers and snow sticking to the crampons slides out from between the points with each step.

Crampon Technique

Modern crampon technique has evolved from two older complementary techniques, "flat-footing" and "front-pointing." When the two are combined and used under appropriate circumstances, they enable the climber to move efficiently and with minimum fatigue over the variations in terrain. Generally, flat-footing is used on lower-angled slopes and where point penetration is easy; front-pointing is most common on slopes steeper than about 50 degrees and on very hard ice.

Flat-Footing

Flat-footing involves a logical and natural progression of coordinated body and ice ax positions to allow the climber to move steadily and in balance while keeping all vertical points of his crampons biting into the ice. The weight is carried directly over the feet, the crampon points stamped firmly into the ice with each step, and the ankles and knees flexed to allow boot soles to remain parallel to the slope.

On gentle slopes the climber simply walks where he chooses — usually straight up the hill. His feet are naturally flat to the slope and the ax is used as a cane. If pointing the toes uphill becomes awkward, they are turned outward, duck-fashion.

As the slope steepens, the climber must turn his body to face across the slope rather than up it. His feet may also point across the slope, but additional flexion and greater security are gained by pointing the lower foot downhill. The ax is used only to maintain balance and may be carried in the cane position or the arrest grasp with either the pick or point touching the slope. Movement is diagonal rather than straight upward and the climber takes advantage of natural irregularities and locally lower-angled slopes, just as in slab climbing.

Changes in direction are accomplished as in step-kicking on snow: by planting the downhill foot, turning the body towards the slope to face the opposite direction, and stepping off with the new downhill foot. On gentler slopes, the flat-footed approach is used throughout, but it is more secure and easier on steeper slopes to initiate the turn by kicking in the front points and briefly front-pointing through the turn. At some point in the turn, the grip on the ax must be reversed. The exact moment for this depends on the preference of the climber and the specific situation; however, the one important consideration is the security of the climber's

Fig. 153. Ascending with crampons and ax.

footing – his stance must be solid when he temporarily relinquishes his third point of support.

On very steep slopes, those which approach the limit of practical use of this style of ascent, the climber begins to rely on his ax for the security of a hold as well as for balance. The ax is held in the arrest grasp with one hand on the head and the other on the shaft, above the point; the well-sharpened pick is planted firmly in the ice at about shoulder height to provide one point of suspension while a foot moves forward and the crampons are stamped in.

Descent follows the same general progression of foot and ax positions: descend the fall-line, gradually turning the toes out as the slope gets steeper; as the angle increases, widen the stance, flex the knees, and lean forward to keep weight over the feet; and finally, face sideways and descend with the support of the ax in the arrest position. On very steep or hard ice it may be necessary to face the slope and front-point backwards.

When flat-footing downhill, all crampon points should be stamped firmly into the ice. It may be necessary to shorten the stride to take very small steps which allow the climber to remain in balance as he moves; long steps require major weight shifts to adjust balance. The "bannister grasp" of the ax (hand grasping shaft just below axhead and pick pressed into the ice) permits the climber to descend steep pitches while still facing out.

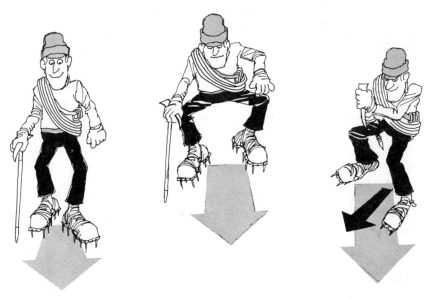

Fig. 154. Descent with crampons. *Left* to *right:* gentle, moderate, and very steep slopes. Grey arrows point downhill. Travel is directly downhill except at right where a black arrow shows climber's traversing path.

Fig. 155. Descent with ax in "bannister" position.

Front-Pointing

Front-pointing enables even average climbers to quickly overcome steep pitches which would call for the utmost in skill from practitioners of a purely flat-foot technique. The climber ascends by kicking in the front points of his crampons and stepping directly up on them. Rarely is extremely hard or repeated kicking needed to gain purchase; usually a firm kick directed straight inward is all that is necessary. Standing straight up utilizes the body weight to force the front points of modern 12-point crampons into the ice.

A third point of support is obtained by lodging the pick of the ax firmly in the ice. The ax is held about shoulder high in the arrest grasp and is used more for balance and security in the event of a slip than as a hold. Alternatively, the ax may be held by the head, in one hand only, and the pick used at shoulder height as a dagger or for down-pressure at hip level. On short pitches or when used with an ice hammer, the ax may be swung overhead like a hammer to sink the pick deeply in the ice. On the very steepest ice climbs, the ax may be left behind or carried in the pack and the climber may use two hammers to supplement his front points.

Front-pointing is tiring and the legs, especially, must be in excellent condition before the climber can hope to proceed in this manner for any great distance. To ease the strain on aching calf muscles, the flat-foot and front-point techniques may be combined, that is, one foot front-points while the other is placed flat on the slope. On long climbs, the advantages of stiff-soled boots and rigid-frame crampons become readily apparent, reducing as they do the amount of muscular effort needed to stand on the small bearing surfaces of the two front points of each crampon. Thus, the experienced ice climber selects and uses his equipment and varies his techniques so that he can climb routes of considerable steepness and difficulty without becoming too exhausted to descend safely.

The skilled ice climber, whether flat-footing or front-pointing, displays the same deliberate calculation in his movements as the rock climber on a difficult slab. He must carefully place his points of contact with the slope and transfer his weight to them smoothly and decisively. Essential to skillful cramponing is boldness — exposure must be disregarded and concentration focused solely on the climbing.

Boldness is not blind bravado nor is it a blend of the beginner's naive faith in his equipment added to his discovery, while attempting a severe ice climb, that the techniques he read about seem to work pretty well — so far. Instead, it is a confidence born of experience, developed in many practice sessions on glacier seracs and ice bulges in frozen gullies and followed by ascents of gradually increasing length and difficulty. Only in this manner can the boldness, decisive confidence, and skill be acquired rationally; these attributes are a result of time and practice, *not* reading, enthusiasm, and intestinal fortitude.

Fig. 156. Front-pointing.

Under ideal conditions, experts have extended the flat-foot technique to slopes of 60 degrees and front-pointing to overhanging bulges, using hammers for holds; however, the average climber is unlikely to be able to perform at this level for long periods of time and may desire the additional security of chopped hand and footholds while leading difficult or exposed pitches on steep ice.

STEPCUTTING

If the party is without crampons, has elected not to put them on for occasional short icy stretches, or if the slope has become so steep that members no longer feel secure cramponing, they will cut steps and, perhaps, handholds. Stepcutting must be done rhythmically to minimize fatigue and decisively to get the most out of each whack.

Most frequently, the steps are cut in a path leading diagonally up and across the slope, switchbacking from time to time; only occasionally is it necessary to cut steps straight uphill. Thus, the climber normally stands sideways to the slope, his body erect and the weight carried mostly on the advanced foot. His other foot may be placed as an outrigger to maintain balance or he may rest his inside knee against the slope. If possible, the ax is held with both hands near the spike; however, extremely steep slopes may require one-handed stepcutting. The wristloop is *always* worn for extra wrist support and to prevent loss of the ax if it slips from wet mitts and tired hands. On long, steep, or exposed slopes, the leader should be belayed and the belayer firmly anchored.

On hard snow the adze is used, first cutting a hole at the heel end of the step. Additional blows, chopped progressively toward the toe end of the step, raking the snow out and towards the climber, enlarge the step until it will take the whole foot. If steps are being cut straight uphill, the step need only be large enough to accommodate the front half of the boot.

The pick does most of the work in cutting steps on ice. Two or three hard two-handed blows may be sufficient; however, if more are needed, the first two or three are directed horizontally to form the tread of the step and the next two or three vertically to cut the riser or inside edge. A clean-up stroke or two with the pick may be needed to finish the step before raking

Fig. 157. Stepcutting.

the chips out with the adze. Whether cutting straight up or diagonally across the slope, the step should be large enough to accommodate the boot and crampon and no larger, although on very steep slopes room must be cut for the calf and knee to allow the climber to stand up.

Despite the satisfaction obtained from watching the ice fly, it is unnecessary to bring the shoulders and torso into the blow, woodchopper style, which literally blasts steps out of the ice. Furthermore, such violent efforts can render balance precarious and pitch a chopper out of his steps. Most of the force should come from arm motion, particularly at the end of the swing, when a slight snap of the wrist aids in flaking out ice. Greater efficiency is gained by using a full swing of the ax — utilizing the momentum of the ax head in place of muscular effort. Thus the climber usually cuts two or three steps ahead of his stance to get a full swing with arms and ax.

Water ice, which is usually laminated, presents special problems: sharp ax picks stick as if glued in place and dull ones glance off ineffectually. Even when the problems can be dealt with, the ice may flake off in layers or "dinnerplate" (shatter conchoidally), leaving dents instead of steps. Finally, even when steps can be formed with the ax, the climber's weight on his crampon points may pry off the outer layers of ice, removing the step and climber from their positions. Steps in this type of ice must be *carved* — gently, delicately, and carefully — and the climber must use them carefully, transferring his weight smoothly and without wrenching his crampon points about in the step.

In cutting steps diagonally uphill, a single line of steps is most efficient and easiest to walk in; on steeper slopes, where passing the inside foot between the slope and the outside foot would be awkward, two parallel lines of steps are cut, one for each foot. The optimum distance between steps varies with the slope and individual, but each step should make the greatest possible gain in distance and altitude consistent with ease and efficiency of movement.

When the route must go straight up, the steps are cut to take boots pointed straight in. Again, a full swing with the ax fashions the step with the fewest blows, so the climber must cut steps well above his head. Cutting the tread is awkward and excessive zeal in the downward strokes can split out the step. A short ax is probably easier to use when cutting straight up and makes it possible to rough out the steps with overhead blows and finish them with the adze when the steps are at about waist height.

Atop the crest of a knife-edged ridge, steps can be made with a single blow of either adze or pick; however, balance is so precarious that often it is better to cut lines of steps on both sides of the ridge, using the crest as a handhold.

Cutting steps downhill is slow, tiring, and awkward. The best stance usually is sideways with the upper, or inside, foot bearing most of the weight and placed slightly ahead of the lower or outside foot. The leader on such descents *must* be belayed. On extreme pitches, leaders have been lowered to the full length of the rope and re-ascended, cutting steps for the rest of the party to climb down; however, on such slopes, it may be faster and safer to rappel. Descending in chopped steps is much like climbing down on rock: facing outwards on easy terrain, then sideways as the angle of slope increases; on the steepest slopes, facing in and backing down, using handholds or the pick of the ax or a hammer for additional support.

Handholds in ice are more carved than chopped. The adze is better suited to their construction than the pick, which tends to split them out and requires a longer, less precisely aimed swing of the ax. The hold should be carved as deeply as possible and should be sloped inward to provide the best grasp.

Cutting steps is so slow and tiring a way to gain elevation that conservation of energy and time is supremely important. The leader must select a route that takes advantage of humps and cracks which provide natural steps and should cut steps just large enough for his needs. Additional excavation is left to those following, who generally have plenty of time to elaborate on his outline, especially on steep ice. The lead should be changed at regular intervals, if possible, to keep a relatively fresh step-chopper in action at the head of the team. Despite the fact that stepcutting is resorted to with lessening frequency, it is still an essential skill which even the best climbers may need if, for example, a crampon or strap breaks or if the party without crampons encounters a patch of steep ice.

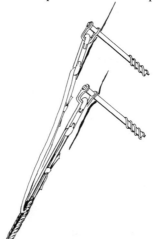

Fig. 158. Ice screw placement. Note, slack sling to second screw allows force to be transferred to second screw as pressure melt weakens placement of first.

PROTECTION ON ICE
Every climbing party should carry a small selection of ice screws if any glacier — or ice — travel is anticipated. These devices can be indispensable in climbing or crossing even the simplest of ice slopes or in overcoming crevasse problems. A full discussion of ice screws and their placement is found in Chapter 15.

Because ice anchors are generally less secure than those used on rock, belays and rappels must be supported with at least two anchors. Placement of ice screws or pitons depends upon the situation, as it does in rock climbing. Generally, on open slopes and in gullies wide enough to allow the leader to climb to one side of his belayer and which are not extremely steep or difficult, only one or two points of protection may be placed on a pitch. The steeper and more difficult or hazardous climbs demand more closely placed protection, provided that it can be placed safely and without leaving the leader too exhausted to continue.

OTHER SAGE OBSERVATIONS
Three generalizations can be made about direct aid climbing on ice: aid techniques should be mastered on rock to attain the necessary speed and proficiency before attempting them on ice; and techniques are most suitable for hard, cold ice, and the climb therefore should be timed to avoid sunlight and warmth on the crucial pitches; and last, since aid climbing is slow at best, routes should be selected to be reasonably free from avalanches and falling rock and ice.

Experts often do difficult climbs with only rope, ax, crampons, and a few ice screws for protection or belay anchors. Novices, on the other hand, have a tendency to bring complex gear into play long before it is really needed and before they are ready to attempt climbs which actually require it. Thus the climber should be trained and experienced enough for the climb he is doing and should limit his equipment to that needed for a reasonable margin of safety; unnecessary items delay the climb and thereby decrease, rather than increase, that margin. In point of fact, time is usually the limiting factor: a slow and inexperienced party can find itself trapped halfway to nowhere, cold and exhausted, with a storm blowing in and no safe retreat available.

As grim as the warnings may seem, ice climbing, when entered into sensibly, can be one of the most exhilarating facets of mountaineering.

Supplementary Reading:

The best information on up-to-date ice-climbing techniques can be found in periodical mountaineering literature of established reputation and merit.

XIV. On ice. *Left*, front-pointing. *Right*, flat-footing. (Sean Rice)

 PART FIVE

Safe Climbing

XV. Sentinel Peak; Glacier Peak Wilderness Area. (Bob and Ira Spring)

19　*

CLIMBING SAFETY

As MOUNTAINEERING is among the most rewarding of sports, so too it can be among the most demanding. The dangers, like the rewards, are found on both physical and psychological levels; disregard or ignorance of any of these hazards may cause the loss not only of the pleasurable benefits, but even of life. This book would be incomplete if it did not outline how to recognize and avoid the hazards and how to realize the ultimate goal of returning safely from the mountains.

From the very outset *every* climber should realize that the burden of safety and accident prevention rests with him. He has the ability, through skill, knowledge, suspicion, and caution, to reduce the probability of his having an accident almost to nil.

ELEMENTS OF DANGER: THE STATISTICAL PICTURE

Sooner or later in his career the climber encounters situations of potential accident, and it is well for him to be forewarned of the most common factors which contribute to mountain accidents, and to reflect upon the basic sources of mountaineering hazards.

Since 1947 the American Alpine Club has published annual descriptions and analyses of climbing accidents in North America. These are available in booklet form and demand close study by every mountaineer. During the 1951-60 decade, 345 accidents were recorded in the United States, 122 of which were fatal; in the 1961-70 decade, 756 accidents were listed from the United States and Canada, with 209 people killed. Only true climbing accidents are included in these totals, as distinguished from those which merely occur in mountain regions. Moreover, the tally shows only those accidents voluntarily reported. Numerous others, even fatalities, occur each year which are never publicized beyond the immediate vicinity. Furthermore, these recorded tragedies are but a fraction of the total world loss; in Europe and in Japan, where large numbers of people regularly engage in mountaineering, the toll is many times greater than in North America.

The statistics published in these annual reports roughly indicate the elements of danger in the sport of climbing, and they show the basic patterns which recur again and again. The most common causes of the accidents reported were (1) fall or slip on rock, (2) slip on snow and ice, and (3) falling rock or other object. The most common contributing causes were (1) climbing unroped, (2) exceeding abilities (inexperienced), and (3) inadequate equipment.

Although every accident is a little different from every other, many of the contributing factors are surprisingly common, and most of the varied causes involve human frailties. Failure of rappels, ropes, pitons, and knots due to improper use is frequent. Injuries from failure of half-learned techniques in exposed situations are common. Mistakes in judgment are as varied as the personalities of the people who make them.

Study of statistics and evaluations of accidents enable the mountaineer to make use of the unfortunate experience of others to evaluate his own actions. As the climber absorbs the experience of others he begins to realize that the maxims of the Climbing Code (see Chapter 1) are not arbitrary but have been forged from actual misfortune. He develops a sound judgment and an attitude which limits danger to a sane proportion of the endeavor. He understands the demands and accepts the responsibilities and thus he becomes a mountaineer.

CLIMBING HAZARDS

The hazards of mountaineering fall into two basic divisions, and an understanding of the dual nature of the problem is essential for the development of a safe attitude. Perhaps the most easily recognized are the objective or physical hazards inherent in the very structure of the mountains and their environment. No less important, but far harder to evaluate, are the subjective hazards which arise from the complexity of the all-too-human climber.

Objective Hazards: The Physical Dangers

Natural Processes

The objective hazards include all the natural processes which exist or operate inevitably, whether or not man is involved. Darkness, storms, lightning, cold, precipitation, altitude, avalanches, rockfall, "acts of God" — all such impersonal factors fall into this category.

Mountains are turbulent places, full of swift violence, where humans are dwarfed by comparison. The climber who cultivates the dynamic view of the mountain will be amazed at the persistence of the continuous destructive forces but never surprised by the rapidity with which conditions can change. The snow that loosens all day and slides in late afternoon, the little midday cloud that unleashes lightning by 3 o'clock — these are things the mountaineer cannot control and therefore must learn to recognize and avoid. He is awed by the part they play — and wisely arranges to be elsewhere while the game is on.

To avoid destruction by these powerful forces the climber first learns *how to recognize* the impending signs of these hazards and second, *how to avoid* them. If he has learned his lessons from other chapters of this book he knows there are places on a mountain where the surface disintegration proceeds more slowly, with long intervals between avalanche or rock slide. He recognizes the possibility of rockfall and wears a hard hat to reduce his vulnerability. He treads lightly to avoid knocking down loose rocks on his climbing companions, and he realizes that with alertness and mental resolution he can avoid essentially all such man-caused rockfall. He knows where hidden crevasses might exist, he ropes up and chooses a route which minimizes the possibility of falling into one, and he is prepared to extricate himself or his companions in event of snowbridge collapse. He has learned to recognize avalanche-prone slopes and what to do in case of being caught in an avalanche. With experience, he develops the keenness of his observations and the astuteness of his judgment to choose the right route at the right time to avoid being caught by what he calls accidents.

Among the objective hazards confronting the climber, the route- and terrain-type hazards are perhaps more evident — simply because of their physical presence — than the weather-type hazards: cold, wind, rain, snow, storm, lightning, fog, white-out, sun, and darkness. Consideration should be given by the climber to each of these potential hazards although they generally are not catastrophic unless the climber is unprepared. However, two such weather-induced hazards are deserving of the serious attention of every mountaineer, namely, hypothermia and lightning.

Hypothermia

Of the many objective hazards that lurk in the wilderness perhaps the most insidious and least understood is hypothermia — the lowering of the body's inner core temperature by cold, wetness, wind, and fatigue. Cold need not be extreme — deaths have occurred at temperatures well above freezing. Wetness could be caused by rain, melting snow, immersion, or even perspiration. Wind vastly increases the chilling effect of cold and wetness (see wind chill chart, Chapter 2), and fatigue lessens the victim's ability to protect himself.

Understanding the effects of cold on the body aids in understanding the genesis of hypothermia. The first response to exposure to cold is constriction of the blood vessels of the skin and, later, of the subcutaneous tissue. The effect is to decrease the amount of heat transported by blood to the skin, consequently lowering skin temperature. The cool shell of skin now acts as an insulating layer for the deeper core areas of the body; skin temperatures may drop nearly as low as that of the surrounding environment, while the body's core temperature remains unchanged at its normal 99 degrees. However, a drop to 50° F. always numbs the skin so that ultimately all sense of touch and pain is lost, rendering the hands, for example, almost useless in performing fine or coordinated movements. Shivering begins shortly after the initial constriction of surface blood vessels and may continue for several hours if exposure to cold is continued. Although it produces considerable heat, shivering consumes a great deal of energy, and if intense and prolonged can result in exhaustion. Inevitably, if this heat loss continues, the body's inner core temperature begins to fall below 99 degrees. As this occurs, body functions are impaired, the victim loses coordination and eventually consciousness. If the situation is not quickly remedied, he dies.

The insidious nature of hypothermia is its absence of warning to the victim, and the fact that as its severity increases, chilling reaches his brain, thus depriving him of the judgment and reasoning power to recognize his own condition. Without recognition of symptoms by a companion, and treatment, this vicious cycle leads to stupor, collapse, and death.

Details on the prevention and treatment of hypothermia as given in Chapter 21 should be assimilated by everyone who ventures into the mountain environment.

Lightning

Though not one of the principal perils of mountaineering, lightning has caused a number of serious — and mostly avoidable — accidents. The very nature of their sport places climbers on or near the most frequent targets: peaks and ridges help produce the vertical updrafts and raincloud conditions which generate lightning; the prominences serve to trigger the strokes. The climber therefore should understand the basic mechanisms involved and fix in his mind the fundamentals of evasive action.

For all practical purposes the hazards are three: (1) a direct strike, (2) ground currents, and (3) induced currents in the immediate vicinity of a strike.

Electrical potential builds up in a cloud in somewhat the same manner one's body picks up an electrical charge on a dry day. Air is normally a very poor conductor (good insulator) of electricity; trees, rock, or earth are better conductors, more so when wet; the human body is still better; and most metals are best of all. Lightning seeks the path of least total resistance between the cloud and earth — the shortest possible line through the air. Ordinarily the closest ground point is directly below the cloud, but a summit off to one side can be closer and become the bull's-eye.

Air ceases to be a good insulator when subjected to a sufficiently high electrical pressure; it *ionizes* and thereupon loses its insulating quality and becomes a conductor. The ionizing breakdown around a conducting projection often gives off a crackling noise (notorious in the Alps as the "buzzing of the bees") caused by small sparks. The distinctive odor of ozone is usually noted. A bluish glow or *corona* (St. Elmo's Fire) may be seen. If a person's head is the projection, the hair (if any) crackles and stands on end. Corona discharges have often been observed when the nearest cloud seemed too far away to be at all relevant. The sound or sight of corona does not necessarily indicate danger, but lacking more precise indication should be regarded as a warning, especially when thunderclouds are nearby. Additionally, any atmospheric activity symptomatic of commotion should stir suspicion. A sudden rush of cold air perhaps announces a strong cold front with possible lightning. A cloudburst of enormous raindrops or monster snowflakes or huge hailstones almost certainly means a cumulonimbus is overhead.

Lightning is, of course, electricity, which is a stream of electrons. When the more than 100 billion billion electrons in an average bolt strike a peak or a tree they do not just lie there in a puddle, but immediately spread out in all directions. In the process considerable damage can result. Two factors determine the extent of human injury: the quantity of current, and the part of the body affected.

The worst threat is the passage of electricity *through* the body in a way which impairs some vital function such as heart, brain, or breathing action. A current from one hand to the other through the heart and lungs, or from head to foot through virtually all organs, is most dangerous, even if relatively small; one can survive a larger current from one foot to the other through the legs.

The climber faces other potential hazards: large currents can cause deep burns at points of entry and exit; a mild shock may momentarily startle him or set off muscular spasms, or he may move about in semiconsciousness, and in either case may fall off a cliff.

First thought should be given to avoiding areas which might be hit. The governing rule is to seek a location with nearby projections or masses which are somewhat closer than one's own head to any clouds which may drift by. In a forest the safest shelter is amid the shorter trees. The middle of a ridge is preferable to the ends; avoid shoulders.

An electrical discharge at a strike point instantly radiates outward and downward, with the intensity of the flow, and consequently the danger to climbers, decreasing rapidly as the distance from the strike increases. On firm rock, especially when wet, the major path in most cases is along the surface. Lichen patches, cracks, or soil may hold moisture and thus provide easy paths. High-voltage currents tend to jump across short gaps, as in a spark plug, rather than take a longer path around.

Current flows because of a voltage difference between two points along its path. A person bridging two such points with some part of his body presents a second, and probably better, path for the current, some portion of which is therefore diverted through his body. The wider the span the greater is the voltage difference and the greater the flow through the body.

With this background, several precepts can be listed:

1. Avoid moist areas, including crevices and gullies.

2. Span as small a distance (occupy as little area) as possible. Keep the feet close together; keep the hands off the ground.

3. Sit, crouch, or stand on insulating objects if possible — a coiled rope or a sleeping bag, preferably dry.

4. Stay out of small depressions; choose instead a narrow slight rise. A small detached rock on a scree slope is excellent.

5. Stay away from overhangs and out of small caves. Large caves are very good if one keeps clear of the walls and entrance. However, a cave might well be the lower terminus of a drainage crevice, and in such case should be avoided.

6. When on a ledge, crouch at the outer edge, hopefully at least 4 feet from the rock wall. If there is danger of falling off in event of a shock, tie in *crosswise* to the prospective flow of current. Make the tie short and avoid placing rope under the armpits.

7. Rappelling when lightning is imminent should be avoided, but may be a valid calculated risk if it is the quickest way to escape a danger zone. Dry synthetic rope presents the minimum hazard.

8. Contrary to popular belief, metal objects do not attract lightning as such. However, in the immediate vicinity of a strike, metals in contact with one's person may augment the hazard from *induced currents,* the nature and mechanism of which lie beyond the limits of the present discussion. Induced currents usually are quite small, but when added to ground currents may mean the difference between life and death. Thus, it is best to set aside all metals, but to keep them close by (don't worry about articles buried in the pack). A metal pack frame might well be positioned to provide a more attractive path for ground currents beside and past one's body. At distances greater than 100 feet from a possible strike there is no need to divest oneself of metal objects.

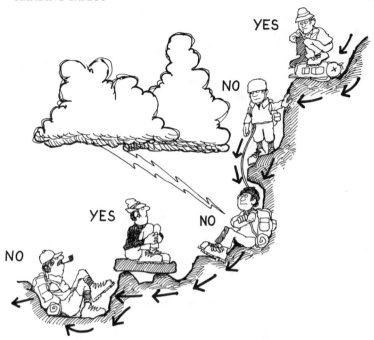

Fig. 159. Body position and location in an electrical storm indicating relative safety from ground currents. (Arrows show probable paths of ground currents.)

The Subjective Hazard: The Climber

Man cannot control the physical nature and the *objective hazards* of the mountains, nor can he completely control the psychological factors which make up the *subjective hazards.* Looking back on an accident one always finds both objective and subjective causes — neither alone is sufficient. The destructive forces daily at work on the mountain are inconsequential unless a human being is in their way at the crucial time. The subjective and controllable factors seldom in themselves cause death; but they do sometimes set the climber on a collision course with one of the objective hazards. It is the combination which is dangerous. A slope may be ripening to an avalanche tomorrow — a climber, ignorant of snow structure, may trigger it today. A rock, slowly weakening by natural processes, may be preparing to fall next week — the weight of a careless climber may pull it loose today. This subjective factor, which brings a particular climber to a given danger point at just the perilous time, is nearly always at the root of a climbing accident.

A climber seeking to control the mountain danger will ask himself which factors of the subjective hazard he *can* control. There are subjective elements in every phase of a climb: the party management, the choice of route, companions, equipment, and techniques, the effort spent in acquiring skill and knowledge, the pre-conditioning, even to a great extent a basic philosophy of approach to mountaineering. If all these elements are under thoughtful control the potential physical danger may never strike.

Of all the psychological hazards the most deadly is *ignorance* — inexperience, climbing beyond one's abilities, unpreparedness, lack of necessary equipment, lack of confidence because of fear or apprehension, poor judgment — and second is its partner, *overconfidence*. The perils of ignorance can be avoided by study and experience; the background of mountaineering knowledge which a climber should have is the scope of this book. However, even the educated and experienced climber can be guilty of overconfidence.

The person with show-off tendencies may be driven by ego to climb beyond his abilities with no margin of safety for the unexpected. A more subtle form of overconfidence arises from familiarity with a given climb: people have been killed because a strong experienced leader thought he could repeat with novices a climb he had made before with experts. Group overconfidence — the fallacious belief that there is safety in numbers — is an insidious danger, one which is the task of leadership to control. Another attitude, not peculiar to climbers but common to nearly every individual, is the feeling that *he* dwells under an umbrella provided by his own special providence, while accidents happen only to the other fellow.

An additional aspect of overconfidence is the generally recognized fact that an individual's ability does, through elusive psychological and physiological factors, vary from time to time. Every experienced mountaineer can remember days when his climbing lacked the usual "feel" and when he had difficulty with pitches well below his normal standard. If a false pride prods him into persisting on a difficult climb during one of his off days, danger can develop. The prudent climber learns to recognize bodily limitations such as inadequate conditioning, overexertion, fatigue, muscular cramps, altitude sickness, dehydration, and incipient blisters, and his temporarily lowered ability, and reacts to them promptly to prevent their becoming a contributing cause or aggravation of an accident, perhaps choosing an easier objective, with no loss of enjoyment.

Subjective dangers are present on every climb. Their control lies in awareness of all the varied factors which influence judgment and decision-making in the mountains. A climber who gains this perspective is never content to fumble or gamble his way up or down a mountain.

Cumulative Factors

Although many accidents occur like "a bolt out of the blue," others, in retrospect, can be seen to have developed, step by inexorable step — following a sort of remorseless logic — until they culminate in the final tragedy.

A typical example might begin with the climber who oversleeps and, in the rush to make up lost time, leaves home without his ax. On the climb the surface of the snow is soft enough to lure him onward, although his companions must belay him. The party dozes on the summit, extending the stay there by another half-hour; descent begins 3 hours later than planned. Perhaps the return proceeds without mishap, but a fall, a sudden storm, and the party is without the time, daylight, and equipment it needs to ensure the survival of all its members.

Occasionally these potential accidents can be recognized while developing, but not always. An alert leader can turn back his minimally-equipped party in the face of obviously-worsening weather, but there are those days which seem to start wrong and get worse, and on such days — and everyone, climber or not, has them — it might be well to temper valor with discretion and select more modest objectives or simply go for a nice walk in the woods.

THE SAFE ATTITUDE: A BASIS FOR CONTROL

To this point the endeavor has been to analyze the dual nature of climbing danger, and to emphasize some of the knowledge fundamental to a safe attitude on the part of the climber, an attitude which permits no more than a reasonable proportion of danger on any climb.

The development of a safe mountaineering attitude proceeds along three lines:

First, each climber must be instilled from the very beginning with a respectful attitude toward mountains, a realization of the basic relationship between their hazards and his limitations.

Second, each person must develop the climbing skill and knowledge of specialized techniques and equipment which supplement his natural abilities.

Third, each must encounter — preferably vicariously — the actual situations which teach him the distinction between safety and danger and enable him to evaluate his margin of safety at all times.

The development of all three lines is parallel: with increasing knowledge and practice of technique comes experience in practical mountaineering situations as well as an intellectual investigation of the fundamentals of the sport. Progress is made when the climber comprehends the reasons for a Climbing Code and resolves to follow its rules. Further study and experience bring understanding of the danger inherent in both the mountain and the climber himself. Using this knowledge the mountaineer can evaluate any climbing situation and is equipped to recognize the fundamental causes — the seeds — from which an accident can grow.

By the time he has understood this much about climbing danger, the mountaineer will have some definite ideas on the kind of climbing he wants to do and how he wants to do it. These ideas make up his attitude toward the sport, in which a paramount element is his consideration of safety.

Of first importance is an attitude of continual suspicion. There is always something in the complex situation that he could have overlooked. Ever alert, he thinks his way up a mountain, analyzing and evaluating, basing decisions on sound reasoning, continually probing for hidden peril and planning ahead to meet it, above all forever suspecting there is something undetected just beyond the limits of his awareness.

As a corollary to his suspicion, every climber must be thoroughly familiar with both the preventive and the corrective safety technique. The safe climber is ready to deal with danger should it develop. High on a glacier far above timberline he asks himself, "Could I survive here if something unforeseen should happen, if we were unable to descend on schedule and were forced to remain all night?" Study of first aid and rescue technique, plus adequate equipment for emergency, should enable him to either answer "Yes" or prompt him to descend and return another day when conditions are more in his favor.

One element of the safe attitude is a generality which applies to every hazard ever encountered in the mountains, and that is always to minimize the time of exposure to danger. Often a calculated risk cannot be avoided, such as when retreating from the peak in a sudden storm. Whatever the reason for taking the risk, it is no more than common sense to better the odds of survival by moving through the danger area as quickly as is consistent with safe travel.

"Margin of safety" is a concept often discussed by climbers, and the individual's evaluation of this margin most fully embodies his attitude toward climbing danger. No one can predict infallibly the boundary of safety, the exact demarcation between routine travel and catastrophe, and the wise mountaineer allows for this uncertainty by keeping the margin of safety as a cushion between himself and peril. The margin is not an absolute thing; it changes character continually to meet changing conditions, but ideally it affords a constant degree of protection for the climber.

Since safety rests upon a number of factors, whenever a weakness appears in one respect the margin must be maintained by adding strength somewhere else. For example, ignorance of the precise breaking strength of rock, or the exact friction between boots and wet vegetation, leads the climber to add the rope. When the moving team might be unable to catch a fall, he adds a belay. If the security of the belayer is in doubt, he adds an anchor for the belayer and pitons for the climber. In doubtful weather he carries extra clothing, food, even bivouac gear, and marks the route carefully. Knowing that rappels sometimes fail, he uses the technique with caution and belays the rappeller. If a member of the team is weak or inexperienced, a balance of strength is maintained by the addition of another strong companion — or by choosing a less difficult objective. The list can be elaborated endlessly, but the principle is always the same: the weakness of one safety factor is neutralized by the strengthening of others.

Such are some of the elements of mountain safety. Only the innocent ignorants are content to set forth blindly on a haphazard struggling journey. The well-trained climbing party proceeds safely into the mountains skillfully directed by responsible leadership that has planned carefully for every reasonable eventuality. At the same time, each member of the team is prepared to cooperate, if need be subordinating his own will; the group responsibility found among mountain climbers is seldom matched in any other human endeavor.

Setting a proper margin of safety and controlling climbing danger — the supreme test of a climber's attitude — depends on his knowledge and his judgment. His judgment determines how he uses his knowledge to remain always within the boundaries established by his never-forgotten Climbing Code. Out of his understanding of the dangers and responsibilities grows a deeper appreciation of the rewards of mountaineering.

Supplementary Reading:

Accidents in North American Mountaineering. Annual report of the American Alpine Club, 113 E. 90 Street, New York City.

Lathrop, Theodore G., M.D. *Hypothermia: Killer of the Unprepared.* Portland, Oregon: The Mazamas, Revised edition, 1972.

Paulcke, Wilhelm, and Helmut Dumler. *Hazards in Mountaineering.* New York: Oxford University Press, 1973.

LEADERSHIP AND THE CLIMBING PARTY

The Group

In most areas of life, man works in groups to achieve his goals more completely, whether the goals are social or individual. In mountaineering, he climbs in groups because he has found that with the help of others he can climb more safely, more successfully, more enjoyably.

On expeditions to remote areas and in climbing organizations or classes, even the most rugged individualist who wishes to participate subordinates his whims of the moment to the needs of the group so that both their success and his will be achieved. In this way he makes his unique personal contribution to the group, but does so within the framework of the group, and thus the climbing party becomes more than the sum of its members. The individual members feel more confident — more aggressive in ascent and more enduring under stress — when they know they are part of a group. On the other hand, the group cannot exist apart from its members. It is created and sustained by their will; the members have a group only as long as they will to be together, to work together and to sustain each other.

Most climbers, however, tend to be strongly and aggressively individualistic and show little inclination to submerge themselves in a group just for the sake of doing so. Moreover, many of the more experienced climbers tend to prefer small parties of close friends held together by a mutual desire to achieve a specific goal. Even in such groups, there always is a leader — a person who is usually first to verbalize the thought on everyone's mind, one who assumes the initiative more than the others, the individual who most frequently seems to be in the right place at the right time to coax, cajole, and prod his companions.

While the group must have unity, it must also have direction and this involves two things: steering and propelling. The group must steer in one direction and, at the same time, be propelled in that direction, too. This is the aim of leadership.

The Leader

The leader is responsible for the success of the trip and the safety of the party. His knowledge, experience, and climbing skill help him meet these responsibilities, but of far greater importance is his ability to deal with others, to inspire and encourage them and to guide them in the exercise of their own initiative so that their efforts contribute to the achievement of the team goal.

The "born leader" possesses a blend of personality traits and acquired skills which enable him to lead and inspire others, seemingly without conscious effort. Those not naturally endowed with these attributes can acquire the same climbing skills, gain the same amount of experience, and develop those qualities which give others confidence to follow their lead. Thus, leaders may be made as well as born.

Character and intelligence may best summarize the variety of personality traits which must be properly blended in an individual to enable him to lead others. There is no single optimum blend which yields the perfect leader, but all effective leaders must possess, among other traits, sufficient amounts of self-discipline, integrity, decisiveness, objectivity, and adaptability. Above all, every leader must consciously accept the responsibilities of leadership — the certain knowledge that his party will look to him for stability and guidance in a crisis — and prepare himself accordingly.

Although experience is important, it is not the most important quality. The members of a party look instinctively to the person who inspires the most confidence. This may not be the climber with 20 years experience if those years were spent in compulsive climbing motivated by egoism or thrill-seeking. Rather, it might be the person with only 2 years experience if he also has a lifetime accumulation of common sense and good judgment. Physical strength and agility are desirable but not necessary, since the leader may even be the rearguard and not lead a single pitch of the climb; what matters is that the party looks to him for judgment and decision.

As party size and trip length increase, so do the complexities of leadership. On a weekend climb by two close friends, it may be feasible for one person to plan the menu, buy the food, furnish the transportation, do

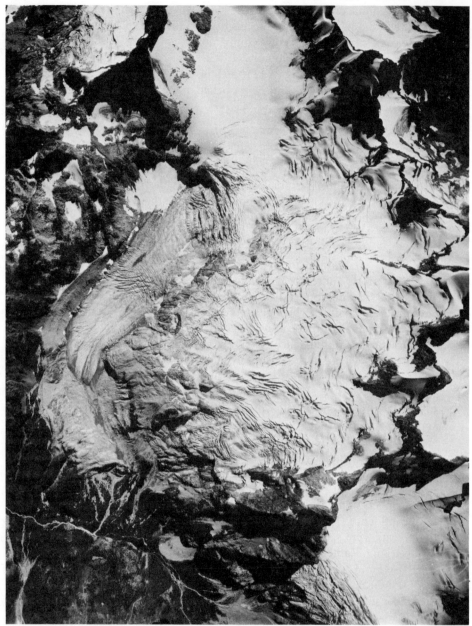

XVI. Chickamin Glacier — vertical view. Dome Peak lower right, Sinister upper right, and Blue upper left; Glacier Peak Wilderness Area. (Austin Post, University of Washington)

XVII. Chickamin Glacier — oblique view. Dome Peak right. Sinister left of center, and Blue left. (Austin Post, U.S. Geological Survey)

the route research and even supply most of the technical climbing equipment; when longer trips and larger groups are involved, this is impractical and probably impossible for one person. The leader cannot do everything nor should he try; rather, he should delegate duties to others whenever possible. Delegation of duties and responsibilities relieves the leader of detail work, enables him to keep the overview of the entire trip, ensures that all tasks are performed, and builds morale by involving the individual members in the climb.

In a large group or in one in which the members are not well acquainted, the leader should appoint an assistant who, if need arises, can assume the role of leader. Next, one person might be assigned the task of planning the meals, another the job of arranging transportation, and a third that of coordinating equipment.

On a climb with others of less experience, the leader may also have to become a teacher and share his knowledge and experience, as others did with him. Techniques may have to be taught and, when possible, time alloted for the "student" to practice these techniques. Inexperienced leaders need — and should be provided — the opportunity to gain experience in all phases of climbing leadership; indeed, helping others learn to lead is the acme of leadership, requiring patience, empathy, and generosity.

While actually climbing, the leader is always thinking ahead, anticipating the problems that may arise and planning their solutions. In camp he is thinking of the climb; on the ascent he is thinking of the descent; in success he plans retreat. His eye is on the horizon, on that little cloud no bigger than a man's hand. He notes symptoms of weariness in his companions and assesses what strength he can count on in crisis. If the party is ascending a face, he studies the ridges on either side; if climbing a ridge, he studies the faces on each side. He plans for bivouacs or alternate routes of descent. He verbalizes problems and solicits alternative solutions, both to relieve his own isolation and to keep the party alert because any one of them may suddenly become leader. Everywhere on the trip, the leader is crossing bridges before he comes to them; and more — he borrows trouble. What to do if a rucksack were lost here, if a belay stance failed to materialize, if a slope were to avalanche? By keeping these things in mind, by being alert and thinking ahead, the leader is, to that extent, master of what happens on this particular climb and he will, to that extent, increase his ability to lead in the future, anywhere he may go.

However, the most common, and the most vexing, problems of leadership are not the major disasters leader fear and for which they have prudently prepared themselves, but rather, the little exasperating mishaps which arise at the most inopportune moments — a lagging, footsore member of the party who dried his boots too well too near the fire, or more seriously, a party member too ill or fatigued to continue the climb but able to descend or stop and wait for the party's return.

There is no set of systematic answers for such trying situations and there is no way of relieving the leader of his responsibility for dealing with them. The only proper recommendation can be to follow the safest, most conservative course. In practice, the leader must use his best judgment as he evaluates the factors pertinent to reaching a decision, then he must make his decision firmly and unequivocally.

Any mountaineering trip involves a rich spectrum of choices and makes continual demands on the will. A route must be found, equipment selected, dangers evaluated, the tired body must be inspired with the will to move. Without leadership, even a strong party may wander aimlessly, sit paralyzed with indecision, or lie abed while only the sun climbs. With good leadership, even a relatively weak party may expect to achieve its goals.

The Party and Its Strength

A party is strong or weak in relation to its goals and several things may make it so: the mountaineering proficiency of the members, the size of the group, and the party's morale. Morale is the most difficult to analyze; in general, a party has good morale when it has good leadership, good "followship," and good luck.

Mountaineering proficiency involves many things, chiefly climbing ability, experience, and good physical condition. A strong party would consist of several experienced, well-equipped climbers in good physical condition, each agile on rock, and each able to handle rope and ice ax with ingrained reflexes. What constitutes a weak party is not so easy to define. In some cases, a party is strong enough if it has only two strong climbers in addition to many weak climbers. In other situations, a group of ten strong climbers and one weak climber is too weak a party. The weak man might merely be clumsy, slow or inexperienced, and yet his weakness might jeopardize the entire party. A party with no experienced members is a weak party in any situation.

In small parties, rope teams are usually formed by tacit agreement among the climbers. In larger parties or in groups where the climbers are relative strangers, the leader may assign climbers to rope teams, basing these assignments on experience, speed, and personality. Each team should have enough strength to rotate the lead, distributing the work of stepkicking and trail building among all and allowing less experienced climbers to expand their fund of experience.

At all times, the leader should know where his most competent climbers are so that he can make their abilities of greatest use to the party. He may need to assign a patient, reliable friend as rearguard to encourage slow or weak members or he may need to send a team ahead to scout or prepare a portion of the route. If the leader is at or near the head of the party, his assistant should probably be near its rear to ensure continuity of control in the event the leader's entire team becomes involved in an accident.

Deciding the most appropriate size of a climbing party requires consideration of many factors. Ideally, the minimum size of a party is the number of people who can handle an accident situation adequately.

Traditionally, a minimum party of three has been standard: if one climber is hurt, the second can stay with him while the third goes for help. Variations from the basic unit of three depend on the particular situation. On difficult climbs where it would be dangerous for one man to go alone for help, four is the safe minimum. On the other hand, if there is a support party nearby, a rope of two may elect to climb alone. On a glacier climb, four to six people are needed where a speedy crevasse rescue may be necessary. A climb in a remote area where there is no support for hundreds of miles must plan for complete self-sufficiency and, therefore, becomes an expedition of relatively large numbers.

A party gains in strength if it has a support team of climbers nearby or if there is another climbing party in the area. The latter case often proves to be merely a parody of safe mountaineering, because the other party might itself be exhausted or need rescue. To be useful, a support party must be willing and able to do rescue work and ready, moreover, to initiate rescue automatically at a prearranged time. In cases where there would ordinarily be no support in the area, the climbing party should arrange in advance to have support available somehow, as near to the area as possible, leaving its plans and time schedule with a responsible person who will dispatch help if the climbers do not return when due.

A mistake to be avoided is the belief that a larger party is a safer party. A larger party can start bigger avalanches and kick down more loose rock. It can retard itself in many ways, both in camping and climbing. No matter how well organized and led, the largeness of the group tends to breed overconfidence and carelessness, even among good climbers. The large parties of 40 to 60 are now a thing of the past; a party of approximately 15 is presently considered to be the maximum number which can impose itself on a wilderness environment without serious damage to the ecosystems.

The Trip

Some climbers like to make adventure their objective and strike out into the wilderness deliberately ignoring "cookbook" information, thus enjoying the challenge of a pioneer ascent on even the most heavily traveled peaks. Most parties, however, aim at a more definite objective and, to attain it, the leader first gathers all the information he can concerning the best approaches, the best campsites, the location of the various climbing routes and their difficulty.

After the party has chosen its objective, plans have to be made for food, transportation, and equipment. Each member should be fully informed of these plans well in advance of the day of departure.

Time is one of the most important considerations in planning any climb. The party will be safe and successful according to how it uses its time.

Other factors, such as proficiency, size, and morale, contribute to the party's strength in many ways, but the most important of these is the way they enable the party to use its time.

A time schedule should be drawn up. Good scheduling requires thorough consideration of many factors and will usually swing the balance from failure to success. In addition to estimating time requirements for the climb itself, the trip planners allow some extra time for minor mishaps, inadvertent bivouacs and the like, before leaving the trip schedule with the support-dispatcher. The extra margin of time gives an extra margin of confidence, for the party can afford to climb more conservatively than if hurrying to meet a deadline.

Consider, for example, a party camped at 5000 feet below an 8000-foot summit. The leader determines that ascending to 7000 feet will be straightforward and will take 2 hours. The next 500 feet is steep ice and may take 1½ hours. The final 200 feet of rock and 300 feet of scrambling will take 3 hours. The ascent will, therefore, total 6½ hours from camp to summit. Descending the rock by rappel will take 1 hour; descending the ice will take as long as the ascent, 1½ hours. The long glissade down the bottom slope should require only ½ hour. Hence, the total descent will require 3 hours, and the total climb 9½ hours. On this particular day, darkness comes at, say, 8:30. The party wants an hour on the summit and 2 hours of daylight left after return to camp, and 2 additional hours must be allowed as a margin of safety. Thus, the starting time from camp in the morning is — despite the moan of the indolent and the cry of the dissenter — 6 o'clock. A similar projection of estimated times along highways, trails, and through the brush will fix the necessary departure time from home in order to reach high camp at a decent hour.

The accumulated experience of the party affects its time use directly. An expert routefinder can choose a route with little wasted time. Likewise, the experienced leader can evaluate situations and make good decisions faster than the less experienced person. Experience adequate for easy trips may be inadequate for harder ones; but, in general, an experienced leader has not only an accumulated store of knowledge to draw on, but also the very habit of decision-making, so that his lack of experience with the details is compensated for by his confidence and shrewdness in on-the-spot decision-making. The more experienced the leader, the less he is slowed and awed by unfamiliar situations.

The climbing ability and physical stamina of the party also affect its time use. If the climb is difficult, all members of the party must be suitably experienced and capable. If the climb is a pre-dawn to after-dark tour, the members must have the endurance to maintain a steady pace for the whole time *plus* reserves of strength for coping with the unforeseen.

On the trail or on the peak, many problems can be avoided by setting and maintaining a good pace. This is not to say that the pace must be fast or slow (relative terms — what is fast for one party might be slow for another and what is fast for one terrain might be slow elsewhere), but that it must be suited to the group and its objective. A small party generally moves faster than a large one and can be more casual in setting its pace; however, a larger party must be kept moving steadily because a greater number of people devour time and tend to exert a braking action on themselves.

Most long climbs involve camping for one or more nights. Camps should be located with the time factor in mind. The higher the camp, the greater the time available next day for the climb (or the later the party can sleep). On the other hand, the scenic camp high on a peak is attained at the cost of a long, pack-laden trudge up from the valley floor.

An extremely important responsibility of leadership is that of keeping the party together or, at the very least, in strong enough units to deal with an emergency. In small parties of equally proficient climbers, little effort is needed to achieve this and when one member or one team lags, the others usually realize a problem has arisen and slow their pace. In larger parties, the leader and his assistants must work together to avoid having their group become fragmented into a number of independently wandering groups. This sort of situation most often arises within organized club outings and climbing courses; leaders of these groups may need to exert considerable control to keep the lead rope from ranging too far afield and to stay in contact with the last team.

Although it is hard enough to keep the party together on the ascent, it becomes even more difficult on the descent and the leader, who is normally the last man off the mountain, must have crystal-clear plans and instructions laid out and issued regarding rendezvous points for regrouping in the event of separation. Glissading has played a major role in the breaking up of many parties on the descent, particularly those with limited experience: the first glissaders frequently take off down the mountain long before the last ones have come down. To prevent this, the leader should require a rendezvous of the entire party reasonably near the end of the glissade.

The climber who leads the descent must keep the party under control and not moving so fast as to cause a separation of the group, thereby dramatically weakening it and creating the substantial additional burden of trying to locate the missing member or members while still endeavoring to maintain sufficient strength to complete the descent. A party which stays together may use its strength for the attainment of its original objective and to return to camp.

The Margin of Safety

In all his planning and in all his decisions, the leader must think in terms of his margin of safety — the reserve of time, energy, and equipment a party has maintained for handling unexpected trouble. Even with the most detailed planning and maximum alertness, there is always the unexpected, and precautions should be routinely taken to insure the ability to deal with it.

The party must be prepared, with surplus food, clothing for colder weather than is anticipated, more rappel slings and pitons than needed, an abundance of extra flashlight batteries and bulbs. To emphasize a point already discussed, in setting the starting time, the leader plans for a reasonable margin of daylight. The leader also takes the precaution of roping his party before it is absolutely necessary, rather than waiting until the very fine line between Class 3 and 4 climbing has been crossed. In making decisions regarding turning back or bivouacking, or in failing to make them, if the leader does not make ample allowance for turning back, the bivouac is sure to follow. If the party is caught by darkness, however, the leader insists that they bivouac while still on easy ground rather than climb until hung up or completely exhausted.

The more experienced a climber, the more he realizes the margin of safety is a good half of the enjoyment. The student need not be experienced, however, to realize that the more efficient the leadership, the more smoothly the climbing party functions as a group and the wider the margin of safety.

Becoming a Leader

There are still two important problems to be considered: how a person can learn to lead and what basic guidelines exist for making leadership decisions.

Becoming a good leader is a do-it-yourself project, requiring desire and initiative. The best way to become a good leader is to lead and to watch others lead, to organize informal private trips with friends on short, familiar climbs and gradually move on to more ambitious projects. If possible, the trainee should climb with more experienced leaders and observe how they plan and how they work with their teams. He should seek assistant-leader positions with these experienced climbers and become involved in the planning and decision-making process. Finally, after leading or assisting on a climb, he reflects on his performance: did he do as well as he could have? What went right? What went wrong? How could things have been improved?

The Climbing Code, discussed in Chapter 1, is the soundest set of guidelines yet advanced for making decisions, general principles which retain their validity under a wide variety of circumstances. As the sole basis for his decisions, it may cost the novice leader some summits, at first, but it is unlikely to cost him his life or the lives of his friends. Later, as he gains experience and insight into the complexities of leadership, he may modify and adapt the individual rules of the Climbing Code to specific situations; however, it is unlikely that he will ever depart radically from it because it is based on a commonsense approach to safe mountaineering.

The challenges of leadership bring about its pleasures as well as its burdens. The rewards are commensurate with the amount of effort expended. As awesome as the responsibilities appear to the first-time leader, the exercise of competent leadership can become surprisingly easy when he has fully accepted these responsibilities, has prepared himself for the task, and can use his common sense in adjusting to rapidly changing situations.

21 *

FIRST AID

THIS CHAPTER IS NO SUBSTITUTE FOR
CURRENT FIRST AID TRAINING

WHEN ACCIDENTS OCCUR away from civilization a doctor's services
are seldom immediately available, and it is therefore the responsibility of
all who venture into the mountains to possess a working knowledge of how
to examine and properly care for disabled persons until professional
services can be obtained. To this end it is highly recommended that ALL
wilderness travelers be trained in current first aid procedures by enrolling
in an advanced first aid course, preferably a mountaineering-oriented first
aid course of recognized merit, or an emergency medical technician
(EMT) training program, for only with supervised classroom and practical
experience will an individual be prepared to handle the emergency situation efficiently and with confidence. Further, emergency care practices
and procedures are continually changing and being improved; therefore
periodic refresher courses are recommended.

There are numerous conditions which can affect a party member,
thereby incapacitating not only him but the entire party as well. This
chapter does not attempt to cover every possibility, but only to *summarize*
the more common problems, with emphasis on life-threatening emergencies, and major injuries which if not treated properly could result in
permanent or long range impairment. It should also be noted that this
chapter focuses on *first* aid — that given in the absence of professional
medical help.

Procedures for dealing with life-threatening emergencies are presented in the order of their importance: pulmonary resuscitation, cardiopulmonary resuscitation, and control of hemorrhage.

GENERAL PROCEDURES FOR
ACCIDENT RESPONSE

Turbulent emotions after an accident frequently confuse those involved. Therefore, knowing exactly what to do and when to do it are extremely important. It is well to memorize an optimum sequence of actions, and to carry an action checklist in the first aid kit. Then, when an accident occurs, a dependable formula is available. For ease in assimilation and reference, the following discussion is presented largely in outline form.

1. Take charge of the situation. Keep cool. Don't panic. Hasty actions, though well meant, may be fatal.
2. Approach the victim safely. Do not approach directly from above if there is a possibility of rock or snow slide.
3. Perform urgently needed first aid IMMEDIATELY — pulmonary resuscitation, cardiopulmonary resuscitation, and control of hemorrhage — since time is of the utmost importance in avoiding certain death.
4. Keep the victim lying down and warm. Always suspect and treat for shock after an accident. Do not move the victim until the extent of his injuries has been ascertained. Keep the victim as comfortable as possible. Reassure him (Tender Loving Care).
5. Check for other injuries. Examine gently and observe for shock, wounds, fractures, dislocations, contusions (bruises), or other irregularities.
6. Analyze the situation. Plan what to do. Preferably the most experienced person should direct the first aid. While he makes a careful examination of the victim, assistants should gather first aid kits and assemble necessary supplies. After the immediate treatment, decide if the victim can be evacuated under his own power. If there is any doubt, assume he cannot. Then decide if the party has sufficient manpower for evacuation or if further aid should be summoned.
7. Carry out the indicated plan. If unable to evacuate the victim, make preparation for bivouacking in the area. If possible, transport the victim to timberline or a sheltered area such as a crevasse. Above all, however, ALWAYS THINK AND ACT IN TERMS OF THE VICTIM. When sending for help, be sure at least two of the stronger members are sent with all the information necessary to effect a rescue. This includes not only information on the victim's condition but the condition of the remainder of the party as well. If possible, complete an accident report of the type shown in Chapter 22 at the scene before leaving. If the party

has sufficient strength, manpower, and expertise to evacuate, the procedures of Chapter 22 should be followed.

PULMONARY RESUSCITATION

In mountaineering, the stoppage of breathing from causes other than death results most frequently from crushing chest injuries, electrocution by lightning, drowning, or drug abuse.

Resuscitation is best carried out by the mouth-to-mouth method. The victim is placed on his back with head tilted backward by pressure with one hand on the forehead and the other beneath the victim's neck, where it is held throughout resuscitation. The mouth and throat are cleared of any foreign material. The first-aider takes a deep breath, opens his mouth wide and places it tightly over the victim's mouth, at the same time pressing his cheek against the victim's nose to form a seal or pinching the nostrils shut with the fingers. The first-aider blows air vigorously into the victim's mouth (any obstruction is readily apparent at this time and should be corrected), then removes his mouth and looks for chest movements associated with the breathing process. At the same time, he

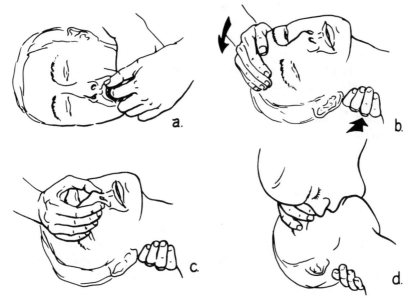

Fig. 160. Mouth-to-mouth resuscitation.

a. Clear mouth.

b. Tilt head back.

c. Pinch off nostrils; take deep breath.

d. Make airtight seal to mouth and blow.

listens and feels for the exchange of air at the patient's mouth and nose. Usually the elastic recoil of the lungs furnishes adequate expiration, but in some cases it is necessary to apply downward pressure on the chest with the free hand. The process is repeated about 12 times per minute for adults and 20 times per minute for children. Note, however, that an adult can rupture a child's lungs, and therefore shallower breaths or even very light puffs are required, depending on the size of the child.

In cases of drug abuse or electrocution by lightning, artificial respiration may have to be performed for a long period of time (1 hour or more) before the victim can resume independent respiration.

CARDIOPULMONARY RESUSCITATION (CPR)

Artificial respiration is only of value if breathing alone will revive the victim; it is of no use if the victim's heart has stopped, since without circulation, oxygen cannot be carried to the vital organs. In this case, heart action must be replaced by external chest compression, called cardiopulmonary resuscitation or CPR. Its use, however, can be quite hazardous. Whereas a victim's weak breathing may be assisted by mouth-to-mouth artifical respiration, if his heart is pumping, even weakly, he will NOT benefit from attempts to assist his heart by compression.

To be successful, closed-chest cardiopulmonary resuscitation depends on thorough and careful training. It is doubtful that one will be able to achieve artificial circulation of oxygenated blood by this method if his only training is from reading written instructions. Further, injury is much more likely when performed by an untrained individual. Fractures of the ribs and sternum caused by improper cardiac massage can cause injury to the heart, spleen, liver, and lungs. The American Red Cross and American Heart Association strongly encourage individuals to obtain training that will qualify them to use this technique.

CONTROL OF HEMORRHAGE

Hemorrhages are of two kinds, arterial and venous. *Arterial bleeding* occurs in pulses or spurts and the blood is usually bright red; since massive arterial bleeding can be fatal in a few minutes, quick and correct action is mandatory. *Venous bleeding* is usually dark and flows smoothly, without spurting. Bleeding injuries should always be examined carefully to determine if they are as severe as they may appear. Many bleeding wounds that at first appear serious may, in fact, be quite minor.

The following steps are taken to control any *major hemorrhage:*

1. Immediately apply direct pressure to the bleeding area! Do not allow severe bleeding to continue while rummaging through packs for sterile dressings; use your bare hand if necessary. When a sterile compress is available, place it directly over the wound. If bleeding continues place

additional sterile compresses on top of the old and continue to apply direct pressure. This stops the bleeding in a majority of instances.

2. If feasible, elevate the bleeding area. Use pressure points if known.
3. Apply cold packs, if available.
4. If these measures fail, and the wound is on a limb, and *only if the bleeding is severe and life-threatening,* apply a tourniquet. Apply it tightly enough to completely stop the bleeding, and once the tourniquet is in place, leave it on; do not loosen it. Tag or otherwise mark the victim to identify that a tourniquet has been placed, the time of placement, and by whom. Remember that a decision to apply a tourniquet is essentially a decision to sacrifice that limb to save the life.

If the wound has been a severe bleeder and transportation is planned, it is advisable to pass a tourniquet beneath the extremity without tightening it. It can then be tightened and fastened promptly if bleeding should re-start and cannot be controlled by any other method. This is particularly necessary if the extremity must also be splinted — it would be difficult if not impossible to apply a tourniquet around or under a splinted extremity.

For small lacerations with *minor bleeding* the area should be thoroughly washed and the edges closed with steristrips, butterfly bandaids, or butterflies improvised from ½-inch strips of adhesive tape. Puncture wounds are not pulled together but are left open and covered with sterile pads. (Sucking chest wounds require special handling and bandaging.) Avulsions (tearing of tissue) and abrasions are simply washed with soap and water and covered with a sterile dressing.

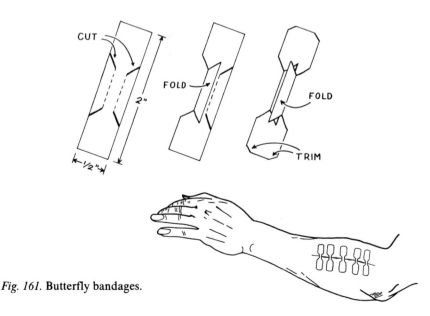

Fig. 161. Butterfly bandages.

SHOCK

Shock is a profound depression of all body processes caused by the failure of the cardiovascular system to provide sufficient blood circulation. It may follow *any* injury, even a relatively minor one, but bleeding, pain, cold, and rough handling are intensifying factors. The victim feels weak and listless and may faint in the upright or sitting position. The skin is cold and clammy, the pulse weak and rapid. Shock actually can be more serious than the initial injury and must be assumed to exist and treated in every casualty.

The following measures are used both to prevent and to control shock:

1. Place the victim in a supine (flat on his back) position to make the blood which is circulating available to the brain, heart, lungs, and kidneys. If the victim has head or chest injuries, it is desirable to raise him about 15 degrees toward sitting position.
2. Keep the victim warm with extra clothing. If he is badly chilled from exposure to cold, apply heat, but not above body temperature; otherwise merely prevent heat loss, using material to insulate from the ground.
3. Minimize shock by controlling hemorrhage, relieving pain and handling gently.
4. Allow victim to drink a weak salt solution (six salt tablets per quart of warm water).
5. If the victim has no injuries to the head, neck, back, or legs, it is desirable to raise the legs by bending the knees to deliver an increased supply of blood to the body core.

COMPLETE VICTIM EXAMINATION

The requirement for this examination is to find the additional (sometimes unseen) injuries that often cause serious complications — the closed undetected fracture that can become an open fracture when the victim is moved, the spinal injury that causes major spinal cord damage when the victim is helped to his feet. This examination must be a "head-to-toe" evaluation with careful checks for specific injuries. A good ten-point examination starts with the head as follows:

1. Check scalp for laceration and contusions, beginning at the back of the neck and working to top of head.
2. Check skull for depressions.
3. Check ears and nose for blood and fluid.
4. Check for neck fractures, feel for lumps and bony protrusions.
5. Check chest region for fractures and wounds, look for movement and feel for fractures.
6. Check abdomen for spasms, tenderness, and discoloration.

7. Check pelvis area for fractures.
8. Check all extremities for fractures.
9. Check for paralysis of lower extremities.
10. Check buttocks for fractures or wounds; be cautious if spinal damage is suspected.

FRACTURES

Fractures are classified in two general categories: closed (simple), with no break in the skin; and open (compound), in which a broken bone fragment has penetrated the skin. One or more of the following signs are usually present: pain and tenderness at fracture site, inability to move or bear weight on the affected part without pain, a grating sensation felt or a grating sound heard during motion of the affected part, and sometimes deformity of the limb or body part. The following are general rules for treatment:

1. When in doubt, treat the injury as a fracture.
2. Splint both the joint above and the joint below the suspected fracture.
3. The extremity may usually be splinted in a position of some deformity. If it is apparent that splinting might result in penetration of the skin (in the case of some ankle fractures), or if splinting or subsequent transportation is not practical in that position, a gentle attempt at repositioning may be made by applying traction and then straightening the deformity.
4. Carefully pad all splints. Make sure the splint is the correct size and shape *before* application. Measure the unbroken extremity and use for a pattern.
5. Check splint ties frequently to be sure they do not interfere with circulation.
6. In the case of an open fracture, the bone end should not be left exposed. Before straightening the limb, thereby allowing the bone to slip back under the skin, examine the end carefully for dirt and debris. Do NOT HANDLE the bone end. If it is dirty, rinse with a saline solution of 1 teaspoon salt or 12 salt tablets in a quart of clean, or preferably sterile, water. (To sterilize the water boil it for 15 minutes.) In all cases, NEVER allow the bone to dry out — keep it wet. Do NOT attempt to push the bone under the skin, but let it slip back of its own accord when the limb is straightened.
7. Above timberline, splint materials are scarce and a good deal of ingenuity is required to immobilize the fracture. Ice axes, piton hammers or uninjured portions of the patient's own body may be the only splints available. Inflatable plastic splints now on the market effectively immobilize lower arm or lower leg fractures; inclusion of these in a group first aid kit should be considered.

Fractures of the jaw are held rigid with roller bandages. Place gauze pads or bits of clothing between the teeth before bandaging to allow for drinking or expulsion of vomitus. *Fractures of the collarbone* are held rigid by roller bandages, cravats or triangular bandages, and by immobilizing the affected arm over the chest. In *fractures of the upper arm or humerus,* the weight of the victim's arms help to overcome the pull of the muscles and reduces pain. The victim's ribs are used as a splint, and the forearm supported in a sling. *Fractures and dislocations of the elbow* are best splinted and supported with a sling in the position of maximum comfort; a position acutely bending the elbow should be avoided, since circulation to the forearm may be cut off. *Forearm and wrist fractures* are best treated by securing to a splint applied on the inner side of the arm, and then supporting the limb with a sling. For *fractures of the hand or fingers,* the hand is folded around a fluffed gauze bandage and fastened with a cravat, webbing, or triangular bandage. *Fractured ribs* are best immobilized by encircling the chest with three to four cravats or pieces of webbing. They should be tightened as the victim exhales. If pain is not relieved upon gentle compression, nothing should be applied since there is some possibility that the ribs are fractured inward, and compression may puncture a lung.

Injuries to the pelvis are most frequently of a crushing sort. There is agonizing pain and possible swelling or bruising at the fracture site. Fractures most frequently occur in the front and a great hazard is perforation or rupture of the bladder. In such case it is essential to limit fluids to less than one pint per day. Pelvic fractures are immobilized by tying the legs together at the knees and ankles with a thick pad of clothing between the thighs.

A *fracture of the femur* is difficult to treat because of the powerful thigh muscles. The broken ends tend to be displaced inward and frequently slip over one another, causing great pain. A splint may be improvised, as illustrated, extending from under the arm on the outside of the leg to below the ankle. The splint must be well padded and held in place by strips of cloth or other material. Under *no circumstances* should a traction splint be attempted; the possibility of causing further damage by impeding circulation is too great.

Fig. 162. Improvised full leg splint.

Fractures of the lower leg, ankle, and foot may be treated by splints improvised from ice axes, alpine trees, or by taping to the opposite leg, making sure to loosen the boot lest the swelling impair circulation. Pad all splinting material and between the legs.

INJURIES TO THE HEAD AND SPINE

Injuries to the head and spine give the alpine first-aider his worst moments. These portions of the anatomy are so delicate that the slightest mistake may cause further injury or death, yet often symptoms are so confusing it is difficult to choose a course of action. Usually indecision revolves around the question of whether or not the victim can safely be moved, or whether medical treatment on the spot is essential. Many climbers, particularly those who have once undergone the agonies of having to make this life-or-death decision, carry a detailed checklist of symptoms in their first aid kit. The sequence of examination and treatment is important, and must be accurate.

Head Injuries

It is first necessary to control any obvious bleeding. This may be done by direct pressure with sterile compresses. Ten minutes is usually sufficient to control most bleeding.

Next the first aider must thoroughly examine the victim.

1. *Unconsciousness* means there probably has been some bruising of the brain tissue by swelling or hemorrhaging, which can create excess pressures within the skull. The length of unconsciousness is roughly proportional to the seriousness of the injury.
2. *Bleeding or secretion of clear spinal fluid* from the ears, nose or eyes are symptoms of skull fracture. If observed, elevate the head to lower blood pressure within the skull and thus lessen bleeding. Caution: ALWAYS suspect a neck injury. Approximately 15 per cent of all severe head injuries are associated with a broken neck (see Injuries to the Spine).
3. *Unequal pupil size or unequal pupilary response* to light indicates possible intra-cranial pressure on the side which is larger or does not react to light. To test for light reaction shade the eye with the hand, then suddenly remove the hand, exposing the eye to bright sun (or to a flashlight). Both pupils should react equally; unequal pupils are an important sign of brain damage.
4. *A very slow pulse* or *noticeable respiratory fluctuation* means there may be hemorrhage within the brain and increased intra-cranial pressure.
5. *A headache generalized over the entire head* may be caused by internal hemorrhage.
6. *Disorientation* by the victim as to when, where, or how he got there may be an indication of serious injury.

If the victim has none of the above-listed symptoms and has no indications of spinal injuries, ask him to stand with his eyes closed. Swaying or falling may indicate damage to the brain or to the labyrinth (balancing organ). If he is stable, he may be evacuated by walking but must be watched during the next 6 hours for evidence of drowsiness, nausea, vomiting, increased headache, bleeding, or unequal pupils. These may occur in injuries where there is an extradural hemorrhage between the skull and the membrane lining the skull.

If the victim has any of the above symptoms, he should be evacuated by stretcher. If his condition is serious, a helicopter evacuation should be considered, and if his condition is progressively deteriorating, speed of evacuation becomes of primary importance.

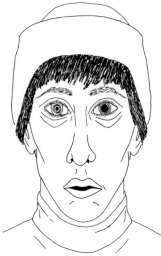

Fig. 163. Eyes with pupils of unequal size.

Injuries to the Spine

Injuries to the spine may be caused by a blow on the head, a fall, or a blow by a falling rock. If there is any doubt as to a possible neck or back injury, examine for it and, if still in doubt, treat it as if it were a fracture. The victim may be able to assist in defining the area of pain. With a cervical (neck) fracture, there usually is a great deal of muscular spasm and the victim will not want to move his neck. The first-aider should check for the loss of muscular and sensory functions in the arms and legs by asking the victim to move them, or by stroking them with a pointed object and asking if any sensation is felt. Always check both right and left sides.

If a fracture of the cervical spine is suspected, splint neck with one pad under the chin to prevent compression of the spinal cord, and others on both sides of the neck to prevent rotation. Alternately, a cervical collar of rolled ensolite or clothing should be applied, with the center directly under the chin, the objective being to prevent hyperextension or flexion positions of the cervical spine. The lateral movements of the neck must also be restricted. For evacuation, log-roll the patient onto his back, being sure his body and head are at all times held in perfect alignment. One person should hold the head and exert slight traction, rotating the head in line with the body as other carefully roll the trunk and legs. EVACUATION MUST BE BY RIGID STRETCHER — not by rope stretcher. If none is available, wait for assistance and proper equipment.

Fig. 164. Cervical collar improvised from sweater.

If a fracture of the back is suspected, slowly and gently roll the victim onto his back with one person keeping the victim's legs constantly in line with his body. Put a small pad under the small of the back to hyperextend it, as there is less likelihood of injury to the spinal cord if the back is returned to the natural arched position. If there is any doubt regarding the extent of injuries EVACUATE BY RIGID STRETCHER.

INJURIES TO JOINTS AND MUSCLES

Sprains

A sprain is a stretching or tearing of ligaments in the region of a joint, followed by hemorrhage, swelling, and tenderness. The most common and distressing type from the standpoint of mountain evacuation is a sprained ankle. If there is pain in the region of the ankle bones or in the region of swelling, the possibility of a fracture is great. It is often impossible to tell without an x-ray if the ankle bones are broken. All severe "sprains" should therefore be treated as possible fractures until proven otherwise. If a sprain has just occurred, the ankle should be elevated and a cold pack applied for 30 minutes to control internal hemorrhage. After that time, if the pain is still excessive, splint as for a fracture.

Strains

A strain is a rupture of the lining covering a muscle, or a tear in the muscular fibers. It is differentiated from a sprain by its occurrence over a muscle rather than in the region of a joint. Localized tenderness is present. Treatment is by warm applications which increase circulation and promote healing.

Dislocations

A dislocation is a tearing of the ligaments around a joint, followed by displacement of the bone from its socket. Most common in mountaineering is dislocation of the shoulder. The shoulder appears more angular, the arm cannot be moved, the muscles are in spasm, and there is considerable pain. A depression can be seen or felt below the tip of the injured shoulder, as compared with the normal side. REDUCTION OF A DISLOCATED SHOULDER SHOULD BE ATTEMPTED ONLY BY TRAINED PERSONNEL, SINCE PERMANENT DAMAGE CAN BE CAUSED BY IMPROPER PROCEDURE.

All dislocations should be treated in the same manner as fractures — by immobilization until medical assistance can be obtained.

HYPOTHERMIA

Many deaths not involving apparent injury have been caused by what the news media refer to as "exposure." Medically, this term is meaningless, for "exposure" is really a condition brought about by a number of factors, one of which, and perhaps the most important, is hypothermia — a lowering of the body's inner core temperature.

To understand hypothermia it is useful to review some basic concepts of how the body can gain and lose heat.

Body Heat Gain

The body can gain or conserve heat in a number of ways, for example, through the digestion of food: the body produces heat by oxidation of food and tissue at a specific rate while resting (called the basal metabolic rate) or at an increased rate while exercising. The body can also gain heat externally from hot food and drink, the sun, fire, another body, and so on, or internally through muscular activity, either by deliberate exercise or by involuntary exercise like shivering. (Shivering produces as much heat as running at a slow pace or the approximate equivalent to the amount of heat generated from eating two medium-size chocolate bars per hour.) Heat is conserved through constriction of surface blood vessels, which reduces circulation at the skin layers and keeps blood nearer to the central core of the body.

Body Heat Loss

The body loses heat in five ways.

Respiration

A large amount of heat escapes when warm air is exhaled. This cannot be prevented entirely but can be reduced by covering the mouth/nose area with wool or fur, thereby "pre-warming" the air as it passes through the material.

Evaporation

Evaporation of perspiration from the skin and moisture from the lungs contributes greatly to the amount of heat lost by the body. Although evaporation cannot be prevented, the amount of evaporation (and therefore cooling) can be controlled by wearing clothing that can be opened easily for ventilation or taken off readily, and wearing clothing that will not absorb water, but will breathe, that is, let the water vapor escape to reduce the cooling effect of evaporation.

Conduction

Sitting on the snow, touching cold equipment, and being rained upon, are all examples of how heat can be lost as a result of conduction. If an individual becomes wet a tremendous amount of body heat is lost rapidly: deaths have occurred as a result of suspension or immersion in water below 40°F — body temperature could not be maintained. Although not as immediately serious in mountaineering situations, perspiration or rain should never be allowed to saturate articles of clothing, thus seriously reducing their insulating properties.

Radiation

Radiation causes the greatest amounts of heat loss from the body from uncovered surfaces, particularly the head, neck, and hands. Coverage of these areas, therefore, is extremely important in keeping warm.

Convection

The body continually warms (by conduction) a thin layer of air next to the skin. If warm air is retained close to the body, it remains warm. If removed by wind or air currents (convection), the body is cooled. The primary function of clothing is to retain this layer of warm air next to the skin, while allowing water vapor to pass outward, by enclosing air in cell walls or between numerous fibers. Heat is lost rapidly with the lightest breeze unless the proper type of clothing is worn to prevent the warm air from being convected away.

Table 10. Effects of Hypothermia.

SIGNS AND SYMPTOMS

Body Inner Core Symptoms	*Observable in Others*	*Felt by Yourself*
Intense and uncontrollable shivering; ability to perform complex tasks impaired.	Slowing of pace. Intense shivering. Poor coordination	Fatigue. Uncontrollable fits of shivering. Immobile, fumbling hands.
Violent shivering persists, difficulty in speaking, sluggish thinking, amnesia begins to appear.	Stumbling, lurching gait. Thickness of speech. Poor judgment.	Stumbling. Poor articulation. Feeling of deep cold or numbness.
Shivering decreases; replaced by muscular rigidity and erratic, jerky movements; thinking not clear but maintains posture.	Irrationality, incoherence. Amnesia, memory lapses. Hallucinations. Loss of contact with environment.	Disorientation. Decrease in shivering. Stiffening of muscles. Exhaustion, inability to get up after a rest.
Victim becomes irrational, loses contact with environment, drifts into stupor; muscular rigidity continues; pulse and respiration slowed.	Blueness of skin. Decreased heart and respiratory rate. Dilation of pupils. Weak or irregular pulse. Stupor.	Blueness of skin. Slow, irregular, or weak pulse. Drowsiness.
Unconsciousness; does not respond to spoken word; most reflexes cease to function; heartbeat becomes erratic.	Unconsciousness.	
Failure of cardiac and respiratory control centers in brain; cardiac fibrillation; probable edema and hemorrhage in lungs. Death.		

TREATMENT

Reduce Heat Loss

Add Heat

Deaths have been attributed to a loss of body heat at temperatures of 40°F, with 30 mph breeze. Under these conditions, the cooling effect on the skin is equal to that of much lower temperatures due to increased evaporation and convection. At lower temperatures and strong winds, cooling occurs even more rapidly. This is why the victim of an accident situation must have wind protection to ensure that his body heat is not carried away. This is why he must also be provided with a great deal of insulation (dead air space) to ensure that body heat is retained at a safe level.

Signs and Symptoms

If heat loss exceeds heat gain, and if the condition is allowed to continue, hypothermia results. The facing table presents a summary of signs and symptoms keyed to the body's inner core (rectal) temperature. The temperatures shown are only approximate, nor can they be measured in the field since normal medical thermometers read only as low as 94°F. However, the table provides an indication of how the bodily functions deteriorate with falling core temperatures. Learn to recognize these signs and symptoms and carefully watch yourself as well as others in your party during exposure to cold, wet, and wind.

Treatment

There are four lines of defense against hypothermia: avoidance of exposure, termination of exposure, early detection, and immediate treatment.

Avoidance of Exposure

In avoiding exposure one should dress for warmth, wind, and wet. When clothes become wet, they lose about 90 per cent of their insulating value. Wind drives cold air under and through clothing and refrigerates wet clothing by evaporating moisture from the surface. Put on rain gear before you are wet; put on wool clothes and wind gear before you start shivering. Do not be deceived by ambient temperatures well above freezing; most hypothermia cases develop in air temperatures between 30 and 50°F, and water at 50°F is unbearably cold — particularly when running down the neck and legs and flushing body heat from the surface of the clothes. Do not ask how cold is the air, but instead how cold is the water against the body.

Termination of Exposure

If you cannot stay dry and warm under the existing conditions, terminate exposure. Don't be afraid to give up your objective and turn back. Get out of the wind and rain. Bivouac early before energy is exhausted and before coordination and judgment are impaired. Eat sweets which are quickly and easily absorbed and keep continuously active to insure adequate heat production.

Early Detection

Any time your party is exposed to wind, cold, or wet, carefully watch each other for the symptoms of hypothermia: uncontrollable fits of shivering; vague, slow, slurred speech; irrational actions; memory lapses, incoherence; immobile, fumbling hands; frequent stumbling, lurching gait; apparent exhaustion, inability to get up after a rest; drowsiness (to sleep is to die). Below the critical body temperature of 95°F the victim cannot produce enough body heat by himself to recover. At this point extreme measures must be taken to reverse the dropping core temperature. Remember that a person may slip into hypothermia in a matter of minutes and can die in less than 2 hours after the first signs of hypothermia are detected.

Immediate Treatment

Although the victim may deny he is in trouble, believe the symptoms, not the victim. Even mild symptoms demand immediate, drastic treatment. First, prevent any further heat loss by getting the victim out of the wind and rain and into the best shelter available. Then remove his wet clothing and replace it with dry garments, insulate him from the ground, and warm him by the most expedient methods available. If the victim is only mildly impaired give him warm drinks and get him into a sleeping bag prewarmed by another member of the party who has stripped to his underclothing in order to transfer a maximum amount of heat from his body to the bag. (Placing a hypothermia victim in a cold sleeping bag, no matter how much down it contains, is not sufficient because the victim's body cannot produce the heat needed to warm the bag and himself.) Well-wrapped, warm (not hot) rocks or canteens also help. Skin-to-skin contact is the most effective treatment, the stripped victim in a sleeping bag with another person (also stripped) or if a double bag is available, between two warmth donors. Build a fire, if possible, on each side of the victim. If he is able to eat he should be fed candy or sweetened foods; carbohydrates are the fuel most quickly transformed into heat and energy. If the victim is semiconscious or worse, try to keep him awake and give him warm drinks (tea, broth, sweetened juice).

FROSTBITE

Frostbite, or freezing of the tissues, most commonly affects the toes, fingers and face. It occurs when an extremity loses heat faster than it can be replaced by the circulating blood or it may result from direct exposure to extreme cold or high wind, as happens with the nose, ears, and hands. Damp feet may freeze because moisture conducts heat rapidly away from the skin and destroys the insulating value of socks and boots. With continued cold or inactivity, the blood circulation to the extremities is steadily reduced, accelerating the freezing process. With adequate equipment, properly maintained and used, frostbite is not likely to occur.

Superficially frostbitten areas are warmed by placing them against warm skin: feet, against a companion's abdomen or in his armpits; fingers, in a person's own armpits. Most emphatically the temperature of the frostbitten area should not be raised much above body temperature, such as by warming near a fire. Such misguided efforts to give speedy relief invariably increase the injury. Further, though the injured part may be snuggled closely, it must never be rubbed, especially with snow, for the additional cooling and the abrasive action of the snow can only cause additional damage to already devitalized tissues. Areas of more extensive or deep frostbite, in which the affected area is white, has no feeling, and appears deeply frozen, should be immersed in 99°F to 104°F water until thawed.

If it is not possible to completely and uninterruptedly thaw the deeply frozen area, no attempt should be made to do so; it is better to await medical assistance than risk incomplete thawing and/or refreezing. In some circumstances, callous though it may sound, no attempt should be made to thaw frozen feet, since it is possible for a person to walk on frozen feet and suffer little or no additional tissue damage; once they are thawed he becomes a stretcher case, creating an obvious burden for the party and perhaps incurring considerable pain.

PULMONARY EDEMA

Pulmonary edema is the leakage of blood plasma into the lungs, which renders the air sacs (alveoli) ineffective in exchanging oxygen and carbon dioxide in the blood. This condition rarely occurs in healthy people below 9000 feet; the average elevation at which it strikes is 12,000 feet in the United States.

The early symptoms of pulmonary edema are similar to those of pneumonia, although pulmonary edema is not precipitated by an infection and there is no fever. Within 12 to 36 hours after reaching high altitude the victim of pulmonary edema experiences extreme weakness, shortness of breath, nausea, vomiting, very rapid pulse (120-160), cyanosis (bluish color), "noisy" breathing which progresses to moist crackling breath sounds, and irritative coughing which produces a frothy white or pink sputum and later blood.

If untreated, the victim rapidly moves into the final phase characterized by unconsciousness and bubbles in the mouth or nose. If the unconscious victim is not immediately moved to lower elevation or given oxygen, he will die. All the early symptoms may be mistaken for "mountain sickness" or fatigue, or may pass unnoticed during the night with the morning finding the victim unconscious in the final phase. (The final stage of hypothermia may also be mistaken for pulmonary edema.) The most effective first aid is rapid evacuation to lower altitude or constant administration of oxygen.

HEAT EXHAUSTION

Heat exhaustion may occur either when an individual is exposed to a hot environment or when he overheats (perhaps because of physical exertion). In heat exhaustion, the blood vessels in the skin become so dilated that the blood to the brain and other vital organs is reduced to inadequate levels. The result is an effect similar to fainting. Lack of acclimatization to heat or even minor degrees of dehydration or salt deficiency make an individual more susceptible to heat exhaustion. All or some of the following symptoms may be present: nausea, cold and clammy skin, faintness, weakness, and perhaps a rapid pulse. Treatment consists of rest, in the shade if possible, with plenty of liquid and salt tablets.

HEAT STROKE (SUNSTROKE)

When exposed to excessive sun the body may become so overheated that it is provided too much blood through the cooling effort of the circulatory system. Symptoms are a flushed, hot face; rapid, full pulse; pain in the head; weakness; dizziness. Sunstroke is relatively rare among climbers since proper headgear usually assures effective prevention. If it occurs, it is EXTREMELY SERIOUS and requires IMMEDIATE treatment by cooling of the head and body with snow or water; administration of cold liquid should be continued until the body temperature drops to near normal.

THE PERSONAL FIRST AID KIT

Mountaineering first aid begins with the first aid kit, an essential which must be carried *by every person on every trip.* The kit should be small, compact, and sturdy. The contents must be waterproof whether the container is or not.

Each person should have the items listed below in his personal first aid kit, plus any medications he needs because of individual medical problems, such as allergies. Parties going on long trips or to regions remote from medical aid may wish additions to their group first aid kit. The majority of these require a doctor's prescription and special instruction concerning their use and hazardous side-effects.

THE MOUNTAINEERING FIRST AID KIT

Item	Quantity and Size	Use
Aspirin	12 tablets — 5 grain	1 to 2 every 4 hours, for pain
Antacid	6 tablets	For indigestion or heartburn; may be Bucladin, Ulcetral, Rollaids, etc.
Antihistamine	6 tablets	1 every 4 hours for insect bites, colds, or hives
Bandaids	12 one inch	For lacerations
Butterfly Bandaids (or know how to make)	6 (various sizes)	For closing lacerations
Carlisle (Battle Dressing)	1 four inch (or sanitary napkin)	For large bleeding wounds
Moleskin	½ pkg.	For blisters
Needle	1 medium size	To remove splinters, etc.
Tincture of Benzoin	1 oz. bottle (plastic)	To hold tape in place and protect the skin
Antibacterial soap or Tincture of Zepherin	1 oz. bottle (plastic)	Mild antiseptic for abrasions, cuts
Razor blade, single edge	1	For shaving hairy spots before taping
Roller gauze	2 rolls 2″ x 5 yd.	For holding gauze flats in place
Safety pins	3 (1 large)	Mending seatless pants
Salt tablets	24	To prevent exhaustion and cramps due to heavy perspiring
Steri-pad gauze	6, 4″ x 4″	For larger wounds
Tape, non water-proof	2″ roll	For sprains, securing dressings, etc.
Triangular bandage	1	For supporting arm, protecting dressing from contamination.

OPTIONAL ITEMS

Drugs	As prescribed by personal physician	If carried, each should be stored in a separate container, and clearly labelled as to dosage, expiration date, type of drug and expected reaction
Elastic bandage	1 three inch	For securing dressings in place. Training in its use is required
Thermometer	1 (-40°F to 120°F)	For measuring temperature
Wire mesh splint	1	For suspected fractures: lower arm, lower leg, cervical

Miscellaneous items may include:
2 dimes and 2 nickels for calling in emergencies
First aid/rescue information
Pencil and paper

COMMON MOUNTAIN MISERIES

Blisters

Blisters result from rubbing of the skin against the socks, either because the boots are too large or laced too loosely, or because the socks are lumpy or wrinkled. To prevent blisters, shoe and sock should be removed at the first sensation of discomfort and the foot examined for reddened skin areas which indicate undue friction. A wide band of adhesive tape, applied smoothly over – and well beyond – the margins of the "hot spot," relieves discomfort and prevents blistering. Application of tincture of benzoin prior to taping makes the tape adhere more firmly and toughens the skin. If preventive measures are not taken in time, a hole may be cut in a piece of moleskin, which is then placed over the blister to protect the area from further direct contact. The moleskin is secured with tape.

Because of the risk of infection, blisters should not be opened unless absolutely necessary. If it must be done the area is washed with soap and water and a needle sterilized with a match is inserted under the blister's edge. Fluid is gently pressed out and a sterile bandage applied. If the blister has already broken it should be washed and bandaged in the same manner and carefully watched for subsequent infection.

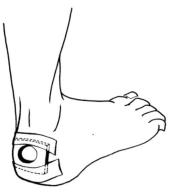

Fig. 165. Blister protection. Circle is cut out of pad to keep pressure off blister.

Headache

Headache in the mountains usually results from inadequate sunglasses, tension in neck muscles, constipation, or some pre-existing physical condition. An occasional cause is "water intoxication," with actual swelling of the brain tissue, when over a period of several days a climber has sweated excessively and drunk great quantities of water without taking salt tablets. In any case of headache the source of the trouble should be sought and eliminated by better protection of head or eyes, stretching and relaxing neck muscles, salt tablets, or a laxative. Aspirin alleviates the immediate pain.

Mountain Sickness

Whenever a person ascends rapidly to an altitude greater than that to which he is accustomed his system adjusts to new conditions: breathing becomes more rapid to extract the necessary oxygen from the thinner air; the blood increases its proportion of oxygen-carrying red corpuscles. In the extreme case, such as when an airplane pilot climbs thousands of feet in minutes, unconsciousness results. The mountaineer, moving upward slowly but steadily, suffers very uncomfortable but less drastic symptoms. First comes general malaise and loss of appetite, followed by increasing weakness and lessening of desire. If forced by social pressure or inner resolution to continue the climb, the sufferer eventually becomes apathetic, nauseated, dizzy, and sleepy.

Symptoms of mountain sickness can occur even at relatively low altitude. Tourists driving in automobiles to 8000 feet sometimes feel lazy or dizzy, or experience palpitations. Climbers generally have more time to acclimatize, and except for shortness of breath usually feel only minor effects until elevations of 12,000 feet or more are reached. However, in regions such as the Pacific Northwest where climbers live at sea level yet ascend to over 14,000 feet on a weekend, mountain sickness of greater or lesser severity is the rule rather than the exception.

Proper use of the rest step is the first remedy. Next come rest stops, with forced deep breathing ("overbreathing") to hyperventilate the lungs. Nourishment in the form of the simple sugars in candy, oranges, or fruit juice should be taken.

Muscular Cramps

Leg cramps caused by an accumulation of lactic acid in the muscles and loss of salt through perspiration sometimes make it impossible for a climber to continue. Such cramps appear suddenly, usually after strenuous exertion for several hours, and the pain is excruciating. During ordinary activity the blood removes lactic acid as it is formed, but in extended exercise a surplus may build up. Resting, to allow the blood to carry away the lactic acid, is the first step in treatment. Deep breathing, and stretching of the cramped muscle as quickly and completely as possible — painful as this may be — give further relief. Salt tablets should be administered immediately to remove the other cause; indeed, many climbers, after finding their cramps quickly dispelled by salt intake, wisely prevent them by using salt tablets at periodic intervals on any climb where they perspire heavily.

SNOWBLINDNESS

Snowblindness is caused by failure to use adequate eye protection (see Chapter 2) during brilliant sunshine on snow or light-colored rock. The eyes are bloodshot, feel irritated and "full of sand." The treatment is application of cool, wet compresses to the eyes, and then having the patient wear two pairs of dark glasses. Aspirin controls the pain. Occasionally it may be necessary to cover the eyes and lead the casualty out by the hand. Recovery may take 2 or 3 days. Snowblindness is not a permanent condition.

SUNBURN

Protection of the skin from the burning rays of the sun is discussed in Chapter 2. At high altitude and on snow nothing but coverage by clothing is completely effective and a degree of burning is inevitable. Lips are particularly vulnerable and some climbers develop severe lip sores unless they exercise special caution. Reflection from snow causes burns in areas not ordinarily affected, such as under the chin, around the eyes, inside the nostrils and ears, and on the roof of the mouth. Lack of a hat when hair is short, thin, or absent may result in scalp burns.

First degree burns with skin-reddening and second degree burns with blisters are not uncommon. The climber often miscalculates the intensity of the sun or is simply too weary to take preventive action. As with any burn — from sun, rope, or fire — if the affected area is large, toxic substances absorbed by the body can cause generalized illness.

Sunburn usually is treated on first notice by further applications of sunburn preventive. In severe cases, and if there is much swelling, cold compresses should be applied. Aspirin may be taken for pain, and warm, salty liquids administered to replenish body fluids.

Supplementary Reading:

American Academy of Orthopedic Surgeons. *Emergency Care and Transportation of the Sick and Injured.* Menasha, Wisconsin: American Academy of Orthopedic Surgeons, 1971.

Grant, Harvey, and Robert Murray. *Emergency Care.* Washington, D.C.: Robert J. Brady Co., 1971.

Lathrop, Theodore G., M.D. *Hypothermia: Killer of the Unprepared.* Portland, Oregon: The Mazamas, Revised edition, 1972.

Mitchell, Dick. *Mountaineering First Aid.* Seattle: The Mountaineers, 1972.

Wilkerson, J. A., M.D. *Medicine for Mountaineering.* Seattle: The Mountaineers, 1967.

22 *

ALPINE RESCUE

ANYONE WHO CLIMBS very often for very long must expect sooner or later to be involved in misfortune, if not his own, then someone else's. The very nature of the sport rules out much chance of help from casual passers-by; climbers usually must be rescued by other climbers, often at great risk and sacrifice. So high a degree of mutual responsibility requires that every mountaineer be familiar with emergency procedures.

Many times a handful of climbers have done a difficult rescue speedily and efficiently using only such labor-saving and safety devices as could be improvised from ordinary climbing tools. This chapter approaches the rescue problem from the viewpoint of a small climbing party.

SEARCH

Search is ordinarily not begun until it is reasonably certain the missing person is not delayed for any normal reason. After straying from the route he may recognize his mistake, retrace his steps, and rejoin the party within a few hours. If he is healthy, experienced, well-equipped, and has been traveling where injury is unlikely, search can even be deferred overnight.

Under some conditions there should be no hesitation. Immediate search is mandatory if the lost person might have wandered onto steep rock or a crevassed glacier, if a potential physical disability such as diabetes is known to be a factor, or if he is very fatigued, inexperienced, or poorly equipped. Similarly, if an entire rope team is missing on difficult terrain, after a lightning storm, or in avalanche conditions there should be not the slightest delay.

A small party may be able to make no more than a hasty search along a limited track. With a half dozen people available there probably can be a perimeter search. If this is found to be ineffectual, a large group must then proceed to comb thoroughly over a considerable area.

Regardless of the method adopted each person must know the full plan before beginning the search. If the party is to divide then each division must know the location of the others. Audible signals such as yodels, yells, and whistles, or visible signs with smoke, mirrors, or lights should be prearranged. All members must know the rendezvous point and the time at which they are to meet regardless of the success or failure of their search effort.

For safety, searchers should travel in pairs or remain always within earshot of one another. This means that a party of two or three people can cover only a narrow strip of ground. Their best chance is outguessing the lost person, putting themselves in his place and visualizing the logical errors. The most likely places such as the exits of wrong gullies and ridges are checked first. Failing there, the party retraces its original trail while casting about for tracks showing where the lost person wandered off. Once such a point is found the searchers proceed swiftly along the most likely path, watching for footprints in snow, mud, sand, or on footlogs. When such track-showing ground is intermittent, the party fans out at broad intervals, calling to each other regularly and pausing frequently to listen for calls from the lost person. If after several hours no clues at all have been found then it probably is time to seek outside help.

AVALANCHE RESCUE

When a companion is swept away, the *rest of the party must not panic,* but must note with respect to fixed objects nearby — trees or rocks — first, the point on the slope where he was caught, and second, the point where he disappeared. At the same time the party watches — until the avalanche stops — the point on the moving surface of the avalanche where he disappeared. If successful in observation they have three points on his path and know he is somewhere on or near the line between the lower two, probably closer to the lowest point.

It is important to keep in mind that sliding snow flows like water, faster on the surface and in the center than on the bottom and at the sides. When an avalanche follows a twisting channel the snow and the victim conform to the turns. Both these facts have obvious influence on search.

After an escape route has been picked and lookouts posted to watch for further slides, the upper two points are quickly marked. The party hurries down the victim's path toward the lowest point, searching carefully as they go, scuffling their feet through the snow to uncover clues — items of the victim's gear, or his avalanche cord. They look especially carefully around trees or outcroppings which might have stopped him, and scan beneath any blocks of snow that lie on the surface. They shout at intervals, then maintain absolute silence while listening for a muffled answer.

If any loose equipment is found on or near the surface, the buried victim probably lies not far uphill, and rescuers immediately begin to probe and dig in the vicinity. If no equipment is found, the party should mark the observed stopping point of that portion of the avalanche debris where the victim disappeared, and quickly search the area just above, where he is most likely to lie. If nothing is found they begin to probe, using blunted willow wands, taped ice axes, or reversed ski poles. Sharp probes must not be used because it must be assumed the victim is still alive. More systematic probing is best done as a team, not by individuals, and hence may be beyond the capability of the small party except on a very limited basis. However even a sole survivor *must* carry out the search to the best of his ability.

Statistics show that 50 per cent of buried avalanche victims suffocate if not uncovered within 1 hour. An excruciating choice must be made — whether to continue search with full party strength or to send for help — based on the size of the avalanche area and the availability of help.

Fig. 166. Slab avalanche. Victims are likely to be at accumulation points (marked by X's).

Probably the best course, if the avalanche is not too large, is to continue the hasty search with full party strength unless organized help such as ski-patrol personnel is near at hand. Once alerted, an organized ski patrol may well be able to dispatch a search team within 10 minutes, but may have to travel some distance to the accident scene. To speed their arrival the messenger must carefully mark the route, especially if snow is falling.

Whatever the size of the party, the search is not given up as long as there is any hope of success. People have lived for a week in dry snow, and in the Cascades a youth once survived burial for some 9 hours in wet avalanche debris, his life saved by an airspace between big blocks of snow. On the other hand, only one out of seven avalanche burial victims survives after being covered for 2 hours.

Once the victim is found, first aid begins unless rigor mortis is positively diagnosed. As soon as his head is exposed, his mouth and throat are cleared and mouth-to-mouth resuscitation started. The first-aider must check for bleeding and mechanical injuries. Head and spine injuries are common and treatment for hypothermia and shock are an absolute necessity.

WHEN AN ACCIDENT HAPPENS

When a climber is injured the first response of his companions often invites further accidents. The victim must be reached quickly but not at the expense of additional accidents. Calmness is essential; excitement can only frustrate the rescue effort. Under rockfall or avalanche hazard those not needed immediately take cover. On difficult terrain only one or two rescuers should be dispatched to reach the victim, not ignoring the need for belays and anchors.

Forceful, competent leadership and strict discipline are requisite to success in alpine rescue. If there has been no recognized leader then one must be selected to deal with the emergency. Once he accepts the task, companions abide by his decisions without argument, though he should remain flexible enough to consider suggestions.

Urgent first aid should be rendered at the first possible moment — bleeding stopped, breathing restarted, shock relieved, and fractures treated. Impending hazards may force the party to move the victim at once to a more sheltered location. However, choice between acceptance of the hazards of the accident site and the risks of moving the victim may be difficult. If he must be moved, methods must be used which do not compound his injuries.

If for any reason an injured person must be left unguarded even for a few minutes he must be tied to the mountain. Too often an injured person left alone has in his confusion fallen or wandered to his death, sometimes untying himself to do so. Companions must anticipate that he may become irrational and secure him so he cannot possibly work free.

When something has gone wrong, swift action may be less effective than correct action. A spontaneous but short-sighted effort has less chance of ultimate success than one more deliberately considered. Therefore, after the initial demands of safety and first aid are satisfied, the leader and his party sit down to plan. In the mountains once any person is beyond voice range of his companions the party has lost control over his subsequent actions; therefore, there must be no hasty separation. Everything must be thought through to the very end, everything prearranged, including what each member is to do under all conceivable circumstances until he has completely played out his part in the rescue operation.

Every aspect of the situation needs cool analysis: seriousness of the victim's injuries, measures necessary to sustain him during evacuation; terrain and distance to the road; and the strength and resources of the party. Then, and only then, should a course of action be selected.

Evacuation by the Party

Sending for outside help means delay and imposes considerable inconvenience upon volunteer rescuers. There are occasions when a party should attempt to remain self-sufficient. If an accident has occurred near a trail and the victim has broken a lower leg or arm, for example, evacuation may be considered after some rest and adequate first aid.

It is generally true that a victim will benefit from a period of rest following an injury. The further trauma of immediate evacuation is seldom justified; therefore, evacuation should be postponed until the victim's condition has stabilized. The victim himself is probably the best indicator as to when evacuation should be started. He should be consulted and his condition closely observed prior to and during transportation. His comfort must be kept foremost in the minds of the party.

Some conditions require immediate evacuation: pulmonary edema, unconsciousness (cause unknown), diabetic coma, and progressively deteriorating condition such as appendicitis, or whenever weather or terrain conditions are life-threatening. Some conditions require that evacuation be delayed until trained rescue personnel arrives (unless such help will be more than 24 hours in arriving): head injuries, neck and spinal fractures, heart attack, apoplexy (stroke), and internal injuries. Evacuation is required but not urgent for all other serious injuries and illnesses.

Obtaining Outside Aid

There are occasions when a party cannot cope with its own emergency. In an area requiring technical evacuation (that which involves any raising or lowering), where injuries are severe, where distances are great or the party size or strength are not sufficient, then evacuation by the party should not be attempted. Rather, help should be sent for as soon as first aid has been given and the victim made comfortable in a safe place. In most areas, help by helicopter is usually about 3 hours away once word gets to the proper authorities. If a ground party is required, help is usually about 8 to 16 hours away. Therefore, if the party is in an area accessible by helicopter, if the party and victim are sheltered, and if the weather is good there is little reason to move the victim unless the injuries require it.

When help must be requested — from climbers on nearby peaks, from people living or working in the region, or from local authorities — then there must be no hesitancy in making the request. At all times a party should know what help it can expect if its own efforts fail, where and how to get it, and how to co-operate with authorities and rescuers.

Going for Help

The party must have a clear grasp of the problem and of its own capacities and needs before deciding how much and what form of aid to request. Once a runner has been dispatched there is no way to control what he does or says. An excited messenger hurrying to reach the road with little idea of his party's needs only causes confusion.

Ideally two climbers should travel out together — partly for safety and partly because two people do a better job of obtaining help. Written instructions should be carried so that nothing is forgotten. Messengers carry a minimum of equipment and travel swiftly, marking a plain trail on the way to facilitate the return.

Once in contact with civilization the messengers call the county sheriff, National Forest or Park Service personnel, or the local authorities in charge of the region. These are asked to relay a message to the local rescue group (Mountain Rescue Unit in the State of Washington) or to provide the needed help themselves.

The messengers' job is not ended here. They must make certain messages are sent at once, accurately, and that they reach their destination. Often the organization of a rescue depends upon a chain of communication, messages relayed from person to person via telephone and radio until finally a rescue leader is reached. Along the way vital information may be lost by non-mountaineers who do not understand the words they are asked to convey. In the interests of efficiency and accuracy, the messengers should talk directly with some trusted fellow climber. The line of communication must not be broken. If the rescue leader cannot be personally contacted, then messengers must be insistent with intermediaries to the point of being obnoxious, if necessary. Messages garbled along the way — or simply nor forwarded — have directly caused a number of tragic rescue failures.

Enough information must reach the rescue leader so that he can devise and execute an effective rescue plan. Since it is extremely difficult to

ACCIDENT REPORT FORM

This form is to be completed in duplicate AT the scene of the accident for each injured member of the party. One copy should be sent with those going for help and the other form retained by the leader.

ACCIDENT	Date:	Time:	AM ☐	PM ☐

LOCATION

Quadrangle:	Section:

Exact Location (include marked map):

Terrain: Glacier ☐ Snow ☐ Brush ☐ Timber ☐ Rock ☐ Trail ☐
Heather ☐ Easy ☐ Moderate ☐ Steep ☐ Other:

COMPLETE DESCRIPTION OF ACCIDENT

Ascending ☐	Descending ☐
Roped ☐	Unroped ☐
Rock Fall ☐	Ice Fall ☐
Avalanche ☐	Illness ☐
Excess Heat ☐	Cold ☐
Equipment Failure ☐	

Witnesses: Other:

INJURED PERSON

Name:	Age:
Address:	Male ☐ Female ☐
Phone:	

Whom to Notify: Relation: Phone:

INJURIES

Overall Condition	Good ☐ Fair ☐ Serious ☐ Fatal ☐
	Unconscious: Yes ☐ No ☐
	If yes, length of time:
Injury 1	Location on Body:
	Type of Injury:
Injury 2	Location on Body:
	Type of Injury:
Other Injuries	Location on Body:
	Type of Injury:

FIRST AID TREATMENT

General:	Bleeding Stopped ☐	Shelter Built ☐
	Artificial Respiration ☐	Warm Fluids Given ☐
	Treated for Shock ☐	Evacuation ☐

Injury 1

Injury 2

Other Injuries:

ON-THE-SCENE PLANS	Will stay put ☐ Will evacuate to trail ☐ to Road ☐ Will evacuate a short distance to shelter ☐ Will send some members out ☐ Other:
PERSONNEL	Number: Inexperienced ☐ Experienced ☐ Intermediates ☐ Advanced ☐ Capability for a bivouac: Yes ☐ No ☐
	ATTACH the pre-trip prepared LIST OF PARTY MEMBERS including names, address and phone numbers to the ACCIDENT FORM BEING TAKEN OUT.
EQUIPMENT AVAILABLE	Tents ☐ Sleeping Bags ☐ Ensolite ☐ Flares ☐ Saw ☐ Hardware ☐ Stove and Fuel ☐ Ropes ☐ Other:
WEATHER	Warm ☐ Moderate ☐ Freezing ☐ Snow ☐ Wind ☐ Sun ☐ Clouds ☐ Fog ☐ Rain ☐ Other:
TYPE OF EVACUATION RECOMND'D	Lowering Operation ☐ Carry-Out ☐ Helicopter ☐ Rigid stretcher ☐ None until specialized medical assistance ☐ Specify:
PARTY LEADER	Name:
MESSENGERS SENT FOR HELP	Names:
FURTHER INFORMATION, IF ANY.	
RECOMMEN-DATIONS FOR FUTURE CLIMBS	Equipment: Leadership: Route: Abilities:

remember all the information required, particularly under the pressure of an emergency situation, it is very helpful for the leader to carry some form of accident report form to serve as a checklist (see sample). The form should be completed in duplicate at the scene of the accident for each injured member of the party. One copy should be sent out with the messengers reporting the accident and given to the responsible rescue agency; the other copy should be retained by the party leader for future reference in making any required reports.

Having established contact with the rescue leader, the messengers should remain by the telephone until the rescue party arrives. The rescue leader may need to contact them for further information, or to advise them of unexpected developments, or to make progress reports. Careful consideration must be given to the matter of informing relatives of people in the climbing party. In a large party this requires making a written list of names and telephone numbers before leaving the accident scene. It is cruel to keep family members waiting in anxiety for hours or days, but it might be well to await the arrival of the rescue leader so his efforts will not be hampered by busy telephone lines. Also, the rescue leader will have had a wealth of experience in dealing with concerned relatives and the public news media.

A last and important function of the messengers is to meet the rescue party at an agreed-upon rendezvous, rested and ready to lead the way back to the accident scene. If they are incapacitated by fatigue or injury it is all the more important that they have marked the trail on the way out for help.

TRANSPORT ON TECHNICAL TERRAIN

On terrain so difficult as to require technical climbing even a minor handicap can render a person incapable of descent without help. With reserve strength and plentiful equipment, a large party may be able to choose almost any route for evacuation, devising elaborate traversing and lifting devices, sending scouts ahead to prepare these in advance of the main party.

The small party has less choice. Though short lifts and traverses can be made, generally the lack of party strength makes it necessary to evacuate by descending the fall line, which uses the least energy and equipment. Frequently the party must descend by a different (and unknown) route, with hidden dangers. The prime object — moving the victim — is naturally uppermost in all minds, yet the safety of each individual must never be forgotten. A rescue inherently is more dangerous than a normal climb over the same ground because attention is focused upon the victim instead of upon the surroundings and one's own movements. Therefore, solidly anchored belays may be required both for the victim and for those aiding

him, even where superfluous under ordinary climbing conditions. If ropes
are in short supply, rescuers can be served by a fixed line to which they
attach themselves with prusik slings. Since in a small party the normal
equipment may be insufficient for rescue purposes, many climbers carry
in their rucksacks — depending on the climb— such emergency items as
extra slings, carabiners, a pulley, brake bar, folding saw, snow shovel, ice
screws, whistle, and plastic tarp — as well as all the basic essentials
described in Chapter 2.

Lowering

A person with slight injuries can climb down under tension from a tight
belay assisted by a companion who helps him place his hands and feet. On
snow or ice large platform steps can be prepared. If the victim has no head
injury or symptom of shock he can sometimes be allowed to rappel — always with a safety belay, of course.

Swami Belt

If neither down-climbing nor rappelling is possible but the victim still
has use of his legs, he can be lowered in his swami belt, preferably rigged
in a seat as though for rappelling. As a companion pays out the belay line
through a braking device, he guides himself down with his feet and hands.
If the swami belt is used and there is some doubt about the victim falling
over, a chest harness can be arranged to provide upright stability.

The victim can also descend on the back of a helper using a single
climbing rope. With a figure-8 knot a small loop is tied into the rope about
3 feet from the helper's end knot. The victim's swami belt is attached to
this figure-8 loop using a separate piece of sling material and snugged up
tight so most of the victim's weight is taken on the rope rather than on the

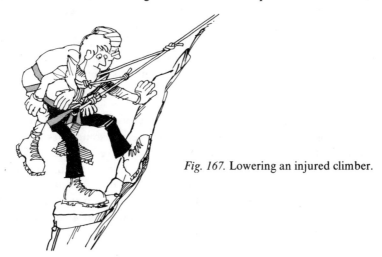

Fig. 167. Lowering an injured climber.

helper's back. Chest loops are provided for both, a simple example being a loop high under the armpits attached to the rope at about face height with a prusik knot. The helper backs down the slope in a rappel stance lowered by others above using braking devices. Both people should be separately belayed with additional safety ropes. The back carry illustrated can also be used.

Friction Braking Devices

The versatile carabiner brake is commonly used to control the descent. It can be doubled for very heavy loads, can be operated from either an upper or a lower station, and can be used for descents of more than one rope length. When available, a brake bar does the same job more simply. The braking action is the same as that for rappelling as described in Chapter 10.

The brake usually is placed near the top anchor, but occasionally it can be more conveniently situated below or at one side. In such case the rope runs from the victim through an upper carabiner or pulley and down to the braking station.

On a long pitch it is sometimes desirable to tie in additional ropes while the load hangs in midair to allow an uninterrupted descent of several rope lengths. The problem is to bypass the joining knot around the carabiners without dropping the load. Two men can accomplish this without difficulty. When only about 2 feet of rope remain, they halt the descent. One man holds the rope while the other attaches a prusik sling just below the brake and then wraps this sling several times around an auxiliary carabiner anchored above the brake. He holds this sling — it must not be tied — while his partner eases the load onto it, threads the new rope through the carabiner brake alongside the first rope, pulls the first rope on through and ties the two ends in a knot below the carabiner brake. The sling which is wrapped around the auxiliary carabiner is then allowed to slide and the load is smoothly transferred back to the climbing rope, permitting descent to continue. (Note the prusik sling must be long enough to allow for the slack introduced in the system.)

Raising

Although lowering puts the force of gravity on the side of the rescuers and thus is preferred whenever possible, there is sometimes no option to raising a victim up a steep face. In such case the rescuers have a choice of two methods: prusik system, which depends upon the victim's own efforts, and the pulley system which can be used to lift even an inert weight. Although they work equally well on steep rock or on snow these systems are usually associated with crevasse rescue and therefore are described in Chapter 17.

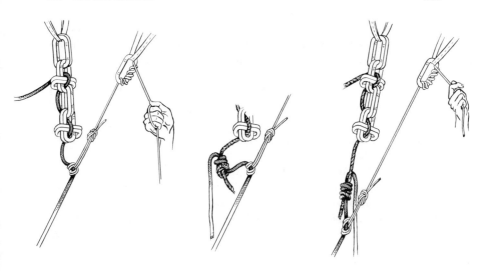

Fig. 168. Attaching a second length of rope when lowering on carabiner brake system.

Traversing

If the descent route must deviate far from the fall line, transport becomes very difficult. A pendulum is useful on terrain where rescuers can traverse overhead. Suspended from an anchored rope, the victim is pulled sideways by a second rope also anchored from above. As tension is gradually released from the first rope he pendulums to a position underneath the anchor of the second rope. The first rope is reanchored farther along for the next pendulum, if required.

Rockfall

Falling rocks are responsible for a large proportion of injuries, and the danger is many times increased during rescue. Loose rock is then a particularly serious hazard because of the many dragging ropes, because the attention of rescuers is focused on the victim, and because the operation may continue into the night. Anyone working above the victim or other rescuers must be doubly careful. Those below, with small chance for dodging, should wear hard hats and pad vital spots with extra clothing. If possible, sentries should be posted to warn of barrages. The first man down attempts to scour the route of loose rocks; if the danger persists, it may be wise to lower an extra man just above the victim – a man with quick reflexes who holds in his hands a well padded rucksack to field flying rocks.

Evacuation On Snow

On snow there is particularly urgent need for protecting the victim from heat loss while administering first aid and planning evacuation. He should be wrapped in extra clothing and insulated from the snow by pads, packs, ropes, or the body of a companion. If he cannot be moved quickly a trench or low wall should be constructed to shield him from the wind. For overnight stays a snow cave should be dug. If possible, the victim should be moved to a sheltered spot or down to timberline where a fire can be built. This should be done as quickly as first aid can be administered and the victim prepared for travel.

The quickest method of travel is by *human toboggan.* An uninjured person dons all available clothing, including a parka with the tail outside his trousers. He lies in the snow with his head in the direction of travel and the victim is laid on top of him, head uphill or down as the injuries require. On a steep slope the two should be tied together. Belayed by the ankles, the "toboggan" is towed by his arms. For hard pulls a tow rope can be added but the load must be distributed over the body with a harness arrangement. If the slope angle permits, the headfirst pull is preferred because the toboggan slides more easily and comfortably. Under proper snow conditions the toboggan allows an evacuation pace little if any slower than that of an ordinary climbing party in a hurry to get home. Usually it is necessary to change toboggans every mile or so – more frequently on rough snow.

Other methods also depend upon sliding rather than carrying the victim. Sometimes the victim can be lowered in a sitting glissade position, well wrapped in extra clothing, perhaps riding in back of a companion who smooths the track – the two tied together and carefully belayed. If injuries are relatively minor and the slope not excessively steep he can be roped in with two or three companions who slide slowly as a team, constantly under control.

Axes having metal shafts are preferred for their greater strength, but even·so the ice ax belay usually is not strong enough for rescue purposes unless two or more are used: if the snow is very hard, the ax will not penetrate; if very soft, the snow will not resist the ax load. Hip belays are preferable, particularly in very hard or very soft snow. Moats often provide superb anchor positions for lowering. In narrow chutes, belay ropes can be run to both sides. Rock islands in the snow are often solid, and sometimes can be made artificially by piling rocks in an excavation. The deadman anchor, the snow fluke, the snow picket or stake, used singly or in combination as described in Chapter 15, also serve as anchors for belayers or for braking devices. The bollard is always worthy of consideration, and a pole buried in a snow trench at right angles to the pull can be a very strong anchor.

TRANSPORT ON NON-TECHNICAL TERRAIN

In many rescues the hardest job begins when the steep terrain is past and ropes are put away. No longer aided by gravity, the party must carry its burden, very fatiguing work on rough ground. Under some conditions, however, a few simple techniques extend the capacity of the small party so that it need not call for help.

The *four-hand seat* is useful for short distances if the two carriers are of the same height. Standing side by side, each grasps his right wrist with his left hand with palms down. Each carrier then grasps the wrist of the other with his free hand to form a seat.

For longer distances the *ice ax carry* is better: carriers wearing rucksacks stand side by side with joined ice ax shafts resting between them in their pack straps; the victim is seated on the padded shafts with his arms over their shoulders.

A strong climber can carry a person on his back for long distances provided the weight is distributed properly. For the *rucksack carry* a large rucksack is slit on the sides near the bottom so the victim can step into it like a pair of shorts. The drawstring is tied snugly around his waist. He rides piggyback, wrists tied over the carrier's chest if need be.

The *back carry*, as illustrated, employs wide nylon webbing to distribute the victim's weight.

Fig. 169. Back carry.

Another method of evacuation is by use of a *rope stretcher*. This can be constructed and used with or without the aid of ice axes and/or branches as follows.

Place the rope, preferably 150-foot, extended, on the ground, and find the center. From the center make 16 180° bends, eight extending on each side of the center. The distance between the bends should be approximately as wide as the victim and the full 16 bends approximately as long as the victim's length. Bring the rope ends around the sides of the stretcher adjacent to the bends. Tie a clove hitch in the rope section adjacent to each bend and insert the bend. Continue tying clove hitches and inserting bends until all the bends are bound. Leave a small loop between the apex of the bend and the knot. Insert the remaining rope through the loops until the entire remainder is coiled around the stretcher. Snug up the knots, tie off the ends, and insert padding from the neck to the hips.

Someone should try out the stretcher, whether it is constructed of rope or branches, before placing the victim on it, to determine the need for additional padding or supporting material without causing discomfort to the victim. CAUTION: evacuation by rope or any improvised stretcher is usually very rough on the victim. If there is a chance that further injury will result DO NOT EVACUATE until trained rescue personnel with proper equipment are available to assist.

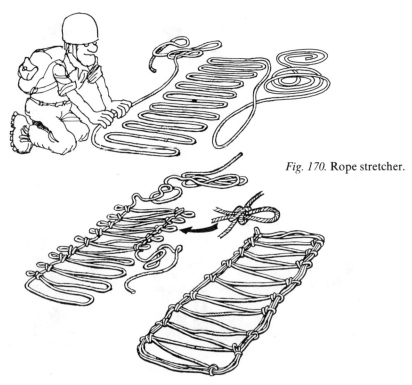

Fig. 170. Rope stretcher.

SPECIALIZED RESCUE EQUIPMENT

Rescue organizations often bring equipment especially designed to make their task easier. Although these items are not standard climbing gear, every climber should know what they are and what can be done with them.

Most important is a rigid metal stretcher such as the Stokes which has a framework of metal tubing and a wire mesh basket that closely fits the body outlines, even to separate troughs for the legs. Some designs are demountable for carrying in sections and have provision for attaching either a wheel or ski. For snow rescues there are several toboggan-type litters designed for use by rescuers on skis or snowshoes. Orthopedic stretchers are mandatory for evacuation of neck or spinal injuries and should be requested by the messengers going for help.

For raising or lowering on steep rock or ice there are portable winches. Whether driven by hand or by engine, these have extensive wire cable systems reaching several hundreds of feet.

Radio Communications

Two-way radio communication, when the gear is both light and efficient, immensely facilitates mountain rescue. The main problem is obtaining reliable transmission and reception despite heavy timber, intervening ridges, long distances, and bad weather.

Air Rescue

The international symbols illustrated are familiar to the majority of pilots and it is well worth a climber's time to jot them down on a slip of paper to be carried in the first aid kit. Symbols should be made 8 to 12 feet in height with a 1-foot line width.

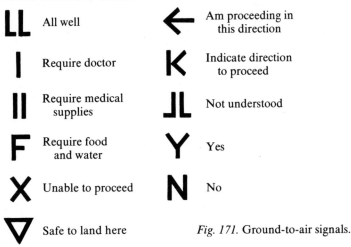

Fig. 171. Ground-to-air signals.

The helicopter has revolutionized mountain rescue. It has plucked persons from cliffs and glaciers and rushed them to hospitals in hours rather than the days required by ground transport — over and over again meaning the difference between life and death. Therefore a climber should know some of the principles of helicopter operation as well as their limitations.

A helicopter can take on a load either by landing, or when that is not feasible, by hovering and lowering a sling or a stretcher on a cable attached to a power winch. The most important factors governing its ability to evacuate are visibility, wind velocity and turbulence, and air density.

In mountain flight continual visual contact with the ground is essential, and thus in poor weather the helicopter cannot operate. It can maneuver safely in winds up to about 35 miles per hour, a wind of about 10 miles per hour being better than still air. Turbulence which usually accompanies high winds is dangerous, although under some conditions steady breezes are actually helpful. The maximum altitude at which a helicopter can operate is determined by air density, which decreases at high altitude and high temperature; less dense air reduces the lifting force of the rotor blades and the power output of the engines.

As a helicopter nears the ground, downwash of the rotors creates a cushion of compressed air on which the craft floats. Only when such a cushion can be built can the helicopter hover or land. When there is no flat surface against which the rotors can push, or when the air is too thin for floating, the helicopter flies by exactly the same principles as a fixed wing airplane — that is, it must keep moving forward to remain airborne. It can stop forward motion and rest on a cushion only when within "reach" of the ground. The reach of most machines is less than 50 feet at sea level, and much less than that at any altitude. Contrary to lingering misunderstanding, a helicopter cannot stop forward progress high in the air and descend vertically hundreds of feet onto a dime.

Because he must make an airplane-like approach, the helicopter pilot must have a clear lane into his proposed landing or hovering area. Windward slopes are desirable for the extra lift provided by steady updrafts; lee slopes with downdrafts are to be avoided. The landing or hovering spot need not be exactly level, but should be reasonably so. The pilot prefers falling off the top or side of a ridge crest or the lower edge of a hanging valley to rising vertically from a valley bottom. From a flat landing spot he may be able to climb only a few feet before losing his cushion and having to fly forward. Thus the ground party must have selected a spot with a clear exit into the wind.

An area around the touchdown pad at least 75 feet in diameter should be cleared of obstacles such as brush and loose objects and made as level as possible, with a slope of not more than 10 per cent. The landing area should be clearly marked with colored tape or brightly colored objects, securely anchored. Streamers, plastic ribbon, or smoke should be used to aid the pilot in determining wind direction, preferably at the edge or downward of the area so as not to obstruct his vision. If the helicopter lowers equipment, allow it to touch ground first to dissipate static electricity. If there is last-minute danger to the helicopter, "do not land" should be indicated by moving the arms from side horizontally to overhead several times. If the party has no streamers or smoke, members should stand with arms extended toward the landing area with the wind at their backs indicating "land here, my back is into the wind." The downwash winds from the rotor approach 60 to 100 mph depending on the size of the machine, so do not stand near the edge of a cliff. Watch out for flying debris, use eye protection, and have all gear safely secured.

Warning: Never approach a helicopter unless signalled to do so by the pilot or a crewman and then duck down and always approach or leave from near the front so the pilot can see you at all times. Stay away from the rear rotor; when spinning it is nearly invisible and can kill an unwary stroller. All other personnel should stay at least 75 feet away from the landing area. Be sure to secure the victim and any gear going with him so there are no loose straps, ropes, or clothing, and shield his face and eyes to protect him from flying debris and assure proper respiration.

RESCUE GROUP ORGANIZATION

In the Alps, with its large corps of professional guides, organized rescue is all part of the business. In North America rescues are carried out largely by amateur organizations. They thoroughly know their local mountains, are able from fragments of telephone information to analyze a situation and decide quickly what action to take, and can direct such action at the accident scene. With the help of a call committee they round up the necessary equipment and manpower — volunteers among local climbers, ready to answer a call at any time, ready to finance their own way, use their own equipment and take time from their jobs.

In most areas, responsibility for rescue now rests with the county sheriff, the National Park Service, or some other comparable arm of government. Volunteer rescue units work closely with such authorities. In the State of Washington, Mountain Rescue Council Units are headquartered in the major cities. Although more people may be peripherally involved, most rescues are accomplished by one telephone calling committee, one rescue leader, and either 18 to 24 stretcher-bearers or one helicopter.

Supplementary Reading:

LaChapelle, Edward R. *The ABC of Avalanche Safety.* Denver, Colorado: Colorado Outdoor Sports Co., 1970.

MacInnes, Hamish. *International Mountain Rescue Handbook.* New York: Charles Scribner's Sons, 1972.

May, W. G. *Mountain Search and Rescue Techniques.* Boulder, Colorado: Rocky Mountain Rescue Group, Inc., 1972.

Mitchell, Dick. *Mountaineering First Aid.* Seattle: The Mountaineers, 1972.

Perla, Ronald I. *Modern Avalanche Rescue.* U. S. Department of Agriculture, Forest Service, Wasatch National Forest, Alta Avalanche Study Center, April, 1968.

 PART SIX

The Climbing
Environment

XVIII. Mt. Daniel and Lynch Glacier; Alpine Lakes region, Cascade Range. (Bob Gunning)

23 *

MOUNTAIN GEOLOGY

WHEN A CLIMBER reaches a summit and looks out over ridge after ridge of peaks he may imagine he is on the crest of a gigantic wave heaved up by a turbulent ocean. His fancy is not so very wrong, for even the geologist often likens mountain ranges to stormy seas, though the storm is inside rather than outside the earth's crust. Nor do the waves of rock ever achieve the perfect form of waves in water, for as fast as the mountains rise they are attacked by elements of the very air they have displaced and degraded by the gravity they defy. Sun and frost, water and wind, tear down the peaks grain by grain.

The tempests in the earth's crust have a duration measured in eons rather than hours, and man clambers about among the crests and troughs for too brief a span ever to see – except in imagination – the rise of mountains from plains and their degradation into plains once more. However, just as the master mariner knows the nature of wind and water so that he can navigate even in the hardest blow, so does the master mountaineer know the nature of the more complex storms that toss up the mountains and tear them down. Some knowledge of mountain geology can make alpine navigation easier, and climbing a much richer experience than any mere athletic exercise.

FOUNDATION OF MOUNTAINS: THE EARTH

According to one theory of the earth's formation, the entire solar system, sun and planets, slowly coalesced from diffuse cosmic dust about 4½ billion years ago. Many scientists believe that as the dust coalesced the pressure produced in the center of the growing mass and radioactivity of the interior caused the spinning solid juvenile earth to heat up and melt. With cooling, chemical compounds formed, the heavier ones gravitating inward until ultimately the earth differentiated into at least three concentric spheres. Others feel that this differentiation could not have taken place in the allowable time before the oldest crustal rocks formed at least 3½ billion years ago. It has even been suggested that the outermost layer of the light shell of the earth — the continents with their mountains — began as great splashes of late-arriving meteoric material.

Whatever the origin of the earth, earthquake (seismic) waves show it to have a relatively rigid crust, a layer of rock some 22 miles thick with an average density of about 2.6 (that is, weighing about 2½ times more than water, which has a density of 1). The middle shell has an approximate density of 5, or a good deal heavier than basalt. Virtually nothing is known about the inner core, by far the major mass of the earth. Having a density of up to 17, it could be a nickel-iron alloy, like some meteorites, but many scientists believe that under the extreme pressure and temperature of the earth's center atoms do not have the same characteristics as in the crust, so that the core is a substance utterly unlike any material familiar to man, having the properties of both a highly compressed gas and a tough metal.

The climber is most interested in the outer shell, the crust that crumples and ruptures to form mountains. Though the highest mountains and the deepest valleys are nothing more to the earth as a whole than the scratches and dust on a billiard ball, man himself is sufficiently small to find the scale impressive.

BUILDING BLOCKS OF MOUNTAINS: MINERALS AND ROCKS

The Minerals

Mountains are made of rocks and rocks of minerals, compounds not broken apart except by chemical action, so that a climber can begin his study of mountain construction considering minerals as the basic building blocks. Over 2000 are known, but less than 20 are common, and of these, seven, known as the *rock-forming* minerals constitute most of the earth's outer shell: quartz, feldspars, white and black micas, amphiboles, pyroxenes, and calcite. The element silicon is as ubiquitous in rock as carbon in living things, 90 per cent of the crust being either silicon dioxide (*silica*) or compounds of silica and other elements (*silicates*). Among the rock-forming minerals, only calcite does not have silicon in its molecule.

Igneous Rocks

Now and again within the crust, internal friction, heat of radioactive decay, and/or release of pressure creates *magmas*, melts of silicate minerals which on cooling solidify into igneous rocks. If the process is completed deep in the earth with a gradual loss of heat, the minerals crystallize slowly and develop well, forming a coarsely grained *plutonic* rock. If in addition the melt moves upward, propelled by its own lesser density, perhaps dissolving and incorporating the overlying masses, or forcing them aside, an *intrusive* rock results. Should the liquid erupt onto the surface and cool rapidly the mineral crystals have little opportunity to grow and develop, and the rock that results is called *volcanic* or *extrusive*.

Plutonic or Intrusive Rocks

Slow crystallization from deeply buried melts generally means good climbing, since the minerals formed are relatively large and interwoven into a solid mat. Weathering develops protrusions of relatively resistant minerals which either make for a rough-surfaced rock with excellent friction, or, if the resistant crystals are very much larger than the enclosing mat, one with numerous knobby holds. Many of the rock routes in the Cathedral Peak area of Yosemite afford just such crystal climbing.

Pieces of foreign rock included in the plutonic body while it was rising and crystallizing, or clusters of segregated minerals, may weather differently than the main rock mass and form "chicken heads." These delightful features may dot an otherwise unclimbable wall.

Intrusions are variously named according to location and size. Very large masses of plutonic rock are called *batholiths* and small ones *stocks*, being with rare exception in the *granite* family: granite, granodiorite, tonalite, diorite, and others, all similar in composition and formation, differing only in the relative amounts of minerals contained.

There is a core of such batholiths in every major mountain system in the world. In the Alps, Sierra Nevada, North Cascades, British Columbia Coast Range, and most other ranges this core is at least in part exposed, providing some of the finest and steepest rock climbing.

Small bodies are *sills,* forced between sedimentary strata, and *dikes,* fissures which crosscut the strata. Many small intrusive bodies are quickly cooled, and thus may look like extrusive rocks.

Volcanic or Extrusive Rocks

Explosive eruptions, most characteristic of melts with a chemical composition producing rhyolite, eject molten rock so abruptly into the atmosphere that it hardens into loose airy masses of fine crystals and uncrystallized glass. When this ash is bound together, either while still partially molten or after cooling, it is called *tuff,* a weak rock that disintegrates rapidly and erodes easily. Loose ash, or *cinders,* are of no interest whatsoever to the rock climber.

Quieter eruptions with the molten rock flowing from large fissures as *lava* are most characteristic of melts producing *basalt*. The plateau of eastern Washington and Oregon is composed of innumerable basalt flows extruded and accumulated over a few million years. The peculiar "pillow" lavas of the Olympic Mountains are similar, but were formed by basalt spreading out beneath shallow seas.

Volcanoes built almost exclusively of basalt flows have broad bases and gentle slopes, such as Mauna Loa in Hawaii, while those explosive in origin are steep cinder cones. Many are complex, their history including eruptions of flows and ash ranging from basalt to rhyolite in composition. Examples are Fujiyama in Japan and the Pacific Coast volcanoes, from Lassen in California to Garibaldi in British Columbia. On these peaks snow and glacier routes are usually preferred; the nightmarish slopes of shifting cinders and ice-carved cliffs of rotten andesite rarely tempt a climber.

Jointing

The importance of joint systems to the climber has been discussed in Chapter 7. In plutonic rocks, joints or cracks are caused by internal stresses such as from contraction during cooling or expansion when overlying rock is eroded away. Some joints tend to follow a consistent pattern throughout an entire mountain and their existence can often be predicted. For instance, when a ledge abruptly terminates the climber does well to look around the corner, for perhaps the joint — and thus the ledge — resumes.

When molten rock extrudes onto the surface of the earth as a lava flow or even when it intrudes into a cold surrounding mass as a dike or sill, the contraction from rapid cooling commonly causes such a profusion of joints that, in contrast to plutonic rocks, the climbing is most treacherous. However, not infrequently the jointing is so regular as to present the appearance of massed pillars, the classic example being the Devil's Tower in Wyoming, where most routes are strikingly vertical.

Sedimentary Rocks

Igneous rocks originate deep in the earth, but sedimentary rocks are born high on the mountains, where the erosive forces pluck away debris and pass it along to rivers for transportation to places of deposition in valleys, lakes, or arms of the ocean. As sediments accumulate, the underlayers are solidifed by pressure and by mineral cements precipitated from percolating groundwater. Gravel and boulders are transformed into *conglomerates*; sandy beaches into *sandstone*; beds of mud into *mudstone* or *shale*; shell beds and coral reefs into *limestone* or *dolomite*. Sedimentary rocks may also form by direct chemical precipitation (mainly from warm, shallow seas); examples are the Dolomites and the Eiger.

Though in general sedimentary rocks are much more friable than those cooled from fiery magmas, pressure and cementing often produce very solid rocks. Indeed, by sealing up cracks cementing can result in a disturbingly flawless surface, particularly in limestone. Most of the high mountain ranges have some sedimentary peaks. The Canadian Rockies are almost exclusively so, and offer every degree of sturdiness. However, in general sedimentary rocks do not offer high-angle climbing comparable to that of granite.

Metamorphic Rocks

Pioneer geologists quickly became adept at distinguishing between rocks of fiery and aqueous origin, but not so quickly did they recognize that many rocks — though grossly resembling igneous or sedimentary rocks — have been so profoundly changed by heat or pressure that they have become something quite different. These are the *metamorphic* rocks, that is, changed rocks. No rock is fixed in a permanent state; all change in time. Sand does not become sandstone without pressure — and what constitutes a magma if not melted older rocks? Metamorphic rocks bridge the gap between sedimentary and igneous, though on either side the boundaries are ill-defined.

After sediments are solidified they may be subjected to such great pressures and high temperatures, meanwhile being permeated by hot water, that the minerals recrystallize. The bedding may at the same time be distorted by folding and squeezing. Shale is transformed into *slate* or *schist*, sandstone and conglomerate into *quartzite*, limestone into *marble*. The changes may be slight, producing slightly-altered sediments, or so considerable as to produce *gneiss*, hardly distinguishable from igneous rock. Indeed the end result of continued pressure and heat and circulation of hot water is a rock with all the characteristics of granite even though it has never been melted.

Most rocks called metamorphic have a recognizable ancestry in sedimentary rocks, but some can be traced back to an igneous origin. *Greenstone* or *amphibolite* may be metamorphosed basalt or andesite. Even gneiss can be derived from rhyolite or a crushed and squeezed granite, and many of the favorite climbs in the North Cascades are just such gneissic granite.

Metamorphic rocks may have not only joints and bedding, but *cleavage* or *foliation*, a series of thinly-spaced cracks imparted to the rock by the pressures of folding. Blackboards were once made from cleaved slabs of slate. Because of this cleavage, the lower grades of metamorphic rocks may be entirely unsuitable for climbing, the mountains quickly wasting away to uninteresting low angles, or if steepened by glaciers, altogether too rotten for pleasure — the rock routes on Mt. Shuksan being a prime example. However, the higher degrees of metamorphism or metamorphism of the right rocks provide superb sport. An example of low-grade metamorphism of the right rocks is the Northwest Ridge of Sir Donald in the Southern Selkirks, composed of a durable quartzite sound enough to stand solidly at high angles and yet so well broken by bedding, jointing, and cleavage that rarely is much investigation needed to find the next hold or the next belay. The opposite side, because of incline of the rock bedding, presents loose holds and downsloping slabs. Similar examples occur in the metamorphic rocks (gneiss) of the Pickets, Sloan Peak, and Bonanza, which offer excellent slab climbing on one side and on the other steep, difficult faces with holds weathered off.

MOUNTAIN BUILDING: THE GRAND PATTERN

Two steps are necessary in the building of a mountain. First a land area must rise above sea level. Second, erosion must dissect the crustal protuberance. Both are essential, for mere altitude does not make a mountain. The high plateaus of Colorado and Tibet, not yet deeply eroded, are of little interest to the climber. An understanding of how mountains are built and sculptured will sharpen the climber's perception of mountain forms and the effects they have on climbing strategy and tactics.

The Theory of Mountain Building

Little is known of the *why* behind the crustal motions which produce mountains. The most prevalent theory is that of *continental drift*, in which it is speculated that all continents were once part of a single land mass, gradually separating and being set adrift by some force, perhaps one connected with the rotation of the earth. There is evidence, for instance, that Africa, South America, and Antarctica were once joined, ultimately splitting apart and floating to their present positions. The stresses produced in the continental margins, or plates, as they plow through the denser substratum of the earth or drift against one another could give rise to the mountain ranges. For example, there is some evidence to suggest that the Alps, composed of the world's most strongly squeezed rocks, have been caught between the crustal blocks of central Europe and Africa.

The Internal Structure

The various horizontal and vertical stresses that act on the rocks of mountains commonly produce complex patterns. However, each kind of stress, if left to itself, would produce a certain ideal *structure*; some ranges can be described in terms of these simple structures.

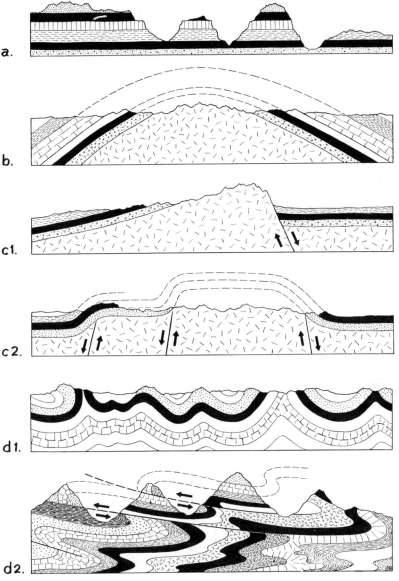

Fig. 172. Internal mountain structures.

a. Plains-plateau mountains: Canadian Rockies.

b. Dome mountains, eroded to expose granite core: Raft River Range, Utah.

c1. Fault block mountains, one sided faulted: Sierra Nevada.

c2. Fault block mountains, deep-seated faults: Southern and Middle Rocky Mountains.

d1. Fold mountains, gentle folds, highly eroded: Appalachian Mountains.

d2. Fold mountains, tight folds and overthrust fault: Alps.

The first mountain structure to be considered is called with apparent incongruity *plains-plateau,* where sedimentary strata have been lifted upward and dissected without being tilted much from the horizontal. Some sections of the Canadian Rockies evidence such a simple history, but perhaps the best example is the mountain range now being sculptured from the Kaibab Plateau, where the Grand Canyon is the first good cut, so to speak. As erosion progresses in future eons there will be steadily more peaks and less flatland.

A simple upward bulge of the crust forms *dome mountains* such as the Ozarks of Arkansas and Missouri, and in a more complicated way, the Olympic Mountains of Washington and the High Uintas of Utah.

Often accompanying upwarp is faulting, or cracking of the crust into large chunks, resulting in *fault block mountains.* A great variety of forms are created by motion of these chunks along the faults. The ranges of the desert country of California, Nevada, and Utah present most striking instances of faulting; the breakage extends to the surface and often during an earthquake — caused by slippage between the blocks — fresh scarps many feet high develop. Sometimes a block is faulted on both sides and rises or falls as a unit, but the Tetons of Wyoming and the Sierra Nevada are faulted on one side only: along the single zone of faults the range heaves up impressive steep scarps, while on the other side the mass bends but does not break, leaving a gentler slope from the base of the range to the crest. Blocks may drop as well as rise. A clear example is Death Valley, which is below sea level and thus most certainly could not have been carved by erosion. The adjacent upfaulted block bears Telescope Peak, 12,000 feet above the floor of Death Valley. Motion is not always merely up and down — slippage along the notorious San Andreas Fault of California is essentially lateral, and elsewhere are instances of blocks that move both horizontally and vertically.

More subtle examples of fault block mountains are the ranges of the Central and Southern Rocky Mountains, from Wyoming to New Mexico, elevated by faulting but with the planes of breakage deeply buried under the surface strata, which are bent above the faults but commonly unbroken — a condition not always easily distinguishable from compressive folding.

Perhaps the most common architectural style is a rococo of complex folds. When erosion strips down the geosynclinal pile that has risen out of the ocean, the folds and contortions are most evident. The Alps are one example of *fold mountains.* The Appalachians are another, but much older; the rocky summits are remnants of resistant strata.

When the squeezing of a range is intense, the rocks of the mountain mass first fold but may then break and parts of the rocks be pushed sideways and override others. Eons later when the geologist attempts to decipher the history of the region he may well be puzzled, finding older rocks perched atop younger ones. Isolated blocks of the *overthrust* mass may form when erosion strips away links connecting them with their place of origin. The rocks of the Alps have been shoved to a large extent into foreign locations.

But an overthrust structure may also form in another way. As a large mountain range rises very high, large masses of rock, measured in miles, creep out over the lowlands at the base of the mountain. These may be likened to a landslide, and although their motion may be of a geologic slowness, they may move considerable distances. In the North Cascades Mt. Shuksan (greenschist) overrides younger volcanic rocks on Shuksan arm — part of a very large overthrust originating near what is now the crest area of the Cascades and extending westward to near Bellingham. Almost every range of folded mountains in the world exhibits an overthrust of one sort or another.

Volcanic mountains are in a class by themselves, an exception to the rule that both uplift and dissection are needed to produce peaks. The Pacific Belt includes the Rim of Fire — from Katmai in the north to Aconcagua and Tierra del Fuego in the south, from Rainier and Popocatepetl on the east to Fujiyama and Krakatoa on the west. However, the Pacific has no monopoly on volcanoes; Kilimanjaro in Africa and Etna in Europe are no mean examples.

Mountains can be categorized by ideal structure for convenient description, but most ranges are *complex mountains*, with portions that have been simply moved upward without tilting, with other portions folded, domed, and faulted, frequently with a sprinkling of volcanoes. Moreover, the processes described occur both on a large and a small scale. A single gigantic fold may form an entire mountain peak, but there are also folds measured by a rope length, and tiny folds confined within a handhold. A single fault may build a mountain front, but the climber encounters smaller faults that form ledges and gullies.

MOUNTAIN SCULPTURE: WEATHERING AND EROSION

Having surveyed the processes that elevate portions of the crust, it is time to consider the sculpturing of highlands into peaks and valleys; although the uplift of the mountains has been discussed separately, it is well to remember that the minute a land area rises above the sea, the forces of erosion begin to tear it down. Were it not that uplift gains an edge, the mountaineer would have nothing but broad rolling hills for his pleasure.

Two processes cooperate in carving the mountains. *Weathering*, both mechanical and chemical, breaks the rocks into smaller particles without moving them. *Erosion* encompasses all the activities of gravity, wind, water, and ice which not only break or grind the rocks but transport the degradation products.

Weathering

The consequences of weathering to the climber in choosing his route are considerable and have been mentioned in Chapter 7. *Chemical weathering* constantly attacks exposed rocks, since many minerals, which crystallized within the hot earth, are unstable at the cooler surface where they are exposed to air and water. Chemical weathering is not uniformly intense on all rocks in all places. Some minerals, such as quartz, are extremely stable, so that quartzite or quartz sandstone are little affected. Feldspars and other complex silicates, on the other hand, break down readily into clays, while calcite dissolves. Water is the prime factor in chemical weathering; a limestone cliff is very durable in a desert but rapidly crumbles in a humid climate. Carbon dioxide and humus acids in solution immensely increase the power of water to dissolve, so that weathering is accelerated in the presence of vegetation, attaining its fastest tempo below timberline in a moist climate.

By way of contrast, *mechanical weathering* is particularly severe high on the mountain peaks, especially *frost-cracking* or *wedging* by water that trickles into minute cracks and in freezing exerts a tremendous expansive force. Many high summits consist entirely of shattered rock; some areas are aptly called a rock ocean. In arctic ranges cracking is so intense that often no unshattered rock is found, merely heaps of loose rubble. In more temperate climates the climber does well to keep in mind that even routes thoroughly "cleaned" by generations of travelers may present new dangers after the freeze and thaw of winter.

Exfoliation does much of the sculpturing in granitic areas: created by pressures built up during cooling and crystallization of magmatic rock deep beneath the surface then released as the rock mass is exposed to the low pressure environment at the surface, its results are quite distinctive. By chemical and mechanical action curved flakes of the surface are loosened and break away from bedrock. A combination of exfoliation at the surface and tension jointing deep in the rock produces the spectacular granite domes of Yosemite Valley. On a smaller scale, exfoliation alone makes the characteristic rounded and flaking boulders often seen on high mountains.

Gravity and Wind Erosion

Gravity does its very best to clean up the peaks, and by rockfall indefatigably clears away fragments loosened by weathering and climbers. More terrifying, though rare, are *landslides*. In December 1963 a series of landslides on the north side of Little Tahoma on Mount Rainier delivered some 14 million cubic yards of broken rock to the glacier below, via a climbing route, and sent debris 4 miles down the valley at rates up to 90 miles an hour. Evidence of a recent landslide is an unweathered cliff or slope standing out in sharp contrast to darker and more vegetated surrounding surfaces, or a heap of tangled trees and rocks and earth where a timbered slope has slid from the bedrock. Landslides are usually set in motion when the ground is saturated and thus lubricated with water, such as after heavy rains or when the winter snows are melting, good times to avoid steep and unconsolidated slopes such as those on river terraces and moraines. *Mudflows,* especially wet landslides which act like viscous streams of water, are common on the flanks of volcanoes; climbs of volcanic peaks often begin on gentle ramps of mudflow debris.

All loose soil and rocks steadily *creep* downhill under the pull of gravity. In steep meadows creep produces striking patterns of contoured terraces. These wrinkles in the hillside are usually attributed to animals; actually both game and humans help transform them into "trails," but their origin is quite different.

A special kind of creep promoted by freezing and thawing of ice deep in a pile of coarse rock rubble produces *rock glaciers.* These streams of rock, found in many deglaciated cirques, advance downstream like a glacier and are commonly mistaken for concentric arcs of terminal moraine. Geologists are not agreed as to whether they are actually related to a preceding glaciation or not. Examples abound in the Colorado Rockies.

Wind is least significant of the erosional agents, though playing an important role in deserts, sandblasting rocks into weird forms and impelling sand dunes in their steady march.

Stream Erosion

In all but the iciest or driest ranges, ultimately every particle of every mountain, however it begins its downward journey, enters a stream of

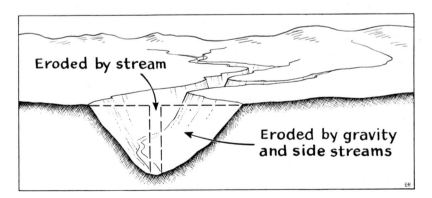

Fig. 173. Erosion by a stream

water and is ground boulder against boulder, pebble against pebble, grain against grain until — given sufficient time — nothing remains but sand and silt. Meanwhile, the stream carries steadily its burden of milling rubble to the sea, moving the mountains piecemeal to the seeding places of a future range.

Though the highest and most interesting peaks are chiefly carved by glaciers, streams retain an important role. Glaciers rarely if ever originate valleys, rather tending to follow and modify those previously dug by rivers. Actually the digging of the river valley is a complex business. The stream or river saws a notch into the rock, using the rubble it carries for abrasives. As the notch deepens, weathering, gravity, and side streams all work to eliminate the steep walls of the notch, ultimately producing a V-shaped valley. The climber, whether fording a rushing stream or following a river to its alpine headwaters, constantly must cope with erosional effects of streams. In some places, indeed, such as the cliffs along the Great Falls of the Potomac and the impressive Dalles of the Columbia, he finds practice climbs on rocks whose steepness is almost entirely due to sculpturing by the load carried in the stream.

Unladen water running downhill gains velocity and thus energy — energy to transport; the swift water seizes hungrily on any loose material until fully *loaded*. If the gradient of the hill lessens, the velocity and energy must decrease; the stream is overloaded and drops its load of sand and gravel, building a new and steeper gradient.

The supreme aim of a stream is to make its bed form a smooth curve from its headwaters to its mouth, or *baselevel,* a curve steep at the upper end, flat at the lower. When the ideal curve is achieved, the stream uses all its energy to carry all the debris dumped into it by side streams and gravity, and the stream is said to be at *grade*. Since perfect grade is elusive, a stream is always in flux, rarely satisfied for long. Lakes and waterfalls are particularly abhorrent. To fill the former the stream slows down (it must) and drops its load; to eliminate the latter it speeds up (it must) and picks up more tools to gouge away at the steep face, causing the falls to migrate upvalley, and leaving behind a deep gorge.

The mountaineer soon learns to avoid the temptation of trail-less riverside routes when marching into the hills, realizing that he may arrive at an impasse of cascading water and damp, sheer cliffs. A lake or waterfall acts as a *temporary baselevel,* and the stream above grades itself in relation to it, meanwhile trying to remove the lake or fall from the true grade curve.

A river issuing from the front of a retreating glacier is almost invariably overloaded, since the melted ice is charged with rock debris picked up by the glacier and the gradient in front of the glacier is very low. The river drops part of its burden, thereby obstructing its own course, moves to a

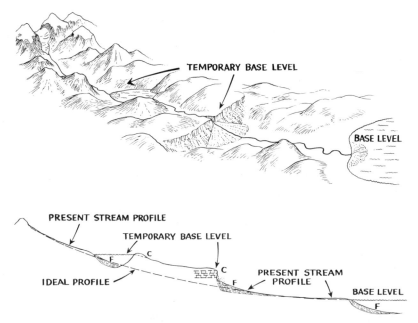

Fig. 174. Graded stream profile and baselevels. Stream is cutting at C, filling at F. Dashed line is ideal profile.

new course and in turn fills that up with debris, finally creating a system of braided channels and the wide plains of gravel commonly encountered below a glacier terminus.

A river flowing at grade may have built itself a flat flood plain. Rejuvenation — by a new uplift of the land or a change of baselevel, such as the elimination of a lake downstream — causes the water to slice deeply into the sand and gravel it had previously deposited, leaving remnants of its abandoned flood plain perched high above the river. Often the mountain traveler can make good use of these *terraces* or benches, which provide smooth pathways along the valley. However, such benches are not unmixed blessings, for both the main stream and its tributaries gouge into the old fill, making steep and unstable gravel or sand cliffs that are sometimes troublesome.

Glacier Erosion

Of all erosional agents, glaciers are most significant to the climber. Many mountaineering routes are largely the work of past glaciation; others lie upon the surface of presently-active ice. A knowledge of glacier habits is indispensable. The ultimate beginnings of a glacier are described in the next chapter, which describes the metamorphosis of snow into ice.

The Hierarchy of Glaciers

A *cirque glacier* is one confined to its place of origin, either because it has not yet gathered sufficient mass to venture farther, or because it has retreated from a previously greater extension. As a climbing problem it may be no more severe than a snowfield. If the place of origin is on a steep cliff, a *hanging glacier* results, perhaps consisting entirely of icefalls. When the pressure of increasing snow layers on the underlying ice becomes too great it flows down from the cirque, becoming a *valley glacier*. If ice advances downvalley to the plains beyond the mountain front, a *piedmont glacier* forms. Vast regions of ice lower the average temperature so that more and more snow falls and less melts. The valley glaciers thicken and spill over divides to merge with other ice streams, the piedmont glaciers advance steadily, and ultimately only the highest peaks rise above an *ice cap*.

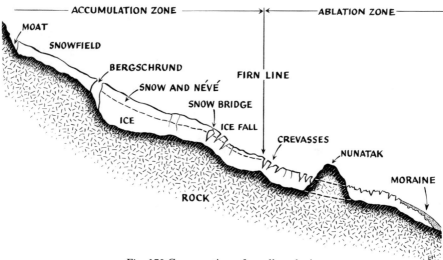

Fig. 175. Cross section of a valley glacier.

Features of Glaciers

In the *accumulation zone* of a glacier, annual snowfall exceeds annual melting; in the *ablation zone* melting predominates. The boundary between the two is called the *firn* or *névé* line, though usually it is a wide belt rather than a narrow line. The vitality of a glacier depends on at least as much ice flowing from the upper zone as melts in the lower, and the location of the firn line is a good indication of whether the glacier is advancing or retreating. Many glaciers of the Canadian Rockies, for instance, are chiefly bare ice, *dry glaciers*, with only small patches of snow

Fig. 176. Glacial features.

Ice features
A. Moat
B. Bergschrund
C. Firn line
D. Crecentric crevasses
E. Nunatak
F. En echelon crevasses
G. Marginal crevasses
H. Terminus or snout
I. Braided outwash stream

Moraine features
1. Lateral moraine
2. Medial moraine
3. Terminal moraine
4. Outwash plain (and ground moraine)
5. Erratic
6. Old terminal moraine
7. Old lateral moraine

at their upper limits; these are extremely unhealthy, steadily retreating. If the firn line marches down toward the glacier *front, snout,* or *terminus,* a growth or advance of the glacier may be expected.

The depths of a glacier are solidly compressed and without cracks but the brittle surface layers fracture under the strains and stresses of motion down steep slopes, around corners, and along rock walls. These *crevasses* are rarely deeper than 200-250 feet but even when much shallower, as is usual, they are the major problems of glacier travel. Specific climbing tactics have already been discussed in Chapter 17, but understanding what controls crevasse formation is immensely helpful in planning a route.

Crecentric crevasses develop wherever the ice increases its rate of flow, commonly where the glacier bed steepens. The change in angle may be so small it is not evident on the surface and is only indicated by belts of crevasses forming long arcs concave downvalley, at right angles to the direction of flow.

If the incline is very steep an *icefall* forms, the surface broken into a profusion of crevasses extending every which way, with large ice towers or *seracs.* Below a sharp declivity crevasses are often absent, since the glacier is slowing down after its plunge, but sometimes pressure from the cataract above buckles the surface into *pressure ridges,* with attendant crevasses. In a steep icefall a considerable portion of the downward advance is by avalanches, a hazard that influences routes both through a fall or anywhere underneath one.

Lateral marginal crevasses are opened by the faster motion of a glacier's center relative to its sides, where friction along the valley walls has a restraining effect. Lateral crevasses invariably trend upvalley. The characteristic of both crecentric and lateral fractures to angle upstream toward the glacier center is frequently useful in guessing the hidden extension from a single surface hole. Crevassing, however, is not so simply methodical, for minor surface stresses produce random fractures which follow no pattern whatsoever. Protuberances of rock through the ice, *nunataks,* usually have a halo of crevasses and thus are best avoided, but if the rock does not quite reach the surface, the crevasse pattern may completely baffle the routefinder. The only general rule applicable to crevasse location is that they can occur anywhere and anyhow on a glacier.

Crevasses are most hazardous to the climber in the zone of accumulation, where they are frequently bridged by snow. New snow may completely fill the depths, or with the assistance of a cornice-building wind, build an arch over inner emptiness. The entire structure may melt away or collapse of its own weight during the summer, leaving an obvious pit. Often glacier motion widens the crevasse and by stretching the bridge cracks it open; the climber who assumes the visible thin fissure respresents the entire width of the chasm can be unpleasantly surprised.

At the glacier's upper limit is a giant crevasse, the *bergschrund,* formed between the glacier and the rock by the movement of the glacier and melting or both. Sometimes the bergschrund is the final problem of the ascent, with the summit only a short stroll above. If the glacier is diminishing, the surface lowers, leaving a steep arcuate precipice above, which may be capped by hanging glaciers with still more menacing crevasses and bergschrunds. Above the highest bergschrund there is often perched a snowfield separated from the rock face by a *moat,* formed partially by melting and partially by creep, thus being similar in origin to a bergschrund and frequently every bit as difficult to cross.

A glacier continually receives debris from its headwall, from its bed which it scrapes and gouges, and from valley sides; it incorporates and carries all this burden along. In the ablation zone the glacier thins and the rubble emerges on the surface; when the ice is entirely melted the debris is dumped in *moraines.*

If the glacier terminus remains in one place for a long time a *terminal moraine* is built, a steep ridge generally concave upvalley in accordance with the usual shape of a glacier front. Deposits along the sides of the glacier, on and off the ice, are *lateral moraines.* When two valley glaciers come together the lateral moraines merge into a *medial moraine.* When a glacier swiftly retreats, debris is widely and thinly scattered, leaving a formless *ground moraine.* The unstable rubble of moraines is usually a nuisance, but sometimes lateral or medial moraines provide easier walking than the surface of the glacier.

Whereas running water sorts sediments so fastidiously that in any one bed particle size may lie within a narrow range, ice carries along particles sized from the *rock flour* produced by milling of rock against rock, all the way to boulders as big as small mountains. Such unsorted deposits are called *till,* the general term for all the material found in moraines. The boulders, when left perched far from their source, are called *erratics.* The flour gives to glacier streams their characteristic opaqueness and when carried in suspension is the *rock milk* which makes fording a blind and chancy job. Within till there are usually inclusions of bedded sand, gravel, and clay, evidence of a vanished river or lake at the margin of the re-treating ice.

Land Forms Produced By Glacial Erosion

Few unglaciated mountains have any attraction for the climber. Glaciers deepen the valleys and steepen the slopes, and thus create the sharp relief called "mountainous."

A cirque glacier erodes headward in a complex way. Most of the damage to the rock wall of a bergschrund is done by the freezing and thawing of ice; the loosened blocks fall down into the bergschrund and become incorporated in the glacier. The bottom of the cirque is lowered by the scratching, scraping, and gouging of rocks frozen in the ice: a glacier is a giant rasp. Even in the northern Appalachians and the hills of Britain, where glaciation was never prolonged, whatever cliffs exist have been provided by headward cirque erosion, which produces *biscuit-board* terrain, generally gentle of profile interrupted by occasional cirques.

When glaciation is more prolonged and two cirques work toward each other they lower the divide into a razor-sharp *col*. Three or more cirques plucking backward into a common mass of rock make a *horn*, which in ideal form has three cirque walls, three *aretes* separating them, and culminates in a steep sharp summit. The Matterhorn is the classic example. Forbidden Peak in the North Cascades (see Figure 15) and Sir Donald in the Selkirks are splendid American horns.

A distinction must be made between a *valley*, which represents erosion under the leadership of a stream of water or ice, and a *channel*, the actual space occupied at any time by that stream of water or ice. Cross-sections of both river and glacier channels are U-shaped. However, ice moves much more slowly than water, and a glacier requires a much larger channel than a river to drain a watershed. For a given amount of precipitation, a river might have a channel 100 feet wide and 5 feet deep; a glacier might need a channel — the U-shaped valley — 1 mile wide and 2000 feet deep.

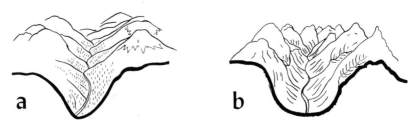

Fig. 177. Stream- and glacier-cut valleys.
a. V-shaped, stream-cut valley.
b. U-shaped, glacier-cut valley.

Abandoned glacier channels are very widespread in today's mountains and give the traveler some interesting moments. Typically in the North Cascades, the wide flat floor of the U is a swampy tangle of brush and morainal hillocks, and the walls are steep. In many ranges it is not always easy to distinguish a glacier channel from a water-carved valley, for talus and alluvial fans rapidly obscure the U, smoothing it into a V. Such modifications often provide ramps through the cliffs of the U.

Tributary glaciers with their smaller flow cannot keep pace in downcutting with the main valley glacier, and *hanging valleys* are characteristic of ranges once heavily glaciated. Reaching these valleys from below can be as challenging as ascending the peak.

A glacier-cut valley is seldom an evenly-graded highway to the alpine country. Most commonly the history of glaciation includes the birth and death of several generations of glaciers which when born as cirque glaciers did not always form at the same elevation. Thus *multiple cirques* are occasionally encountered. In the North Cascades, the upper cirque may still support a glacier, while the steep cliffs of the lower cirque, plucked by vanished ice, are stoutly defended by waterfalls and cedar trees. Mountaineers tend to devalue these pitches with humor, feeling the effort demanded to overcome them is considerably less noble than that needed to scale clean rock crests, but in truth the lower cirque is frequently the crux of the climb.

More commonly the valley is broken into cliffs or *steps* due to differences in rock resistance, the glacier more rapidly eroding the weak rocks than the strong ones. Commonly in jointed granite terrain, large blocks of rock are quarried by the ice, leaving a vertical step along the joint plane when the ice is gone. Steps may also form where several tributary glaciers join a main one, the additional ice volume increasing the erosive power. Any rock protuberance overridden by a glacier, especially one on the edge of a step, is plucked and steepened on the downvalley side and streamlined on the upper side, leaving a *roche moutonée.*

Glaciers, being viscous masses with some strength, have the ability to flow uphill and thus erode a sizable depression in their bed — a feat only achieved by water when it gains extra energy by falling off a cliff to dig a plunge pool. *Grinding down at the heel* is quite typical of glacial erosion and has produced such features as the deep fjords of Norway and British Columbia, long lakes in glaciated valleys such as Lake Chelan of Washington and the Finger Lakes of New York, and the round lakes or *tarns* in evacuated cirques.

Glacial Cycles

World climate has fluctuated radically in past ages. A lowering by only several degrees in mean annual temperature of the atmosphere is sufficient to cause a general advance of glaciers; such fluctuations have occurred many times in the geologic past and with them have come ages of ice.

The ultimate reasons for the coming of an ice age are not known exactly, though responsibility has been assigned to a variety of things. Popular for many years have been theories which more or less assign a single cause, such as clouds of dust which shield the earth from the sun, either the passing of the solar system through a cosmic cloud or clouds produced by accelerated vulcanism on earth. Current thought favors more complex relationships which not only involve changes in average summer and winter temperatures due to orbital and rotational eccentricities of the earth, but the configuration of mountain belts and distribution of hot and cold ocean currents.

Whatever the cause, the world is now either in or emerging from a cycle of glaciation, the Pleistocene Ice Age, which is one of the most extensive ever to have occurred. The glaciers were most widespread between 10,000 and 25,000 years ago, at which time a continental ice cap covered all of Canada, most of Alaska, and much of the northern United States. Another reached from Siberia and Scandinavia far south into Europe. The Antarctic cap was thicker and bigger than it is today and extensive systems of valley and piedmont glaciers entwined all mountainous regions of the world.

Subsequent to the time of maximum ice cover, the world glaciers have been in general retreat. The so-called "climatic optimum" of 4000 to 6000 years ago, when all but a few ice caps disappeared, provided warmer and drier climates the world over than have been enjoyed since. Following that period the climate has fluctuated several times, sending mountain glaciers charging down their valleys. Records in Europe show considerable advances in the 16th and 17th centuries. Near Chamonix, the glaciers of the Mont Blanc chain descended into the main valley and overwhelmed several villages.

In the United States the record is less complete. There appears to have been a rebirth and growth of mountain glaciers in the high cirques of the Northwest about 2500-2000 years ago and several resurgences since then. While Europeans explored and settled the New World the ice revived, reaching a maximum in the 18th century; throughout the Northwest mountaineers commonly encounter moraines from that period. Another lesser advance climaxed around 1900, and since then recession has been general and worldwide with but minor exceptions. However, glacier lovers have been excited recently by the general resurgence of ice in the Cascades and Olympics. It would be premature to herald a new age of ice, for so local a phenomenon could be the effect merely of a temporary shift in storm tracks. It would also be unwise to suppose that the Ice Age is over; only time can tell whether contemporary glaciers will increase their dominion or become extinct.

Certainly the world is not so chill as it was earlier in the Pleistocene Epoch, but it is much colder than it has been during most of the geologic past. The Antarctic continent is almost completely submerged in an ice cap of some 5 million square miles and locally almost 3 miles thick. The Greenland ice cap, though only an eighth as large, has been estimated to be almost 2 miles thick. Continental North America is blessed with over

30,000 square miles of glacier, mostly in Alaska and Canada, but also sprinkled in generous samples through the Cascades and Olympics of Washington, and in meager bits through the Rockies and Sierra Nevada.

THE MOUNTAINEER AS GEOLOGIST

It is interesting that much early climbing was done by geologists who sought the secrets of mountain origin. The novice climber asks what ancient geologic history has to do with his struggle to reach the register book. The devout mountaineer answers that freedom of the hills comes only with understanding. The next handhold, the next belay, the next twist in the route, all express the interplay over millions of years of the forces that both build and destroy mountains. Whether the climber seeks his sport high on granite spires that are the remnants of a magma once buried deep in the crust, or navigates the ice avenues of a glacier, he can choose his route with more confidence, and gain a more intimate feeling for his mountains, if he knows their history and present state of flux.

Supplementary Reading:

Easterbrook, D. J., and D. A. Rahm. *Landforms of Washington.* Bellingham, Washington: Western Washington State College, 1970.

Ekman, L. C., *Scenic Geology of the Pacific Northwest.* Portland, Oregon: Binfords and Mort, 1962.

McKee, Bates. *Cascadia: The Geologic Evolution of the Pacific Northwest.* New York: McGraw-Hill, Inc., 1972.

Milne, Lorus, and Margery Milne. *The Mountains.* New York: Time, Inc., 1962.

24 *

THE CYCLE OF SNOW

WHEN THE CLIMBER leaves behind the rock crags and cliffs and ventures into the zone of perpetual snow, he passes from terrain of stable, known, and reasonably predictable character to a region where change is the rule and where, as a consequence, his previous experience is often of little avail. He enters a world where snow and ice invest high mountains with a beauty foreign to lower peaks, mold their form and character, at the same time presenting him with some of his more strenuous difficulties, unpredictable hazards, and most thrilling moments. The almost infinite variety of conditions which snow and ice can assume at different times of day and season, and in different locales, confronts him with an infinite variety of problems. The techniques necessary to deal successfully with these elevate the skill of an adequate climber to the craft of a competent mountaineer.

Complete familiarity with the behavior of snow and ice, if attainable, would require a lifetime spent dwelling above the snowline, for the first rule the climber learns is that mountaineering on snow and ice is indeed a craft, and must be learned by direct participation rather than from books. However, his apprenticeship will be shortened if he departs for the hills equipped with a basic understanding of the way snow behaves, how it becomes ice, and the manner in which meteorological factors affect the entire process. The following sections are intended to provide the background for this understanding. Emphasis is placed on presenting fundamentals which will enable the mountaineer to face intelligently the problems of snow and ice travel wherever he may go, and in whatever season. Once the basic physical laws which govern snow behavior are understood, logical explanations can be drawn for phenomena observed in the field, a method established for their prediction, and a firm foundation set up for the training of an experienced craftsman.

THE HYDROLOGIC CYCLE

The conditions of geology, climate, and life on this planet are determined by the existence of a temperature range wherein water, the commonest substance on the earth's surface, can exist in all three states of matter — solid, liquid, and gas. It is difficult to conceive what the face of the earth would look like if the cycle of evaporation, condensation, and runoff were eliminated by temperatures high enough to keep all the water in the form of vapor, or low enough to keep it all in the form of ice. Because the temperatures that do prevail permit water to pass readily from one state to another, a complex hydrologic cycle exists. All three states of water are active participants in the hydrologic cycle, but the solid state — snow and ice — represents a temporary storage on the earth's surface of water substance which is not immediately available to the continuous cycle of evaporation, condensation, and liquid runoff. This storage may be of short duration, as in the temporary winter snowcover, or it may be for centuries or millennia when the solid state takes the form of glacier ice. In either case, water owes its perpetuation in the solid state on the earth's surface to the fact that a great deal of energy is required to return it to the liquid state once it has been deposited as a solid. The amount of heat required to melt a given weight of ice, without any change in temperature, is seven times that required to melt the same weight of iron, and thirteen times that for the same weight of lead.

The various forms which water assumes during the solid phase of the hydrologic cycle are displayed in Figure 178, and are discussed in the following sections.

FORMATION OF SNOW IN THE ATMOSPHERE

Snow may occur whenever water vapor is precipitated at temperatures below freezing. Snow crystals are known to form around centers of foreign matter in the air, such as microscopic dust particles. The first step is collection around the nucleus of a small ice crystal, which grows by the deposition of additional ice from water vapor in the atmosphere. (The transfer of water directly from the vapor to the solid state, or vice versa, is known as *sublimation*.) Recent investigations suggest that minute water droplets (i.e., diameter around 1 micron) may also contribute to the growth of snow crystals. These crystals in general assume a hexagonal pattern, but variations in size, shape, and form are almost limitless. A general classification according to form divides snow crystals into stars,

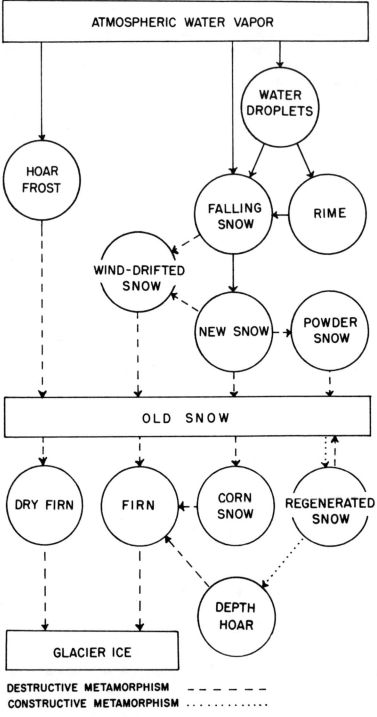

Fig. 178. Solid phase of the hydrologic cycle.

Term	Remarks	Examples
Plates	also combinations of plates with or without very short connecting columns	
Stellar crystals	also parallel stars with very short connecting columns	
Columns	and combinations of columns	
Needles	and combinations of needles	
Spatial dendrites	spatial combinations of feathery crystals	
Capped columns	columns with plates on either (or one) side	
Irregular particles	irregular compounds of microscopic crystals	
Graupel (soft hail)	isometric shape. Central, crystal cannot be recognized	
Ice pellets (sleet)	ice shell, inside mostly wet	
Hail		

Fig. 179. Types of solid precipitation, from International Snow Classification.

needles, columns, and plates. Combinations of these forms may occur, and irregular crystalline aggregates are found. The particular form developed in the atmosphere depends on the air temperature and the amount of water vapor available. When a snow crystal falls through different air masses with different temperature and water vapor conditions, the more complex or combined types may develop. Crystals formed in, or falling through, air whose temperature is near the freezing point stick together to become aggregates of individual crystals, or *snowflakes*.

When snow crystals fall through air which contains water droplets, these droplets freeze to the crystal as a *rime* deposit. As the amount of rime on a crystal increases, the original shape is obscured and a rounded ball results, giving rise to the type of snow commonly known as pellet, or tapioca. The technical term for these rimed crystals is *graupel*.

The percentage of water in new-fallen snow prior to settlement may range from 1 per cent to 30 per cent or higher. The average for mountain snowfalls is from 7 to 10 per cent, depending on climate. For some extremely maritime climates, this average may be as high as 25 per cent. The lightest snow is deposited under moderately cold and very calm conditions. At extremely low temperatures a fine, granular snow is deposited with somewhat higher densities. The highest new snow densities are associated with graupel or needle crystals falling at temperatures near the freezing point. In general, new snow density increases with air temperature, but density can vary widely in the range of $20°$ to $32°F$. As air temperature falls, density variations become smaller and lower densities predominate. High winds break up falling snow crystals into small fragments which pack together on deposition to form a dense, fine-grained snow structure.

FORMATION AND CHARACTER OF THE SNOW COVER

Formation of the snowcover is in some ways analogous to the formation of sedimentary rocks. Solid precipitation from the atmosphere (*sedimentation*) builds up the snowcover layer by layer, yielding a stratification that displays the history of weather variations which occurred during its development. With the passage of time, structural and crystalline changes within the snowcover (*metamorphism*) obscure the original stratigraphic differentiation and convert the snow into new forms.

The metamorphic process within the snowcover is a continuous one which begins when the snow is deposited and lasts until it melts. The normal path of metamorphism tends to destroy the original forms of the deposited snow crystals and gradually convert them into rounded grains of ice (*destructive metamorphism*). This process is also called equi-temperature metamorphism because it is the one which prevails in the absence of

large temperature difference within the snow cover. When the crystals of
new snow have been altered by this conversion so their original form is no
longer recognizable, it becomes, by definition, *old snow.* The physical
process causing these changes is not entirely understood, but transfer of
water vapor by sublimation from the points of the crystal branches to the
more central portions of the crystal appears to play an important role. The
process is strongly influenced by temperature, and proceeds at a rapid rate
when the temperature is near freezing. At extremely low temperature
metamorphism is very slow, virtually stopping below -40° C. All types of
crystals tend to approach the uniform conditions of rounded grains as this
process takes place, and the snowcover becomes more homogeneous. The
rate of metamorphism is influenced by pressure as well as temperature
(*pressure metamorphism*), and the weight of additional snowfalls over a
given snow layer causes acceleration of the crystalline changes within it.

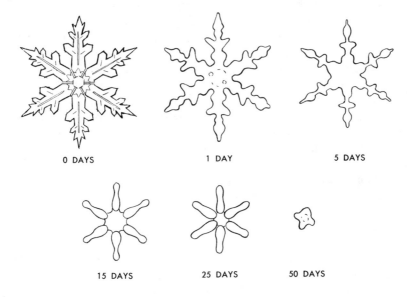

0 DAYS   1 DAY   5 DAYS

15 DAYS   25 DAYS   50 DAYS

Fig. 180. Destructive metemorphism of a snow crystal.

The destructive metamorphism of the snow crystals results in a reduction of the space a given amount of ice occupies. With this increased
density the snowcover shrinks, or settles. *Settlement* is a continuous, visible
indication of metamorphism. Rising temperatures cause an increase in the
settlement rate.

Constructive metamorphism, or temperature-gradient metamorphism,
may also take place in the snowcover. This occurs when water vapor is
transferred from one part of the snowcover to another by vertical diffusion

and is deposited in the form of ice crystals with different characteristics from those of the original snow. These crystals often have a scroll or cup shape, appear to be layered, and may grow to considerable size (several millimeters in diameter). They form a very fragile mechanical structure which loses all strength when crushed and which becomes very soft when wet. The snow form produced by this type of metamorphism is known as *depth hoar* and is sometimes popularly referred to as sugar snow. The necessary conditions for its formation are a large difference in temperature at different depths in the snow (large, or steep, temperature *gradient*) and sufficient air spaces in the snow so that water vapor can diffuse freely. These conditions are most common early in winter when the snowcover is shallow and unconsolidated.

Because of its plastic nature, whenever snow is situated on a sloping surface it tends to move slowly downhill under the influence of gravity. The snow layer deforms internally, the upper layers moving downhill faster than those next to the ground. This internal deformation, called *creep*, proceeds most rapidly at the freezing point and diminishes with falling snow temperature. The entire snow layer also *glides* on the ground if the interface between snow and earth is at the freezing point. If the ground surface is smooth (grass, for instance), gliding is the dominant form of snow motion. The slow combined motions of creep and glide often go unnoticed by the casual observer, but they cause the snowcover to exert enormous forces on obstacles in its path. These forces increase with the square of snow depths and may achieve magnitudes of several tons per square yard. Such forces must be taken into account when designing mountain installations such as avalanche barriers, ski lift towers, and snow sheds. The stresses produced by uneven creep of snow are an important factor in avalanche formation.

Variations in the strength of snow are among the widest found in nature. The hardness of windpacked old snow or frozen firn may be as much as 50,000 times that of light, fluffy new snow. Tensile strength also varies widely. Strength characteristics continually change as a result of metamorphism, and also depend on temperature for a given snow type. When snow is disturbed mechanically and then allowed to set, it undergoes a process known as *age-hardening*. This results in a gradual hardening of the snow for several hours after it has been disturbed. The greatest source of mechanical disturbance in nature is the wind, and an increase in hardness is always associated with wind-drifted snow.

THERMAL PROPERTIES OF THE SNOWCOVER

Properties of snow that have been mentioned are all functions of temperature. Indeed, the thermal properties of snow are the key to its whole behavior and its stability.

There are three basic characteristics of snow which strongly influence its thermal properties. First is the high heat of fusion of ice already mentioned. For each gram of ice at the freezing point, approximately 80 calories are required just to convert it to liquid water without any change in temperature. The second is a very low heat conductivity, especially for dry, new-fallen snow. The heat conductivity of snow ranges from about .0001 to .0007 calories/cm-sec-°C. For comparison, the heat conductivity of copper is 1.0 calories/cm-sec-°C., some 10,000 times greater than that of snow. The third characteristic is the presence of water in the vapor and/or liquid states as well as the solid state. Vapor and liquid water play an important part in heat transfer within the snowcover.

The heat supply at the bottom of the snowcover is relatively minor. The internal heat of the earth provides a small but steady heat supply at the ground surface, and is sufficient to melt about 1 centimeter of ice each year. A larger amount of heat is stored in the surface layers of the earth each summer, and this heat will melt some of the winter snow as it is deposited. If cold weather precedes the first snowfall, some of this heat may already be dissipated by frost. In any case, an appreciable snowcover serves to insulate the ground surface from external heat exchanges, and the internal and stored heat, even though relatively small in quantity, is still sufficient to melt some snow throughout the winter. For this reason the base of the snowcover is almost always at 0°C., or 32°F., throughout the temperate zones.

Heat is both lost and gained in much larger quantities at the snow surface, and the temperature undergoes wide fluctuations below the freezing point. Because water cannot exist in a solid state at temperatures higher than the freezing point, the temperature of the snow surface, which is composed of particles of solid ice, can never be higher than 32°F., though a thermometer placed on the snow surface will often give a misleading value higher than 32°F., because of solar radiation. The principal media of heat transfer at the snow surface are heat conduction, radiation, condensation-evaporation-sublimation, and precipitation. Conduction, radiation, and vapor exchange may either add or subtract heat, while rainfall can only add it, as liquid water will always be at a temperature equal to or higher than that of ice.

The medium of heat exchange with the largest potential is the air. Heat may be conveyed to or removed from the snow surface in large quantities by the process known as *eddy conduction*, a transfer of heat accompanying turbulence; being dependent on the motion of air over the snow surface it does not occur with completely calm air. Under this latter condition heat is transferred between snow and air only in very small amounts. When the air is warmer than the snow surface, heat is transferred to the snow, and as the difference in temperature increases, so does the amount of heat transferred. With air colder than the snow surface, heat flow is in the opposite direction. The turbulent transfer of heat depends on wind velocity — that is, the higher the wind velocity, the greater is the amount of heat transferred. The amount of snow that can be melted in a given period by a strong, warm wind, such as a Chinook wind, is much greater than can be melted by any other natural source, including solar radiation.

A great deal of energy arrives at the earth's surface as short-wave (visible) radiation from the sun, but only a small portion is available to snow because of its high reflectivity. Up to 90 per cent of the short-wave radiation arriving at the surface of freshly fallen snow is turned back by reflection. This figure drops to about 60 per cent for wet spring snow, and may be even lower if there is any appreciable dirt on the surface.

In contrast to its behavior under short-wave radiation, snow is the most nearly perfect absorber of long-wave (infra-red) radiation in nature — or to put it another way, is the nearest approach to an ideal "black" substance. This means that snow is also an excellent radiator of infra-red, and thus can lose heat rapidly through this medium as well as gain it. When skies are clear, snow loses heat to space by long-wave radiation, the amount depending on the quantity of water vapor and carbon dioxide in the air, both of which have strong effects. Under overcast conditions snow will also lose heat by long-wave radiation to clouds if the cloud temperature is lower than that of the snow surface. Clouds of any appreciable thickness also behave as black bodies to infra-red, and if temperatures of cloud and snow surface are known, the amount of heat exchanged can be estimated. When the clouds are warmer than the snow surface, the process is reversed and the snow gains heat by long-wave radiation. This latter condition is most common in spring or summer when the air and clouds are warm, but the snow surface remains at 32°F.

The effects of long- and short-wave radiation add algebraically to produce the net radiation balance of the snow surface. The net balance is usually positive (snow gains heat) in the day and negative at night during clear weather. Occasionally, under conditions of clear skies at high altitudes in winter, when the sun angle is low, even at midday the outgoing long-wave radiation may exceed the short-wave radiation absorbed by the snow, which will actually be cooled while the sun is shining. Maximum positive radiation balance is not achieved on clear days, for then the outgoing infra-red radiation subtracts from the solar radiation available to the snow surface. The maximum amount of heat in the form of radiant energy is received by the snow under conditions when *both* infra-red and short-wave radiation are delivered to the snow surface. This usually occurs with a partly overcast sky.

The behavior of water vapor as a medium of heat exchange at the snow surface is determined by the high heat of vaporization of water. The conversion of 1 gram of water from liquid to vapor without change in temperature requires 600 calories of heat. If water is converted directly from solid to vapor (sublimation), the heat of fusion must be added to this figure, giving a heat requirement of 680 calories per gram. It is thus seen that, even though the heat of fusion is large, the heat of vaporization or sublimation is very much larger. Accordingly, addition or subtraction of material at the snow surface through the medium of water vapor must always be accompanied by the exchange of large quantities of heat. This means, first, that evaporation can take place only if enough heat is available to supply the heat of vaporization. Heat in such quantities is not ordinarily available to the snow surface, and evaporation losses are always quite small. Significant amounts of evaporation can occur only when extremely dry air with temperature well above that of the snow surface is accompanied by high winds, provided that the condition for evaporation described below is satisfied. A second corollary is that condensation of water vapor on a snow surface can be a large source of heat, for when condensation takes place, the heat of vaporization is given up to the snow. The transport of water vapor to or from the snow surface is governed by laws similar to those governing the turbulent transfer of heat, and increases with increasing wind velocity.

Whether evaporation or condensation occurs depends on a simple physical law. When the dew point of the atmosphere is lower than the snow surface temperature, evaporation is possible. When the dew point is higher than the snow surface temperature, condensation can take place. If the air and snow surface temperatures are below freezing, the exchange takes place as sublimation. Conditions most frequently favor condensation in spring or summer, when air temperatures (and dew points) become higher, while the snow temperature remains at 32°F.

Rainfall rarely delivers more than a minor amount of heat to the snow surface. It takes 1 calorie of heat to raise the temperature of 1 gram of water 1°C. Each gram of rain which falls on a snow surface and is cooled to the freezing point gives up only 1 calorie for each degree Centigrade it is cooled. Since the heat of fusion of snow and ice is 80 calories per gram, it naturally follows that deluges of rain — rare in the high mountains — are needed to melt any significant amount. The heavy snow melt sometimes associated with rainstorms can usually be attributed to the accompanying warm wind and condensation.

The flow of heat within the snowcover is a complex phenomenon, due to the presence of all three phases of water. Part of the heat is transferred by molecular conduction, and part is transferred by circulation of air in the spaces between the snow grains. The air itself carries some heat, but the water vapor with it carries more. It has been estimated that in some environments up to half of the heat flow in snow is due to sublimation and diffusion of water vapor. Because of the high heat of sublimation of water, only small quantities of water vapor are required to transport appreciable heat in this manner. In any case, the total amount of heat transferred within the dry snowcover is quite small, due to its overall low conductivity. This picture is altered, however, when appreciable amounts of liquid water are present. The downward percolation of liquid water through a snowcover transports heat very rapidly, and a sudden thaw or rainfall which produces free water at the surface will quickly warm the whole snowcover to the freezing point. When water percolates into snow below the freezing point, the water refreezes and gives up its heat of fusion. Heat is thus transported through the snow by the physical penetration of water, circumventing the otherwise low conductivity of snow.

SPECIAL FORMS AND FEATURES OF SNOW AND ICE

Certain forms of falling or deposited snow have already been described and their origin explained; there are other special snow and ice forms of interest to the mountaineer.

The term *powder snow* has been so widely applied in the United States to light, fluffy, new-fallen snow that this usage has gained some measure of authority. However, powder snow is also more specifically defined as new snow which has undergone a certain degree of crystalline change, having lost some of its cohesion due to the recrystallizing effects of steep temperature gradients (constructive metamorphism) in the surface snow layers. These changes can occur only during periods of persistent low temperatures. (The widespread phrase among skiers, "cold powder snow," has its basis in fact.) Such snow is loose and powdery, commonly affords good skiing, often better than the original new snow at the time of deposition, and may form dry loose-snow avalanches.

After the advent of melting in early spring, a period of fair weather may be followed by the formation of coarse rounded crystals on the snow surface. When this *corn snow* thaws out each morning after the nightly freezing it offers an excellent skiing and stepkicking surface. These coarse crystals are formed from the alternate melting and freezing of the snow by the diurnal temperature changes during fair weather. The melting each day must be just sufficient to form some free water among the snow grains; if too much melting occurs part of the surface is ablated away, and the process must start afresh with another layer of snow the next day. Only when the same surface layer of snow is exposed to the alternate melting and refreezing does true corn snow develop. For this reason, corn snow formation is less frequent later in the spring and summer, when surface ablation is greater. A surface similar to corn snow is common on summer snowfields, or firn; but this is usually an ice layer exposed and disintegrated by ablation.

Rotten snow is a condition of snowcover, sometimes found in the spring, and characterized by a soft, wet snow in the lower layers of the snowcover which offers little support to the sometimes-firmer layers above. In its most pronounced forms it will not support even the weight of a man on skis. Snow conditions which promise good spring skiing early in the morning, while some strength remains in the diurnal crust, may later in the day deteriorate to rotten snow, the disappointed skier finding himself sinking in to his knees. This type of snow forms when layers of depth hoar in the lower part of the snowcover become wet and lose what little mechanical strength they originally possessed. Wet loose-snow or slab avalanches running clear to the ground frequently occur. Continental climates such as those of the Rockies are most productive of rotten snow formation, which is much less likely to occur in the more stable maritime snowcovers of the Pacific coastal ranges.

Crusts form in several ways. The simplest is the so-called *sun crust*, which hardens when water melted at the snow surface by solar radiation is refrozen and bonds the snow crystals together into a cohesive layer. This sequence of events can take place at any time of the year, on either snow or firn surfaces, whenever the radiation balance becomes positive during the day and causes melting, followed by a cooling of the snow surface at night to cause freezing. This cooling may be caused by heat loss from the snow surface to air below the freezing point, or it may occur as radiation cooling even when the air temperature is above freezing. In winter and early spring the thickness of a sun crust is usually determined by the thickness of the surface layer where free water is formed in otherwise dry snow. In later spring and summer (firn conditions) when free water is found throughout the snowcover, the sun crust thickness is determined by the amount of cooling at night.

This type of crust might better be included under the more general term *meltwater crust*. Melting due to warm air or condensation at the snow surface, followed by freezing conditions, produces a crust similar to that caused by the sun. The only difference is the source of heat.

In distinct contrast is the *wind crust* caused by mechanical action of the wind, often without the presence of meltwater. Once the surface snow layers are disturbed by the wind, age-hardening is initiated and these layers become harder than the undisturbed ones underneath. Furthermore, the snow crystals are broken and winnowed by wind transport, and the fragments are deposited compactly together when they come to rest, adding a further mechanical process of hardening. The hardening is compounded when the wind provides a source of heat as well as mechanical action, particularly through the medium of water vapor condensation. Even when there is not enough heat to cause melting, the warming of the disturbed surface layer, followed by cooling when the wind dies, provides additional metamorphic hardening.

Rime is the dull white dense deposit derived from freezing of droplets of liquid water on objects exposed to the wind. Rime deposits are always built up *toward* the direction from which the wind blows, and may form large feathery flakes, as well as a solid incrustation, but regular crystalline patterns are absent. This is in contrast to the distinctly crystalline nature of hoar deposits.

Hoarfrost, on the other hand, is formed by sublimation of water vapor from the atmosphere onto solid objects and has distinct crystalline shapes — blades, cups, and scrolls. When deposited on the snow surface, it is known as *surface hoar*, generally produced during a clear cold night when strong radiation and conduction losses can carry away the heat of sublimation from the snow or other surfaces. It is easily recognized by the fragile, feathery appearance of the crystals, which often reach a centimeter or more in length, and the brilliant sparkle of these crystals in sunlight. A heavy deposit of surface hoar makes a very fast and excellent skiing surface.

Crevasse hoar occurs within the snowcover in such enclosures as crevasses. Like surface hoar it is a product of sublimation, but because of a protected location and available free space, it can grow slowly over long periods of time, the crystals often attaining considerable size, sometimes a length of several centimeters. They may assume a cup or scroll shape similar to that of depth hoar, but on a larger scale.

Firnspiegel, or "firn mirror," is the thin layer of clear ice sometimes observed on snow surfaces in spring or summer. Its reflection is so highly specular that under suitable conditions of sunlight and slope angle it produces the brilliant sheen of "glacier fire." Firnspiegel forms when solar radiation can penetrate the surface snow layers and cause melting just *below* the surface at the same time that freezing conditions are prevailing *at* the surface. Once formed, it acts like a greenhouse, and can permit melting of the snow surface underneath while the transparent ice layer itself remains frozen at the surface. After a clear, cold night, miniature crevasse hoar crystals may be found growing from the underside of this thin ice layer into the hollows which were formed beneath it by melting on the previous day.

Verglas is a layer of thin, clear ice derived from liquid water freezing on a rock surface. A combination of a thaw to form the liquid water followed by a freeze is needed — most commonly encountered at higher elevations in the spring or summer. The water may come from melting snow or firn fields and flow down over the rock, from rain, or perhaps most commonly from the melting of a fresh fall of snow. Radiation cooling can cause the freezing, as well as chilling by air which is below the freezing point. Verglas may also be formed directly by supercooled rain drops freezing as they fall onto exposed objects ("freezing rain," also sometimes called — inaccurately — "silver thaw").

After melting has begun in spring, dendritic *drainage patterns* appear on snowfields, formed in snow — as on the ground — by the runoff of liquid water. However, the flow takes place *within* the snowcover, unlike the surface channels on the ground. As water is formed at the snow surface by melting it percolates downward until it encounters impervious layers (including perhaps an ice layer) which deflect its course, or highly permeable layers which it can easily follow. Much of the water also reaches the earth beneath, and either flows along the surface or else penetrates farther and becomes groundwater. That water which flows along the layers within the snowcover tends to establish a dendritic pattern of channels just as does water flowing on soil. The reason the pattern so quickly becomes visible on the snow surface is that the flowing water locally accelerates the snow settlement around its channels, which in turn are soon outlined by depressions at the surface. The dirt which collects in these depressions absorbs solar radiation and accentuates them further by differential melting.

Suncups are depressions in the surface of summer firn, varying in depth from an inch to 2 feet or more. They never occur as isolated depressions, but always as an irregular pattern covering an entire snowfield. They form whenever weather conditions combine to accentuate irregularities in the snow surface. There must be motion of air to cause greater heat and mass transfer at points or ridges of the snow surface than at the hollows. The air must be dry enough to favor evaporation (dew point cooler than snow surface). There must be an additional source of external heat; usually this is solar radiation, but need not necessarily be so. Under these circumstances, more heat reaches the points than the hollows, but a larger proportion goes to cause evaporation than melt. Because evaporation of a given mass of snow demands 7½ times as much heat as melt, less mass is lost from the point or ridges as vapor than is lost from the hollows as meltwater. The hollows get deeper faster than the points melt away, and suncups form. Why suncups take the shape and size they do is still unexplained. Once formed, they are further enhanced by differential melting when dirt in the hollows absorbs extra solar radiation. Because the sun is not directly overhead (except in the tropical latitudes), the suncups melt faster on the south sides of the ridges (in the northern hemisphere) and the whole suncup pattern gradually migrates northward across its snowfield. Warm, moist winds tend to destroy suncups by causing faster melt at the high points and edges. A prolonged summer storm accompanied by fog, wind, and rain will often erase a suncup pattern completely.

They immediately start to reform with the return of dry fair weather.

Nieve penitentes (Spanish for "penitent snow") are the pillars produced when suncups are so pronounced that the cups intersect to leave columns of snow standing between the hollows. They are peculiar to snowfields at high altitudes, where radiation and atmospheric conditions conducive to suncup formation are particularly intense and reach their most striking

Fig. 181. Surface features on snow. *Top*, suncups. *Lower left*, nieve penitentes and *lower right*, sastrugi.

development among the higher peaks of the Andes and Himalaya, where they may attain a height of several feet, with consequently difficult travel. The columns often slant toward the midday sun.

The surface of dry snow may develop a variety of *erosional forms* when subjected to scouring by winds, minor examples being the small ripples and irregularities on winter snowcover. On high ridges and treeless arctic wastes, where the full sweep of the wind is unimpeded, these erosional features can attain considerable relief. Most characteristic are the wavelike forms, with a sharp prow directed toward the prevailing wind, known as *sastrugi,* from the Russian (singular: *sastruga*), or *skavler,* from the Norwegian. A field of sastrugi is difficult to travel not only because of their depth, which may be as much as several feet, but because like wind crusts they also are usually very hard and unyielding. High winds over featureless snow plains also produce *dunes* similar to those found in desert sand, with the crescentic dune, or *barchan,* being most common.

Cornices are deposits of wind-drifted snow on the lee edge of ridges or other exposed terrain features. They offer a particular hazard to the mountain traveler because they often overhang to the lee, forming an

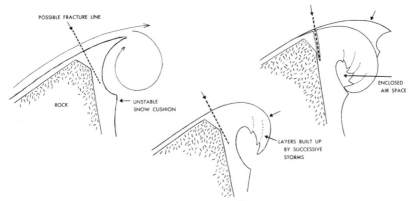

Fig. 182. Cornice development. *Left* to *right:* young, middle and mature.

unstable mass which may break off either from human disturbance or natural causes. Falling cornices, in themselves a large and dangerous mass of snow in motion, in addition are frequent causes of avalanches. Depending on wind and snow conditions, cornices vary from those soft and easily broken to structures extremely hard which remain solidly attached to the mountain throughout the winter. The stability of a cornice is best determined by test or inspection — there are too many complicating factors for advance prediction from consideration of snow and wind data, even if these were available. Probing with an ice ax or reversed ski pole may indicate whether the snow is solid, or weak and poorly compacted. Such probing can also help to locate the crack, if there is one, between a mature cornice and solid snow or bedrock. Where such a space — often hidden by surface drifting — has developed, even a very solid, hard cornice may be on the verge of detaching from the ridge, and great care is indicated. When the climber approaches the cornice from the windward the extent of its overhang and the danger it offers are often hard to judge; in the case of a mature cornice the probable line of fracture may be many feet back from the edge. Though, as with all snow phenomena, it is unwise to generalize too widely, a rather reliable rule is that the fracture line of a well-developed, unstable cornice is usually farther back from the lip than examination from the windward would lead an observer to expect.

Cornices are formed by drifting snow. During storms the precipitated snow furnishes material for cornice formation wherever appropriate eddies form to the lee of ridges. If a snowfield lies to the windward, additional material can be gathered by wind drift. Cornices form during fair weather as well, but here the only source of snow is that picked up to the windward and hence the presence of a source such as a snowfield or other accumulation area becomes essential. As a general, though not universal, rule, cornices formed during snow storms are softer than those produced by wind drift alone.

THE FORMATION OF GLACIERS

Discussion to this point has been confined largely to the nature and behavior of a transient winter snowcover. Whenever climatic conditions during the melting season provide a supply of heat insufficient to remove completely the snow deposited during the winter, a certain part of the winter snowcover is carried over to the next season. If the climatic conditions leading to this annual carryover of snow are sustained for a long enough time, the successive annual increments will eventually form a glacier.

The process leading to the formation of glacier ice from snow is called *firnification*, during which snow is converted to *firn* (or *névé*) and firn to glacier ice. The exact point when firn turns into ice is clearly defined – it becomes ice when the pores become noncommunicating. To put it another way, firn becomes ice when the air spaces between the grains become sealed off from each other, so that the mass becomes airtight. The point at which snow becomes firn is not so easy to state, for this is purely an arbitrary division, and different authorities recognize the formation of firn on different bases. Firn can be defined as snow which has survived at least one season of ablation – i.e., snow which is carried over from one year to the next. This is probably a convenient definition for the mountaineer, as the difference between snow and firn on this basis can be easily recognized without any special instruments. In terms of the processes involved, firn can be more generally defined as old snow in which destructive metamorphism of the original snow crystals is complete, any further changes leading to the formation of glacier ice. The transition takes place at densities of around 0.55 to 0.60 grams per cubic centimeter.

The process of change, or metamorphism, observed in newly fallen snow continues throughout the time the water substance remains in a solid state. The wet, granular snow of spring is by no means an end product; changes continue to take place until it once more returns to the liquid state, whether it be in a few hours, or over a period of centuries. Diurnal melting and refreezing during spring and summer is the first step which carries old snow towards the formation of firn and eventually glacier ice. Once a snow layer has been carried over through a second winter, it is shielded from daily changes by the newer snow on top of it, but the melting and refreezing part of the metamorphic process continues on an annual basis with the alternate penetration of winter chill and percolating summer meltwater. Reinforcing this process are the changes effected by increasing pressure as subsequent burdens of snow are added each season. Together they gradually compact the snow, increase its density, reduce its pore volume, and lead to the formation of ice.

Part of the ice developed from layers of firn is formed by the refreezing of percolating meltwater each spring when the subsurface layers are still at temperatures below the freezing point. This refrozen meltwater is usually concentrated at certain levels within the snow to form discrete *ice layers.* Thus, by the time compaction and metamorphism have prepared the general body of a snow layer for conversion to ice, it may already contain irregular bodies of solid ice. Under certain subarctic conditions this refreezing of percolating meltwater is the predominant factor in converting snow into glacier ice.

The process most commonly encountered by climbers in the mountains is the one described above, but it does not apply in all cases. Under polar climatic conditions at high latitudes, the formation of glacier ice sometimes takes place without the presence of liquid water at any time. The metamorphism of snow through firn to ice is then controlled entirely by pressure and subfreezing temperature, with the melting and refreezing process entirely absent. Such glaciers are known as *polar glaciers,* where *dry firn* is produced by the process of *dry metamorphism.*

Once ice has been formed, metamorphism does not cease. Through crystallographic changes some of the ice grains continue to grow at the expense of their neighbors, and the average size of the ice crystals increases with age. The mechanical effects of ice flow in a moving glacier influence this growth, so that crystal size can serve only as a very relative indicator of ice age. In large glaciers, where the ice has undoubtedly spent centuries in its journey to the glacier terminus, crystals sometimes are found several inches to a foot or more in diameter — gigantic crystals which have grown from minute snow particles.

The climatic conditions which control the formation and preservation of glaciers – that is, the conditions which determine whether or not some winter snow will be left over at the end of each summer melting season – are complex in themselves, and are further complicated by the influence of topography. Recent studies have given some insight into the manner in which various weather factors influence glaciers, but the causes of the climatic changes which in turn affect these weather factors are obscure. Many theories have been advanced to explain the periods of glaciation which have occurred repeatedly throughout geologic time, but no single, positive explanation has yet been found. Even though factors which cause present-day glaciers to advance or retreat are not always clear, it is possible to discuss in a general manner how a glacier is formed and sustained.

The amount of snow deposited on the ground each year at any particular point on the earth's surface is determined by the climate and topography. Given a fixed climate and location, the amount of snow which would fall each year on a level surface varies with the altitude of that surface above sea level. Generally, this amount of snow increases up to a certain elevation, and thence decreases with increasing altitude. Also, given the same climate and location, the amount of snow on a level surface which can be melted by the heat available each year varies with altitude, usually being maximum at sea level and decreasing with height. For the given conditions, there will then be some particular altitude at which the snow which can be melted will equal the snow deposited. Above this altitude not all of the snow falling on a level surface each year will be melted away, and accumulation will result. If the altitude at which deposition and melting of snow are equal is postulated for each point over the earth's surface, it is possible to conceive of it as a surface in the form of a rough sphere surrounding the earth, being farthest above sea level in the vicinity of the equator, and closest to sea level near the poles, but varying considerably from point to point with local climatic conditions.

Over most of the earth this *cryosphere* is an imaginary surface, but wherever the real surface of the earth intersects it, it becomes real, and perpetual ice (glaciers) form. For a glacier to form where none existed before it is obvious that the level of the cryosphere must by some climatic change be depressed in elevation so that it will intersect an actual land mass and become real. It may be depressed by a decrease in the amount of heat available each year, by an increase in the amount of snow precipitated, or both.

It was pointed out in the previous discussion of the thermal properties of snow that there are several ways in which the heat supply can be altered. For instance, an increase in the average cloudiness reduces the amount of heat available from the sun. A decrease in the mean air temperature reduces the heat supply to the snow surface. More important, given the same air temperature, a reduction in the mean wind velocity also lowers the heat available from the air.

Snow accumulation, on the other hand, can be greatly altered by variations in the mean position of storm paths during the winter months. The prevailing direction of storm winds can ultimately determine which lee slopes will accumulate the greatest amount of snow. Increased snowfall goes along with the climatic changes brought about by the geological process of mountain building in the path of already-established storm tracks. This latter situation illustrates the earth's surface rising up to meet the cryosphere as it is depressed by climatic change.

To cite a specific example of such changes and their effects on glaciers: the general reactivation and advance of glaciers observed in western Washington state from 1945 to 1958 appears to be due to a combination of increased winter precipitation and lowered mean annual temperatures. In this case the general trend of recession of alpine glaciers was reversed; indeed in some places small cirque glaciers which had practically disappeared were reconstituted. Obviously the process can work both ways. An elevation of the cryosphere, or depression of the earth's surface, can lead to the recession or even elimination of glaciers.

One way to demonstrate the factors which affect glacier behavior is to follow the steps in the formation and development of an idealized glacier. The formation of a simple valley-type alpine glacier will serve as an illustration.

Consider a mountain in the northern hemisphere presently free from glaciation, and suppose a climatic change sufficient to cause snow to persist from year to year in a sheltered spot on a northern exposure. From the first, snow deposited on the mountainside will tend to flow valleyward in the slow motion of creep. As new layers of snow are added each year, the snow patch will grow in depth (and probably in extent) and the amount of snow in motion will increase. This creeping snow will tend to dislodge the soil or weathered rock beneath it, and the melting, refreezing, and flow of water around and under the snow patch during part of each year will add to the mechanical action of the snow patch on its surroundings. This small-scale process of erosion is known as *nivation,* and will eventually lead to the formation of a hollow where the winter snows can be deposited in deeper drifts. With the climate continuing to favor accumulation of snow each year, the snow patch will continue to grow, and as it becomes deeper its downslope flow will become more pronounced. When the depth approaches a hundred feet or so, the lower layers will be nearing the state of ice, and the increasing pressure of the many layers of firn will cause the plastic flow to accelerate.

In short, a glacier is born. With continued nourishment from heavy winter snows it flows toward the valley as a stream of ice. At some point in this descent of the mountainside it will reach an elevation low enough so that the melting each year will exceed the annual accumulation of snow. Then the excess heat supply left after each annual snowcover is melted away will melt some of the ice which has been carried down from above. Because ice has a much lower reflectivity for solar radiation than snow, it will absorb more of the available heat than snow.

Eventually the glacier will reach an even lower elevation where the supply of heat is sufficient to melt all the ice carried down from above. Until climatic conditions once more undergo a change, this will represent the lower limit of the glacier. The amount of snow gained on the upper reaches each year will equal the amount of ice melted away on the lower parts, and the glacier will have reached a state of equilibrium with its environment.

At the elevation on the surface of this idealized glacier where annual melting equals the annual snowfall, a feature will be developed known as the *firn limit*. This is the line across the glacier above which it gains material each year, and below which it loses material. Such a line is found on all real glaciers which descend from a region of accumulation to a region of ablation. In practice it is not usually a sharply defined line, but rather a narrow, irregular zone whose position may vary from year to year, but whose average elevation remains more-or-less constant as long as the climate remains unchanged.

The elevation of the *regional snow line* is defined as the elevation above which annual accumulation exceeds annual ablation on a level surface. It thus corresponds to the position of the cryosphere at any given point. On a regional, rather than a point-to-point basis, however, the snow line obviously must be an average of wide fluctuations. In the first place, the idealized case of the definition, a level surface, is the exception rather than the rule in the mountains. In most places the annual snowfall is deposited on slopes whose orientation, and position in respect to other terrain masses, determine the amount of heat they receive, and the annual melting. Glacier formation and the persistence of snow patches from year to year occur on sheltered northern exposures well below the regional average of the snow line. On the other hand, southern exposures which receive the full benefit of solar radiation remain free of snow well above the regional average.

Because of these wide variations, describing the mean elevation of a regional snow line in any given mountainous area is often difficult. A more convenient indicator of the general level of glaciation in a given area may be the elevation of firn limits on existing glaciers, for it takes into account the effects of wind — drifting, exposure, etc. The firn limit is usually confined within relatively narrow boundaries of elevation on any given glacier, and often exists at comparable elevations on several glaciers

XIX. Ice encrusted rocks in upper Blue Glacier cirque on Mt. Olympus. (Bob and Ira Spring)

of a region. Even so, the firn limit elevations can be described only in general terms over any very large region.

The lowest firn limit elevations in the contiguous United States are found in the Olympic Mountains of western Washington. In the vicinity of the Mount Olympus massif, they presently lie between 4500 and 5500 feet. Eastward in the Cascade Range and the volcanoes of Washington, the firn limit elevations rise to between 6000 and 8000 feet, with considerable variations from north to south. Southward through Oregon and California the average level of the firn limits rises rapidly until in the Sierra Nevada they are found at 12,000 to 13,000 feet on a few tiny glacier remnants in the high sheltered cirques. Northward along the Pacific coast the firn limits descend rapidly to elevations of around 3000 and 4000 feet in southeast Alaska.

Only a few small glaciers exist today in the Rocky Mountains of the United States, although at one time these peaks were rather extensively glaciated. The concept of a firn limit can hardly be applied to the few scattered perennial snow patches found among the many 14,000-foot peaks of Colorado. In fact, in this area the regional snow line may properly be placed at elevations higher than the summits of the peaks. Farther north in the Rockies some true glaciation exists in the Wind River Range of Wyoming, where firn limits are found in the neighborhood of 12,000 feet. Near the Canadian border the peaks of Glacier National Park boast a few small glaciers with firn limits between 8000 and 9000 feet, but these glaciers owe their precarious existence at this elevation to heavy deposits of wind-drifted snow in certain localities. As in the Colorado Rockies, the regional snow line in this area is actually higher than the peaks. Still farther north, however, the Rocky Mountains of Canada support a much more extensive glaciation with firn limits no higher than 7000 to 9000 feet.

The regional snow line, and the firn limits on glaciers, over the earth as a whole vary more widely in altitude than the few examples from North America. In the tropical zones perpetual snow is able to exist only at elevations higher than all but the highest peaks of this continent while, at the other extreme, firn limits are found at sea level in such places as northeast Greenland. The earthwide visible manifestations of the cryosphere are thus found to vary extensively with altitude, but even greater are the variations with time, illustrated by the great continental ice sheets of past ages.

A *temperate glacier* is one which is at the melting point of ice throughout its bulk. (The melting point decreases slightly under pressure, hence even a temperate glacier is a little colder at the bottom than at the surface.) During the winter, sub-freezing temperature causes the glacier to freeze at the surface. Penetration of this winter *cold wave* varies from a few feet to many dozens of feet, depending on climate and thickness of the insulating winter snowcover. All glaciers of the United States are temperate except those in northern Alaska. A *sub-polar glacier* is at subfreezing temperature throughout its bulk except for a surface layer which experiences warming to the melting point during the summer. Its thermal regimen is thus just the opposite of a temperate glacier. A *high polar glacier* lies in a climate cold enough to prevent melt even in summer and thus is subfreezing the year around. Much of the Antarctic ice cap belongs to this category.

The *mass balance* of a glacier is the annual difference between accumulation and ablation of snow and ice. It is usually expressed in equivalent volumes of water, either for the glacier as a whole or for a unit area at some specific point on the glacier. If a glacier gains mass in the course of a year, it is said to have a positive balance; if it loses mass the balance is negative. In order for a glacier to grow and advance, it must experience a sustained period of positive mass balance. The mass balance each year is determined by an intricate combination of weather and climate elements. In maritime climates with abundant snowfall, the mass balance is sensitive to temperature. In cold, polar climates where melting is slight or absent, variations in the usually light precipitation are the dominating influence.

Glacier behavior varies all the way from stagnant masses with little motion to vigorously flowing rivers of ice which annually transport large masses from higher to lower elevations. The concept of a glacier *activity index* is intuitively obvious in terms of the amount of mass which is added each year in the accumulation zone and the amount removed by melt in the ablation. The larger these quantities are the more mass must be transported by flow through the firn limit; and the greater their difference in elevation, the faster this flow must be. Formulated in physical terms, this activity index turns out to be the vertical gradient of specific mass balance. In other words, the faster accumulation increases with altitude (or ablation decreases), the more actively the glacier must flow to sustain its shape.

Temperate glaciers flow both by internal plastic deformation and by sliding on their beds. Velocity distribution is somewhat like that in a river, fastest at the center and surface and slower at the sides and bottom where bedrock creates a frictional drag. The basal sliding depends on plastic deformation to get the ice around large obstacles and *regelation* (melting and freezing) to surmount the small ones. Meltwater, including that involved in regelation, plays an important and not completely understood role. There seems to be some evidence, for example, that the velocity of glacier flow depends to some extent on the amount of meltwater produced at the surface. When the climate is sufficiently polar to cool the glacier below freezing clear down to its base, the flow of meltwater is cut off, regelation is blocked, and the glacier is frozen to its bed. Basal sliding is severely inhibited if not stopped entirely and the glacier is forced to flow by internal plastic deformation alone. Small polar glaciers present a striking difference in appearance from their temperate cousins; the former look much like flowing molasses, while the latter are rivers of broken ice.

Glaciers do not respond smoothly to changes in climate which alter their mass balance. Often they tend to advance in spurts, overreaching new equilibrium positions and then stagnating in their lower reaches. One reason is that glaciers are unstable in zones of *compressive flow* which commonly occur below the firn limit. Compressive flow occurs when velocity decreases down-glacier and more mass is carried into a volume element on its uphill side than flows out on the downhill side (the difference is removed by ablation). In these circumstances a climate-induced thickening tends to cause the glacier to grow even thicker, while thinning causes the glacier to react by becoming even thinner. Another cause of erratic behavior is the development of *kinematic waves* in glacier ice. Suppose an excess of ice thickness develops in the accumulation zone. This may descend the glacier as a wave of thickening which travels at a velocity substantially greater than that of the ice flow. If the wave reaches the glacier terminus (diffusion tends to prevent this), the terminus may suddenly advance, sometimes overriding or invading a zone of stagnant ice. Large glaciers with valley ice streams of gentle gradient many miles long sometimes develop a *glacier surge*. A vast quantity of ice is suddenly displaced downvalley as much as several miles in a few months. Surface levels in upper parts of the stream may drop a hundred feet or more. Such large ice streams are known from a theoretical standpoint to be unstable, but the mechanism by which so much ice is moved so far so fast is still unclear.

STABILITY OF THE SNOW COVER

Like everything on the earth's surface, snow is continually under the influence of gravity. Because snow is composed of an irregular aggregate of independent particles, often mechanically weak, and is subject to constant change, it often yields to this influence. Upon a level surface this yielding is confined to settlement, or compaction. Upon an inclined surface, the effects of gravity may have results ranging from slow creep to a violent and destructive avalanche. The stability of snow determines its power to resist the force of gravity tending to carry it down a mountainside, and the correct estimation of this stability is essential to safe travel in the mountains, especially in winter.

It must be emphasized at this point that to attain familiarity with avalanche conditions there is no substitute for personal experience in the field. No mountaineer will become an expert by reading this or any other book — he must learn by first-hand experience the feel of snow under his skis, the resistance it offers to his ice ax, the instinct that warns of danger even when the "rules" say that the snow underfoot should be safe.

Here space permits only a cursory treatment of a subject deserving elaboration in a separate volume. For further details the reader is referred to publications dealing specifically with avalanches. (See references at the end of this chapter.) It is possible here to present only a broad outline of conditions affecting snow stability, and their recognition, but a discussion of safe conduct through snow under hazardous circumstances will be found in Chapter 16.

This topic may be divided into two parts — stability of snow considered as an aggregate of individual particles, and stability of snow en masse. In terms of the active expressions of instability, avalanches may be divided into two major types: *loose snow* and *slab*. Each type may be further classified as *wet* or *dry*, depending on whether liquid water is present in the snow. Avalanches in motion may consist of snow sliding only on the ground, snow carried only through the air as a dust cloud, or a combination of the two.

Avalanche types are customarily classified according to conditions prevailing at the point of origin. Obviously, more than one kind of snow may be involved in an avalanche falling over a long slide path with a large difference of elevation. For instance, a slide might originate as a dry slab avalanche, and then assume the characteristics of a dry loose-snow avalanche once in motion. Such an occurrence is actually fairly common in the high mountains in winter. In spring an avalanche originating in dry snow, either loose or slab, will often involve predominantly wet snow as it descends to lower elevations.

Regardless of the type of avalanche considered, the stability of the snow, the manner in which it changes, and the duration of any instability are all determined by the metamorphism of individual snow crystals. This metamorphism is controlled by the temperatures prevailing within the snowcover, and the temperatures are determined in turn by the processes of heat transfer described previously. Once the initial mechanical conditions have been established at the time of deposition, duration of any instability is controlled primarily by the snow temperature. If the mountaineer had to choose a single instrument to serve as a guide to snow stability on a winter expedition, that instrument might well be a thermometer.

Loose Snow

Loose snow is defined as the condition wherein individual snow crystals are free to move in respect to one another. This condition can lead to instability, and in dry snow, to the commonly observed small powder snow avalanches of winter. Wet snow may also satisfy the same definition when the bond between individual particles of snow disappears.

Consider the behavior of a material such as dry sand which is composed of particles free to move in respect to one another. For any such material there is some angle of a sloping surface with the horizontal, above which the force of gravity acting parallel to the surface will exceed the cohesion of the individual particles. This angle is known as the *angle of repose* for each given material, and when a material is deposited on a slope with an angle greater than its angle of repose, it will tend to run off under the influence of gravity. If dry sand, for instance, is placed on a board at less than its angle of repose, it will be stable, and it is possible then to increase carefully the angle of the board with the horizontal beyond the critical angle for the sand without the sand sliding off. However, any slight disturbance of the sand in this position will cause it immediately to slide off or seek its angle of repose. When in this elevated but undisturbed position, it may be said to be in a condition of *unstable equilibrium* — any outside force acting on it will cause it to seek a new, and stable, position.

The behavior of loose snow is analogous to that of sand, but complicated by the fact that the cohesion between particles varies with snow type, manner of deposition, and with metamorphism. As new snow is deposited during a storm it may, especially if accompanied by wind, form a snow layer whose individual crystals are sufficiently well-bonded together so that they will never move in respect to one another under the influence of gravity, except for the slow movement of creep and settlement. Occasionally such conditions prevail that this intercrystalline bond is low in the newly deposited snow, as when the snow has low density and there is relative absence of wind. Such snow falling on slopes steeper than its natural angle of repose will tend to run off in loose-snow avalanches. Usually a slight bond will exist between the snow crystals sufficient to permit a certain amount of snow to build up an unstable equilibrium before it starts to slide. Very often, however, light fluffy new snow will run off very steep slopes, cliffs, etc., almost as fast as it falls. This actually has a stabilizing effect on slopes of lesser angle below, as the small sloughs running off the steep slopes dislodge the snow below before it can build up to any great depth. Occasionally the snow will be deposited in such a manner that a considerable depth may accumulate as an unstable layer before it is set in motion by some exterior disturbance. Then a loose-snow avalanche of great magnitude may occur, especially on long, steep slopes. *Wild snow* illustrates the most extreme case of this kind. This is new snow deposited under very calm, cold conditions, and its water content may be as low as 1 per cent. At the slightest disturbance it flows down the mountainside almost like water, for wild snow represents deposition of material under extreme conditions of unstable equilibrium. Fortunately, true wild snow is quite rare, and is almost unknown in the coastal alpine zone of the United States.

Instability in loose snow may develop in other ways than by the deposition of new snow with little original cohesion between crystals. New

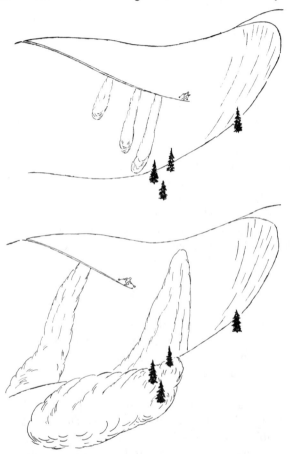

Fig. 183. Instability in loose snow. *Top,* minor surface instability — harmless sloughs. *Bottom,* highly unstable — large quantities of snow involved.

snow frequently has considerable stability, due to the interlocking of snow crystal branches and arms. As metamorphism proceeds, these interlocking branches tend to disappear, and with them the intercrystalline bonds. As a result a condition of unstable equilibrium is introduced in a snow layer which originally showed no inclination to avalanche. A slide may then be precipitated by some external disturbance, such as a lump of snow falling from a tree, or the metamorphism may simply proceed to the point where the snow can no longer support itself on the slope. The latter is the frequent cause of a cycle of small loose-snow avalanches observed to run a day or two after a fall of new snow. However, this phenomenon is not to be expected after every snowfall. The introduction of instability in loose snow by metamorphism depends on the original type of snow crystals. It most commonly occurs with stellar or dendritic crystals whose branches form a good initial bond, but one which can subsequently be weakened. With more granular types of snow, and with snow whose crystals carry any significant amount of rime, a period of decreasing stability during metamorphism is less likely to occur.

Wet loose-snow avalanches are common in the spring when significant amounts of melting take place at the snow surface. At this time of year metamorphism is usually well advanced, and the snow crystals have for the most part become rounded, isometric grains. Meltwater formed at the snow surface percolates downward and provides a lubricant between the individual snow grains, so that snow which has previously been stable is disposed to slide. Small wet loose-snow slides are common on southern exposures in spring, when the sun has reached sufficient elevation to provide a strong source of heat to the snow surface. During clear weather these slides are likely to occur only around midday or in the afternoon when the production of meltwater is at a maximum; each night the snow becomes stable as the surface freezes. Wet loose-snow slides of large and destructive proportions are more likely to occur during warm cloudy weather and wind or rain, when melting proceeds both day and night and large quantities of liquid water penetrate deep into the snowcover. Shallow snowcovers with a large proportion of depth hoar are particularly apt to produce wet loose-snow avalanches with the advent of melting conditions in the early spring.

Regardless of the type of loose-snow avalanche, the instability which produces it is usually of a transient nature. Frequently the processes which lead to the original instability can be counted on to carry the snow through to a more stable condition — for instance, by precipitating an avalanche in the case of newly-fallen snow, or by stabilizing the snow through settlement in the case of metamorphism, though the latter process may be quite slow if temperatures are very low (well below 0°F.). In any case, instability in loose snow is more easily detected than is that in slab avalanches. For a given snow condition where such instability exists, there will usually be a certain slope angle above which the snow can be set in motion by the mechanical disturbance of a ski or ice ax. The skier or climber has only to test the snow on sufficiently steep slopes to see whether or not it is in immediate danger of sliding.

Snow Slabs

When the individual particles of the snowcover cohere sufficiently to behave as an aggregate, the development of instability takes on an entirely different character. Most frequently snow which has lost its loose nature and become a cohesive mass has increased in stability, for once the snow has gained mechanical strength it is able to resist for a time the force of gravity, instead of yielding to it immediately. However, this very cohesiveness bears within it the seeds of instability. Resistance in turn enables snow creep to build up tensions within certain snow layers, and when they finally break, the rupture may come with explosive suddenness.

Unlike the loose-snow avalanche, which begins at a point and involves more and more snow as it descends, the slab avalanche is characterized by

Fig. 184. Instability in slabs. *Top*, minor instability. *Bottom*, grave instability.

an extensive area of snow starting to slide at the same time. The types of snow which may exhibit this characteristic when set in motion, ranging from soft, dry new snow through hard wind drifts to wet spring snow, are so varied that it is possible to apply the term *slab,* strictly speaking, only to the description of a type of instability, rather than to any particular type of snow.

A snow slab is a mechanical state which cannot be correlated with any specific physical appearance. The dull, chalky surface of certain types of wind-drifted snow (popularly called "wind slab") is not a universal indicator of unstable snow slabs — slab avalanches may and do develop in this type of snow, but many more develop in snow which is neither dull nor chalky in appearance. The action of the wind is a major factor in the formation of most slab avalanches, but wind is not a necessary condition. Under certain circumstances dangerous instability in a snow slab may develop through the action of metamorphism alone. Regardless of how a snow slab is developed, its hazard to the mountaineer is further increased if it is hidden under a subsequent snowfall. It must be emphasized here that there is no sure way in which an unstable snow slab can be distinguished from stable snow on the basis of physical appearance alone.

Whether or not a snow slab will actually become detached from the mountainside and descend as an avalanche depends on its adhesion to the underlying layer, the support it has at the bottom, and the strength with which it is attached to stable snow or fixed objects at the sides and top.

Gravity acting on the weight of the slab layer develops a component of force acting parallel to the slope on which it rests. This force has a shearing effect at the bottom of the slab where it rests on stable snow or earth. If the attachment of the slab to the underlying layer, or a weak snow layer in between, has a shear strength less than this force, then the basic condition for release of the slab is established. Whether or not it actually is released depends on the many complex variables involved in its support and attachment on the mountainside.

Both snow slabs and stable types of snow tend to flow down any incline with the slow movement of creep. The velocity of creep depends on the snow type, snow temperature, and slope angle. When a slab is anchored at the top and there is creep in its lower portions, the uneven motion develops a tension, and the snow undergoes elastic deformation. The amount of deformation depends on the snow type and its strength characteristics, and is actually quite small, but nevertheless, a snow slab in this condition is under tension just as much as a stretched rubber band. When the slab breaks off, the release of this tension causes it to fracture over an extended area, and a large body of snow is set in motion. It is the possibility of creep tension that gives the slab avalanche its dangerously unpredictable character and can cause an entire mountainside to erupt in an avalanche when only a small section of the slope is disturbed.

The uneven creep which produces tension may arise in other ways than from a slab anchored at its top, as discussed above. A common source of uneven creep is a slope with a convex profile, for the snow on the lower, steeper part will creep faster than the snow higher up. In contrast, differential creep on a concave slope produces a compressive force on the snow and is less likely to form an unstable slab. Snow which is drifted onto a slope so as to be thicker at the bottom than at the top will develop creep tension, for the deeper snow will creep faster at the surface than will the thinner layers. Layers within the snowcover consisting of different types of snow, or at different temperatures, will also creep at different rates and introduce tension.

When snow temperatures are near the freezing point, creep is rapid, and dangerous tensions in snow slabs may develop very quickly. However, at these temperatures snow is also able to relieve the creep tension by more rapid plastic deformation. The result is that slab avalanche danger can develop quickly under warm conditions, but the period of danger also passes quickly and the snow soon assumes a stable state. On the other hand, with low temperatures the creep process is retarded, but the snow can less easily relieve the tension by plastic flow. The consequence is persistence of unstable conditions over a long period of time at low temperatures ($0°$ F. and lower).

In many cases a snow slab will develop an unstable condition, and then gradually return to stability through settlement and metamorphism if no outside force provides the trigger for its release at the critical moment. Avalanches do not "just happen." Though the degree of instability developed may be very high, in the last analysis something must actually set the snow in motion. In the case of snow slabs, this trigger may be any one of a number of effects, some of them complex.

The simplest triggering force is the mechanical breaking of a slab layer by a falling rock, a piece of cornice, or the weight of a skier. The weight of a new fall of snow can have the same effect, or a slide of new snow running on top of a slab may develop enough dynamic force to dislodge it. Metamorphism or penetrating meltwater can weaken the slab or its attachment to an underlying layer. Sudden changes in snow temperature can release slab avalanches by causing a rapid change in the creep process, which sets up force exceeding the mechanical strength of the snow. The support of a slab may be removed by the undercutting action of another avalanche running nearby. Sound waves of sufficient amplitude, such as the shock wave from an explosion, can release a delicately poised slab, and it is theoretically possible that weaker disturbances, such as the sound of the human voice, could do the same, although such an extreme degree of instability must be very rare, if indeed it ever occurs.

There are three different types of slab avalanches against which the mountain traveler must guard. These are the *soft, hard,* and *wet* slabs.

Soft and hard slabs are usually found in dry snow conditions. The dividing line between them is more-or-less arbitrary. A convenient indicator is the resistance of the snow to a weighted ski. A man on skis will sink into the snow of a soft slab, but will stay on the surface of a hard slab.

Soft slabs are most frequently encountered during snow storms, when the snow is fresh and unconsolidated. At times the snow may appear so light and fluffy as to suggest the possibility of a loose-snow avalanche, but the characteristic fracture of a slab avalanche can sometimes be observed even when the snow is so soft a skier sinks to his knees. In these cases the avalanche usually assumes the appearance of a loose-snow slide once it is in motion, and no blocks or large segments of snow are found in the debris when it comes to rest. Soft slab avalanches form from a combination of wind and heavy snowfall, and usually run during or immediately after a storm. They sometimes form without regard to wind direction, and may be found on windward as well as lee slopes. This is the type of avalanche most frequently encountered in the coastal alpine zone of the United States, with its maritime climate and frequent falls of deep, heavy snow. Unstable conditions in soft slab do not usually persist as long as they do in hard slab, for there is greater scope for alterations which may be effected in the snow by metamorphism and settlement.

Hard slabs are the most dangerous and unpredictable of all unstable snow conditions. This unpredictability stems from the fact that they may persist in an unstable form for long periods of time, and from the high mechanical strength of the snow involved, which enables the slab to withstand the triggering action of weaker external forces. With soft slab, the weight of a ski or boot breaking through the snow is often sufficient to set an avalanche in motion. A hard slab, on the other hand, will often support the passage of several persons, appearing to be stable and safe, and then will suddenly break loose with the addition of only one more small triggering force. One case is on record in Switzerland of a slab avalanche being dislodged by the last 3 men of a 34-man military patrol which crossed a steep slope. A fatal avalanche accident in the Canadian Rockies involved a slope on which a number of people had been skiing all day just prior to the slide.

Hard slabs are the product of high winds and low temperatures. They are more commonly found above timberline, where the full sweep of storm winds is unimpeded and the higher altitudes bring persistent low temperatures in winter. High winds alone are sufficient to form hard slabs (wind slabs) on lee exposures, and dangerous conditions often develop even when no new snow falls. Their occurrence in the United States is more common in the Rocky Mountain regions, where high winter winds and sub-zero temperatures are common. In the coastal ranges, extensive hard slab formation from wind action alone is usually restricted to exposed areas of the higher peaks.

The snow of hard slabs has enough cohesion to preserve pieces of the slab as angular chunks and blocks as the slide descends the mountain, and the presence of such blocks in the debris serves as positive identification of a slab-type avalanche and of hard slab in particular. It must be pointed out that the line of demarcation between hard and soft slab is not always sharply drawn, and the mountaineer must bear clearly in mind that slab avalanches can occur in soft, light new snow, in hard windpacked snow, and in all the gradations between.

Strictly speaking, *wet slabs* are rather the product of structural changes in the snow than of the conditions prevailing at the time the snow was deposited. The snow which becomes part of wet slab avalanches is often deposited in stable layers, but some weaker layer within the snowcover develops which still has enough strength to support the overburden while dry. With the advent of melting conditions in the spring, water penetrates the snowcover, lowers the mechanical strength, and greatly reduces the shear strength of the weak layers. In addition, the free water itself provides a lubricating action. The instability leading to slab avalanche formation is thus introduced into a previously stable snowcover. Such a phenomenon most frequently occurs in a snowcover which is poorly consolidated. Because percolating liquid water is refrozen when it reaches snow layers which are at temperatures below the freezing point, wet slab avalanches (and the same applies to wet loose snow) cannot form until the snow layers involved have become isothermal at 32°F. This provides the opportunity for a quantitative check on the development of wet slide conditions. If measurements with a thermometer show that sub-freezing temperatures exist within the snowcover, then the conclusion may reasonably be drawn that wet-snow avalanches are not likely to run, no matter how brightly the sun is shining. It must be remembered, however, as previously discussed, that the snowcover can be warmed up very quickly by percolating meltwater and the penetration of solar radiation.

The formation of slab avalanche conditions by metamorphism of previously stable snow in a dry, and therefore cold, snowcover is extremely difficult to discern in the field, and at times can be anticipated only if a good record of previous snow, weather, and avalanche conditions is available. One example of how such conditions may develop will be cited here as an indication of the complexity of the problem. Consider a fall of light, dry snow deposited to an appreciable depth (say 3 feet) in the middle of winter. This fall of new snow may have some tendency to slide as a loose-snow avalanche at the time it is deposited, but it soon undergoes rapid settlement and becomes stable. If such snowfall is on top of a deep and stable base of old snow, it may be expected to become incorporated as a stable part of that base and provide no further source of avalanche hazard. However, if it falls on a very shallow base — say on a slope which has been partly denuded of snow by previous avalanching — then an entirely different situation can develop. If the period following its deposition is one of cold weather, a sufficiently steep temperature gradient may be set up in this layer to initiate constructive metamorphism. (Such a gradient would not readily form where the new snow was on top of a deep base.) Constructive metamorphism then need not proceed to the formation of depth hoar, but only far enough to weaken the mechanical structure of the snow layer in question to the point where it could break loose as a slab avalanche. This might take place 1 or 2 weeks after it had been deposited as new, loose snow with no indication of any slab development.

From the foregoing paragraphs it can be seen that slab avalanches are complex in nature, and that analysis of the factors leading to their formation is sometimes difficult. Even more difficult is the quantitative evaluation of forces developed by creep tension. In fact it must now be apparent that the determination of avalanche hazard cannot be made by applying a fixed set of book rules, or by seeking a certain fixed sequence of physical events, or by external appearances alone. There are certain general principles for anticipating hazardous conditions and these are discussed in the next section, but, especially where slab avalanches are concerned, snow conditions must actually be tested in the field before reliable conclusions can be drawn, and even these must depend to a great extent on the personal experience of the observer.

RECOGNITION OF INSTABILITY IN THE SNOWCOVER

The first and most common cause of avalanches is a heavy new fall ot snow, and this is the first warning sign the mountain traveler heeds. As little as 6 or 8 inches of new snow may create a hazard, a foot or more should always be regarded with suspicion, and greater depths must always be treated with caution.

The total depth of snow existing on the ground affects the development of avalanche hazard. The deeper the snow, the more covered up are terrain irregularities, and the smoother the slide paths. With deep snows, fewer natural obstructions break the surface to hinder the release of avalanches, or reduce their size once in motion.

The rate at which new snow falls is an important factor. A 2- or 3-foot snowfall spread out over 3 or 4 days may produce little hazard, for settlement will often stabilize the snow faster than it builds up. On the other hand, only a foot of snow falling within a few hours may become very dangerous, for the stabilizing effects of settlement will not have had time to act. No hard-and-fast rule can be drawn, for conditions vary widely with the type of snow, but snowfall rates greater than 1 inch per hour can usually be regarded as a possible source of hazard.

With other factors equal, the development of unstable conditions will become much more likely as wind velocity increases. Wind is one of the prime agents in the formation of slab avalanches, and may build up dangerous conditions even when no snowfall occurs. In this case, hazardous areas are local and generally confined to high-angle lee slopes where heavy wind deposition of snow is taking place. This is not necessarily true when high winds accompany a heavy snowfall. In such cases slab avalanches sometimes may form without respect to exposure, and whole areas of a mountainside, both windward and lee, will become unstable.

The precipitation intensity, or rate at which water (in the form of snow) is deposited during a snowstorm, is an important key to snow stability, though it is more difficult to measure in the field. Very high rates of water deposition, accompanied by high winds for prolonged periods, are almost always followed by avalanche action. Qualitatively, heavy snowfalls of a dense or heavy type of snow (graupel, for instance) must always be suspected as a potential source of avalanche danger, particularly if winds are high. Quantitatively, observations of many storms have shown that 1/10 of an inch of water per hour is about the critical rate of deposition if the snowfall lasts long enough to precipitate an inch or more of water. The greater the rate above this, the more likely it is that hazardous conditions develop.

Temperature is an important key to both development and duration of avalanche danger. Storms which begin with high temperatures and a damp, sticky type of snow which bonds well to the old snow surface, and then gradually turns to a drier type of snow with falling temperatures at the end, will be less likely to cause avalanching than will a storm which starts with a cold, dry type of snow and then warms up to produce a heavy, wet snow toward the end. In the latter case the light snow which fell first provides a poor bond between the old snow and the heavier snow which comes later. The lower the temperature after a storm or high wind, the longer will unstable conditions prevail. Hard slabs formed at low temperatures may remain dangerous for days, or even weeks, if the temperature remains well below 0°F. Clear cold weather early in the season when the snowcover is shallow will often lead to the formation of depth hoar within the snowcover. This is not always dangerous in itself, but provides a weak base which may fail to support a subsequent heavy snowfall.

An important clue to the formation of slab avalanches is the appearance of cracks in the snow underneath the foot or ski. This is particularly true of soft slabs forming during a storm. Local cracks around a ski formed by the breaking of the snow are not generally a sign of serious hazard. Cracks which run out ahead of foot or ski for several feet are a definite indication that slab conditions are forming. Whether or not a slide will actually occur on a given slope depends on many factors, such as the bond between the snow layers, shape of the slope, etc., but an avalanche is always possible under these conditions, and caution is indicated. When cracks are observed to run out 30 or 40 feet ahead of skis in snow of any significant depth, it is time to return to safe terrain with all possible haste. Once snow has cracked without sliding, any tensions existing in the snow slab are relieved, and it will usually stabilize in place after a day or so.

Regardless of how carefully snow conditions are studied and all the factors leading to instability considered, it is not possible to predict with any real certainty just when and if a given slope will avalanche. Nevertheless a mountaineer often finds it necessary to get the answer to this very question, as he may be about to cross a suspected slope where a miscalculation could be disastrous. If his estimation of the avalanche hazard can actually be put to test, he will be able to proceed with more confidence.

The tests ordinarily available to the climber are described in Chapter 16. There always exists the possibility, however, especially with hard slabs, that the test procedures will fail to reveal a significant hazard. Such situations must always be borne in mind and a certain amount of judgment exercised whenever slab avalanche conditions are encountered. When selecting routes the wise mountaineer will allow sufficient margin of safety to compensate for errors in estimation of avalanche hazard, and when, on occasion, he deems it necessary to take calculated risks in crossing avalanche terrain, he will first assure himself that the risks are indeed calculated, and not foolhardy.

In conclusion it should be emphasized that a knowledge of theoretical considerations involved in avalanche formation will stand the climber in good stead, but that actual testing and observation in the field must be the basis for practical decisions concerning avalanche hazard — with the reservation that the only reliable test of snow stability is the shock of high explosives.

THE HIGHER CRAFT

This chapter has presented in very brief outline some of the characteristics of snow, and how these characteristics affect the formation of glaciers and the stability of the snowcover. The more serious student may continue his research by referring to the bibliographies published from time to time in alpine journals, which will serve as a guide to the extensive literature on snow and avalanches. For the skier or climber who would rather not delve into technical details there is still the best teacher of all — nature itself. An alert observation of snow in its many phases, coupled with at least a rudimentary comprehension of the processes which affect it, can develop within him a better understanding of an important part of his mountain environment, and with this understanding will come the making of a better mountaineer. Then will he learn what Geoffrey Winthrop Young meant when he wrote: "The higher craft of mountaineering begins above the line of perpetual snow."

Supplementary Reading:

Atwater, M. M. *The Avalanche Hunters.* Philadelphia: Macrae Smith, 1968.

Fraser, Colin. *The Avalanche Enigma.* London: John Murray, 1966.

Gallagher, Dale (editor). *The Snowy Torrents: Avalanche Accidents in the United States 1910-1966.* Alta, Utah: Avalanche Study Center, U. S. Forest Service, 1967. *The Snowy Torrents (Vol. 2): Avalanche Accidents in the U.S. 1967-1972* expected to be available in mid-to late-1974 through the U.S. Government Printing Office in Washington, D.C.

LaChapelle, Edward R. *Field Guide to Snow Crystals.* Seattle and London: University of Washington Press, 1969.

LaChapelle, Edward R. *The ABC of Avalanche Safety.* Denver, Colorado: Colorado Outdoor Sports Co., 1970. A pocket summary by the author of this chapter.

Post, Austin, and Edward R. LaChapelle. *Glacier Ice.* Seattle and London: University of Washington Press, 1971.

Seligman, Gerald. *Snow Structures and Ski Fields.* London: 1936. Though written at a time when the subject was just beginning to be systematically studied, this remains the basic introduction.

25 *

MOUNTAIN WEATHER

WEATHER is of prime concern to the mountaineer, since his comfort and possibly his safety are dependent upon it. Weather can not only change with astonishing rapidity in the mountains, but its patterns and effects may be surprisingly local: hypothermia has claimed victims caught unprepared for wind and rain on exposed alpine slopes, while just a few miles away others have sweltered in lowland summer heat. After an early attempt on the Matterhorn, Edward Whymper reported being driven back by a fierce storm within a cloud high on the mountain; skeptical villagers in the valley below recalled only warm sunshine under clear skies.

At 5000 feet and higher, snow can fall any time of year; excessive snowfall brings avalanche hazards to exposed slopes and can force retreat from a major peak, even in summer. Rain, snow, and verglas can present unwelcome problems to the rock climber. Fog can completely frustrate routefinding. Lightning is a particular hazard on exposed peaks and ridges. Climbs of major peaks such as Mt. McKinley frequently require several weeks due to periods of bad weather. Minor emergencies, such as simple evacuation of an injured climber, can become major problems in the face of a mountain storm. Even fair and warm weather can introduce peculiar problems such as melting snow bridges and rising streams which in the afternoon obliterate routes climbed successfully in the morning.

While the mountaineer can do nothing about the weather directly, he can learn to recognize signs of impending changes, so that he will not be caught unprepared. Even lacking weather instruments or current Weather Service reports, he can learn much about approaching weather merely by observing clouds. If he is carrying an altimeter, his prognosis can be confirmed through observation of barometric changes: the decreasing pressure, or falling barometer, often announcing an approaching storm, register on an altimeter as a gain in altitude unjustified by physical progress up the mountain. Barometric changes are easily observed when the party remains at the same elevation, as in an overnight camp or bivouac.

WEATHER FORECASTS

The time to become concerned about the weather is not at the first rumble of thunder, but before leaving home. Local Weather Service observations and forecasts are timely and informative. Weather maps published in newspapers help in anticipating possible developments, but the information in these maps is a forecast of anticipated weather based on older data. TV weather maps presented with the evening news, on the other hand, are generally based on the most recent information released by the Weather Service, and have the additional advantage of being presented in an easily understood manner. Many include satellite pictures showing cloud patterns over large areas. Other sources of weather

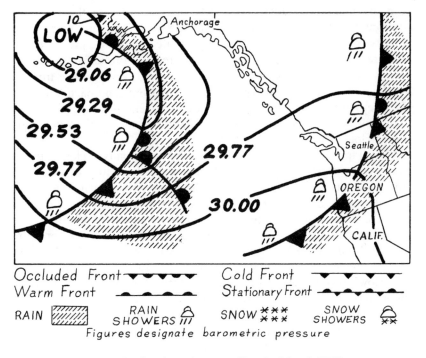

Fig. 185. Regional weather map (Seattle, May 6, 1973).

forecasts are prerecorded telephone messages and continuous Weather Service reports on the VHF-FM public-service band (either 162.4 or 162.55 MHz.). In any case, weather signs read in the clouds are more meaningful when considered in reference to recent Weather Service forecasts.

Weather at higher elevations in the mountains may be substantially different from weather observed even a few miles away in the lowlands. Low stratus clouds causing an overcast but dry day at home may be forced up mountain slopes, causing a heavy drizzle. Conversely, a cloudy, drizzly day at home may be due to low stratus clouds, or fog, with the mountains rising above this low overcast into clear, sunny weather. While it is sometimes difficult or impossible to anticipate the extent and significance of a heavy overcast, or the weather above an overcast, an aviation weather forecast may resolve these points. Aviation weather observations and forecasts are available on telephone recordings and are also broadcast on the long-wave aircraft frequencies (200-400 kHz and 108-110 MHz). They are especially helpful in identifying cloud levels.

ORIGINS OF WEATHER

In the middle latitudes, major weather patterns are the result of confrontation of cold, relatively dry polar air with warm, moist air. These air masses meet along a *front,* usually identified by clouds, precipitation, temperature change, and a trough of low pressure. Fronts are the boundaries between air masses of different densities. Low-pressure troughs develop along fronts so that pressure falls as fronts approach and rises after they pass. Wind direction shifts clockwise (veers) as a cold front passes in the northern hemisphere (in the southern hemisphere, the wind shifts counterclockwise).

Most important weather changes usually accompany cyclonic storms associated with frontal waves. Development and dissipation of a cyclonic storm is illustrated in Figure 186. As the storm (frontal wave) develops, cold air pushes under a warm air mass, while the displaced warm air rides over the cold air mass. The cyclonic frontal pattern of Figure 186 is characterized by wind movement counterclockwise around a low-pressure center. Winds follow approximately the direction of the isobar lines (isobars connect places of equal barometric pressure), so that the location of the low-pressure center can be estimated from the wind direction. In the mountains, unfortunately, surface winds are often unreliable indicators and upper-level clouds must be relied upon to indicate wind direction. An easily remembered generalization is that in the western United States southerly winds preceed and accompany most storms.

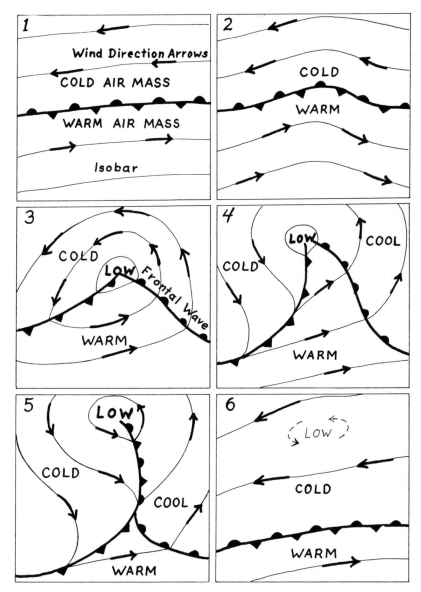

Fig. 186. Development and dissipation of a cyclonic storm cell.

Because a cold front travels about twice as fast as a warm front, the cold front ultimately overtakes the warm front, becoming an occluded front. This is the final stage before dissipation of the cyclonic weather pattern.

FORECASTING WITH CLOUDS

The best way to forecast weather in the mountains, as previously mentioned, is to start at home by reviewing the latest weather maps and Weather Service forecasts. Armed with knowledge of the general weather pattern, the mountaineer is better prepared to predict local weather several hours in advance by observing cloud types, pressure changes, and wind direction. Clouds indicate what is going on in the atmosphere, always demonstrating that a layer or body of air has cooled before its dew point so that some of its vapor has condensed into liquid or solid form. This moisture becomes condensed in only two ways: air, with invisible water vapor contained therein, must be lifted and thereby cooled until the vapor condenses, or there must be horizontal countercurrents of air of different temperatures. By contact, the warmer air is cooled and clouds form. Clouds tend to repeat themselves in familiar patterns because atmospheric processes tend to repeat themselves, giving visible evidence in the clouds.

Cloud Types

Clouds are defined by their appearance as belonging to the *cumulus* family, with a billowing shape, or to the *stratus* family, with pronounced stratification. The two varieties are further classified by their altitude.

Cirrus clouds, formed of ice crystals, are at very high altitudes, usually 20,000 to 35,000 feet in the middle latitudes. They can give 24 hours warning of approaching bad weather hundreds of miles in advance of a warm front. Frail, scattered tufts are a sign of fair weather, but prognostic types, such as mares' tails or dense cirrus bands, may be a prelude to approaching lower clouds and finally the arrival of precipitation and the front.

Alto-family clouds are the middle clouds, extending from about 8000 to 20,000 feet. Altostratus sheets or veils and altocumulus clouds should be observed for indication of approaching bad weather. When these thicken, especially if preceded by prognostic-type cirrus, precipitation within 6 to 10 hours is probably indicated.

Stratus clouds are low-level clouds, ranging from the earth's surface to about 8000 feet. If they reach the ground they become fog. Mountaineers frequently find the heavy overcast in the morning is low-lying stratus, or valley fog, which is left behind after a few hour's climbing brings the party

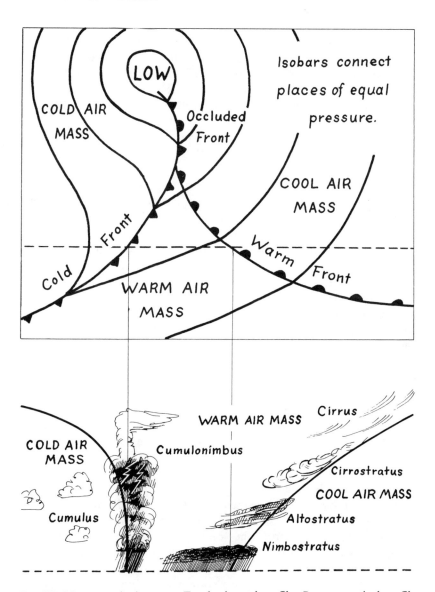

Fig. 187. Mature cyclonic storm. *Top,* horizontal profile. *Bottom,* vertical profile taken along dashed line in upper illustration.

to upper slopes bathed in sunlight. *Nimbostratus* is the cloud that yields steady rain.

Cumulus are tall clouds with vertical development, formed in moist, unstable air. Cotton puffs of cumulus are fair-weather clouds but should be observed for possible growth leading to *cumulonimbus,* or thunderstorm clouds. Great amounts of energy arc released in a cumulonimbus cloud as strong updrafts carry moist air upward for thousands of feet to be condensed, yielding heavy precipitation as snow, rain, or hail. Cumulonimbus activity is typically associated with cold fronts and can occur at any time of year, although more common in summer. Cumulonimbus also form along ridges or peaks on summer afternoons. Some mountains are more prone to produce afternoon thunderstorms and in some areas of the Rocky Mountains, for instance, prudent climbers get an early start to assure being off the peak by the time the afternoon thunderstorm develops.

Cloud caps sometimes form above prominent peaks, indicating moisture aloft. A cloud cap is not of immediate concern unless it is descending on the climbing party's objective; in this case a cold and windy summit can be anticipated. A growing and descending cloud cap foretells approaching bad weather. High winds can produce a *lenticular cloud banner* extending downwind from a peak or ridge, sometimes for several miles; such phenomena should also be watched for indications of worsening weather.

Cloud development should be observed over a period of time to reduce confusion over misleading patterns. When winds are due to circulation about high or low-pressure centers and not due to mountain or valley winds or land or sea breezes, typical weather patterns can be generalized in cloud orientation rules. These rules apply only in the northern hemisphere and are subject to variation due to local weather patterns.

Cloud Orientation Rules

1. High or middle clouds moving from the south are an indicator of deteriorating weather. Movement from the north indicates fair weather (except possibly under an arctic air mass in winter).
2. Low clouds moving from the south indicate deteriorating weather, especially if moving fast. Movement from the north indicates fair or improving weather.
3. When clouds are absent, a strong north wind indicates fair weather.

LOCAL WEATHER PATTERNS

Local weather patterns tend to complicate weather prediction in the mountains but are an important part of local mountain lore. Familiarity with local weather can contribute substantially to the success of a climb. In fact, it is almost impossible to accurately predict weather in the mountains without knowledge of local orographic or terrain effects.

Regional weather patterns can be determined by consulting local meteorologists. Any climber in the Tetons, for instance, should be aware of the predictable afternoon thunderstorm and plan his schedule to be off the summit before lightning strikes. Winter climbers in New Hampshire's Presidential Range are apprehensive of a northeaster bringing in moist air off the Atlantic resulting in heavy snowfall, an apparent exception to the cloud orientation rules. Climbers in the Cascades frequently find that dreary, rainy weather on the western slopes can be avoided by selecting an objective on the sunny eastern side of the range.

Seasonal weather variations are also of interest. Major Himalayan ascents are frequently timed for the brief period between severe winter storms and the summer monsoons bringing storms off the Indian Ocean. Weather in the Cascades, while generally sunny for several days at a time in summer, frequently has rapidly moving fronts passing through almost daily in winter, almost twice as fast as in summer. Summer weather in the Cascades, although generally predictable, is subject to occasional thunderstorm activity, indicated by middle and high clouds of moist, unstable air moving out of the south or southeast.

A weather phenomenon observed wherever winds must pass over mountains is *adiabatic cooling and heating* of the air. As an air mass is lifted over a mountain range, it is cooled due to decreasing pressure; as it descends the other side of the range, it is warmed due to increasing

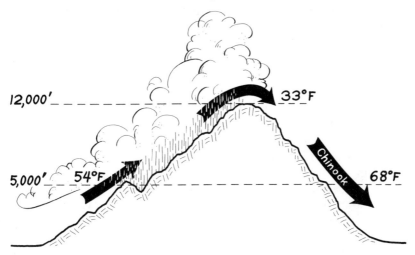

Fig. 188. Example of adiabatic lapse rate in an air mass moving over a ridge.

pressure. The drop in temperature with altitude, or dry adiabatic lapse rate, is about 5°F for each 1000 feet. If precipitation accompanies the elevation gain, heat given up to the air through condensation of water vapor reduces the adiabatic temperature drop to about 3°F per 1000 feet.

Knowledge of the adiabatic lapse rate is useful in estimating clothing and equipment suitable for the colder temperatures encountered at a higher elevation. For example, if rain is falling and the temperature is 41°F at one location, the rain will turn to snow about 3000 feet higher. A 15,000-foot summit may be 25 to 40°F cooler than the trailhead at 5000 feet. On the other hand, a temperature inversion may occasionally produce relatively warm temperatures on a lofty summit.

Chinook winds are a peculiar occurrence resulting from adiabatic cooling of moist air ascending a mountain barrier followed by adiabatic warming as the air descends the opposite side. The temperature drop of the ascending air is reduced due to heat released by condensing water vapor. However, when this air mass descends the leeward slopes, it still gains 5°F per 1000 feet of descent. Therefore, there is a net temperature gain at the base of the leeward slopes. If the quantity of precipitation released on the windward side is large, the temperature on the leeward side is considerably warmer.

Mountain and valley winds are a local weather phenomenon. As the sun warms the slopes, the air near the ground is heated and rises, creating an "upslope canyon" wind; but as the sun descends and the slopes cool, the cooling air flows back down the canyons into the valleys. Temperature changes and moderate winds may be experienced in the paths of mountain and valley winds. They generally pose little problem except for confusing attempts at recognizing the real wind pattern. This is especially true near mountain passes where winds attempting to cross the mountains are funneled through the path of least resistance, frequently with increased wind speed and change of direction.

FURTHER STUDY

The study of weather is a complex science, involving a composite of the net effects of multiple contributing factors. Even professionals are so frequently frustrated by its vagaries it is rumored they resort to dart-board forecasting.

It should be apparent that one short chapter can only briefly generalize about mountain weather and its prediction. As a practical matter, however, using the preceding information and the actual evidence around him during the approach and while gaining a peak, but *before* the start of any technical difficulties enable the climber to decide whether or not to go on in the face of developing weather.

Fig. 189. Cloud formations. *Left, Mares' tails cirrus,* earliest warning of possible approaching storm center. *Right,* fair weather *cirrus* over Yakima Peak. (Roger Wilcox)

Fig. 190. Fair weather *cumulus* over Mt. Assiniboine. (Austin Post, University of Washington)

Fig. 191. Cloud cap on Mt. Rainier, indicating a cold, windy summit. (T. M. Green)

Fig. 192. Cumulus dissipating adiabatically over Shuksan Arm. Moist marine air formed clouds as it rose over Shuksan Arm. This is not an indicator of bad weather. (Roger Wilcox)

Fig. 193. Mt. Baker rising above *stratus;* fair weather above but foggy below. (Roger Wilcox)

Fig. 194. Cumulus conjestus over Snoqualmie Mtn. The occluded peaks are wet and foggy.

Fig. 195. Cumulonimbus — more commonly observed in conjested patterns, the source of lightning storms.

Fig. 196. Sunset under *altocumulus*. Storm passed through the next day. (Roger Wilcox)

Fig. 197. Lenticular cloud over Mt. Rainier. A growing and descending lenticular cloud indicates deteriorating weather. (Bob and Ira Spring)

Fig. 198. Lenticular altostratus over Tatoosh Range — a growing lenticular cloud pattern which warned of the storm that passed through the next day. (Roger Wilcox)

Fig. 199. Banded cirrus over Mt. Baker. Warning of approaching bad weather. (Roger Wilcox)

Supplementary Reading:

Aviation Weather for Pilots and Flight Operations Personnel, published jointly by the Flight Standards Service of the Federal Aviation Agency and the Weather Service, Superintendent of Documents, U.S. Government Printing Office, Washington, D.C. 20402.

Cantzler, George L. *Your Guide to the Weather.* New York: Barnes and Noble, 1964.

Clouds. Superintendent of Documents, U.S. Government Printing Office, Washington, D.C. 20402. Publication No. ESSA/P1680002.

Watts, Alan. *Weather Forecasting Ashore and Afloat.* London: Adlard Coles, 1967.

Whelpley, Donald A. *Weather, Water and Boating.* Cambridge, Maryland: Cornell Maritime Press, 1961.

Zim, Herbert S. *Weather.* New York: Golden Press, 1960.

APPENDIX 1

FOOD REQUIREMENTS FOR CLIMBERS

ENERGY EXPENDITURE IN THE MOUNTAINS

Climbing is one of the more strenuous human activities and demands a great deal more energy than the average everyday occupation. The increased food requirement can be calculated approximately by considering the body in its role as a machine.

In city or mountains or wherever, each individual expends a certain amount of energy merely breathing and circulating the blood and otherwise carrying on basic life processes. This *basal metabolism* uses about one "large" calorie per kilogram of body weight per hour, or approximately 1100 large calories per 100 pounds of body weight per day. (The "large" calorie is the unit of food calculations, equivalent to 1000 "small" calories — the latter being the amount of energy needed to raise a gram of water 1°C. in temperature. Throughout this discussion the calorie mentioned is the large one.) The rate of basal metabolism varies with height, age, sex, race, altitude, and other factors, but in relatively-insignificant degree. To find the energy requirements for a climb, the amount used to do external work is added to the basal rate.

The activities in Table 11 are those of "irreversible work," done against friction. Lifting the body to higher elevations is theoretically "reversible work," since the potential energy of the body is increased. Unfortunately the body is incapable of utilizing this potential energy on a descent (except in the undesirable way of falling) and indeed must work to climb down a mountain, though nowhere near so hard as in climbing up. The efficiency of the body in doing work over and above basal metabolism varies from 20 to 40 per cent. Assuming an average value of 30 per cent efficiency, the *energy needed to raise 100 pounds 1000 feet of elevation is about 110 calories.*

Table 11. Energy Rate Over and Above Basal Metabolism.

Activity	Calories Per Hour Per 100 Pounds of Body Weight
Walking 2 mph (on smooth level pavement) . . .	45
Walking 3 mph (" " " ") . . .	90
Walking 4 mph (" " " ") . . .	160
Eating	20
Sitting quietly	20
Driving an automobile	40
Sawing wood	260
Swimming 2 mph	360
Rowing in race	730
Shivering	up to 220

Source: Carpenter, T. M., Tables, Factors, and Formulas for Computing Respiratory Exchange and Biological Transformations of Energy. Carnegie Institute, Washington, D. C., 1939.

The final factor in calculating energy requirements is the *specific dynamic action*, or "SDA." During metabolism from 6 to 10 per cent of the calorie content of food is released as heat, and thus is not available for doing work.

Table 12. Estimated Daily Energy Expenditure of 170-Pound Man at Office Job.

Activity	Calories Per Hour	Hours	Total
Basal metabolism (1100 x 1.7)			1870
Eating	34	1.5	50
Driving automobile	70	1.0	70
Working	90	8.0	720
Leisure and miscellaneous	40	5.5	220
Subtotal			2930
SDA (7% of subtotal)			200
Total			3130

Using such methods the energy expenditure on any proposed trip can be roughly calculated, and thus the food requirements. The "roughly" must be emphasized, since even professional nutritionists vary somewhat in their findings. The standard ration of the United States Army is 4500 calories for strenuous work, 3500 for garrison duty.

Table 13. Estimated Energy Expenditure of 170-Pound Man
Climbing Mount Olympus in Washington State

To simplify calculation it is assumed the pack weighs uniformly 30 pounds throughout, making a constant total of 200 pounds. The walking energy rate from Table 11 is thus multipled by a factor of 2. In addition it is multiplied by a factor of 1.5 to correct for rough trail. This factor may be several times larger for bushwhacking, boulder-hopping, snow-slogging, etc.

Activity	Calories Per Hour	Hours	Total
Day No. 1			
Basal metabolism			1870
Eating	34	1.5	50
Driving (Seattle to road end)	70	6	420
Hike from Jackson Guard Sta. to Elk Lake			
15 miles @ 3 mph	270	5	1350
1600 ft. elevation gain			350
Pack, unpack, make camp, etc.	100	3	300
Subtotal			4340
SDA			300
Total			4640
Day No. 2			
Basal metabolism			1870
Eating	34	1.5	50
Hike from Elk Lake to summit and return			
14 miles @ 2 mph	135	7	950
5400 ft. elevation gain			1190
Side trips, camp chores, etc.	100	6	600
Subtotal			4660
SDA			330
Total			4990

Activity	Calories Per Hour	Hours	Total
Day No. 3			
Basal metabolism			1870
Eating	34	1.5	50
Hike to car	270	5	1350
Driving	70	6	420
Pack, unpack, etc.	100	3	300
Subtotal			3990
SDA			280
Total			4270

R. W. Gerard, in *Food for Life*, University of Chicago Press, 1952, estimates that general factory work requires about 3000 to 4000 calories daily. The Juneau Ice Field Research Project, in various reports published by the American Geographical Society, 1949-51, tells of several differing dietary experiments; on one trip it was later calculated that the average intake per man had been 4085 calories per day.

COMPOSITION OF FOODS

The three major food components are proteins, fats, and carbohydrates. Each provides energy, but also other essential values more-or-less understood at present. In addition the undigestible portion, the pure bulk, has a function. No less important are the trace quantities of vitamins and minerals needed for various vital body processes. All must be supplied in approximately the right amounts to maintain health of body and mind.

Proteins

Proteins are broken down in the digestive process into their constituent amino acids which are in turn recombined by the body to make new proteins, such as muscles and other body tissue. Animal proteins such as meat, milk, cheese, and eggs are called "complete" because they yield exactly the amino acids in the exactly correct proportion the system requires. Cereals such as wheat and oats and legumes such as peas and beans yield varying amounts of amino acids, though their proteins are "incomplete," lacking several amino acids. However, the addition of a little milk or cheese renders vegetable proteins "complete," the combination supplying all essential amino acids.

Protein requirement per day is nearly constant regardless of activity. The body steadily renews itself, replacing old muscles. Hard work does not accelerate the process, which continues at the same rate during sedentary office work and violent manual labor. The recommended daily allowance is 70 grams of protein, at least half of it *complete,* distributed over the entire day. The body cannot utilize its entire daily requirement at any one meal; amino acids in excess of what can be immediately used, and "incomplete" groups of amino acids, are not stored. Having been rejected for tissue-building purposes they are converted into fuel or stored as fat.

Fats

Fats are used primarily for energy, but also supply the fat-soluble vitamins. In addition there are certain unsaturated fats with an imperfectly understood but apparently vital function. It is recommended that a minimum of 20 to 25 per cent of the total calories be supplied by fat. Major sources are meat fats, butter, margarine, cheese, egg yolks, and nuts.

Carbohydrates

Carbohydrates supply nothing but energy but in a form so easily used that most nutritionists recommend their use for half the caloric intake. Carbohydrates include all sugars, starches, and celluloses, found in cereals, legumes, milk, vegetables, fruits, bakery goods, and candy. Only sugars and starches are digestible by man. Cellulose is digested by the browsing animals but in man passes through the system chemically unchanged, providing bulk, or roughage, in many people seemingly necessary for regular elimination.

Vitamins

Vitamins yield enzymes which catalyze various chemical reactions and physiological processes. The quantities required are small, but when lacking, deficiency diseases result. Vitamins are broadly classified as to their solubility in fat or water, which determines their source. The principal fat-soluble vitamins are A, D, E, and K. The water-soluble vitamins include the B complex and C, found in cereals, vegetables, fruit, and meat both fresh and dehydrated. The fright-propaganda of proprietary drug manufacturers notwithstanding, any ordinary balanced diet supplies enough of all of these. However, body storage of water-soluble vitamins is slight, and though deficiency diseases such as scurvy and beriberi are unlikely to afflict a climbing party, the earlier symptoms of deficiency can occur, such as irritability and mental depression. Thus on any long trip with a possibly unbalanced diet, the inclusion of vitamin pills should be considered.

Minerals

The mineral parts of food include salts of calcium, phosphorus, iron, sodium, copper, chlorine, and a host of other elements, some of whose functions are unknown. All are water-soluble and thus provided by meats, vegetables, and fruits, and in sufficient amount by a balanced diet.

METABOLISM

The mechanism of food usage by the body is extremely complex and not completely understood in detail. All food on digestion contributes to the common metabolic pool. The amino acids needed to build tissue are extracted, the remainder after a further digestive process being contributed to the fuel supply, which also includes the derivatives of carbohydrates and fat. Some of the fuel is used for immediate needs. Some is converted into glycogen, a starch that is stored in small quantities in the liver and muscles and converted to glucose for fuel on quick demand. The remainder is manufactured into body fat for long-term storage.

The end-products of food oxidation for energy are water and carbon dioxide and lactic acid. During hard work these accumulate while fuel dissipates, resulting in weariness. The function of rest is to allow blood and lungs to remove end-products and replenish oxygen and fuel.

Heat is a byproduct of work. Virtually all the energy of basal metabolism and specific dynamic action is converted ultimately to heat. Since the body is on the average only 30 per cent efficient in using its "work calories," the remaining 70 per cent are also converted to heat. Together these maintain body temperature. Excessive heat released by metabolism, SDA, and work is dispersed by perspiration. During inactivity in cold weather, metabolism and SDA may not supply enough heat; when the lower limit of the thermostat is touched the body sets the muscles to shivering.

Conditioning

During exercise the body improves its capacity for exercise. Metabolism becomes more efficient, the blood moving more rapidly to carry waste products away from the muscles and bring them new fuel. Glycogen storage is increased slightly, and also the speed of its conversion into energy. The harder a person works today the harder he can work tomorrow.

Before bursts of extreme and extraordinary exertion a simple life is best. How a person feels on a strenuous weekend climb depends partly on how hard he worked on a previous weekend — but also very largely on what he has been doing during the week. A well-balanced regular diet with steady moderate exercise and plenty of rest puts the system in finest tuning. Exotic foods and irregularity of meals and rest upset body chemistry and reduce physical performance for hours or days.

During the climb itself the only physiological requirements are energy and water. Theoretically, then, the most efficient diet during the period of heavy work is sugar and water — and indeed some mountaineers go hours at a time on fruit juice and candy. For various reasons cited herein fats and proteins are generally consumed in addition. Whatever the components, all meals immediately before and during a climb should either be small or followed by a long rest. The blood cannot serve two masters, lungs and stomach; attempting to set a vigorous pace just after a feast causes rubbery legs or stomach upset or both.

Frequency of Meals

Carbohydrates are most rapidly and efficiently converted into energy, and thus starches and sugars most immediately replenish the fuel supply. The rapidity of conversion, however, means that a diet high in carbohydrates requires frequent meals, as many as eight a day.

Proteins and fats are most slowly digested but release their energy over a longer period of time. An egg at breakfast contributes nothing to an energetic start but steadily helps the forenoon struggle. Similarly, peanut butter at noon powers the making of camp at sunset, and Goteborg at supper makes it possible to rise on the morrow. The body can adjust to very infrequent meals when the fat and protein content of the diet is high. Arctic explorers such as Vilhjalmur Stefansson consider one meal a day ample, and only two meals a week no excessive hardship.

Hunger pangs are symptomatic of an empty stomach, not of an empty energy reservoir, since there may still be ample body fat available. Even in the person of average weight this reserve is sufficient to sustain a high level of activity for several days; fasts as long as a month have been made without lasting body damage. During transition from a city diet high in bulk to a relatively concentrated mountain diet it is well to endure mild hunger for a few days while the stomach shrinks; attempting to fill up on concentrated foods leads to obesity, or even illness. Extreme hunger is of course unpleasant, and to be avoided. A meal of carbohydrates passes entirely out of the stomach in 1 or 2 hours, while a meal high in fat remains as long as 6 or 7 hours. Bulk in the stomach gives a feeling of satisfaction; foods high in fat and protein "stick to the ribs."

From what has been said, obviously the optimum frequency of meals depends on the kind of food eaten. In addition there are great variations between individuals. Some people work best on almost constant intake of carbohydrates. Others attain top performance with one or two meals a day, high in fat and protein. Every climber should experimentally establish his own best frequency, and limits of variation. Most parties achieve the greatest happiness of the greatest number by planning only the main evening meal in common, letting adherents of the three-squares-per-day and the one-square-plus-constant-nibbles factions adjust the remainder of the diet to individual needs.

Food Efficiency

On a short outing the ratio of calories to pounds scarcely merits consideration, since even with pure carbohydrates (with no water) 2½ pounds per day suffices, a weight relatively small compared to that of equipment. Most overloading of the commissary comes simply from carrying more food than necessary to satisfy energy requirements of the trip. Another key consideration is choosing foods low in water content, either naturally or through processing. The majority of mountains are quite liberally endowed with liquid resources, and it is pointless to backpack water long distances. Similar objections can be raised to hauling excess metal in the form of cans.

Table 14. Energy Values of Food.

	Calories Per Gram	*Calories Per Pound*
Protein	4.0	1800
Fat	9.0	4100
Carbohydrate	4.0	1800

As is apparent from Table 14, an increased proportion of fats in the diet is very desirable on long backpacking trips. A single pound of pure fat very nearly supplies the daily energy requirement, though such a menu is undesirable for various physical and psychological reasons. However, the case of pemmican is instructive, and a climber would do well to read the works of Vilhjalmur Stefansson, including *The Friendly Arctic,* Macmillan, New York, 1953, and *Fat of the Land,* Macmillan, New York, 1956. Pemmican was invented by the Plains Indian, and used by him on long hunting and war expeditions. Adopted by the early fur traders it made possible the economic penetration of the West, and by a later generation, exploration of the Arctic. Pemmican is composed of equal parts of dried, powdered, lean meat and rendered fat, and despite denunciations by experts who have proved by formula that a man living on pemmican will surely waste away and die in a few weeks, ample testimony to the contrary is provided by the history of the fur trade and Arctic exploration, which cites innumerable instances of men working hard and healthily and happily many months at a time on no other food than pemmican. During World War II, theory and experience conflicted in a "Pemmican War," the worst result of which was the production by the U.S. Army of a fruit-nut confection libelously labelled "pemmican." Genuine pemmican is expensive and rare, but with it the traditional limit of approximately 2 weeks for a backpack trip without relaying supplies could be extended to 4 weeks, the equivalent weight being half that of a conventional high-carbohydrate diet.

The virtues of pemmican appear only on a long trip, since like any other unfamiliar diet it requires a period of adjustment. In general it is best for a climber to eat in the mountains approximately the way he does in everyday living to avoid the unpleasantness of physiological conversion. The psychological values of food thus are particularly important on short outings. There is no physical necessity for hot meals, leafy vegetables, spices, and sweets, but if the craving for them is not satisfied morale suffers. This has been most strikingly demonstrated on high-altitude expeditions, leading many expeditions to synthesize from processed foods, at considerable trouble and expense, a diet approximating the one to which the members are accustomed at home. Even during a week in the Cascades it is usually worthwhile to carry a few such luxuries; the food value may be small, but the contribution to pleasure immense.

Table 15. Values of Representative Mountaineering Foods.

Food	Energy Value	Composition of Edible Portion		
	Calories per ounce	% Protein	% Carbo- hydrate	% Fat
DAIRY PRODUCTS				
Butter	203	0.6	0.4	81.0
Margarine	204	0.6	0.4	81.0
Whole milk	18	3.5	4.9	3.9
Whole buttermilk	10	3.6	5.1	0.1
Malted milk, dry powdered	116	14.7	70.8	8.3
Milk, dry skim	103	35.8	51.6	0.7
Milk, dry whole	142	26.4	38.2	27.5
Milk, evaporated, unsweetened	39	7.0	9.7	7.9
Milk, condensed, sweetened	91	8.1	54.3	8.7
Cheese, cheddar	113	25.0	2.1	32.2
Cheese, Swiss	105	27.5	1.7	28.0
Cheese, processed	105	23.2	1.9	30.0
FRUITS				
Orange	10	1.0	12.2	Insignifi-
Banana	16	1.1	22.2	cant in
Apple, raw	13	trace	12.0	most
Apple, dried	78	1.0	71.8	
Apple, dehydrated	100	1.4	92.1	
Apricot, dried, sulphured	74	5.0	66.5	
Avocado, fresh	49	1.8	5.6	16.7
Date, dried	78	2.2	72.9	
Fig, dried	78	4.3	69.1	
Peach, dried, sulphured	74	3.1	68.3	
Prune, dried	64	2.1	67.4	
Raisin	82	2.5	77.4	

Table 15 (cont.)

Food	Energy Value	Composition of Edible Portion		
	Calories per ounce	% Protein	% Carbo-hydrate	% Fat
FRUIT JUICES				
Apple	13	0.1	11.9	Insignifi-
Applesauce, sweetened	26	0.2	23.8	cant in
Grape	19	0.2	16.6	all
Grapefruit, sweetened	15	0.5	12.8	
Orange	14	0.7	10.4	
Pineapple	16	0.4	13.5	
Prune	22	0.4	19.0	
Tomato	5	0.9	4.3	
Lemon juice concentrate, frozen, unsweetened	33	2.3	37.4	
Orange concentrate, canned	63	4.1	50.7	
Lemonade concentrate, frozen	55	0.2	51.1	
Fruit cocktail, canned, in syrup	22	0.4	19.5	
VEGETABLES, DEHYDRATED				
Cabbage	87	14.4	72.5	Insignifi-
Carrot	97	6.6	81.1	cant in
Potato	100	8.3	80.4	all
Sweet potato	107	4.2	90.0	
Tomato flakes	97	10.8	76.7	
NUTS				
Almond	170	18.6	19.5	57.7
Brazil	185	14.3	10.9	66.9
Cashew	159	17.2	29.3	45.7
Coconut, dried, sweetened	155	3.6	53.2	39.1
Peanut butter	167	27.8	17.2	49.4
Peanut, roasted	165	26.0	18.8	49.8
Pecan	195	9.2	14.6	71.2
Walnut	159	14.8	15.8	64.0
GRAIN PRODUCTS				
Breakfast Cereals				
Bran flakes, 40%	85	10.7	82.1	3.6
Cornflakes	109	7.9	85.3	Insignifi-
Oatmeal, uncooked	110	15.0	78.5	cant in
Rice, puffed	113	6.0	89.5	most
Farina, enriched, uncooked	103	11.4	77.0	
Wheat, puffed	103	15.0	78.5	
Wheat, shredded	104	9.9	79.9	
Wheat germ	102	26.5	47.0	10.3

Table 15 (cont.)

Food	Energy Value	Composition of Edible Portion		
	Calories per ounce	% Protein	% Carbo-hydrate	% Fat
Other Grains (Uncooked)				
Barley, pearl	99	8.4	78.8	Insignifi-
Macaroni	105	12.5	75.2	cant in
Noodles, egg	110	12.8	72.0	all
Spaghetti	105	12.5	75.2	
Rice, brown, raw	102	7.5	77.4	
Rice, white, raw	103	6.7	80.4	
Rice, precooked	105	7.5	82.5	
Pancake mix, wheat	101	8.6	75.7	
Pancake mix, buckwheat	93	10.5	70.3	
Baked Goods				
Bread				
Rye	69	9.1	52.1	
White	77	8.7	50.5	
Pumpernickel	70	9.1	53.1	
Whole wheat	69	10.5	47.7	
Boston brown	60	5.5	45.6	
Cooky, sugar	126	6.0	68.0	16.8
Doughnut	111	4.6	51.4	18.6
Fig bar	101	3.9	75.4	5.6
Triscuit	125	12.0	?	?
Rye wafer	98	13.0	76.3	1.2
Logan bread, moist	100	7.0	60.0	10.0
Logan bread, dry	112	8.0	67.0	12.0
MEAT, FISH, EGGS				
Beef				
Corned, canned	75	23.5	0.0	18.0
Dried, chipped	58	34.3	0.0	6.3
Hamburger, cooked	81	24.2	0.0	20.3
Pork				
Bacon, lean, cooked	173	30.4	3.2	52.0
Bacon, Canadian, cooked	79	27.6	0.3	17.5
Bacon, canned	194	8.5	1.0	71.5
Ham, smoked	87	23.0	0.0	30.6
Fish				
Salmon, canned	43	20.8	0.0	7.1
Sardines in oil, drained	47	24.0	0.0	11.1
Tuna, canned, drained	47	28.8	0.0	8.2

Table 15 (cont.)

Food	Energy Value	Composition of Edible Portion		
	Calories per ounce	% Protein	% Carbo- hydrate	% Fat
Processed Products				
Baked beans	35	6.1	19.0	2.6
Bologna	86	12.1	1.1	27.5
Chili con carne, without beans	57	10.3	5.8	14.8
Hash, corned beef with potato	51	8.8	10.7	11.3
Liverwurst	86	16.2	1.8	25.6
Luncheon meat, pork	83	15.0	1.3	24.9
Frankfurter	88	12.4	1.6	27.2
Vienna sausage	68	14.0	0.3	19.8
Bouillon cube	34	20.0	5.0	3.0
Eggs				
Egg, fresh	41	12.9	0.9	11.5
Egg, dried, whole	168	47.0	4.1	41.2
CANDIES AND SWEETS				
"Candy bar"	141	9.2	59.6	25.3
Candy, bulk (hard candy)	139	8.2	64.2	22.5
Candy, peanut	146	11.3	60.5	22.2
Chocolate, unsweetened	143	10.7	28.9	53.0
Chocolate, milk	147	7.7	56.9	32.3
Chocolate, sweet with almonds	151	9.3	51.3	35.6
Cocoa mix	111	9.4	73.9	10.6
Butterscotch	113	0.0	94.8	3.4
Caramel	113	4.0	76.6	10.2
Fudge, plain	113	2.7	75.0	12.2
Peanut brittle	119	5.7	81.0	10.4
Honey, strained	86	0.3	82.3	0.0
Jam	77	0.6	70.0	0.1
Mincemeat	61	5.3	34.4	6.4
Molasses, cane	66	0.0	60.0	0.0
Sugar, brown	106	0.0	96.4	0.0
Sugar, granulated	109	0.0	99.5	0.0
Ice cream, plain	59	4.0	20.6	12.5

Source: Adapted from Watt and Merrill, *Composition of Foods, Raw, Processed, Prepared — Agriculture Handbook No. 8,* U. S. Department of Agriculture, Washington, D. C., revised December 1963. This handbook was compiled from all research data available, and is considered by experts to be authoritative. The above table lists several items for which information was derived from other sources. Unfortunately, it has not been possible so far to gain data on the values of the specially-packaged foods which nowadays constitute an important component of the mountaineer diet.

APPENDIX 2

SAMPLE MEALS

BREAKFAST

Weights accurate to ¼ ounce. Greater error in the dry measure.

	One Serving		Four Servings	
	Ounces	*Cups*	*Ounces*	*Cups*
COLD CEREALS				
Wheat Chex	2 to 2.5	1 crushed	8 to 10	4
Grapenuts } combined	{2	{½	{8	{2
Grapenut Flakes	.75	¼ crushed	3	1
	2.75		11	
Birchermuesli (Familia) (Cereal food including nuts and fruit. No sugar needed.)	3.5 to 4	¾ to 1	14 to 16	3 to 4
All-Bran	2 to 2.5		8 to 10	
Wheatgerm (May be added to all)	.25 to .5		1 to 2	
Milk, whole (Can be premixed)	.75	¼	3	¾
Sugar, white granulated (Can be premixed)	1	2 tblsp.	4	½ plus

	One Serving		Four Servings	
	Ounces	*Cups*	*Ounces*	*Cups*
HOT CEREALS				
Cream of Wheat (quick-cooking)	1.5 to 1.75	3½ to 4 tblsp.	6 to 7	¾ to 1
Wheat Hearts	1.4 to 1.75	¼ to ⅓	5.5 to 7	1 to 1⅓
Instant Ralston	1.4 to 1.75	¼ to ⅓	5.5 to 7	1 to 1⅓
Roman Meal (instant)	1.5 to 1.75	⅜ to ½	6 to 7	1½ to 2
Rolled oats (quick-cooking)	1.5 to 1.75	½ to ⅝	6 to 7	2 to 2½
Sugar, brown To be added to cooked cereal	1⅓	3½ tblsp.	5½	⅞
Powdered cream product	⅓	1½ tblsp.	1½	⅜
OR				
Whole milk To be added to cooked cereal	.75	2 tblsp.	3	½ plus
Margarine May be added in addition to or in place of milk	½ to 1	1 to 2 tblsp.	2 to 4	¼ to ½
FRUITS, sun-dried and vacuum-dried				
Raisins (sun)	1		4	
Date nuggets (vacuum)	1		4	
Apple nuggets (vacuum)	1 to 1.5		4 to 6	
Banana flakes (vacuum)	⅓ to ½		1⅓ to 2	
Mincemeat (sun)	1.5		6	
Apricot-raisin (sun)	1.5		6	
Prunes (sun or vacuum)	1 to 1.5		4	
Peaches (vacuum)	1		4	
Fruit cocktail (vacuum)	1 to 1.5		4 to 6	

These fruits may be mixed with cereals, hot or cold, or stewed separately with some sugar (⅔ to 1 ounce per serving) if desired. Cinnamon and nutmeg can be used to season fruits, also dried lemon peel or lemon crystals. Combining stewed fruits adds interest.

FRUITS, freeze-dried Fruit cocktail Peach slices Apricot slices Strawberries	⅔ to ¾			
STARCHES				
Pancakes (mix with milk and eggs)	2.5	½	10.5	2
Pilot biscuits	2 to 3	2 to 3 biscuits		
Logan bread	2 to 3			
Cinnamon-nut roll	2 to 3			
Margarine	1 to 2 (on breads and pancakes)			
Honey or jam	1⅓ to 3			

	One Serving		Four Servings	
	Ounces	*Cups*	*Ounces*	*Cups*
EGGS				
Omelets, freeze-dried	1 to 2	½ to 1 pkg.	4 to 8	2 to 4 pkgs.
Scrambled, freeze-dried	1.5 to 2		6 to 8	
MEATS				
Ham, freeze-dried	.5 to .8		2.25 to 3.25	3 to 4 tins
Prefried bacon	1.6	4 slices	6.5	1 tin
Corned beef	2 to 3		8 to 12	1 tin
Chopped meat product	2 to 3		7 to 12	1 tin
Bacon bar, dried	.75 to 1.5	¼ to ½ bar	3 to 6	1 to 2 bars
Meat food product bar, dried	.75 to 1.5	¼ to ½ bar	3 to 6	1 to 2 bars
Margarine for cooking eggs	.5 to 1 (less when meat fat available)			
BEVERAGES				
Milk, dry, skim	.75	⅓	3.2	1⅓
Milk, dry, whole (Kraft, Darigold, Milkman)	1	¼ to ⅓	4	1 to 1⅓
Cocoa, ground, with sugar	.75	⅛	2.75	½
Mix with milk	1.	¼	4.	1
	1.75		6.75	
Cocoa, premixed with milk	1.5	⅜	6	1½
Ovaltine, plain or chocolate	.75	¼	3	1
Mix with milk	1.	¼	4.	1
	1.75		7	
Malt, plain or chocolate	.75	2½ tblsp.	3	⅔
Mix with milk	1.	¼	4	1
	1.75		7	
Breakfast Drink Carnation Instant Breakfast, variety of flavors.	.6 to 1.2	½ to 1 pkg.	3.75	3 pkgs.
Mix with milk	1.	¼	4.	1
	1.6		7.75	
Orange Breakfast Drink (Tang)	1.25	3 tblsp.	5	⅔
Jello	1.5	½ pkg.	6	2 pkgs.

LUNCH

Amounts given in ounces per man-day.

MEAT — 2
- *Sausages*
  - Choose dry hard varieties that are well-cured.
- *Canned*
  - Tuna fish
  - Sardines
  - Corned beef
  - Deviled meats
- *Meat bars, compressed*
  - Bacon
  - Meat product
- *Chip beef*
  - Cellophane-packaged types are quite moist and don't keep long.
- *Jerky — 1*

CHEESE — 2

Moist types are preferred for eating
but keep less well than dry.
Moist
   Monterey Jack
   Kuminost (caraway)
   Danish cheeses
   Blue

Intermediate
   Cheddars
   Swiss
   Edam
Dry—Keep very well
   Provoloni
   Romano
   Kasseri

DRIED FRUIT — 2 sundried, 1 to 1½ vacuum-dried

Raisins, dark or bleached
Dates, vacuum-dried or sun
Figs
Peaches, vacuum-dried or sun
Pears
Prunes, pitted, vacuum-dried or sun
Mincemeat, dried
Fruit cocktail, vacuum-dried
Apple nuggets, vacuum-dried
Apricots, vacuum-dried or sun

NUTS — 2
Cashews
Mixed
Peanuts
Almonds
Pecans

CHOCOLATE OR CANDY BARS—2

Solid baking-type chocolate is
   preferred for its higher melting
   temperature.
Candy bars of most sorts
Candy-coated milk chocolate bits
Fudge
Caramels

HARD CANDY — 1
Lifesavers
Sourballs
Mint bar

BREAD — 3

Pumpernickel types
   Choose the darkest and hardest
   breads for keeping and packing
   qualities.
Logan bread
Can up the weight and eliminate
   fruit and/or nuts in this lunch.
Cinnamon roll
   Same note as Logan bread

BEVERAGES
Premixed with sugar
Artificially-sweetened types
Citric powders plus sugar
Instant tea (sugar)
Powdered milk
   Plain
   Malted
   Chocolate

CRACKERS — 2

Rye krisp
Unleavened breads
Wheat Thins
Triscuits
Pilot biscuits

GLOPS
Old Reliables

Amounts per serving. Measure is ounces unless otherwise stated.

	Soup (Choose one)	Meat (Choose one)	Margarine—1	Cheese—1	Comments
RICE-AND-MEAT Rice, pre-cooked 2⅓ (⅔ cup dry measure)	½-¾ (¼-⅓ pkg.) Any quick-cooking vegetable soup—tomato vegetable, onion, tomato, etc.	Tinned—4 Corned beef Roast beef Chopped pressed meat Sausage, bulk—4 Meat bars—½ to 2 Freeze-dried Hamburgers—1½ Beef patties—1⅓ Meat balls—1⅓	Margarine—1	Cheddar	About 9 total for tinned meat dinners. Add gravy mix for soup quantities greater than 4 people. May add milk powder.
CREAMED-STYLE RICE (*Variation of above*) Rice, pre-cooked 2⅓ (⅔ cup dry measure)	*Soup* Mushroom, leek, or chicken rice	Tinned—4 Tuna Salmon Ham	Margarine—1	Cheddar	*Variations* Freeze-dried mushrooms, particularly with mushroom soup.

GLOPS

Old Reliables (*cont.*)

Amounts per serving. Measure is ounces unless otherwise stated.

Chipped beef—2
Freeze-dried
  Pork patties—1⅓
  Ham—½ to ⅔
  Shrimp—½ to 1
  Chicken—
    ½ to ⅔

Comments
Ala King: green peppers—2 tblsp. for 4; onions—¼ cup flakes
Curry: 1 tblsp. for 4, dried onions, garlic powder

MACARONI AND MEAT

Macaroni—2
5-to-7 minute varieties

Soup (Choose one)
1 pkg. for 3 or 4 servings
  Chicken noodle
  Tomato
  Cream soups:
    Mushroom
    Leek

Meat (Choose one)
Tinned—4
  Tuna
  Salmon
  Ham
Chipped beef—2
Freeze-dried
  Pork patties—1⅓
  Ham—½ to ⅔
  Shrimp—½ to 1
  Chicken—½ to ⅔

Margarine—1

Cheese—1

Comments
May add dried milk powder.
Variations for creamed rice dinners suitable.
Creole: with tomato soup add onions, green pepper.

GLOPS

Old Reliables (*cont.*)

Amounts per serving. Measure is ounces unless otherwise stated.

MACARONI-AND-CHEESE

Macaroni—3	Soup	Dried Milk	Margarine—½	Cheese—3	Seasoning
	Chicken Bouillon— 1 cube or 1 tsp.	¼ cup		Cheddar	For 4: Onions—¼ cup Dry mustard— 1 tsp. Oregano—½ tsp.

POTATO

Potato, mashed—2	Soup (Choose one)	Meat (Choose one)	Margarine—1	Cheese—1	Milk
	Cream type for creamed dishes, any meat Onion or Vegetable with beef	Tinned Roast beef Corned beef			⅓ cup for 4 With corned beef use Dry cabbage— ¾ oz. (¾ cup) for 4 Onions—¼ oz. (¼ cup) for 4

Specialties

Amounts given in ounces for 4 servings.

SPANISH RICE	*Ounces for 4*	*Comments*
Spanish rice mix, precooked	12 (2 pkgs.)	
Tomato soup or tomato sauce		
mix	1 pkg.	
Meat (Choose one)		
Bacon bars	6 (2 bars)	
Bulk sausage	16	
Shrimp—tinned	12	Heavy in water pack
freeze-dried	2	
Tuna, tinned	16	
Freeze-dried		
Hamburger	6.5	
Meat balls	4	More would be desirable—on
Beef patties	4	the order of 5 to 5⅓.
Margarine	4 (1 cube)	
Parmesan cheese, grated	2	Optional

CHINESE RICE		
Rice	9⅓ (2⅔ cups)	
Chicken rice soup	1 pkg.	
Tuna	12	
and chicken, tinned, boned	4-5	
or freeze-dried chicken	6.5	
Margarine	4 (1 cube)	
Cashews, broken	4	

CHILI RICE		
Rice, precooked	9⅓ (2⅔ cups)	
Tomato soup *or*		
tomato sauce mix	1 pkg.	
Meat (Choose one)		
Compressed meat bars	6 to 8	
Roast beef, tinned	16⎰	Add 4 oz. tin Vienna sausage
Chopped meat, tinned	16⎱	to 12 oz. tin.
Bulk sausage	16	
Freeze-dried		
Hamburger	6.5	
Meat balls	4	More would be desirable.
Beef patties	4	More would be desirable.
Margarine	4 (1 cube)	
Cheese, cheddar type, grated	4	
Onions, dry	½ (¼ cup)	
Chili powder	1½ tblsp.	Those who like it hot will want more.

ALA	*Ounces for 4*	*Comments*
Ala	8 (1⅓ cups)	Slow cooking—15 minutes.
Beef soup, beef noodle soup, or onion soup	1 pkg. and 1 bouillon cube	
Meat suggestions and amounts same as chili rice dinner above.		
Margarine	4 (1 cube)	
Cheese, cheddar	4	
Oregano	½ tsp.	

BEEF STEW

Potaoes, cubed, sliced, or diced	8	Slow—soak with vegetables.
Tomato *or* beef soup	1 pkg. and 1 bouillon cube	
Meat (Choose one)		
Roast beef, tinned	16	Add one 4-oz. can Vienna sausage to 12 oz. tin.
Freeze-dried		
Hamburger	6.5	
Meat balls	4	More is desirable—on order
Beef patties	4	of 5⅓ oz.
Margarine	4 (1 cube)	
Dried vegetables		
Carrots	1	Soak
Onions	¼ (¼ cup)	"
Celery	¼ cup	"
Green pepper	2 tblsp.	"
Parsley	1 tblsp.	
Mixed herbs	1 tsp. (½ tsp. marjoram, ½ tsp. thyme)	
Pepper	⅛ tsp.	

SPAGHETTI

Spaghetti, quick-cooking	8	
Tomato soup	1 pkg.	Add chili powder—2 tsps., onions—¼ oz., and herbs.
or		
Spaghetti mix with tomato	1 pkg.	Choose quick-cooking type—not too spicy.
Meat (Choose one)		
Freeze-dried		
Meat balls	4	Larger quantity desirable.
Beef patties	4	Larger quantity desirable.
Hamburger	6.5	

SPAGHETTI (cont.)   *Ounces for 4*   *Comments*

Roast beef, tinned	16⎫	Add one 4 oz. can Vienna
Chopped beef, tinned	16⎭	sausage to 12-oz. tin.
Bulk sausage	16	
Compressed meat bars	6 to 8	
Margarine	4 (1 cube)	
Parsley, dried	1 tblsp.	
Herbs	½ tsp. basil	
	½ tsp. oregano	
	dash thyme	
Parmesan cheese, grated	2	

CURRY DINNER, BEEF

Rice, precooked	9⅓ (2⅔ cups)	
Beef bouillon	4 cubes or 4 tsps.	
Meat (Choose one)		
Roast beef, tinned	16	
Freeze-dried meats can be used but unspiced meats are preferred.	5 to 6	
Margarine	4 (1 cube)	
Raisins	3 (½ cup)	Soak fruits and vegetables.
Apples, dried sliced	2	
Green pepper	2 tblsp.	
Onion	½ (¼ cup)	
Lemon peel, dried	1 tblsp.	
Curry powder	1 tblsp.	
Marjoram	½ tsp.	Mix spices at home and pack-
Thyme	½ tsp.	age together.
Garlic powder	¼ tsp.	
Lemon crystals or citric acid crystals	½ tsp.	
Cornstarch	1 tblsp.	

CURRY DINNER, SHRIMP

Chicken bouillon	4 cubes or 4 tsps.	
Shrimp (Choose one)		
Canned	12	Heavy in water-pack.
Freeze-dried	4.5 (1 #2½ tin)	
Other ingredients the same as above.		
Coconut, dried	¼ cup	May be added to herbs and spices.

CHICKEN OR SHRIMP JAMBALAYA

	Ounces for 4	Comments
Rice, precooked	9½ (2⅔ cups)	
Tomato soup	2¼ (1 pkg.) plus 1 chicken bouillón	
Meat (Choose one)		
Freeze-dried		
Chicken	6.5 (#2½ tin)	
Shrimp	4.5 (#2½ tin)	
Margarine	4 (1 cube)	
Dried vegetables		
Onions	.25 (¼ cup)	Soak vegetables
Green pepper	1 tblsp.	
Celery	2 tsp.	
Thyme	½ tsp.	
Cayenne	dash	
Parsley	1 tsp.	
Chili	½ tsp.	

THE LAST WORD — JERKY

Long a favorite item in the mountaineer's diet, jerky is high in protein and low in weight. For those who object to the high cost and/or preservatives of commercially prepared jerky, here are instructions for preparing it at home.

Slice any lean piece of boneless beef into ⅛-inch strips, trimming off as much fat as possible. (Cut with the grain of the meat for chewy jerky, across the grain for crumbly jerky.) Lay strips on rack, with foil or pan underneath to catch drips, and salt — lightly or heavily, as desired. Dry in oven set at lowest temperature (150°), leaving door slightly ajar, for 8 to 12 hours. Turn several times for even drying, taste-testing occasionally.

For those who like a more highly seasoned flavor, the meat may be cut and marinated overnight in the following combination of ingredients (enough for 1½ pounds of meat):

1 tsp. *each* salt and seasoning salt
½ tsp. *each* pepper, onion powder, and garlic salt
¼ cup *each* soy sauce and worcestershire sauce

Dry as above. Vary the marinade as experience and personal taste dictate.

INDEX

Ablation, 400-01, 406; zone of glacier, 382
Accidents, 325-36, 351-52; prevention, 303, 304-13; report form, 326, 354-56; statistics, 303-04
Accumulation zone, glacier, 382, 414
Addresses for ordering maps, 71, 74
Adiabatic temperature, 436; lapse rate, 435
Aid climbing, 209-18; equipment, 157-80, 209-11
Aid, outside, in rescue, 352-56
Aiming the belay, 131-43
Air rescue, 363-65
Alpine rescue, 348-66
Altimeter, 75, 429
Altitude: cooking and eating, 55, 56; and hypothermia, 305; and pulmonary edema, 341-42; and mountain sickness, 345-46
Amphiboles, 370
Amphibolite, 373
Anchors, 312, 351, 358; aid, 212, 213, 214, 217, 218; ax as, 256-57; belay, 128-34, 136, 140, 141, 239; deadman, 130, 360; glacier, 284, 287; rappel, 119, 142, 144, 152-53; rock, 158, 170, 175; sling, 143; snow, 242, 267
Andesite, 372, 373

Angle pitons, 170, 175
Approach observations, 101-04
Arete, 386
Arm lock jam, 196
Arm rappel, 145
Arrest: and ice ax design, 230-32; grasp of ax, 268, 293; in wild flight, 264; limits of, 266; on ice, 266; position, 262; self-, 261-66; team, 267; techniques, 95, 245, 261-69; variations, 265; (see also Self-arrest)
Arterial bleeding, 328-29
Artificial: aid climbing, 209-18; anchors on rappel, 142; chocks, 110, 111, 163-65, 168, 177, 213, 222 (see also Chocks)
Ascenders, mechanical, 157, 271, 281
Attitude: mountaineering, 3-4, 183; safe, 311-13
Avalanche, 106-07, 125, 126, 271, 299, 305, 351, 400, 405, 414-15, 418; conditions, 247-52; cushions, 261; fans, 82-83; hazards, 247-52, 351, 424; loose snow, 415-16; probability, 249; rescue, 251, 349-51; slab, 401, 415, 419-24; tracks, 83
Avoiding: avalanche, 248-52; brush, 83-84; crevasses, 275; exposure, 339; hazards, 104, 305; lightning, 306-08